THE ROLE OF LANGUAGE IN PROBLEM SOLVING 2

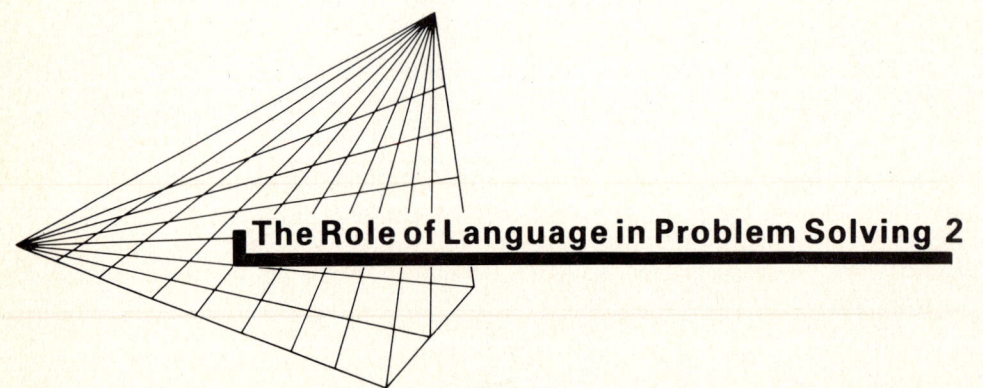

Symposium logo by courtesy of:
Angelika Peck
TIR Group
The Johns Hopkins University
Applied Physics Laboratory

THE ROLE OF LANGUAGE IN PROBLEM SOLVING 2

Edited Proceedings of the
Johns Hopkins University Applied Physics Laboratory
Second Symposium on the Role of Language in Problem Solving
held in Laurel, Maryland, 2–4 April, 1986

Editors:

J. C. BOUDREAUX
Center for Manufacturing Engineering
National Bureau of Standards
Gaithersburg, Maryland, U.S.A.

B. W. HAMILL
The Johns Hopkins University
Applied Physics Laboratory
Laurel, Maryland U.S.A.

and

R. JERNIGAN
Decision Resource Systems
Columbia, Maryland, U.S.A.

1987

NORTH-HOLLAND
AMSTERDAM · NEW YORK · OXFORD · TOKYO

© Elsevier Science Publishers B.V., 1987

All rights reserved. No part of this publication may be reproduced, stored in a retrieval system, or transmitted, in any form or by any means, electronic, mechanical, photocopying, recording or otherwise, without the prior permission of the copyright owner.

ISBN: 0 444 70114 1

Published by:
ELSEVIER SCIENCE PUBLISHERS B.V.
P.O. Box 1991
1000 BZ Amsterdam
The Netherlands

Sole distributors for the U.S.A. and Canada:
ELSEVIER SCIENCE PUBLISHING COMPANY, INC.
52 Vanderbilt Avenue
New York, N.Y. 10017
U.S.A.

Printed in the Netherlands

PREFACE

This volume comprises the proceedings of The Johns Hopkins University Applied Physics Laboratory Second Symposium on The Role of Language in Problem Solving, which was held at the Laboratory's Kossiakoff Conference and Education Center on April 2-4, 1986.

The goal of this Symposium was to bring together investigators and practitioners from a variety of disciplines to address issues relating to language and its use in and effects on solving problems in science and engineering. The focus was on how language influences the problem solver. In particular, we sought to address such topics as knowledge representation, formal and "natural" notation systems, heuristic methods, and issues related to the design of workstations, programming environments, and supercomputing systems.

The papers and panel sessions of the Symposium address these issues in several ways, including formal theoretical analysis, theoretically-based empirical investigation, structured system design, and both formal and informal application-oriented development. The perspectives represented are primarily those of computer scientists and computer programming practitioners attempting to find effective ways to support the cognitive activities involved in solving scientific and technical problems in their respective domains of interest.

A natural consequence of these perspectives is that the "language" aspect of the Symposium topic tends to emphasize languages for programming computers, although broader conceptions of language are also present. Two metaphors for programming computers predominate here: one is the language metaphor, that is, using languages and notational systems for computing; the other is the "computer-as-toolkit" metaphor, that is, the idea of the computer system as a programming and problem-solving environment containing a collection of tools to be selected and used on an interactive basis by the problem solver in approaching solutions to domain-specific problems. Underlying both of these metaphors is the goal of putting into the hands of problem solvers, in the most natural and convenient possible way, the power and diverse capabilities of specialized computer-based systems.

The papers in this proceedings volume are grouped around the principal themes of the Symposium.

Knowledge Representation comprises a set of papers addressing fundamental issues in using knowledge for solving problems both in general in the software development process, and specifically in problems of reasoning about language, discourse processing, and relating knowledge bases.

Formal Approaches underlying problem solving include analogy and intensional logic in programming, an ontological view of computation, software validation based on transformation from formal representation of domain knowledge into software, and linguistic and cognitive factors influencing inferential reasoning.

Panel: Theoretical and Empirical Approaches addresses relationships between theory and empirical results for understanding how people solve problems in various domains and for guiding the development of software and hardware systems designed to support problem solving.

Design Issues includes papers concerned with a range of topics including formal aspects of marker-passing, automated programming, graph theoretic formalisms for problem representation, very high level query languages, and requirements for programming parallel processors.

Panel: Applications, Language, and Architecture: Dimensions in Problem Solving presents a discussion of the interactions of problem requirements, computing languages, and computer architectures.

Programming Language Environments comprises papers describing studies of several systems designed to aid in the programming process in various domains, including automated manufacturing, Pascal program code debugging, efforts of novices using different programming languages, and high-level application-oriented interfaces.

Panel: Open Questions: An Agenda for Language in Problem Solving is a discussion of several of the themes and issues arising in the Symposium, with suggestions of topics for a future symposium on the subject.

We thank The Johns Hopkins University Applied Physics Laboratory for financial and facilities support. We gratefully acknowledge the inspiration provided by Robert Rich, George Weiffenbach, and David Weintraub, the publicity efforts of Connie Finney, and the skillful supporting efforts of Vicky Franke, Brenda Laub, Linda Sussman, and Susan Testerman in preparing for and conducting the Symposium and in preparing this volume.

Finally, we wish to recognize the considerable contribution of Barbara Northrop, who served once again as Symposium Coordinator. The success of the Second Symposium event in

April and the production of this proceedings volume reflect her well tested patience, diligence, and skill. To her we express our special thanks.

Laurel, Maryland   J. C. Boudreaux
June 1986   Bruce W. Hamill
                                              Robert Jernigan

TABLE OF CONTENTS

Preface   v

Symposium Committee   xiii

KNOWLEDGE REPRESENTATION

Problem Spaces, Dimensionality, and Representation
    Issues in the Software Process
B.I. Blum   3

Knowledge Representation for Reasoning About Language
J.G. Neal and S.C. Shapiro   27

Abduction in Discourse Processing: A Parsimonious
    Covering Model
V.R. Dasigi and J.A. Reggia   49

Relating Two Knowledge Bases: The Role of Identity
    and Part-Whole
R. Rada, L. Darden, and J. Eng   71

FORMAL APPROACHES

Analogy in Program Development
S.R. Dietzen and W.L. Scherlis   95

Intensional Programming
A.A. Faustini and W.W. Wadge   119

Computational Ontology
J.C. Boudreaux   133

A Constructive Approach to Validation
G. Arango and P. Freeman   161

Language and Reasoning: Sorting Out Sociopragmatic
    and Psychopragmatic Factors
M. Dascal   183

PANEL:
THEORETICAL AND EMPIRICAL APPROACHES   201

Panel Chairman: R.P. Rich
Panel Members: V.R. Dasigi
                     S.L. Epstein
                     B.W. Hamill
                     W.L. Scherlis
                     B. Shneiderman

DESIGN ISSUES

Issues in the Design of Marker-Passing Systems
J. Hendler   227

The Automated Programmer System: Language Design
    Issues for Scientific-Mathematical-Engineering
    Applications Programming
M. Klerer, F. Grossman, and R. Klerer   245

Languages for Problem Solving in Graph Theory
S.L. Epstein   261

Symbolic Translation and Very High Level Query
    Languages
W.H. Guier and R. Jernigan   301

Programming the Parallel Processor
G. Lyon   321

PANEL:
APPLICATIONS, LANGUAGE, AND ARCHITECTURE:
    DIMENSIONS IN PROBLEM SOLVING   337

Panel Chairman: G. Lyon
Panel Members: J.W. Carr, III
                     R. Jernigan
                     B. Kowalchack
                     A. Lazanoff

PROGRAMMING LANGUAGE ENVIRONMENTS

AMPLE: A Programming Language Environment for
    Automated Manufacturing
J.C. Boudreaux   359

Drs.: A Language Oriented Diagnostic Run-Time System
B. Kowalchack and M.V. Zelkowitz   377

The Effect of Graphical Representation of Programming
    on the Conceptual Bugs in Novices' Programs:
    A Comparison of FPL and PASCAL
N. Cunniff, R.P. Taylor, and S. Taylor   391

Languages and Software Parts for Elliptic
    Boundary-Value Problems
R.F. Boisvert   411

PANEL:
OPEN QUESTIONS:
    AN AGENDA FOR LANGUAGE IN PROBLEM SOLVING   435

Panel Chairman: B.I. Blum
Panel Members: G. Arango
                R. Jernigan
                B. Shneiderman

Author Index   455

Subject Index   463

SYMPOSIUM COMMITTEE

Symposium Chairman   Bruce W. Hamill
Program Chairman   Robert Jernigan
Symposium Coordinator   Barbara Northrop
Publicity   Connie Finney
Advisor   George C. Weiffenbach

Program Committee   J. C. Boudreaux, Chairman
    Saul Amarel
    David Barstow
    Bruce Blum
    Gordon Lyon
    Roy Rada
    Ben Shneiderman
    David Weintraub

Referees   William H. Guier
    Thomas W. Jerardi
    Vincent G. Sigillito
    Robert L. Stewart
    Ralph F. Wachter
    Richard L. Waddell, Jr.

KNOWLEDGE REPRESENTATION

PROBLEM SPACES, DIMENSIONALITY, AND
REPRESENTATION ISSUES IN THE SOFTWARE PROCESS

Bruce I. Blum

Johns Hopkins University
Applied Physics Laboratory
Laurel, Maryland 20707

This paper considers language properties as they relate to the software process. A description of the process is presented, and the key transformations are identified. The problem spaces used during the process are described, and the concept of dimensionality for software process models is defined. Finally, some observations are made about linguistic representations and the process. A major conclusion is that the software process still is largely a cognitive one; therefore, the representations (and tools) used should reflect the structure of the problems being solved rather than more precise formalisms that may mask the structure.

1.0   INTRODUCTION

This paper examines some issues in the dimensionality of and representations for the problem spaces referenced during the software process. In an earlier paper, it was suggested that the language used to describe a software product would be better (in some sense) if the language reflected the views of the application domain rather than the implementation domain.[1] This paper builds upon the earlier one by examining the domains (i.e., spaces) used during the software process. We then view the complexity and structure of these spaces and conclude with a discussion of some issues in the representation of the spaces used during problem solving.

The thesis of this paper is that the software process is a complex one in which a poorly defined model of user needs (of high dimensionality) is transformed into a collection of (a) sequences of computer instructions, (b) human processable text and (c) machine processable data. The latter collection is also of high dimensionality. The agent for this transformation is the human mind supported by methods and tools. Some of the transforming tools, such as compilers, are completely automated and some of the methods, such as HOS, JSP or SADT, may have automated support. Nevertheless, the key agent in the transformation from a model in the application space into one in the implementation space remains the human mind. It is hypothesized, therefore, that a better understanding of the models and representations in these three key spaces (application, problem solving, and implementation) will lead to a better understanding of how the software process can be improved.

2.0   PROBLEM SPACES

This section considers the problem spaces (domains) associated with the software process. Two are obvious:

- Application space. This is the problem space for both the real world environment and the implemented software product.

- Implementation space. This is the space that contains all knowledge of the operations of computers and the transformations of design statements into executable sequences of operations.

There is also a third space that is frequently overlooked: the problem solving space. All transitions from the application space to/from the implementation space must be evaluated in the problem solving space. Currently, for human controlled problem solving, this is constrained by the cognitive process. In the future, systems using artificial intelligence may overcome these limitations by implementing other modes and representations, but that is not of immediate concern here.

In what follows, we first provide an overview of the software process and then examine each space in additional detail.

2.1   The Software Process

In an earlier paper at this conference, we presented a naive overview of the software process. It was described as three transformations: one from the real world (or application, A) to a problem statement (or specification, S), a second from the problem statement to an implementation statement (i.e., the design process), and finally, one from the implementation statement to the executable system (i.e., compilation, assembly, etc.). In this view the final outcome is a product, P, that is isomorphic to the implementation statement. In the traditional waterfall flow, the second transformation includes all activities after analysis and up to operations and maintenance.

For the purposes of this paper, it will be convenient to formalize this by using the model of the software process as described by Lehman.[2] In this model, the process is viewed as two transformations:

- Abstraction: A transformation from the application statement A to the specification S.

- Reification: A transformation from the specification S to the product P.

The abstraction process has not been studied in much detail. On the other hand, Lehman, Stenning and Turski have developed a detailed model of the reification process.[3] This is seen as an iteration of a canonical step. In each step, the specification is a theory from which a model in another linguistic form will be produced. Many models may be produced, and one must be selected. Following the selection there is verification (in which it is demonstrated that the model is correct with respect to the theory) and a validation obligation (in which the behavior of the model is evaluated with respect to the application's needs as suggested by the specification). If correct and valid, the model becomes the theory for the next iteration. An example of a sequence of linguistic transformations might be Functional Specification, Module Specification, PDL, code.

Thus, we see that the software process can be described as a sequence of transformations

$$A \rightarrow S \rightarrow P \rightarrow A' \ldots$$

where A' represents modified application needs resulting from either changes introduced by the product P or other external changes. The $S \rightarrow P$ transformation can be decomposed into

$$S \rightarrow S_1 \rightarrow \ldots S_n \rightarrow P$$

where S_n is a model that is isomorphic (or more accurately, idiomorphic) to the product P, e.g., S_n is source code. Notice that if the initial specification S was complete, no S_i models would be required and P would be defined fully by S. Obviously, that is almost never the case. Turski uses the term "permissive" to describe the incompleteness of S.[4] The specification, he suggests, must contain the essential behaviors of P; the designer is free to make decisions that do not impact those behaviors.

Given this model of the software process, it can be seen that all abstraction transformation actions (i.e., $A \rightarrow S$) and all validation actions are problem solving activities. That is, there is no mechanism to prove the actions are (logically) correct -- they are assumed to be good actions based upon judgment and experience. Where a transformation from a theory to a model can be verified objectively, such transformations (or their verification) may be automated to eliminate human judgment. However, where the verification process (or the specification) is not formal, we must rely upon subjective determinations, i.e., on problem solving decisions.

To summarize informally, the software process can be decomposed into the following three activities:

1. Deciding what the product should do. Before a product exists, this is called analysis and the result is a requirements specification. Once a

product exists, this is called evolution or maintenance, and the result is a change order.

2. Deciding if it was done correctly. This is a comparison of the product with respect to some specification. If the specification is formal, then one may objectively establish the correctness of the product. Otherwise, verification is subject to interpretation and is a subjective process.

3. Deciding if the product conforms to the application needs. This is always a subjective judgment; the decision is ultimately made -- in part -- by the persons who requested the product.

Work in formal specifications will reduce the uncertainty in item 2. There also is a potential for artificial intelligence to shrink the space of all three activities in selected problem domains. Nevertheless, for the near term, virtually all of the software process activities rely upon human problem solving decisions. By extension, therefore, much of the software process is a judgmental (and probably not a formalizable) activity.

2.2 Application Space

We have separated knowledge into two spaces: one that characterizes what is known about the problem to be solved (application) and the other that represents what is known about the solution environment, i.e., computers and transformations into computer processable codes. In reality, however, there is an overlap between the two. That is why Curtis, drawing upon experience in cognitive science, states that "programming skill is specific to the application being considered."[5] Barstow echoes the same conclusion from a perspective on automatic programming.[6]

> The primary conclusion of our initial studies is that domain knowledge plays a critical role in the programming process. This role is so important that automatic programming systems without considerable domain knowledge will be neither usable by non-computer scientists nor feasible for non-trivial domains.

This overlap of domains explains why organizations with experience in implementing compilers find the building of an accounts receivable package difficult, and visa versa.

It will be useful, therefore, to decompose the application space as follows:

- Specific application domain. This includes all knowledge and information regarding a specific application to be implemented and the environment in which it will be used. The space may include factors regarding the use of an existing software product by a new set of users, the definition of a product to meet a specific set of needs, a generally perceived set of needs for which it is believed that a computer based solution can be constructed, etc.

- Generic application domain. This includes knowledge and information common to a generic class of applications, e.g., information systems, patient monitoring systems, lift control systems, etc. This generic application knowledge is usually available within the development team; that is why RFPs request statements of previous experience.

There is no clear boundary between the two application domains or -- for that matter -- between the application and implementation spaces.

2.3 Implementation Space

Implementation space, in this definition, contains all knowledge regarding the use of computers to effect a solution. The space may be decomposed into two layers. The first is the tool space that contains all tools and representations used by the designers in implementing a solution. The second layer, the transformation space, contains all knowledge of transformations from some formal representation into computer executable sequences. We shall only consider this second layer; it can be decomposed as follows:

- Heuristic domain. This includes all knowledge, methods, and information used in the creation of a software product that do not rely upon precise, closed, repeatable transformation rules. Most of the software process is based upon heuristics.

- Algorithmic domain. This includes those well defined, repeatable transformations that are used to produce executable sequences of code. Examples are a compiler and a report generator.

These spaces also can be subdivided by paradigms. For example, there are differences between the heuristics and algorithms used in an AI/LISP environment, a DP/COBOL environment and a mathematical/FORTRAN environment. Moreover, within an environment, there are many different (and conflicting heuristics), e.g., the Jackson, Orr, and DeMarco design methods. The algorithms always tend to be available in some automated form. Although human judgment or heuristics may be required in the selection of the proper algorithm, once one is selected the output will be determined exclusively by the algorithm.

Figure 1 summarizes the software process in the form of its three basic transformations: Analysis, Implementation and Translation. Because the specification produced by Analysis is not complete, i.e., it is permissive, Implementation must add further details in order to produce the final product. These details are added for one of three reasons:

- Clarification -- gaining additional understanding of the application problem space in order to implement a solution. The decisions made should be permissible (in the Turski sense).

- Optimization -- improving the structure to satisfy non-functional requirements for an effective product.

- Housekeeping -- adding necessary transformation space details that are not specified by the product. In many cases, the style of the algorithmic transformation establishes the scope of housekeeping. (See Reference 1.)

Activity	Transformation	Problem Space				Process		
		Appl. Spec.	Appl. Gen.	Heur. Trans.	Algo. Trans.	Judgment	Heuristic	Algorithm
Analysis	$A \rightarrow S$	M	M	m		M	m	m
Implementation	$S \rightarrow S_n$							
(a) Clarification		m	M	M		M	m	
(b) Optimization			m	M	m	M	M	M
(c) Housekeeping			m	M	m	m	M	M
Translation	$S_n \rightarrow P$				M			M

M - Major   m - Minor

Figure 1

Software Process Activities

For each task or subtask the figure indicates the problem space used and the type of process involved. Three processes are identified:

- Judgment: a cognitive activity.

- Heuristic: an activity defined by a general method or approach.

- Algorithm: an activity defined as a formalized, repeatable process.

Note that there is not a match between the heuristic and algorithmic spaces and the processes. Heuristically defined transformations may apply algorithms without their being considered algorithmic transformations. Naturally, the assignment of importance indicators in this matrix is somewhat arbitrary. It is asserted, however, that the diagonal trend from upper left to lower right is a valid representation of the software process.

3.0 PROBLEM SOLVING SPACE

The problem solving space may be viewed as orthogonal to the previous two spaces. All judgmental processes take place in this space. The arena for problem solving (currently) is the human mind. The application and implementation spaces are recorded as the result of experience (learning).

There is a growing literature on cognition, conceptual structuring and computer science. Among the broadly accepted findings are that humans have a short-term memory that can retain five to seven chunks of information for immediate recall and a larger, associative long-term memory from which chunks may be retrieved into short-term memory for use. Pattern recognition to key recall is affected by the size of the encoded schema (i.e., the experience of the observer). Experienced programmers, for example, will recognize structured constructs and consequently can recall, after a brief exposure, far more meaningful code than inexperienced programmers. (See References 7, 8).

The knowledge used by the individual is acquired by learning, and the following understanding of the learning process is emerging.[9]

- Learners look for meaning and will try to construct order even in the absence of complete information. This means that naive theories will always be formed as part of the learning process.

- Understanding is based upon relationships to established knowledge. This knowledge is organized as a schemata; information isolated from these structures is lost or forgotten.

- All learning depends on prior knowledge. Learners try to link new information to established schemata -- even if they represent naive theories.

It follows, therefore, that a problem solving method, which is in fact a learning process, must reflect the user/analyst's schemata and avoid the inadvertent development of inappropriate, naive structures. As an understanding of the problem is gained (i.e., knowledge is bound to the application space), the schemata change and formerly irrelevant facts may now have meaning. (This is one reason why Newell and Simon felt that knowledge should be organized as structures to be reused by the information processing system.[10])

Elstein and his colleagues studied how clinicians perform medical problem solving -- a task similar to systems analysis -- and developed the following hypothetico-deductive model:[11]

- Cue acquisition. This includes taking a history, performing a physical examination, reviewing test results, etc.

- Hypothesis generation. Retrieval from long-term memory of alternate hypotheses of the diagnosis.

- Cue interpretation. The data are now considered in the context of the hypothesis previously generated.

- Hypothesis evaluation. The data are weighted and combined to determine which hypotheses are supported or ruled out.

The process is iterative. It may result in a decision that more data are required (i.e., tests and procedures are to be ordered) or that a probable diagnosis (and recommended therapy) are suggested, or both.

In analyzing this model, the researchers found that the generation of early hypotheses has considerable natural force; medical students generated early hypotheses even when asked to withhold judgment. The number of hypotheses is usually around four or five and appears to have an upper bound of about six or seven. The generation of hypotheses was based more consistently on single salient cues rather than on combinations of cues. Very few cues seemed to be used, and hypothesis selection is biased by recent experience. (That is the source of the joke so common in medical schools: when one hears the sound of hoof beats, one immediately thinks of zebras.) They also found that cue interpretation tended to use three measures: confirm, disconfirm or noncontributory; the use of seven-point weighting schemes had no greater explanatory power. Finally, the accuracy of cue interpretation was related to the accuracy of diagnostic outcome, but it was independent of the thoroughness of cue acquisition. The lack of thoroughness is not as important a cause of error in diagnosis as problems of integrating and combining information.

This discussion suggests that the problem solver (e.g., analyst) can best comprehend the problem space when it is represented as small chunks within an established schema. Since the schemata for the application and implementation (transformation) spaces will be different, it can be expected that the analyst will have some difficulty in navigating between the spaces (or between different representations in the same space). Moreover, where a problem is incompletely understood, the analyst may construct naive theories to guide his judgments. It is hypothesized that the analyst's task will be facilitated (a) when the models of the external (i.e., application and transformation) space conveniently map onto the models in the internal (i.e., cognitive or problem solving) space and (b) when, by experience, the schema is expanded to guide navigation across boundaries. This implies that an understanding of the complexity of and representations for these three spaces will provide insights into the kinds of methods and tools that will improve the software process. This is the focus of the next sections.

4.0 DIMENSIONS

All models are abstractions that simplify some properties of an entity in order to evaluate other behaviors of that entity. The software process can be viewed as a modeling activity that culminates with a model in the form of computer codes to be embedded in the application space. As Lehman put it, "any program is a model of a model within a theory of a model of an abstraction of some portion of the world or some universe of discourse."[12]

Two types of models can be identified:

- Behavioral models that describe what the application is to do and how it is to be used.

- Structural models that describe how the application is to be constructed in order to accomplish its goals.

In most cases there is considerable overlap between the behavioral and structural models, but it is convenient to think of them as different entities. For well understood problem domains it may be sufficient to produce a behavioral model in a form that can be used to infer some of the structural decisions in order to produce a working model. This is what application generators do with their non-procedural languages;[13] this is also a goal of the operational approach to system development.[14] In general, however, the structural model must be produced during a separate development process.

We use the term "dimension" as a measure of the complexity of the model. Although this is a mathematical term, we shall use it casually. Because the behavioral and structural models are quite different, each will have a different concept of dimensionality.

4.1 Behavioral Dimensionality

Clearly, the "real world" is too complex to model. It changes over time, and the changes are ephemeral. Any attempt to produce a "complete" temporal model necessarily would be larger than the entity modeled. Therefore, the first activity in modeling is a conscious decision to ignore aspects of the universe of discourse. Thus, the initial steps in behavioral modeling (i.e., the abstraction transformation as defined in the software process section) are based on judgment and experience. The quality of the model (and the finished product) will depend largely upon the quality of these initial decisions, and quality evaluation itself is a cognitive action. Consequently, the development and evaluation of a behavioral model is based upon inexact criteria; outcome frequently is measured by "marketplace" factors.

We shall define the dimension of a behavioral model as the number of distinct views required to present it fully. A view here is considered a unifying property that links some subset

of the model's behaviors. For example, if we are modeling a
house, one would expect separate views for the plumbing, the
electrical, and the structural subsystems. One would also
expect a spatial view that considered only the spatial relationships of the above subsystems. One might also require a
temporal view to establish the construction sequence. The
behavioral model would incorporate all views within an
integrated whole; it also would provide separate access to each
required view.

We have been building houses for centuries using these behavioral models. The final blueprints and drawings are structural
models derived from the behavioral models. However, because of
our extensive experience, the behavioral models now tend to be
minimal: for example, an architect's drawing. The heuristics
are so refined that most architects work in the structural
modeling domain.

There are some application classes in the computer systems
domain that are sufficiently well understood to be modeled
behaviorally with ease. Examples are simple DBMS applications,
the use of a computational subroutine library, or the preparation of a standard graphic display. Where the application also
is well understood, heuristics can be used to generate the
structural model (and hence the target application) automatically. Where the application is not well understood, heuristics
can be used to produce prototypes that can be experimented with
in order to refine the knowledge of the application (and its
behavioral model). Of course, if the computer process is not
well understood, few heuristics may exist, and the completion
of the behavioral model will depend upon the designers'
judgment.

In summary, the behavioral modeling of an application relies
upon judgment, and there are no provable steps. Where there is
considerable experience, the judgments can be formalized as
heuristic transformations and automated. Where the experience
is limited, the heuristics will be incomplete or untrustworthy.
The complexity of a behavioral model is suggested, in part, by
the number of views it must support. For an interactive information system, three views may be sufficient:

>   What functions are to be supported.
>   What process sequences are necessary.
>   What entities are to be modeled in the database.

For a real time, embedded system, additional views may be
required, e.g.,

>   What are the external interfaces/constraints.
>   What are the timing constraints.
>   What computations are required and with what accuracy.

4.2   Structural Dimensionality

The structure of an operational system may be modeled as a
transition network in which the nodes represent a system state

or instantiation of the internal and database variables, and the edges are sequences of machine instructions that will alter the state. If one assumes bounded and terminating loops and finite storage, the network is finite. The level of detail represented by this network will depend upon the level of abstraction used. For example, the network could represent the state changes for each bit in the computer. Alternatively, it could represent each state change in a compiled (assembly language) representation of a system. Finally, it could detail only the state changes explicit in the source code that produced the assembly language.

Each level of abstraction adds detail. Some of this detail is the output of a problem solving activity; other detail is simply housekeeping. For the purposes of this paper we shall assume that the lowest level of abstraction of interest is that from which all subsequent levels of abstraction can be derived fully by algorithms in the transformation space, e.g., compilers, application generators.

Figure 2 illustrates how a network can be simplified by the process of fusion. In the example, nodes u and v are fused into a new node (u) and the edge is eliminated. The fusion of nodes c and u in the second example will produce a tree. If we define a (higher) level of abstraction to be formed by a reduction of some previous network by a set of independent fusions, then the dimension of a structural representation can be defined as the number of levels of abstraction necessary to transform that structure at the lowest level of interest into a hierarchy (tree).

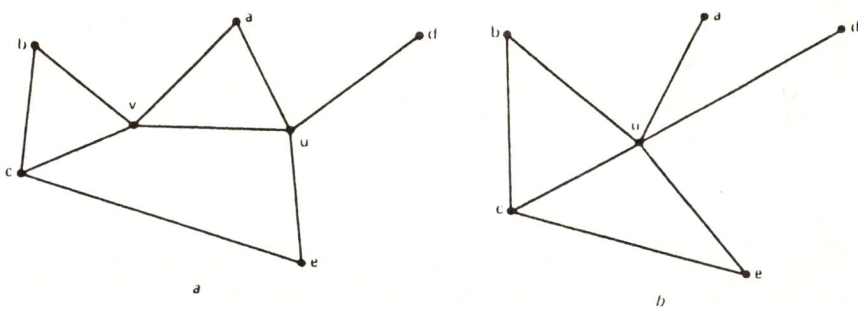

Figure 2

Reduction Process (a) Before and (b) After Fusion of v With u

Because there are a finite number of possible reductions, the minimal number of reductions can be computed. With this definition, the dimension can be computed only after the product is available. This is also true for many other measures, e.g., those presented in software science. However, the complexity of calculation and the dubious utility of a structural dimension make it of use only conceptually.

Using this method, the levels of abstraction can be constructed with a bottom-up tracing algorithm. Before the product has been created, the levels of abstraction may be constructed by a top-down process sometimes called stepwise refinement. (In the software process model presented above, the abstractions correspond to the linguistic levels constructed during reification. Another example is Dijkstra's hierarchy of virtual machines used to explain his model of stepwise refinement.[16]) For well understood problem domains, transformation heuristics exist that guide the developer in this top-down process. In poorly understood problem domains, on the other hand, it is generally accepted that the problem solving is not performed in such an orderly sequence. For example, consider Jackson's comment.[17]

> Top-down is a reasonable way of describing things which are already fully understood. It is usually possible to impose a hierarchical structure for the purposes of description, and it seems reasonable to start a description with the larger, and work towards the smaller aspects of what is to be described. But top-down is not a reasonable way of developing, designing, or discovering anything. There is a close parallel with mathematics. A mathematical textbook describes a branch of mathematics in a logical order: each theorem stated and proved is used in the proofs of subsequent theorems. But the theorems were not developed or discovered in this way, or in this order; the order of description is not the order of development.

Dijkstra refers to the mapping between the model and the reality being modeled as the intellectual distance between the problem and its computerized solution.[18] As we have seen, for well understood domains implementation may be possible in a top-down fashion. In this case, each level of abstraction in problem solution should correspond to a dimension created by fusion. For poorly understood domains, on the other hand, there will be many more levels of abstraction during problem solving than there will be dimensions in the final product. One, therefore, may consider the ratio of problem solving levels of abstraction to product dimension as a measure of "intellectual distance." Of course, it is not possible to compute this measure; most of the problem solving abstractions represent cognitive acts that cannot be recorded.

4.3   Summary

This discussion of dimensions implies that there are different concepts of dimension for the problem statement (S) and the implemented product (P). One may assume that the higher the dimension of an object, the more difficult the modeling process. Therefore, dimension might be considered a complexity metric.

For behavioral models, dimensionality was described in the context of views. This implies that dimensionality will be strongly dependent upon application type, i.e., the number of views necessary to describe it. A weakness of this definition is that it does not measure the complexity of a description within a view. In this case, the volume of the description within a dimension is the true complexity measure.

The concept of dimensionality for structural models was based upon the effort required to transform an operational product in the form of a network into a hierarchical representation with abstractions. Using this concept of dimension, it is clear that one can reduce the dimensionality of a problem by providing an implementation language that supports higher levels of abstraction. (This is the system style concept of Reference 1. The concept is also consistent with abstract data types and other forms of abstraction.) One must be careful, however, to distinguish between dimensions of the process and those of the product. The number of phases, linguistic levels, and virtual representations generally are dimensions of the process and not the product.

If the behavioral and structural models have different purposes and different concepts for dimension, then it stands to reason that they also will have different representations. This is the topic of the next section.

5.0   REPRESENTATIONS

All languages may be described by three intertwining concepts:

- Syntax that defines the valid relationships among the elements in a language.

- Semantics that prescribe the meaning of a sentence by its originator.

- Pragmatics that represents the meaning received by the listener or reader.

In programming languages the domain is constrained so that pragmatics are not an issue. In the software process, on the other hand, pragmatics are involved in the transcription of real world needs as a behavioral specification and in the translation from a behavioral specification to a structural specification.

We assert in this paper that the gap between the semantic intent of the originator and the pragmatic meaning received will be small whenever the representations used by the originator and receiver are similar. For example, the syntax and semantics used in mathematics are well defined. Thus, the gap between intent and understanding is relatively small. (Examples of the gap are seen in false theories and incorrect proofs.) The syntax and semantics of musical notation also are reasonably precise; yet anyone who has listened to a player piano understands the gap left to interpretation.

In the case of the software process, there are some application domains in which the problems are well defined. In these instances, heuristics and representations exist that reduce this intent/understanding gap. For example, there are conventions for the definition of a data model and data type formats. There also are models for semantically describing a database (the Entity-Relationship Model) and for describing process flows (the Data Flow Diagram). In each case, the representation used is not intuitively obvious; it must be learned in the context of the software process, but once learned the result is a reduction in the gap.

For software application domains that are not well understood, fewer tools have been developed, and the gap can be expected to be relatively large. Moreover, the selection of semantic/pragmatic representations that inherently clash with each other probably will not contribute to narrowing this gap. Therefore, the representation problem may be stated as follows. There is a multidimensional behavioral entity that must be codified as a behavioral model using tools that can be managed by human minds. This behavioral model must then be transformed into a multidimensional structural model in another form. Again there are constraints imposed by the cognitive process. The question, then, is can we find "natural" representations or serviceable tools that can facilitate the translations of each modeling step.

5.1 Diagrams Considered Harmful

Figure 3 summarizes the problem spaces previously identified and visually represents the concepts of behavioral and structural dimension. The transformation between these two dimensional representations must be managed by a human agent, e.g., the designer. For the designer, there is a natural preference for a hierarchical structure. There are several reasons for this.

- A printed document is always in the form of a hierarchy (outline). There are two dimensions, index points of reference and sequential length, and the document may be accessed in small linear chunks.

- The final software product may be traced backwards and organized in a tree structure. This reflects the tendency to describe what is known in a top-down way.

- Every search sequence (with backtracking) describes a tree structure. Program call trees also are presented as hierarchies even though repeated instances of calls to utilities indicate that a network is being described.

- Hierarchies contain conceptually useful properties. Inheritance is one frequently used example.

- Because cognition depends on a limited number of short term registers, there are typically only 7 (or 5) plus or minus 2 active concepts at a time. Such small numbers of objects naturally arrange themselves as a tree. Moreover, navigating through long term memory is a search process which defines a tree.

Thus, in Figure 3 the problem spaces are shown as a hierarchy even though there are overlaps that obviously produce a network.

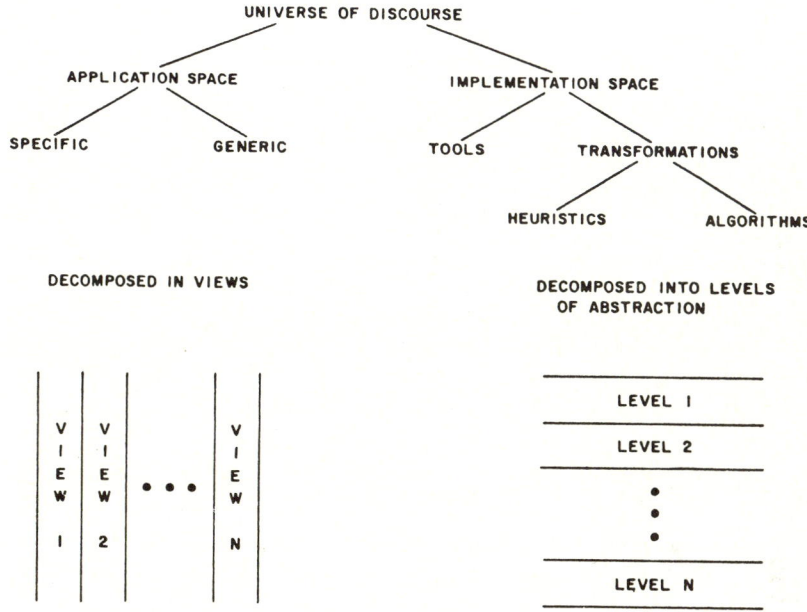

Figure 3

Problem Spaces and Dimension Concepts

The designer also has a natural tendency to use diagramming techniques. As we have seen, short term memory has a fixed number of registers that hold chunks of knowledge. Small collections of knowledge can be organized as a chunk for short term memory; these chunks can be retrieved from long term memory as needed. This chunking principle allows a two dimensional medium (paper) to represent three dimensions as follows: there are the two dimensions displayed by the spatial characteristics of the paper and the third dimension symbolized by the abstractions of each diagrammatic entity; i.e., the boxes or lines. (Newell and Simon refer to this as External Memory.[10]) Where the abstraction (contents of the box) is well defined, e.g., "set x=x+1," the notation is precise. On the other hand, when there is a high level of abstraction, e.g., "initialize," the abstraction is subject to different interpretations by different viewers at different times. These views may conflict and result in contradictory lower levels of abstraction; that is, as a result of the intent/understanding gap, the views may diverge.

Dijkstra has been quoted as saying that pictures (diagrams) are useful only (a) when one does not understand something or (b) when one wants to explain something.[19] If one accepts that the systems being modeled have a complexity greater than what can be organized in the three dimensions of a diagram, then the diagram can be seen as a three-dimensional projection useful for understanding or explaining. The value of a diagram, however, may be ephemeral. Once the concept has been established by use of a diagram, the diagram may not be the best way for representing the concept. Indeed, Orr proposes the use of his entity diagrams simply to go from fuzzy thinking to clear thinking; they then are discarded.[20]

This raises a basic question regarding the use of diagrams as a formal representation for the problem solving process: does the diagram reflect the structure of the objects in the application or implementation spaces, or is it simply a working document built upon abstractions designed to obscure detail? A personal fear is that bit-mapped displays and color are leading us into a high tech domain of icons, trees and nested windows that may obscure rather than clarify. Recall that Elstein *et al*. found that a seven-point scale was not significantly better than the three-point scale of confirm, disconfirm and noncontributory. They also found that clinicians had difficulty in integrating and combining data. People tend to use relatively little information in decision making, and it is not certain that the four dimensions of a color graphics diagram will help in understanding the problem to be solved. In fact, it may simply contribute to the information overload. Furthermore, whenever the graphic representation does not reflect the structure of the entities being modeled, then the use of such diagrams even may be misleading and harmful.

5.2 An Example: Representations for Interactive Information Systems

If diagrams are not the answer, then what is? The author is not bold enough to attempt an answer. Yet for some half dozen years we have been working with diagramless system development environments for interactive information systems. We have had success with one system in implementing complex production systems with a relatively small effort.[21] Therefore, it may be useful to consider how this system represents the information that describes the application and implementation domains.

The diagram in Figure 4 shows that there are three levels of representation.

- Descriptive level. This is a behavioral model that describes what the system is to do. In the present system, this is maintained in the form of

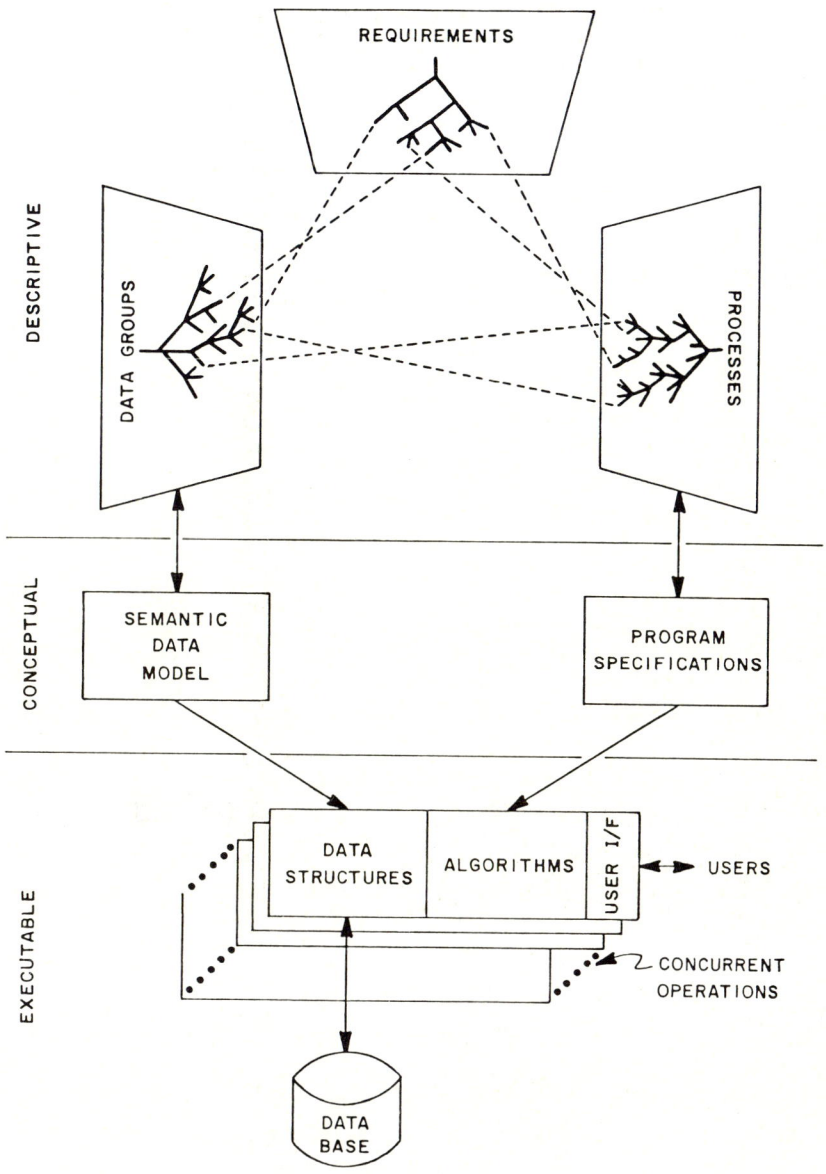

Figure 4

Three Levels of Representation For Information Systems

text; another environment is under development which will represent the information more formally so that the next level can be inferred from it.[22]

- Conceptual level. This is a behavioral model that formalizes the text descriptions of the higher level. It is a complete specification. Therefore, some objects also describe how the entities are to be implemented in the computer environment. In the latter case, the behavioral model is expanded into a structural model in order to satisfy performance requirements. There is a single notation for both behavioral and structural models at this level.

- Executable level. This is a set of executable code sequences generated from the conceptual level using transformation algorithms. The form is a set of transition networks.

Of particular interest for this discussion are the structure of each level and the links between levels. The descriptive level is presented as three views:

  Requirements: the functions to be supported.
  Processes: the flow within the application.
  Data Groups: the objects to be represented in the database.

Although the words "processes" and "data groups" imply design, each of the three is a view of what the target software is to do. In effect, these are the three dimensions of the behavioral model. Internally, each view is structured as a two-dimensional (hierarchical) projection of the project (application) space onto that viewpoint (dimension). The limitation to two dimensions for the internal representation is mandated by the need to list the information in the form of a document without redundancy. Links between nodes of the different views also are recorded. This structure is too complex to be printed; however, it is possible to display relationships, within a context, as hierarchical forms in the small. This kind of organization seems to reflect that of the human mind.

At the conceptual level, the objects have no inherent structure. They are stored as independent chunks. Each may be viewed as (a) a self-contained description of some described need, (b) a higher level of abstraction for some generated sequence of code, or (c) the definition of an entity or relationship in the data model. Links among the descriptive and conceptual objects are defined subjectively. (The system described in Reference 22 will use heuristics to describe some of the associations.) Links from the conceptual to the executable objects are established by the transformation algorithms.

For example, assume that there is a process called "Register patient." The designer can subjectively decide which conceptual programs support this function. Some programs may be key to this process, others may be used in only certain situations, and some may be general utility programs. The recording of the links produces a road map for use in understanding the structure of the final product. The designer must make a subjective judgment regarding relative importance and the need to suppress excessive detail. Once the programs are specified, however, they will be transformed into operational code, and all executable program and database links will be recorded. The executable recording is objective and has no means of limiting detail.

Notice how this type of representation tends to reflect the dimensional concepts of the application and implementation spaces. For the system under review, all representations are maintained in an integrated database organized by target application. There are facilities to provide local views and to navigate through the database using the links. Navigation goes from one dimension to the next in either the behavioral or the structural model. Limitations to this system include the informality of the text descriptive representations, the absence of tests to identify contradictions at that level, and its limitation to a single application domain. Nevertheless, the success of the environment in its target domain suggests that this perspective on spaces, dimensionality and representation is worthy of further exploration.

6.0 CONCLUSIONS

This paper addresses the question of how to represent the objects used during the software process. A "computer science" style exists in which the implementation objects can be formalized with only the control structures of sequence, iteration and selection. Complementary logical notations also are becoming increasingly popular. These forms have grown from a mathematical heritage that aims at precision in the definition of transformation heuristics and algorithms. Yet much of the software process is a cognitive activity operating outside this domain. The development of languages and representations that address the formal aspects of application development is a necessary part of progress in the field. But it is not sufficient.

Most of the software process depends upon human judgment and decision making. Some of that process will be formalized as heuristics and algorithms; however, as the scope and complexity of new applications grow, increased demand for judgmental support will follow. Consequently, knowledge of the problem domains and their representations will facilitate the development of better tools. Moreover, a recognition of the cognitive dimensions of the process should deter attempts to formalize aspects of the process that are inherently judgmental.

As a final note, I would like to point out that I see this paper as little more than the opening of an exchange. This version of the paper was finished, not because the author was comfortable with its contents, but rather because the publication schedule demanded it. Another six month incubation period is required. Of course, the value of conferences such as this is that one can test partially formed ideas and learn in the process. By way of a closing disclaimer, I will admit that I am less satisfied with my definitions of dimension with each draft. But I do not believe that this alters the thrust of the paper, a concept that I think I probably really accept with some certainty.

7.0 REFERENCES

[1] Blum, B. I., Language, Problem Solving and System Development, *The Role of Language in Problem Solving*, North-Holland, pp 237-252, 1985.

[2] Lehman, M. M., A Further Model of Coherent Programming Processes, *Software Process Workshop*, pp 27-34, 1984.

[3] Lehman, M. M., V. Stenning and W. M. Turski, Another Look at Software Design Methodology, *ACM SIGSOFT SEN* (9,2), pp 38-53, 1984.

[4] Turski, W. M., Completeness and Executability of Specifications: Two Confusing Notions, *Software Process Workshop*, pp 155-156, 1984.

[5] Curtis, B., Fifteen Years of Psychology in Software Engineering: Individual Differences and Cognitive Science, *Proc. 7th Inter. Conf. Software Eng.*, pp 97-106, 1984, p.100.

[6] Barstow, D., A Perspective on Automatic Programming, *The AI Magazine*, pp 5-27, Spring 1984, p 26.

[7] Shneiderman, B., *Software Psychology*, Winthrop Publishers, 1980.

[8] Sowa, J. F., *Conceptual Structures*, Addison-Wesley, 1984.

[9] Resnick, B., Mathematics and Science Learning: A New Conception, *Science*, 220:477-478, 1983.

[10] Newell, A. and H. A. Simon, *Human Problem Solving*, Prentice Hall, 1972.

[11] Elstein, A. S., L. S. Shulman, S. A. Sparafka, et al., *Medical Problem Solving*, Harvard University Press, 1978.

[12] Lehman, M. M., Programs, Life Cycles and Laws of Program Evolution, *Proc. IEEE* 68:1060-1076, 1980.

[13] Horowitz, E., A. Kemper, and B. Narasimhan, A Survey of Application Generators, *Software*, (2,1):40-54, 1985.

[14] Zave, P., The Operational Versus the Conventional Approach to Software Development, *Comm ACM*, 27:104-118, 1984.

[15] Goodman and Hedetniemi, *Introduction to the Design and Analysis of Algorithms*, McGraw-Hill, 1977, p.45.

[16] Dijkstra, E. W., Notes on Structured Programming, in Dahl, O. J., E. W. Dijkstra, and C. A. R. Hoare, *Structured Programming*, Academic Press, p.49, 1972.

[17] Jackson, M. A., *System Development*, Prentice Hall, 1983, p. 370.

[18] Cited, Fairley, R. E., *Software Engineering Concepts*, McGraw-Hill, p.3, 1985.

[19] Parnas, D., personal anecdote.

[20] Orr, K., *Structured Requirements Definition*, Ken Orr and Assoc., 1981.

[21] Blum, B. I., Experience With an Automated Generator of Information Systems, *Int. Symp. on New Directions in Computing*, pp 138-147, 1985.

[22] Blum, B. I. and V. G. Sigillito, Some Philosophic Foundations for an Environment for System Building, *1985 ACM Annual Conference*, 516-523, 1985.

QUESTION AND ANSWER PERIOD

<u>WEINTRAUB</u>

Toward the end, Bruce, I had this problem of frustration, not with you, but with the subject matter. In my mind it solidified in the slide where you said there were some things which cannot be handled in an objective domain. I used to work in submarine analysis where the problem was defined in terms of computers because we were doing analysis of other people's computer mistakes. The problem in that domain was that when the perception of need was based on data which was already very objective in its form, there sometimes is an objectiveness to the need. The way I got myself in trouble in that analysis was by realizing that these very well defined, very hard models were completely wrong. They were based on a verification that had been done years before by people who did not understand how the systems was really working. What I realized as you were finishing up was that this frustration is something which is going to last in the computer application field for quite a while because things which are really well defined and really solid and really fully understood are usually completely wrong.

<u>BLUM</u>

This points out one of the things I was trying to get at. There is a major difference between verification and validation. We can verify things and have them all correct in the small, but most of the problem solving that we do is in the large, and there we are dealing with validation. There is also a cultural difference. When we started with computers, most of the people were trying to solve well-defined and well-understood problems that were tool-constrained; that is, we said, "If I had a tool that would allow me to compute these things I could solve my problem." Many of the early applications went along those lines. However, as we start to solve today's problems, we have to recognize that it's our understanding of the problem and the selection of the appropriate tools that is now probably more important than the definition of the smaller tools and the definitions of correctness.

<u>WEINTRAUB</u>

Taking that one step further, the advantage of higher level languages is that we can manage more by saying less. For example, for a sort algorithm, I don't have to worry about how the sort works; here is the result of the sort. Fifteen years ago someone approaching this problem, unless you were working in APL, would have to consider sort routines, there might be 47 of them, and worry about which to use and why it might work best. The point is that our ability to abstract is very much affected by what terms we can handle and by what languages we've learned to think in.

BLUM

I think that there is a major difference between writing programs and designing a system. And I believe that we are getting to the point where, in the next ten years or so, the computer industry is going to subdivide itself into those who are like engineers (implementing solutions, writing programs, working in a very, very structured and formal domain to write programs) and those who are working in the application domain (who use those tools to solve application solutions). I am frankly more concerned with the application solutions than I am with the details of writing programs. Clearly, you have to understand both in order to be able to do either.

DOYLE

I was interested in the two steps of the process that you had drawn with the arrows: abstraction and reification. I suppose everyone who does this a lot has a pretty sure feel that once you have some kind of solution statement that you can reduce it stepwise into programs and into statements. But I think a lot of people when they draw the arrows that move from, "there's a need out here" to "some solution and programs" get a sense that the same thing is going on at those two arrows, as though almost there's a functionality occurring. Certainly, in the second step of the process anyone who does a lot of programming has a sure feel that there is functionality going on and that there is a close connection there. There's not a close connection, however, in the first part, and it seems to me that abstraction is a fundamentally creative process; as though as opposed to a closed system we have an open system. And that system is as open as and as creative as anyone wants to be with it, as opposed to mere abstraction, taking something out. Now, it seems to me that the challenge in that fundamentally creative process is to control it and to guide it. My experience is that most of the programming solutions that come acropp are not because people can't write in a programming language, but because what they produce doesn't have a lot of correspondence to what solving that need requires. Any thoughts about controlling that creative process; any thoughts about getting us from being artists, if you will, and making things up, to better definition in that area?

BLUM

Obviously, like everyone else I have my own solution. But with only two minutes I can't tell you all about it. That's why the diagrams contain two types of feedback; there's a difference between verification and validation. Validation is a thing that's looking at that creative process and trying to constrain it. Even when the people talk about abstraction and reification, they have a very good model for reification and basically no model for abstraction. I think that you should have to have a good model of the cognitive process and an understanding of the domain to build tools. (Clearly, abstraction is going to be different in different domains.) Then, if you have some tools that reflect the domain with the model of how you can implement things, you have a much better chance of controlling and channeling the process so that people don't reinvent wheels.

SCHERLIS

I generally was very happy with your conceptualization of the program design and development process, but most programmers spend most of their time modifying and adapting existing code. My question is, to what extent does your conceptualization support the modification process, and what are the right notions to support adaptation; what is the right representation of past experience?

BLUM

Turski says that this canonical model is valid for changes that occur after delivery. If you want to take a look at maintenance, which represents maybe 60 to 80 percent of the total life cycle cost, this same model can be used. I think of maintenance as being design with lots of constraints. The model that I've shown you has a separation of concerns. We look at the process in a very static way, and we don't really worry about the changes. If you view it as a static model, it is as valid for maintenance as for initial development. However, one has to recognize that even when you're doing your initial development, one is working with a moving target. Barry Boehm has what he calls a spiral model. He represents development as spiralling out, with each layer in the spiral leading to another prototype, learning from that prototype, starting another spiral, until you learn enough to be able to implement the system. Then evolution, enhancement, maintenance, whatever you want to call it, is just the next iteration. Rather than having a prototype that you build on, you're building on a finished system. That's in the large when you have no problems; in the small when you have all of those nagging problems that you have to solve, one frequently loses the clarity of the model.

KNOWLEDGE REPRESENTATION FOR REASONING ABOUT LANGUAGE

Jeannette G. Neal

Calspan Corporation
4455 Genesee Street
Buffalo, New York 14225

Stuart C. Shapiro

Department of Computer Science
University of Buffalo
Buffalo, New York 14260

This paper discusses the representation of language processing knowledge for use by an Artificial Intelligence (AI) system which treats language understanding as (part of) its problem or task domain. The benefits of treating language understanding in this manner are also discussed. Our work focuses on development of knowledge representations and natural language methodology to enable a system to understand input expressions in its accepted language L which are about the same language L. We are particularly concerned with instruction that extends the language L, with the instruction expressed in language L itself. This ability of a language to serve as its own meta-language is an extremely significant feature of any natural language. The extendability of the language requires that its representation be non-static. We therefore use a system whose processing mechanism is an inference engine and which reasons according to the rules of its dynamic knowledge base. This paper also discusses the PARSNIP system which we have implemented based upon the approach indicated above. We discuss the semantic network representation of the system's knowledge; summarize the system's core knowledge and kernel language; develop an example to illustrate the system's use of a language as its own meta-language.

1.0 INTRODUCTION

Language, whether artificial or natural, is a means of communication. However, language and language understanding knowledge can also be treated as objects of thought, reasoning, and discussion. Our approach is to treat language in this dual manner: (a) means of communication and (b) task or problem domain. In this paper we focus on the representation of language processing knowledge for use by an Artificial Intelligence (AI) system which treats language understanding as (part of) its problem or task domain. We assume that all processing, including language processing, is a form of reasoning or inference for the knowledge-based AI system. In particular, our emphasis is on the use of a language as its own meta-language. This approach is exemplified in the PARSNIP language understanding system that we have been developing.

There are many benefits and reasons for a system to treat language understanding as (part of) its task domain and explicitly model its linguistic knowledge and the analysis of input utterances. For example, as computer programs, particularly expert systems, become more complex, it is increasingly important for these systems to explain their line of reasoning, justify their results, and be able to answer questions about their task domain. Language understanding systems should have the same explanatory abilities and therefore these systems must model input utterances and their analyses.

Another reason for treating a system's linguistic knowledge as domain knowledge is to provide for extensibility. That is, a major concern with regard to language processing systems and knowledge-based systems in general is that the system's knowledge or processing capability be extendable. The UNIX consultant (UC) [Wilensky et al., 1984], for example, includes a component called the UC Teacher which accepts input in a subset of English to extend its language processing capability. The UC Teacher, however, is a separate component of UC with its own knowledge base. This contrasts with our approach which consists of the system having just one integrated knowledge base containing linguistic and non-linguistic knowledge and also having just one language which serves as its own meta-language.

We have been particularly interested in the fundamental requirements and problems entailed in providing a system with the ability to use a language as its own meta-language. That is, assuming that the system accepts and understands some language L, we are interested in enabling the system to understand input expressions in language L which are about the same language L. Our primary motivation for this interest is to enable a system to understand instruction that extends the language L, with the instruction expressed in language L itself.

This ability of a language to serve as its own meta-language is an extremely significant feature of any natural language. Common examples of a natural language being used as its own metalanguage include: (a) children receiving classroom instruction about English expressed in English; (b) the dictionary definition of an English word given in English; (c) a textbook about a certain language written in the same language; (d) a person explaining the meaning of a word or phrase to his conversational partner in an informal setting. Our approach requires that the language which the system accepts not be static as in a compiled program. Therefore, in our implementation, the system's processing mechanism is an inference engine which reasons according to the rules of its knowledge base. At any time during processing, new knowledge can be added to the knowledge base and this new knowledge is immediately available for use by the system.

2.0   SYSTEM OVERVIEW

PARSNIP is a knowledge-based AI system in the role of an educable cognitive agent whose domain of expertise is language understanding and whose task domain includes its own language knowledge. PARSNIP has been implemented using the SNePS semantic network processing system (Shapiro, 1979a; Shapiro et al., 1983). This language understanding system is similar to the Prolog-based systems of Warren and Pereira (1982), Dahl (1979, 1981), Dahl and McCord (1983), McCord (1982,1985), and Pereira (1985) in that it is implemented in a logic based system in which processing is a form of inference. The SNePS inference package (Shapiro et al., 1982), however, is not based on a backtracking strategy as is Prolog, but on a multi-processing approach (Kaplan 1973; McKay and Shapiro, 1980; Neal and Shapiro, 1985) incorporating a producer-consumer model. PARSNIP's knowledge is retained in a semantic network representation and new knowledge can be added at any time and immediately used by the system. The system's core consists of certain predefined categories, objects, relations and a kernel language, which are discussed in Section 4. Included in the system's core is an interpretational mapping which maps from parsed surface strings to the representation of their interpretations. Both the syntax and the semantics of the system's language is available for extension by the user at any time.

Our system is unique in its ability to use a language as its own meta-language. The properties of PARSNIP that enable it to do this are: (a) Language processing knowledge is integrated in the system's one knowledge base with whatever other domain knowledge the system may have; all processing, including language processing, is a form of inference in PARSNIP and this integrated knowledge base is the source of rules and facts that guide the system's reasoning during processing; (b) our system incorporates the use-mention distinction for language (Quine, 1951); our representations reflect the fact that the meaning of a token or surface string is distinct from the token or string itself; thus one can talk to the system about both the syntax and the semantics of language; (c) rules and facts of the knowledge base are stored as a set, i.e.,, no order on the rules or facts is assumed, maintained, or used; (d) the simulated multi-processing form of control provides for all applicable rules to be used in simulated parallel fashion during inference processing; (e) PARSNIP's knowledge base is not static and the user can extend the syntax of the system's language definition at any time (i.e., the user can add lexical categories, string categories, and parsing rules); (f) a new rule or assertion can be added to PARSNIP's knowledge base as the interpretation of an input string that has been recognized as being in the domain of the interpretational mapping; (g) the user can extend the system's interpretational mapping; (h) the knowledge base representations for the predefined concepts (e.g., phrase structure constituent relation) are available to the system-user to incorporate in extensions to the system's interpretational mapping; (i) RULE-STATEMENT is a special category in the domain of the interpretational mapping; the PARSNIP core has special knowledge about how to build a rule in the semantic network knowledge base, including universal and existential quantification of variables, so that the structure will be recognized and usable by the inference system.

3.0 KNOWLEDGE REPRESENTATION TECHNIQUES

A SNePS semantic network is a directed graph with labeled arcs in which nodes represent concepts and the arcs represent non-conceptual binary relations between concepts. It is generally agreed that the nodes of a semantic network represent intensional concepts (Woods, 1975; Brachman, 1977; Maida and Shapiro, 1982). A "concept" is something in our domain of interest about which we may want to store information and which may be the subject of "thought" and inference. Since each concept is represented by a node, the relations represented by the arcs of our system are not conceptual, but structural (Shapiro, 1979a).

If there is a path of arcs from node N to node M, N is said to *dominate M*. Two important types of nodes are *molecular* and *atomic* nodes. Molecular nodes are nodes that dominate other nodes. Atomic nodes are simply not molecular. Atomic nodes can be *constant* (representing a unique semantic concept) or *variable*. Variable nodes are used in SNePS like variables are used in normal predicate logic notations. Network nodes can also be categorized as in the following table.

Node Category	Type of Concept
Non-dominated (asserted) molecular node	Asserted proposition which is "believed" by the system
Dominated molecular node	Proposition or structured object which is a participant in a proposition
Atomic node	Object

Figure 1

Table of Node Categories

A propositional molecular node N together with the arcs incident from the node and the nodes $M_1,..,M_k$ immediately dominated by N correspond to a case frame (Fillmore, 1968; Bruce, 1975) where the arc names correspond to the slot names, and the nodes $M_1,..,M_k$ represent the slot fillers. Undominated molecular nodes in a SNePS network represent propositions believed by the system. Concepts such as the following are propositional and are represented by molecular nodes: a certain lexeme being a member of a certain category; a string being a constituent of another string; a lexeme having a certain number (i.e., singular or plural). Simple examples of propositional nodes are M1 and M2 of Figure 2. Node M1 represents the proposition that B1 represents the concept expressed by the word "NOUN" and M2 represents the proposition that the lexeme "SNOW" is in the category called "NOUN".

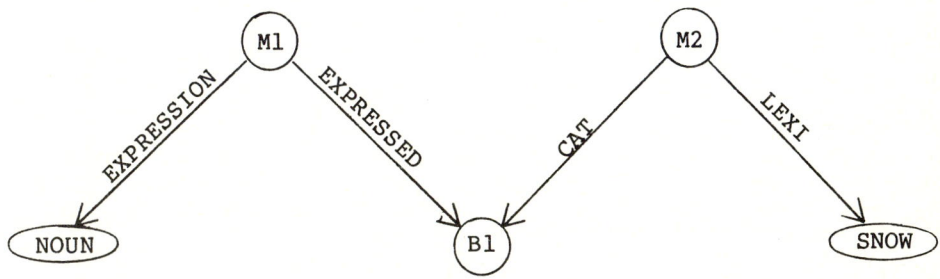

Figure 2

M1 and M2 are Simple Examples of Propositional Nodes

The syntactic objects represented in our network knowledge base include morphemes, surface strings, and nodes of parse trees. Individual morphemes are represented as nodes whose identifiers or print names are the morphemes themselves. The representation of a surface string utilized in this study consists of a network version of the list structure used by Pereira and Warren (1980). This representation is also similar to Kay's charts (1973) in that whenever alternative analyses are made for a given substring of a sentence, the sentence structure is enhanced by multiple structures representing these alternative analyses. Retention of the alternatives avoids the reanalysis of previously processed substrings which occurs in a backtracking system. Our basic representation of a surface string is illustrated in Figure 3.

Nodes identified by the atoms B0, SNOW, IS and WHITE are atomic nodes and represent objects: the empty string, and tokens "SNOW", "IS", and "WHITE", respectively. Node M4 is molecular and represents the initial string SNOW". M5 is also molecular and represents the initial string "SNOW IS", and similarly for node M6. A node such as M6 that represents an object would typically be dominated in our system by some node representing a proposition about it.

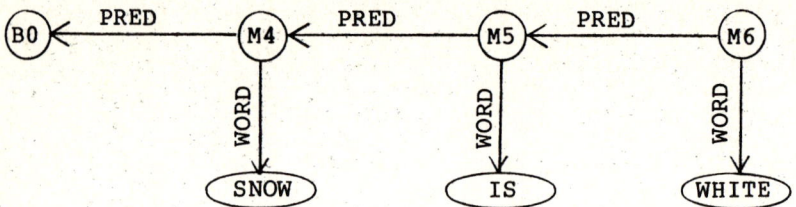

Figure 3

Network Representation of a Surface String

As each word of an input string is read by the PARSNIP system, the network representation of the string is extended and relevant rules stored in the SNePS network are triggered.

Interpretations of surface strings are also represented as nodes of our network knowledge base. The PARSNIP kernel language enables the user to define case frame structures and to begin to define rules to guide the system in interpreting input utterances.

Rules to be used by the system to perform inference are represented in a SNePS semantic network by **rule nodes**. A rule node represents a formula of predicate calculus and dominates a set of molecular nodes using arcs to represent one of the four nonstandard connectives: V-entailment, &-entailment, AND-OR, THRESH (Shapiro, 1971, 1979a,b). A rule node of a SNePS network may also have universally or existentially quantified variables associated with it, using either the AVB of EVB binding relation representing universal or existential quantification, respectively. The PARSNIP system primarily uses the &-entailment type of rule.

4.0 CORE KNOWLEDGE AND KERNEL LANGUAGE

Since our objective has been to design a system which includes its language in its discourse domain and accepts instruction to extend its language, then the system can start with a small core knowledge base and a kernel language (KL) that can be used to bootstrap to a robust self-referential target language. This is the approach we have taken and, as a result, there are conceivably two types of users of our system: (a) a "teacher-user" who instructs the system in language understanding, starting with just the core knowledge in the system's knowledge base, and (b) a person who is a user of the system after a robust language has been "taught" to the system and the discourse is primarily about a domain other than language.

The core of the PARSNIP system consists of certain predefined categories, objects, relations, and functions. The fundamentals of *syntax* typically include lexical classes, string classes, terminal symbols, non-terminal symbols, sequences of symbols or words forming strings, rules defining the syntax of a language, phrase structures, and constituent relations. Provision for syntactic entities has been included in the core.

To provide for the acquisition of syntactic knowledge, the pre-defined *categories* include: L-CAT, the category consisting of the names of lexical classes; S-CAT, the category consisting of the names of string classes; VARIABLE, the category consisting of the identifiers that the user chooses to use as variables.

The predefined kinds of *objects* of the system's core are (i) the Initial String, which can be recursively defined as consisting of a word or token concatenated onto the right end of another Initial String that may be the null string; (ii) the Bounded String, which consists of a surface string with a beginning word and a last word, where the beginning word precedes or is identical to the last word. For example, nodes M1 and M2 of Figure 4 represent Initial Strings and node M3 represents the Bounded String consisting of the string "A NOUN-PHRASE".

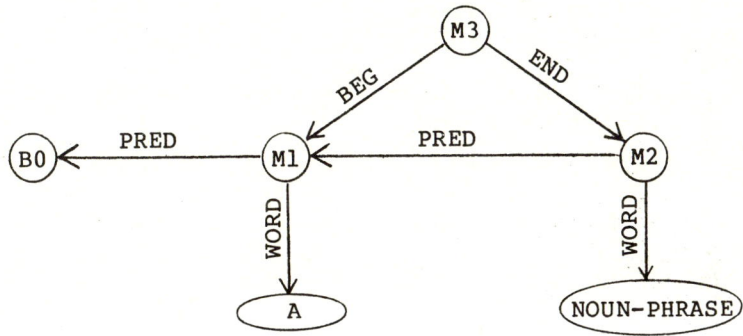

Figure 4

Network Representation of Initial and Bounded Strings

The following are the syntactic *relations* included in the system's core and their semantic network representations are illustrated in Figure 5: (i) Lexical Membership: a lexeme L being a member of a certain lexical category C; (ii) Phrase Structure Relation: Bounded String B being in category C and this phrase structure or parse of the string B being represented by concept N, analogous to a node of a parse tree; (iii) Constituency Relation: Phrase Structure S1 being a constituent of another structure S2.

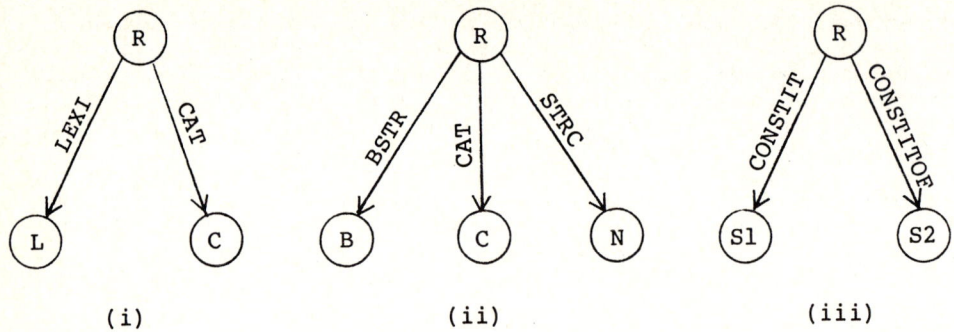

Figure 5

Network Representations for the Syntactic Relations

In order to provide the teacher-user with core fundamentals with which to instruct the system in the *semantics* of her target language, the PARSNIP core contains categories and relations pertaining to the semantics of language.

The predefined *categories* include: RULE-STMT, the category consisting of strings recognized by the system as conditional rule statements; RULE-INDICATOR, a string category which enables the user to explain to the system which input utterances are to be processed as rule statements and interpreted appropriately.

We have striven to make the core of the PARSNIP system simple and unbiased with regard to linguistic theory. Therefore, the system has no concept of coreferentiality. The system has a simple mechanism to enable the user to refer to a previously mentioned entity. This mechanism is the use of a VARIABLE as an appositive to a "main phrase". Thus VAR-APPOSITION-PHR and MAIN-APPOS-PHR are two predefined string categories with a limited predefined syntax and semantics which enable the user to use a variable as an appositive to a "main phrase" constituent of the VAR-APPOSITION-PHR and have the system remember the variable as an identifier for the main phrase.

The predefined *relations* which pertain to semantics are: (i) a structure or parsed string expressing a certain concept; (ii) one set being a subset of another; (iii) the rule structures of SNePS (Shapiro, 1979a).

The PARSNIP kernel language consists of a language of syntactic and semantic rewrite rules to enable the teacher-user to begin to define a target language. The *syntactic rewrite rules* provide for the establishment of lexical and string classes, making lexical entries, and defining the syntax of the language. The *semantic rewrite rules* enable the user to define the interpretational mapping for the target language.

The *syntactic rules* are of the following three types:

(i) Lexical entry: <lexical-category> ---> <literal>;
(ii) Context free rules of the form

<string-category> ---> $<s>_1 \ldots <s>_k$, k>0

where each $<s>_i$ is either a literal or the name of a lexical category previously made known to the system via a lexical entry into category L-CAT;

(iii) Context-sensitive rules of the form

$<ls>_1 \ldots <ls>_n$ ---> $<rs>_1 \ldots <rs>_n$, n>0

where each element $<ls>_i$ or $<rs>_i$ is either a literal, the name of a lexical category, or the name of a string category.

When a lexical entry is accepted by the system it is interpreted as an assertion that the specified token is a member of the specified lexical-category. The interpretation of a rule of type (ii) or (iii) is a semantic network rule structure which is added to the system's integrated knowledge base.

The *semantic rewrite rules* enable the teacher-user to define the semantics for strings of any given category. The semantic rewrite rules are of two types: (1) *Case-frame-definitions* enable the user to define the semantics of a string from any given string-category in terms of a case frame, with the frame slots filled by the representations of the interpretations of the specified constituents. (2) The *Case-slot-definition* is provided as part of the KL so that the user can define the semantics of a surface string whose interpretation is a slot-filler in a case frame, analogous to a participant in a proposition.

Refer to (Neal, 1985) for a complete discussion of the syntax and semantics of the rewrite rules, their implementation and application by the system. Examples of the use of the rewrite rules will be given in subsequent sections.

5.0   REPRESENTATIONS OF LINGUISTIC AND NON-LINGUISTIC ENTITIES

As indicated previously, we have been developing an AI system that can use its language understanding knowledge both (1) in the process of analyzing language and (2) as the discourse domain. That is, the objective is that the system have the ability to understand utterances expressed in language L that are *about* the same language L and which may extend language L.

Since both syntax and semantics of language are important to language *understanding*, it is critical for our system to distinguish between surface strings (or tokens, words) and their meanings. The system must represent both surface strings and their meanings in its knowledge base in order for the user to be able to instruct the system concerning the syntax and semantics of language.

In order to introduce a simple example of the knowledge representations used by our system, the teacher-user begins by making lexical entries initially using the KL:

```
L-CAT ---> 'NOUN              L-CAT ---> 'BE-VERB
L-CAT ---> 'PROPER-NOUN        L-CAT ---> 'ADJECTIVE
NOUN  ---> 'WOMAN              L-CAT ---> 'PROPERTY
NOUN  ---> 'WOMEN
```

According to the above lexical entries, NOUN is established as a lexical category, and "WOMAN" and "WOMEN" are elements in the category NOUN. The representation of this information in the system's knowledge base is shown in Figure 6.

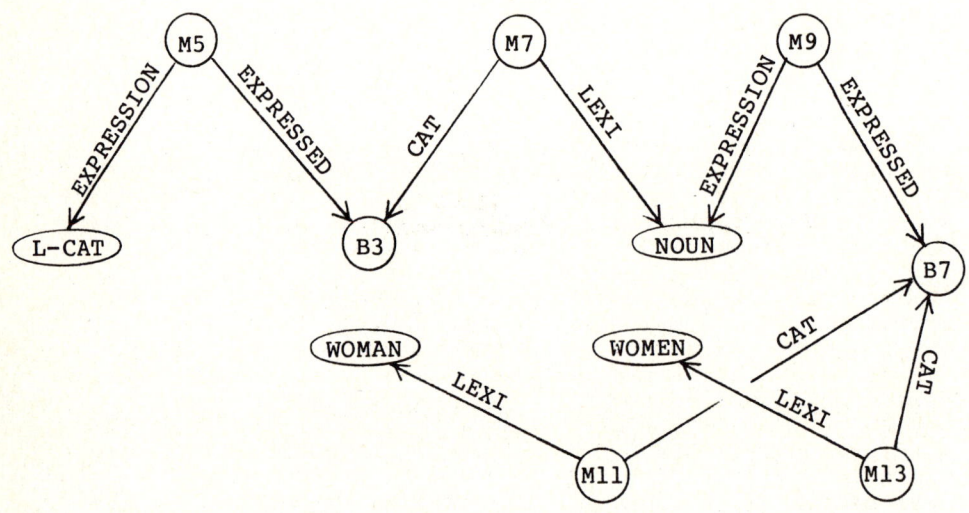

Figure 6

Network Representations for Lexical Entries

As indicated previously, it is critical for the system to distinguish between a word or token and its meaning. This distinction is always maintained by our system and is reflected in Figure 6: a node, distinct from node "L-CAT", is used to represent the category called "L-CAT". Similarly, node B7 represents the category called "NOUN". Node M7 represents the proposition that "NOUN" is in the category L-CAT and node M9 represents the proposition that B7 represents the concept or category expressed by "NOUN". Node M11 represents the proposition that "WOMAN" is a NOUN and, similarly, M13 represents the proposition that "WOMEN" is a NOUN.

We have shown in (Neal, 1985) that after beginning the system's instruction using the KL and building up a definition for a certain small subset of English, the user can input simple utterances about linguistic concepts as well as non-linguistic concepts, as in the following sentences:

(1) " MARY IS TALL "
(2) " 'WOMAN IS SINGULAR "

The system's processing of these statements is governed by the language definition established thus far by the teacher-user. The system interprets each of the above statements as specifying a property of an entity as per the teacher-user's rules which have been omitted since this paper is focusing on representations for language knowledge and also due to space limitations (see (Neal, 1985) for details). The rules, however, enable the system to infer that (1) is about *the entity called "MARY"*, whereas (2) is about *the word "WOMAN" itself*, not the entity called "WOMAN". In each case, the sentence specifies the value of a property of the subject of the sentence, the property being inferred by the system. Figures 7 and 8 illustrate the difference in the representation of the interpretation of words which are mentioned (the word "WOMAN") in comparison to the representation of words which are used (the word "MARY"). Node B70 of Figure 7 represents the concept of MARY, whereas the node labeled "WOMAN" of Figure 8 represents the word itself.

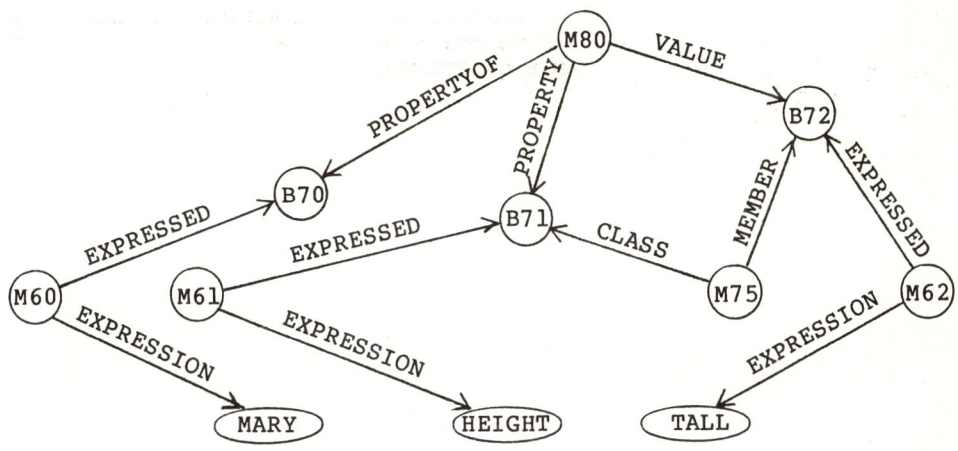

Figure 7

Network Representation of "Mary is Tall"

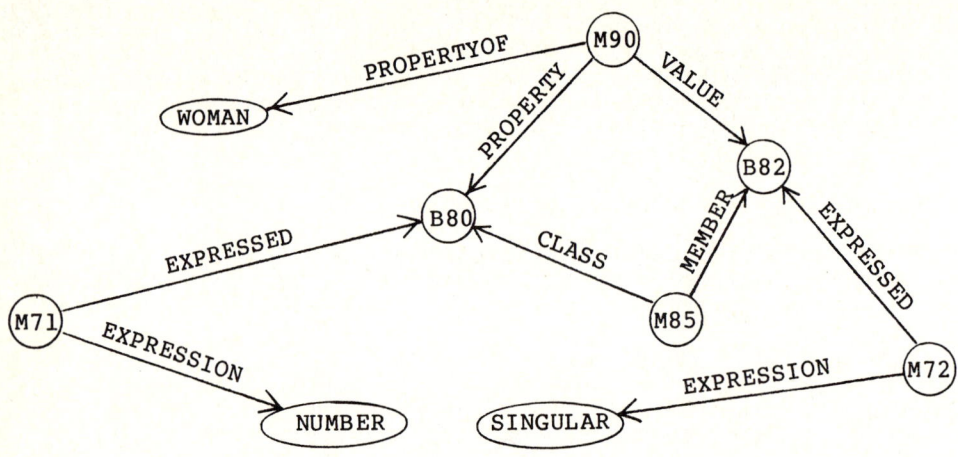

Figure 8

Network Representation of "Woman is Singular"

6.0 DEVELOPING A SUBSET OF ENGLISH AS ITS OWN META-LANGUAGE

Since we treat linguistic knowledge as domain knowledge, the teacher-user can add to PARSNIP's knowledge base by instructing the system as to how to process or understand ever more sophisticated language.

The rewrite rules of the KL are certainly not sufficient for expressing all the rules a user would need to teach the system a target language of her choice. Therefore, one of the most important features that PARSNIP has is the ability to be taught to understand a more general form of rule statement. The syntax of this rule statement is at the discretion of the teacher-user and is determined by rewrite rules input by the teacher-user. This syntax could be an IF-THEN form in a subset of English. In a test of our system (Neal, 1985), we built up the system's language ability such that rules to augment the system's language definition could be entered in a subset of English. The concepts that we have focused on concern features of language such as linguistic number, specificity of determiners and noun-phrases, determinateness, etc. Example rules are:

(3) IF THE HEAD-NOUN OF A NOUN-PHRASE X HAS NUMBER SINGULAR/PLURAL THEN X HAS NUMBER SINGULAR/PLURAL

where "SINGULAR/PLURAL" and "X" are user-declared variables, "SINGULAR/PLURAL" having been used simply for the sake of clarity.

Using concepts of Lexical-Functional Grammar of (Kaplan and Bresnan, 1982), we can specify a condition under which specificity is propagated upward in the functional structure of a phrase structure:

> (4) IF DETERMINER X IS A CONSTITUENT OF NOUN-PHRASE Y THEN THE SPECIFICITY OF Y IS ASSIGNED THE SPECIFICITY OF X;

define indeterminateness for the system:

> (5) IF FUNCTIONAL-STRUCTURE F HAS ATTRIBUTE A AND IT IS NOT DERIVABLE THAT A HAS VALUE V THEN F IS INDETERMINATE;

specify a condition for ungrammaticality:

> (6) IF THE FUNCTIONAL-STRUCTURE OF SENTENCE S IS INDETERMINATE THEN S IS UNGRAMMATICAL.

It is important to remember that we do not advocate that language definitions or language processing instruction for AI systems be expressed in a natural language such as English. What we maintain is that people discuss their language using the self-same language and therefore a computer system should be capable of similar behavior. Furthermore, people extend their knowledge of their natural language by receiving instruction expressed in the same language, and, again, a computer system should be capable of similar behavior.

Let us consider an example to illustrate the system's ability to understand a statement expressed in the same language that the statement is about, the language being a subset of English. The example rule statement to be parsed and interpreted is rule (4) above.

Notice that rule (4) is concerned with specificity of determiners and noun-phrases, and yet the rule itself already uses determiners without a notion of specificity. This is analogous to children using language without knowing all the attributes of the words they use and all the conditions for grammaticality of sentences. They can be taught to become aware of these attributes and conditions and thus become more sophisticated users of language. Similarly, our system can be instructed about these attributes and become a more sophisticated user of language.

PARSNIP's language definition can be built up via instruction so that it can parse and interpret the rules (3) through (6) shown above. Since the teacher-user is provided with the details of the representations of the predefined categories, objects and relations which are summarized in Section 4 (more complete coverage is given in (Neal, 1985)), she can use these (as well as others of her own creation) when extending the interpretational mapping to new string categories of her choosing. Rules (7) and (8), given below, were part of the instruction input to the system to form this language definition when this actual language development was performed with our system. The complete set of input instructions to PARSNIP is not included here due to space constraints, but see (Neal, 1985) for details of a similar experiment.

In building up PARSNIP's language processing ability so that it could understand utterances about its own language, we used a grammar similar to a semantic grammar. Using rewrite rules of the KL, we chose "CONSTITUENCY-CLAUSE" as a non-terminal and defined the syntax of a CONSTITUENCY-CLAUSE to include clauses such as "DETERMINER X IS A CONSTITUENT OF NOUN-PHRASE Y". The syntax of a CONSTITUENCY-CLAUSE was defined by syntactic rewrite rule

(7) CONSTITUENCY-CLAUSE --->
CONSTIT-REF "IS A CONSTITUENT OF" SUPER-STR-REF

and the semantic mapping by

(8) CONSTITUENCY-CLAUSE :: [CONSTIT   CONSTIT-REF
                             CONSTITOF   SUPER-STR-REF]

The above semantic rewrite rule (8) informs the system that the interpretation of a CONSTITUENCY-CLAUSE is to be represented as the case-frame of Section 4 (iii). The CONSTIT slot is filled by the representation of the interpretation of the CONSTIT-REF constituent of the CONSTITUENCY-CLAUSE and the CONSTITOF slot is filled by the SUPER-STR-REF constituent of the CONSTITUENCY-CLAUSE.

Note that the constituency relation is used in two ways during the system's processing of a CONSTITUENCY-CLAUSE. Referring to rule (7), a SUPER-STR-REF is a constituent of a CONSTITUENCY-CLAUSE and its interpretation fills the CONSTITOF slot of the case frame of the semantic representation specified by (8). The constituency relation is also part of the meaning of a CONSTITUENCY-CLAUSE, and therefore the same network representation has been specified by the teacher-user in (8) for the constituency relation as is used by the system during syntactic analysis of any input utterance.

The network representation of the predefined Phrase Structure relation is shown in Figure 5 (ii). This network structure was used by the teacher to define the interpretation of a category she has created and called STRING-REFERENCE to include strings such as "DETERMINER X" and "NOUN-PHRASE Y". The teacher defined the interpretation of a STRING-REFERENCE to be node N of the structure of Figure 5 (ii) with C the referenced category and B the unmentioned bounded string. As a result, the interpretation of strings "DETERMINER X" and "NOUN-PHRASE Y" are represented as shown in Figure 9.

Node V2 of Figure 9 is the representation of the determiner phrase structure being talked about in the surface string and it is analogous to the node of a parse tree. Node M8 represents the assertion that V2 is the structure representing the DETERMINER with associated Bounded String represented by V1. "X" is used as an appositive to the word "DETERMINER" and is not shown in the figure. The system "remembers" node V2 as the

value of "X". This ability to use a variable as an appositive
to a phrase is the only mechanism provided in the system core
for referring to a concept that has already been expressed.
Since the system remembers node V2 as the value of X, the user
can again refer to this DETERMINER by using X as its identifier
as is done in the consequent of rule (2). The use of a variable as an appositive to a phrase is discussed in (Neal, 1985).

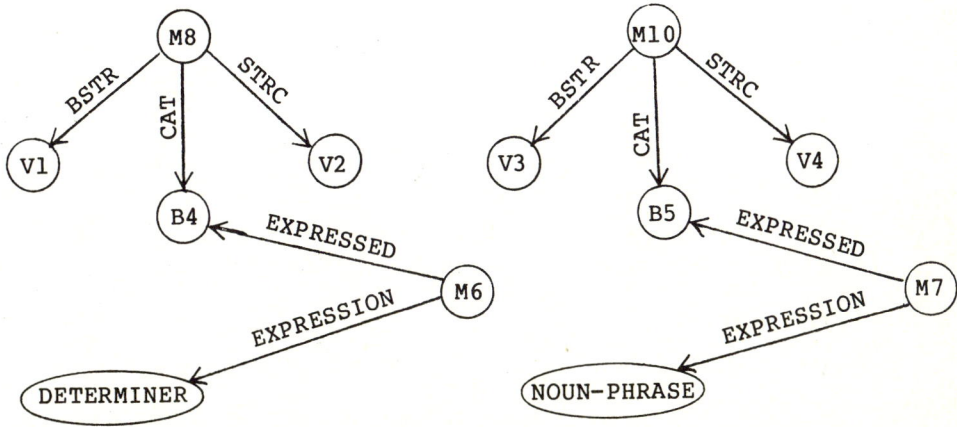

Figure 9

Representation of the Phrases "Determiner X" and "Noun-Phrase Y"

Variable nodes (Shapiro, 1979a,b) V1, V2, . . . are used by the
system in the representation of the interpretation of rule (2)
because the system recognizes the surface string as a rule
statement according to the language definition it has thus far
acquired from the teacher-user.

According to this language definition, the system also recognizes the string "DETERMINER X IS A CONSTITUENT OF NOUN-PHRASE
Y" as a CONSTITUENCY-PHRASE, with the substrings "DETERMINER X"
and "NOUN-PHRASE Y" recognized as a CONSTITUENT-REF and a
SUPER-STR-REF, respectively (these category identifiers chosen
by the teacher-user). Furthermore, the teacher-user has
instructed the system to represent the interpretation of such a
CONSTITUENCY-PHRASE using the core predefined Constituency
Relation representation (of Figure 5 (iii)). Figure 10 shows
the representation of the interpretation of the entire phrase,
accomplished according to the teacher's instructions. Node M10
represents the assertion that Bounded String V3 is a NOUN-
PHRASE with this phrase structure represented by V4. Node M9
represents the assertion that structure V2 is a constituent of
structure V4. To simplify the figure, the notations
R[<expression>] is used to represent the node expressed by the
<expression>. For example, node B4 is expressed by
"DETERMINER" in Figure 9, and is represented as R[DETERMINER]
in Figure 10.

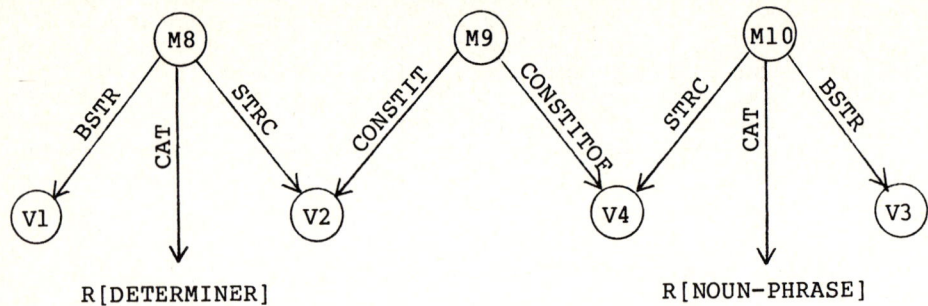

Figure 10

Representation of the Interpretation of the Surface String "Determiner X is a Constituent of Noun-Phrase Y"

The language definition thus far acquired by the system includes representations for functional structures, features such as specificity, feature values and other syntactic and semantic knowledge sufficient for the system to parse rule (4) as a RULE-STATEMENT and to build a network rule structure to represent the interpretation of the rule. The system adds this new structure to its knowledge base and, since the knowledge base is maintained as a set of rules and assertions, this new rule will be just as available for use in processing the next input to this interactive system as the previously acquired rules.

7.0   AN APPROACH TO COREFERENTIALITY

As stated previously, it is not our intent in this paper to present a detailed step-by-step development of a robust language definition that PARSNIP can apply for understanding language. Instead, we present and discuss the fundamental knowledge, representations and abilities which would enable a system to use a language as its own meta-language.

The PARSNIP core is designed with the intent of being unbiased with respect to linguistic theory. In keeping with this approach, we have not endowed the system with a theory/method of determining whether two phrases are coreferential, but have left the development of such a theory to the teacher-user. As a primitive referencing mechanism, the PARSNIP system is able to "remember" a referenced entity when a variable is used as an appositive to a "main apposition phrase". When this mechanism is used, the representation of the entity is stored as the value of the variable used. The variable can subsequently be used to refer to the particular entity.

The kernel language rewrite rules alone are not sufficient to explain a more sophisticated referencing technique. However, by bootstrapping from the kernel language into a subset of natural language, a more sophisticated referencing concept can be explained to PARSNIP. In an experiment to demonstrate this, during the bootstrap process the system was taught the meaning of relation words such as "PRECEDES", MATCHES", and EXPRESSES". INDEF-NOUN-PHRASE was defined to be a simple indefinite noun phrase and a DEF-NOUN-PHRASE to be a simple definite noun phrase. Then we were able to input the following rule to PARSNIP:

>   (9) IF AN INDEF-NOUN-PHRASE X PRECEDES A DEF-NOUN-PHRASE Y AND THE HEAD-NOUN OF X MATCHES THE HEAD-NOUN OF Y AND X EXPRESSES Z THEN Y EXPRESSES Z.

The system's understanding of the rule is demonstrated when it applies the rule in processing the subsequent input statement:

>   (10) A GOOSE IS A GANDER IF AND ONLY IF THE GOOSE IS MALE.

Prior to the input of rule 9, the system has no knowledge of a relationship between the meaning of "A GOOSE" and "THE GOOSE" in rule 10. By applying rule 9, however, the system uses the same representation for the interpretation of the phrase "THE GOOSE" that it has used for the phrase "A GOOSE.

We want to emphasize that we make no claim that the reference concept expressed in rule 9 is adequate or elegant. Instead, the purpose of the example is to demonstrate that if a system initially has only a primitive referring mechanism such as our system's ability to "remember" an entity as the value of a variable when the variable is used as an appositive to a phrase which describes the entity and if the system can understand utterances about its own language ability, then one can explain a sophisticated concept such as conditional coreferentiality to the system.

8.0 SUMMARY

We have been investigating methods of knowledge representation and natural language understanding which would enable an Artificial Intelligence system to use its language knowledge in the dual role of (a) the knowledge applied during the process of parsing and interpretation that enables the system to understand language and (b) the domain of discourse. In this paper we focused on knowledge representation to enable a system to use a language as its own meta-language. We presented an overview of our PARSNIP system and pointed out that all processing performed by PARSNIP, including parsing and interpretation, is a form of inference. We discussed the semantic network representation of its integrated knowledge base of rules and assertions for linguistic and non-linguistic knowledge. We briefly discussed the core knowledge which consists of certain predefined categories, objects and relations. The system's kernel language was described. It includes lexical entries, context-free rules, and context-sensitive rewrite rules with which to define the syntax of a target language. The kernel language also includes semantic rewrite rules with which a teacher-user can begin to define the semantics of her target language. We discussed and presented examples to demonstrate that concepts, not included in the core but commonly used in language processing systems (such as the linguistic number of a noun or noun-phrase), can be "explained" to the system. That is, after bootstrapping up from PARSNIP's core knowledge base, concepts (such as specificity, linguistic number, or coreference of certain expressions) to refine and extend the target language can be defined for the system via rules input in the evolving target language itself. Thus, we discussed the representation of language processing knowledge for use by an AI system which treats language understanding as part of its problem or task domain, with the special ability to use a natural language subset as its own meta-language.

9.0   REFERENCES

Brachman, R. J. (1977), "What's in a Concept: Structural Foundations for Semantic Networks", *Int. J. Man-Machine Studies*, 9, pp. 127-152.

Bresnan, J. (ed.) (1982), *The Mental Representation of Grammatical Relations*, The MIT Press.

Bruce, B. (1975), "Case Systems for Natural Language", *Artificial Intelligence*, Vol. 6, pp. 327-360.

Dahl, V. (1979), "Quantification in a Three-Valued Logic for Natural Language Question-Answering Systems", *Proc. IJCAI-79*, pp. 182-187.

Dahl, V. (1981), "Translating Spanish into Logic through Logic", *AJCL*, Vol. 7, No. 3, pp. 149-164.

Dahl, V. and McCord, M. C. (1983), "Treating Coordination in Logic Grammars", *AJCL*, Vol. 9, No. 2, pp. 69-91.

Fillmore, C. (1968), "The Case for Case", in Bach and Harms, eds. *Universals in Linguistic Theory*, Holt, Rinehart, and Winston, pp. 1-90.

Kaplan, R. M. (1973), "A Multi-Processing Approach to Natural Language", *Proceedings of the National Computer Conference*, AFIPS Press, Montvale, New Jersey, pp. 435-440.

Kaplan, R. M. and Bresnan, J. (1982), "Lexical-Functional Grammar: A Formal System for Grammatical Representation", in J. Bresnan, ed. *The Mental Representation of Grammatical Relations*, The MIT Press, pp. 173-281.

Kay, M. (1973), "The Mind System", in R. Rustin, ed. *Natural Language Processing*, Algorithmics Press, New York, pp. 153-188.

Maida, A. S. and Shapiro, S. C. (1982), "Intensional Concepts in Propositional Semantic Networks", *Cognitive Science*, Vol. 6, 4; reprinted in R. Brachman and H. Levesque, eds. *Readings in Knowledge Representation*, Morgan Kaufmann Publishers (1985).

McCord, M. C. (1982), "Using Slots and Modifiers in Logic Grammars for Natural Language", *Artificial Intelligence*, Vol. 18, No. 3, pp. 327-367.

McCord, M. C. (1985), "Modular Logic Grammars", *Proc. ACL*, pp. 104-117.

McKay, D. P. and Shapiro, S. C. (1980), "MULTI - A LISP Based Multiprocessing System", *Conference Record of the 1980 LISP Conference*, Stanford University, pp. 29-37.

Neal, J. G. (1985), "A Knowledge Based Approach to Natural Language Understanding", Ph.D. Dissertation, Technical Report No. 85-06, Dept. of Computer Science, SUNY at Buffalo.

Neal, J. G. and Shapiro, S. C. (1984), Knowledge Based Parsing", Technical Report No. 213, Dept. of Computer Science, SUNY at Buffalo.

Neal, J. G. and Shapiro, S. C. (1985), "Parsing as a Form of Inference in a Multiprocessing Environment", *Proceedings of the Conf. on Intelligent Systems and Machines*, Oakland Univ., MI.

Pereira, F. C. N. and Warren, D. H. D. (1980), "Definite Clause Grammars for Language Analysis - A Survey of the Formalism and a Comparison with Augmented Transition Networks", *Artificial Intelligence*, pp. 231-278.

Pereira, F. C. N. (1985), "A Structure-Sharing Representation for Unification-Based Grammar Formalisms", *Proc. ACL*, pp. 137-144.

Quine, W. V. (1951), *Mathematical Logic*, Harper and Row, Publishers.

Shapiro, S. C. (1971), "A Net Structure for Semantic Information Storage, Deduction and Retrieval", *Proc. IJCAI-71*, pp. 512-523.

Shapiro, S. C. (1979a), "The SNePS Semantic Network Processing System", In N. Findler, ed. *Associative Networks - The Representation and Use of Knowledge by Computers*, Academic Press, New York, pp. 179a-203.

Shapiro, S. C. (1979b), "Using Non-Standard Connectives and Quantifiers for Representing Deduction Rules in a Semantic Network", Invited paper presented at Current Aspects of AI Research, seminar held at Electrotechnical Laboratory, Tokyo.

Shapiro, S. C. and the SNePS Implementation Group (1983), *SNePS User's Manual*, Dept. of C.S., SUNY at Buffalo, New York.

Shapiro, S. C., Martins, J. and McKay, D. (1982), "Bi-Directional Inference", *Proc. of the Cognitive Science Society*, pp. 90-93.

Shapiro, S. C. and Neal, J. G. (1982), "A Knowledge Engineering Approach to Natural Language Understanding", *Proc. ACL*, pp. 136-144.

Warren, D. H. D. and Pereira, F. C. N. (1982), An Efficient Easily Adaptable System for Interpreting Natural Language Queries", *AJCL*, Vol. 8, No. 3-4, pp. 110-119.

Wilensky, R., Yigal, A. and Chin, D. (1984), "Talking to UNIX in English: An Overview of UC", *Communications of ACM*, Vol. 27, No, 6, pp. 574-593.

Woods, W. A. (1975), "What's in a Link: Foundations for Semantic Networks", in Bobrow and Collins, eds. *Representation and Understanding*, Academic Press, pp. 35-82.

QUESTION AND ANSWER PERIOD

SLATER

One of the problems Quine addressed in set theory is how to construct a sentence out of references as opposed to constructing it out of words? This leads to interesting complications in his work. I was wondering whether it affects your work.

NEAL

Certainly the whole area of interpreting noun phrases, reference in general, is very difficult, particularly the definite references. There has been quite a bit of work done in that area by various people, for example, by Bonnie Webber at the University of Pennsylvania. And I think that we need to do more work in what we've been doing in terms of interpretational mappings to get at that problem. Right now we've been restricting our attention to talking about language. But I think we need to also extend that to talking about other entities and see how that complicates the interrelationship between language domain and non-language domain information and the knowledge structures for those.

ABDUCTION IN DISCOURSE PROCESSING:
A PARSIMONIOUS COVERING MODEL *

Venugopala R. Dasigi and James A. Reggia **

Department of Computer Science
University of Maryland
College Park, Maryland 20742

1.0   INTRODUCTION

'Discourse' refers to several sentences in sequence, related together both syntactically and semantically. When we read a story or a paragraph, or when we take part in a conversation, we do more than understand the individual sentences in isolation. The sentences make a conceptual whole when taken together. Considered separately, the same sentences may not make sense, may be very ambiguous, or their purpose may not be clear. For example, "It was correct" is not very meaningful in isolation, but might make sense in the context of several other sentences.

Understanding sentences in isolation is itself a formidable task, involving such issues as analysis of inflected forms, syntax analysis, conjunctions, word sense disambiguation, modifier attachment, quantification and metaphors [Charniak and Wilks 76, Harris 85, Schank and Colby 73, Tennant 81, Winograd 83]. Discourse understanding adds a new dimension to all of these difficulties, raising complex questions about how to disambiguate anaphors, focus of attention, and so forth. Some past work has tried to produce artificial intelligence (AI) systems that can do discourse processing, but this work has largely been restricted to limited domains or addressed specific aspects of discourse analysis [Grosz 78, Litman and Allen 89, Rieger 79, Rumelhart 75, Sidner 77, Winograd 72]. To the authors' knowledge, no previous studies have tried to provide a unified, domain-independent model of discourse processing based on a formal model of the inferences involved.

We are presently studying a model of the abductive reasoning occurring during natural language discourse understanding using a "parsimonious covering" approach. 'Abduction' refers to plausible inference, and is different from other inference

---

*   Research supported in part by NSF award DCR-8451430 with matching funds from Software A&E and AT&T Information Systems.

** Also with Department of Neurology, University of Maryland at Baltimore.

mechanisms such as induction and deduction. To a great extent, abductive reasoning underlies natural language understanding [Charniak and McDermott 85b]. The goal of abductive reasoning is to arrive at the most plausible explanation or account for a given set of possibly incomplete facts. Abductive reasoning has received increasing attention in AI research during the last decade, primarily through its successful application in diagnostic problem solving [Charniak and McDermott 85a, Pople 73 Reggia et al. 83]. Parsimonious covering, a precise theoretical model of the imprecise notion of abductive inference, has been developed and applied to diagnostic problem solving in the past [Peng 85, Reggia 85, Reggia et al. 85], but has not been investigated significantly in other areas involving abductive reasoning.

In the work described in this paper, we are trying to study and extend the applicability of parsimonious covering theory to the area of natural language processing, and to unify some of the previous approaches to natural language processing within this same framework. In order to circumscribe the otherwise open-ended problem of natural language processing, we are investigating the construction of natural language interfaces to expert systems. This sort of interface can translate a natural language description of a real-world problem into an 'internal' form that is directly usable by an expert system.

Section 2 of this paper briefly relates abduction to natural language processing and presents previous work on parsimonious covering as a model of abduction in diagnostic problem solving. In doing so, several limitations of parsimonious covering as a model of abduction in natural language processing are identified. Section 3 describes our proposed solutions and research. It presents a domain-independent approach to discourse processing and explains the extensions required of the existing parsimonious covering model to make it applicable to natural language processing. An implemented prototype natural language interface is used to illustrate the basic idea of abductive inference in natural language processing and the several extensions which are required. The last section of this paper presents some conclusions derived from this work.

2.0 ABDUCTION AND NATURAL LANGUAGE PROCESSING

Encyclopedia Brittanica defines abduction as "reasoning that derives an explanatory hypothesis from a given set of facts." A more specific, technically motivated definition is, "Abductive inference can be described as probabilistic, parsimonious and context-sensitive disambiguation using associative knowledge, with its goal being the derivation of solutions that best account for given data" [Reggia 85].

Inference using rule-based deduction typically proceeds as follows: If

      P IMPLIES X is known, and P is known,

both with certainty. then X can be concluded with certainty. But, if the premises are not known for sure, or if

> P MAY CAUSE X is known, and X is present

then nothing straightforward can be done deductively. Deductive theory alone cannot adequately address such cases, although implementations of rule-based systems using deduction typically make use of extra-deductive 'certainty factors' to accommodate uncertainties.

But with abduction, in the latter case, it can be hypothesized that P is possibly present. In a more complicated situation, where several different causal associations with X as the effect are given, as in:

> P MAY CAUSE X, Q MAY CAUSE X, and R MAY CAUSE X

and X is known to be present, all of P, Q, or R are inferred to be probably present. Abductive inference thus involves choosing the best of these choices by accounting evidence for or against each of them in a given context. It is this hypothesize-and-test process that makes abduction a powerful inference method. For instance, if the following information is also known:

> P MAY CAUSE Y, Q MAY CAUSE Z, and R MAY CAUSE Z

with Y known to be present and Z known to be absent (or Z's presence or absence is unknown), the plausibility of P being present is higher than the plausibility of Q or R being present.

A simple example in natural language will serve to illustrate the point that abductive inference is an integral part of natural language processing. Consider,

> "It was a colorful ball. The queen attended it too!"

The first sentence is ambiguous; it is not obvious whether the object being talked about is a toy or a formal dance. But in the context of the second sentence, the meaning is indisputable. One of the Images evoked (or hypothesized) by the first sentence is selected by the context of the second. In a more complex situation, more than one interpretation may remain at the end of a discourse. In such a case, the speaker may have intended the ambiguity deliberately (for some special effect such as humor) or clarification may be sought.

Since language comprehension inevitably involves inferences to fill in missing details, an abductive theory of inference appears to be a fruitful area of research in natural language processing. In the following, a formal model of abduction, referred to as "parsimonious covering theory" is introduced and its limitations for natural language processing are also discussed.

In the parsimonious covering model of abduction [Peng 85, Reggia et al. 83, Reggia et al. 85], the underlying knowledge consists of two sets, namely, manifestations and disorders, and a relation 'causes' that specifies which disorders may cause which manifestations. A diagnostic problem is specified by M+, the subset of manifestations that are present. An 'explanation' is defined to be a set of disorders that can 'cover' or account for the observed manifestations M+ and is one of the most 'parsimonious' sets to do so. A set of disorders D is said to cover a set of manifestations M+, if there is no manifestation of M+ that is not caused by at least one of the members of D. A solution to a diagnostic problem is the set of all such explanations (parsimonious covers), or in some cases, might be taken as the few most likely explanations.

The notion of parsimony that qualifies a cover as an explanation deserves some attention. Several alternative interpretations of the notion of parsimony are possible [Josephson 82, Reggia et al. 85 and Thagard 78]. Apart from their intuitive appeal, 'minimality' and 'irredundancy' have been justified as plausible criteria of parsimony by relating them to probabilistic inference [Peng and Reggia 86]. First, a set of disorders that covers M+ can be said to be parsimonious (and hence, an explanation) if it has the smallest possible number of elements in it, i.e., no smaller set can be called an explanation. This is to say that the set is parsimonious if it is of minimal cardinality. An alternative interpretation is based on a notion of 'irredundancy'. A cover C is irredundant if no proper subset of C is itself a cover. Other notions of parsimony are possible [Peng 85].

Depending on the structure of the underlying associative knowledge, at least five types of diagnostic problems can be identified in parsimonious covering theory [Peng 85]. If the knowledge consists of causal associations leading to the manifestations, it is always possible to cover the manifestations and do so parsimoniously. Recent work has extended the original parsimonious covering theory to accommodate causal chaining (causal chaining is the phenomenon of one disorder causing another, which in turn causes another, and so forth), a notion of probability in abductive diagnostic systems, and the ability to assimilate volunteered diagnostic information [Peng 85].

Algorithms for solving diagnostic problems formulated within the framework of parsimonious covering theory and proofs of their correctness can be found in [Peng 85, Reggia et al. 85]. In discriminating among the various alternative explanations, contextual information is accumulated and used. The parsimonious covering algorithms work, in part, by a generalization of the idea of intersecting the sets of disorders evoked by the manifestations in M+. This can be viewed as a generalization of 'marker passing' or spreading activation, strategies used to relate two concepts or disambiguate a concept when knowledge is represented in a semantic network [Charniak 83]. This analogy between the disambiguation mechanisms of parsimonious covering model and marker passing suggests the possibility of modeling abductive inference in natural language interpretation using extensions of the parsimonious covering theory. It even suggests a way of looking at the marker passing strategy as abductive inference.

While parsimonious covering theory is a significant advance, it has not addressed some important issues for abductive problems other than diagnostic problem solving. In particular, although there are strong reasons to believe that natural language processing is a form of abductive problem solving, parsimonious covering theory clearly cannot handle it directly. For one thing, parsimonious covering theory as it is currently formulated is designed to model diagnostic problem solving using unstructured objects to evoke sets of other unstructured objects. While the exact nature of the structure of the concepts or objects in natural language processing is subject to much research [Schank 73], it is certain that these concepts cannot be thought of as unstructured. For instance, a word such as 'he' evokes a concept that encompasses several features, namely, an animate (and possible, a human) referent, one whose sex is male, etc. These features can be thought of as constituting the structure of the object. From a slightly different perspective, it can be said that in the case of diagnostic problem solving using covering, only one type of feature (namely. manifestations of a disorder) is to be covered. But in the case of discourse processing, it appears that several different features (for instance, number, gender, and sense of a word) need to be covered.

In addition, parsimonious covering theory characterizes a problem by, among other things, a **set** of distinguished objects that are said to be present. In natural language processing, the problem is manifested by the presence of a **sequence** of objects (words) whose order is important, and by an interpretation that is a **structured** network of objects (meanings). Also, in natural language, syntactic and semantic processing proceed in parallel. It is not at all obvious how to handle this parallel interplay between syntax and semantics using the existing version of parsimonious covering theory.

Also, in processing natural language, one is usually interested in one "best" interpretation of a given text and not in all possible interpretations. In contrast, parsimonious covering theory comes up with several competing explanations, although inclusion of probabilities into the theory allows significant focusing on a subset of the explanations [Peng 85]. It is not easy to quantify the plausibility notions that arise in the context of natural language understanding into probabilities. Hence, extensions to the parsimonious covering theory to address these problems seem to be a worthwhile research direction in applying abduction to natural language processing.

3.0   A PARSIMONIOUS COVERING THEORY OF DISCOURSE PROCESSING

While parsimonious covering theory does not yet capture the nature of abduction in its full generality, work is currently underway to extend this theory in several directions [Chu 85] and to new areas of application [Ahuja 85]. This section explains how we are extending and applying parsimonious covering theory to capture the features of abductive inference in the area of discourse processing.

The thesis of this work is that with suitable modifications, parsimonious covering provides a good model of the abductive inferences underlying natural language processing. Another aspect of this research is to address the practical issues of natural language processing. Section 3.1 shows how we are circumscribing the otherwise open-ended problem of natural language processing without compromising domain-independence by limiting our work to the context of expert system generators. Section 3.2 presents the top-level design of a natural language interface in this context. An implemented prototype is presented in Section 3.3, and is meant to illustrate the applicability of abduction to language processing. The prototype also suggests several possible enhancements. Section 3.4 gives details of the research currently in progress.

3.1. Circumscribing the Natural Language Processing Task

At least three different courses are available in modeling natural language processing:

(1) Truly domain-independent approach: model all conceivable linguistic and world knowledge. This is too open-ended to be feasible today.

(2) Domain-specific approach: limit the scope of natural language processing to a single application area. This is the other extreme approach, which is feasible since the domain of application is limited. A domain-specific approach has been used by many studies, but is not easily generalizable to other domains and, in this sense, is not very interesting. Also, it is possible that a domain-specific approach can lead to ad hoc solutions.

(3) Domain-independent, but circumscribed approach: limit the scope of the task to a class of problems (e.g., a natural language interface to a domain-independent data management system). This is intermediate in generality between the two extremities represented above. This approach has the advantage that it is applicable to many application areas and hence tends to be much less ad hoc. Another way of characterizing this approach is that it allows concentration on a specific area, but in a way that can be easily extended to other 'similar' areas.

In evaluating the parsimonious covering theory for natural language processing, we are using the third approach above. In particular, we are exploring interfaces in the context of domain-independent expert system generators. Domain-independent expert system generators provide problem-solving ability in many areas. Given a knowledge base for some specific application area, an expert system generator constructs an expert system that attempts to solve problems in the particular area characterized by the knowledge base. This is done by superimposing a pre-defined inference mechanism on the given domain-specific knowledge base. As an expert system is generated from an arbitrary knowledge base, our goal is that a corresponding natural language front-end should be generated simultaneously.

Often, some linguistic information relevant to a specific area of expertise can be obtained from an appropriately designed knowledge base. This is often the case, even when the expert system generator is not at all concerned with the general problem of natural language processing. For example, the names of objects, their properties and the values of these properties are often stored in the knowledge base to expedite asking multiple-choice questions of users. However, typically only a small amount of linguistic information is available. The domain-specific information used in problem solving is not the same as the information that is needed for language processing, and it may not include much of the application-specific vocabulary. The other major omission is the large amount of domain-independent linguistic information that plays a very significant role in language processing.

There is another reason why one would like to test the applicability of parsimonious covering theory to natural language, in the context of abductive diagnostic expert systems. Since abduction underlies the natural language interface as well as the expert system in some applications [Reggia et al. 83], it may be possible to unify the abductive inference in diagnostic expert systems and the abductive inference in natural language.

3.2. Top Level Design

An expert system structured in the conventional way, namely, with a knowledge base (KB) and an inference mechanism (IM), typically accepts information from the user in a restricted format. This might be done by asking the user multiple choice questions about his/her problem, for example. A structure for an expert system which accepts natural language descriptions of the user's problem is shown in Figure 1.

The Natural Language Processor (NLP) acts as the input/output interface. It accepts a paraphrasing of the problem in English and converts it into a form acceptable to the inference mechanism. Also, it converts the output of the inference mechanism, may it be a diagnosis, a justification, or an answer to a user query, into a natural language form.

The NLP is aided in its function by Domain-Specific and Domain-Independent Linguistic Information (DSLI and DILI respectively). It turns out that a significant part of the problem-solving expert knowledge may constitute part of DSLI. For example, in KMS.HT knowledge bases [Reggia et al 83], the names of attributes and their values and the 'synonyms' attachments provide information that is extremely useful for the NLP, and hence is part of DSLI.

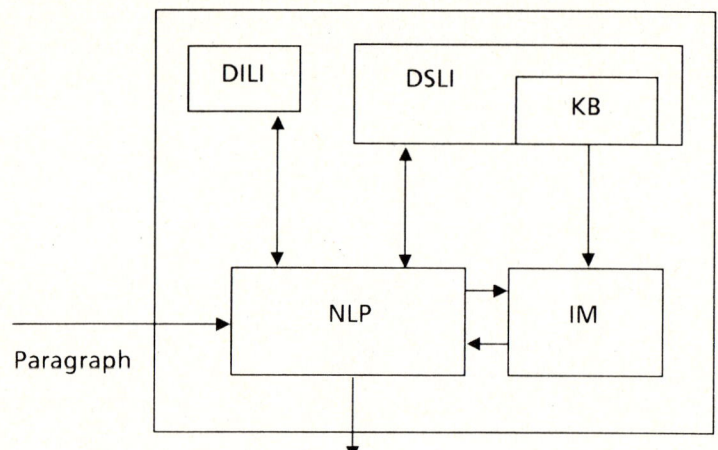

Figure 1

An Expert System With a Natural Language Interface

However, there are other kinds of linguistic information that are typically not present in a knowledge base. If a significant part of this information can be identified at the time of constructing the knowledge base, it can be made either a supplemental part of the knowledge base module or part of the DSLI module. An example of the kind of information needed by the NLP and that is unavailable in knowledge bases of KMS-based expert systems is alternative, equivalent ways of saying the same thing (e.g., a different way of characterizing 'neutral pH' is to say that 'the pH has a value about 7.4'). It appears that a clear separation between the problem-solving knowledge and the non-problem-solving DSLI may be useful. Given a clear separation, we refer to the problem-solving knowledge as the knowledge base and the information useful to the NLP as the DSLI.

The DILI is domain-independent linguistic information. It consists of some form of grammar for English and the inherent vocabulary of the NLP. This vocabulary could comprise a set of closed class words and a set of open words. Closed class words are those parts of language - such as prepositions, articles, auxiliary verbs, etc. - that do not readily admit new words. Open classes, on the other hand, admit any number of new members; for instance, new nouns and verbs can be defined as needed. Even closed class words often have more than one plausible meaning, referred to as 'multiple word senses', and

these senses need to be recorded. Any other conceivable
domain-independent knowledge could go in here, once it is
identified and a suitable representation and usage mechanism
are chosen.

The NLP proper is that part of the natural language understanding system that implements the abductive inference mechanism
translating a given discourse text into some form of inter-
lingua. The NLP has to concern itself with many aspects of
language understanding. These functions range from syntactic
checking through word sense discrimination, anaphora resolution, etc, to intelligent guessing of the user's intentions,
based on the focus of attention. Our organization of the NLP
is as a combination of several layers or stages, each layer
representing the concepts translated from one form into
another, analogous to the causal chaining in diagnostic problem
solving.

3.3. A Prototype

To gain some initial insights into the viability of parsimonious covering for natural language processing, a prototype
based on the ideas of the previous sections was implemented.
It accepts some restricted forms of natural language input,
translates them into KMS.HT commands [Reggia et al. 83], and
performs some simple error checking. It handles several forms
of conjunctions and some forms of negations in the input, and
performs very simple anaphora resolution. It clearly shows the
potential applicability of the abductive approach to the problem at hand. However, this prototype is only a very limited
version of the complete NLP we envision. It does not have a
large vocabulary, it does not distinguish different kinds of
verbs, it does not perform morphemic analysis, it does not
handle KMS.HT elaborations, it assumes the existence of only a
single domain object, and it does not incorporate a detailed
grammar.

A session with this program is shown below in Figure 2. The
prototype works with a chemical spill expert system. The
expert system attempts to diagnose the nature of a spill that
has occurred into a creek, given findings about characteristics
such as the color, appearance etc. of the creek water. The
prototype first asks for the name of the DSLI file. This
"linguistic base" (which forms the DSLI) has been automatically
extracted from a KMS.HT knowledge base (which was written long
ago with no attention to the possibility of a natural language
interface). This DSLI contains LISP functions to create structures corresponding to the object(s), attributes, values etc.
of the KMS.HT knowledge base. It also contains information
about the synonyms of these concepts; the individual words of
the synonyms are indexed back to the appropriate concept structures.

When the linguistic base is loaded (as indicated in the
session), the structure-building functions and the indexing
functions are executed. Then the prototype prompts the user
for the name of the natural language input file and echoes the

<1> parscover

Knowledge base involved: spill.1

Input text file name (Type nil if you don't have one): infile

Input

The water is brown and oily. It is acidic too.
Its specific gravity is ok; spectrometry detects
sulfur, carbon and metal and no radioactivity is
present. The month is September.
What are the chemicals present?

Want a trace of execution? (Y/N : Default = Y) y

TRACING
The phrase "Specific gravity" is covered by:
  specific gravity
The phrase "Chemicals present" is covered by:
  type of spill
The phrase "The water is brown" is covered by:
  assert water color = brown.
The phrase "And oily." is covered by:
  assert water appearance = oily.
  .
  .
  .

The phrase "What are the chemicals present?" is covered by:
  obtain type of spill.
END OF TRACE

Results:
assert month = september.
assert radioactivity = absent.
assert spectrometry = sulfur & carbon & metal.
assert specific gravity = normal.
assert ph = acidic.
assert water appearance = oily.
assert water color = brown.
obtain type of spill.

DONE

Figure 2

A Session With The Prototype

```
input text.   The input text used in the sample session contains
definite noun phrases, several types of conjunctions and very
simple anaphoric references.  The trace of execution shows the
details of which phrase is disambiguated into which concept.
Finally, the results of covering the input text by KMS.HT
assert and obtain commands are displayed.
```

This prototype works by looking for key morphemes such as a period, a verb and a comma, or the word 'and' indicating conjunctions. The important content words are the words that evoke the concept of an attribute or a value of the knowledge base. For example, although the word 'water' (which could really refer to an object, had the knowledge base allowed for it) evokes two attributes, namely, water color or water appearance (and perhaps other concepts too), in this specific case, the context selects only one of these senses. The context may be of two kinds: either the surrounding words, where successive words help disambiguate a concept, or the complete sentence that typically maps into an 'assert' command. Since the knowledge base has information that says that the water color can be brown but not oily and the water appearance can be oily but not brown, the assertional context helps in disambiguation. An anaphor such as 'it' evokes the same concepts evoked by the closest previously mentioned words, of which one is selected by the assertional context - an admittedly naive strategy for anaphoric references. (So, cataphoric references would fail, or are likely to be interpreted incorrectly by this program; but they are relatively rare.) Conjunctions, negations, etc. are handled in the prototype program in an ad hoc manner.

As mentioned before, in this prototype the words appearing in the name of an attribute or a value are indexed back to the name and serve to evoke the relevant concepts (attributes and values respectively). This is a naive strategy, but helps illustrate a few points and provides some useful insights. First, there are two levels of disambiguation involved: the first being the disambiguation of the concept of an attribute or a value, and the second, the disambiguation of an 'assert' command. In the chemical spill expert system, for instance, the word "water" would evoke the concepts "water color" and "water appearance." Here at the word level, no further disambiguation is possible, since this noun phrase has only one word in it. But, the word "brown" in the verb phrase evokes the concept "brown" which can be a value for the attribute "water color," but not for the attribute "water appearance." So at the assertional level, the group of words "water is brown" is disambiguated to mean "assert water color = brown." In a general situation, each word may evoke more than one attribute or value and a group of consecutive words may still not be able to uniquely disambiguate a concept. At the level of assertions, unique disambiguation is possible because certain attributes can have certain values only. In a really general situation even this does not uniquely select an assertion; but the KMS.HT elaboration context will provide some help (not implemented in the prototype).

Next, to the extent that the idea of intersection helps in disambiguation, all of these ideas are implemented in the prototype rather awkwardly, but in a straightforward manner, by applying the notion of sets of unstructured objects as in the parsimonious covering theory. But a different way of viewing the problem is as the disambiguation of structures, and this is the second important point. Each word evokes a structured

object, for instance, an attribute evokes a structure that
indicates that the attribute can take one/some of a set of
possible values and that it is related to a particular object.
Similarly, a property's value evokes a structure that indicates
that the value is associated with a specific attribute of a
specific object, etc. The general idea is like marker passing
(or spreading activation) in semantic networks, but with clear-
cut demarcations. The important difference from marker passing
is that parsimonious covering theory constructs 'generators'
whenever the intersection is nil. When the structure of
concepts is taken into account, unification (on a variation of
it) is needed to aid the process of intersection as the
disambiguation mechanism.

3.4. A More Detailed Look at the NLP: Beyond a Prototype

To apply the ideas of parsimonious covering to discourse
processing beyond a prototype, several significant modifications to parsimonious covering are needed. The framework
within which we are pursuing these extensions is described in
this section.

In modeling abductive problem solving using parsimonious covering, it is useful to identify how the various concepts used in
the process of abductive inference relate to one another. The
concepts at the two extremes, namely, the words/morphemes of
the text and the interlingual representation (which, in the
context of this paper, is currently constituted by KMS.HT
'assert' and 'obtain' commands), are related through a multi-
layered network of concepts as in Figure 3. At intermediate
levels in this network are uninstantiated word senses (e.g., a
noun represented as a structure with "part of speech = noun" or
the word 'she' viewed as a structure with its feature "sex =
female" etc.), instantiated word senses (e.g., simple structures of DILI that are part of a network of linguistic concepts, or sequences of structures evoked by a word such as 'is'
as in Figure 4), and DSLI entities (e.g., objects, attributes
and values).

An example will better illustrate the nature of concepts in
this network. Consider the simple sentence, "The water is
brown." These four words (and the period, although not discussed here) are at the bottom end of the network of concepts,
while at the other end is a KMS.HT assertion "assert water
color = brown." The words of the sentence, in isolation, evoke
several senses, only one of which eventually participates in
the KMS.HT assertion. How does this mapping take place? Figure 9 illustrates the process of covering involved in mapping
the sentence into a KMS.HT assertion.

In Figure 4, the bottommost layer is constituted by a sentence
(a group of words/morphemes -including punctuation symbols - in
order). As one looks up the network, one finds uninstantiated
word senses (e.g., the1-the4, and is1-is4). Further up the
network are senses that are instantiated or domain-specific.
For example, "water1 (x=water1)" is an instantiated sense of
the morphemes "the water." In the covering process, the

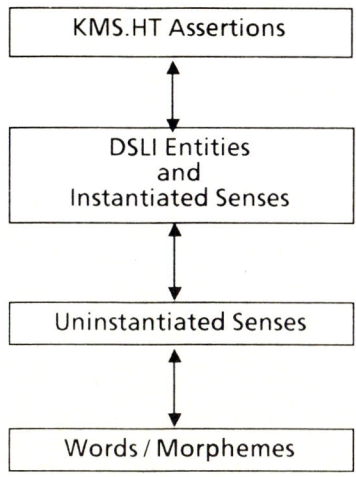

Figure 3

Structure of Linguistic Knowledge in NLP

"simplest/most obvious" choices are made: this corresponds to the notion of parsimony. It can also be observed that in order to instantiate the word senses, some sort of unification is needed.

It is instructive to see how this structure relates to the taxonomy of diagnostic problems. Each level (shown inside a box in Figure 3) is a pseudo-layer according to the terminology of parsimonious covering [Peng 85], and this is thus at least a hyper-bipartite (type 2) problem. In Figure 4, each pseudo-layer corresponds to exactly one level of disambiguation. But, in more complex situations, several and perhaps an unpredictable number of levels of disambiguation may be possible at the same pseudo-layer. (In the phrase, "red ball attendee", the last word selects the 'communist' sense for 'red'; all of these disambiguations are performed at the instantiated senses - or possibly, the DSLI entities - pseudo-layer.) In this sense, the pseudo-layers indicated in Figures 3 and 4 correspond to a group (or class) of pseudo-layers as defined by [Peng 85].

Further, the objects at the highest pseudo-layer are not independent in that they affect the likelihood of one another. This kind of interdependencies cannot be handled by the existing parsimonious covering theory unless the structure of the underlying concepts is taken into account. This complex interaction needs to be fit into the adaptation of parsimonious covering theory, or some other means of handling it is needed to complement the parsimonious covering theory.

Next, the notion of parsimony in natural language does not appear to be as easily quantifiable as in the context of diagnostic problem solving. In natural language processing,

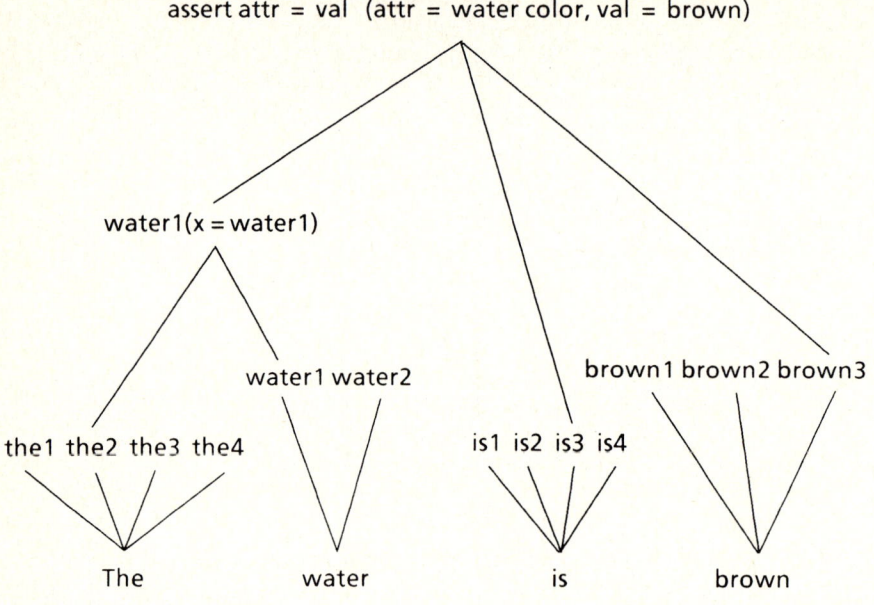

LEGEND: (In the following, names ending in '?' are variables)
the1: the1 x?
    forceful specification of an x? (noun)
the2: the2 x?
    well-known x? (noun / domain-specific thing)
the3: the3 x?
    generic x? (noun that stands for a group)
the4: the4 x?
    the x? (adjective) that follows is used as a noun
water1: domain-specific entity: water color (attribute)
water2: water as a physical object
    (with properties such as: drunk, colorless, etc.)
is1: n? is1
    n? (noun / object) exists
is2: n1? is2 p (n2?)
    n1? is p (prepositional phrase whose noun is n2?)
is3: attr? is3 val?
    attr? (domain-specific attribute) has value val?
is4: n? is a?
    n? (noun) fits description a? (adjective)
brown1: adjective: a dark shade of orange
brown2: noun: a kind of color (dark shade of orange)
brown3: domain-specific entity: brown (value)
    (The difference between the first two senses of brown and
    the third is that the third is directly usable in disambiguating
    an assertion, while the others may have to evoke another DSLI
    entity so as to be indirectly usable in an assertion.)

Figure 4

Mapping a Sentence into a KMS.HT Assertion

usually, a *unique* cover is of interest. Although there are significant differences between the knowledge structures of diagnostic problems and the problem of natural language processing, initially irredundancy is being used as the criterion of parsimony as in ongoing diagnostic problem-solving work.

In natural language processing. It is often required to relate two concepts in a way similar to what is done in semantic networks. While spreading activation from two nodes of a semantic network, the shortest path through which they are connected is often chosen to relate them. This corresponds to the notion of minimality. A minimal path is always irredundant. Other irredundant ways of relating two nodes in a semantic network are through possibly longer (and hence, not minimal) paths that do not contain any other path. This notion of parsimony will be applied wherever possible.

At the level of assertions, other notions of irredundancy are certainly required. For example, consider a patient's description such as, "He feels a definite rotational sensation." The relevant domain-specific vocabulary, as represented in a KMS.HT knowledge base, is shown in Figure 5. In this case, it can be inferred abductively that the definite rotational sensation refers to the attribute 'Type'. But this cannot be asserted without an ASSUMED 'assert Dizziness = present'. In relating two concepts, human beings choose the simplest explanation, namely, one that involves the fewest number of assumptions to be made (of course, without violating any previously known information).

```
Dizziness (val)
    [Elaboration:
        Type (SGL):
            Definite rotational sensation
            Sensation of impending faint
                ...                              ]
```

Figure 5

Part of a KMS.HT Knowledge Base For Dizziness

In the following paragraphs, we take a closer look at the layers of Figure 3. The bottom layer of the NCP is constituted by the outcome of 'preprocessing' of the input text, rather than the text itself. The preprocessor converts the input paragraph an internal form suitable for further processing, preserving the information content. Its functions include separation of a sentence into words, converting the first letter of the first word of a sentence into lower case, handling punctuation, morphemic analysis, changing certain kinds of words into a standard form (e.g.. 'twice' rewritten as 'two times'), identifying unambiguous closed class words and to a limited extent, identifying unrecognizable words, and some obvious spelling error detection and correction.

The second layer up is uninstantiated senses of words, which can be viewed as evoked as part of syntax analysis. The "parsing" is non-deterministic, since all possible semantic categories are evoked at this layer, and their disambiguation is done in conjunction with the semantic senses evoked by the surrounding context. (See Figure 4, where four senses of 'is' are shown, each of which expects certain semantic categories in its context.) A notion similar to semantic categories [Burton 76] is used for this purpose. Two important remarks are in order. First, this phase may not be able to resolve syntactic ambiguities completely. This means that complete instantiation of the senses may not be possible yet. At the following pseudo-layers, semantic senses (either DSLI entities or already instantiated senses) help in syntactic disambiguation.

Second, it has been mentioned that the semantic categories can be viewed as Important senses of words. Semantic categories tend to be domain-dependent. To the extent that they indeed are domain-dependent, a means of representing them in the knowledge base is necessary. This can be done by restricting the 'syntactic categories' to take only certain kinds of values or features via partially instantiated (or uninstantiated) word senses. For instance, a 'semantic category' such as "female" can be represented as a 'syntactic category' "noun" with the feature "sex" instantiated to "female."

The next higher "instantiated senses" pseudo-layer represent partially or totally disambiguated word senses. This pseudo-layer involves looking up meanings, resolving some kinds of ambiguities and inter-sentence references. Identifying the correct sense of any word often involves taking help from the surrounding context. The order of words and the actual words surrounding the word in question (and their complex meaning structures) constitute important aspects of context. A related problem, although often treated separately, is that of anaphora resolution. Each of these layers results from covering one or more concepts of the previous layer parsimoniously, applying the criteria mentioned earlier. DSLI entities are also evoked in this pseudo-layer; they are shown separately to emphasize their dependence on a specific domain. When no further disambiguation is possible (hopefully, when there is a unique cover for the input, representing its meaning in the inter-lingua), the covering process comes to a halt. At the assertional level (topmost level), if a unique cover is not possible, clarification can be sought.

One of the important research issues being examined is the design of representations for objects (right now KMS.HT allows only one kind of object), attributes, values, elaborations, words, word senses, etc. For instance, an attribute of a knowledge base currently has the form shown in the Figure 6. Another important research issue is to decide the details of what constitutes the DILI. It appears that all closed class words and several open class words belong in this category. Apart from this primitive vocabulary, a significant amount of syntax and some general purpose real-world knowledge also helps in language understanding. It is not immediately obvious how

to integrate the representation and use of this knowledge into
an abductive framework. It can be observed that a significant
degree of inference capability using information in the DILI is
needed. Since abduction can be used for this inference, it
appears that unifying abductive inference in the DILI into
parsimonious covering may be a worthwhile direction to pursue.

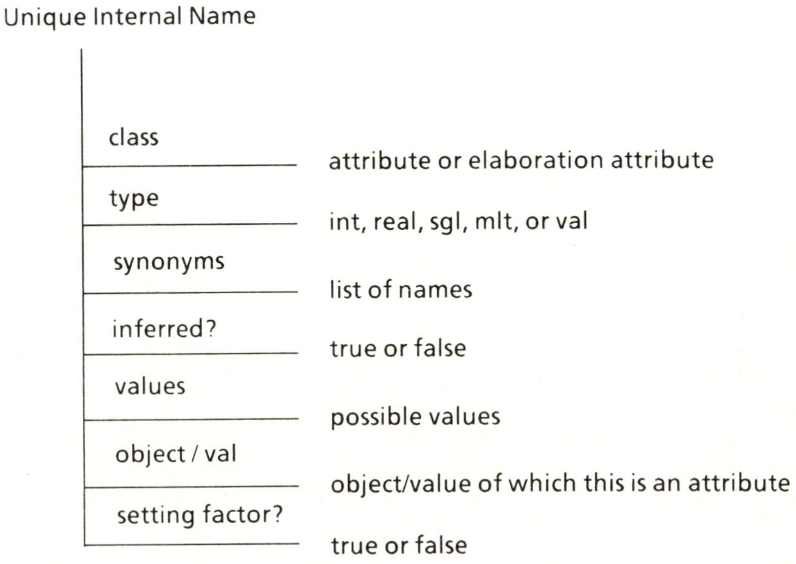

Unique Internal Name

- class — attribute or elaboration attribute
- type — int, real, sgl, mlt, or val
- synonyms — list of names
- inferred? — true or false
- values — possible values
- object / val — object/value of which this is an attribute
- setting factor? — true or false

Figure 6

Structure of an Attribute

4.0 CONCLUSIONS

Many problems of natural language processing can be handled in
an abductive framework combined with an appropriate knowledge
representation. Parsimonious covering has been used to model
abductive inference in diagnostic expert systems and several
useful properties of parsimonious covering have been established earlier. We are currently extending existing parsimonious
covering theory to apply to abductive inference in natural
language understanding. The existing prototype implementation
has proven very useful in identifying several limitations of
the existing theory and in guiding extensions. Our ongoing
work should further illuminate the utility of an extended
parsimonious covering theory as a practical method for natural
language processing.

As mentioned before, abduction has been used as an inference
mechanism in problem solving. Actually KMS.HT can generate,
given appropriate knowledge bases, expert systems employing
abductive inference mechanism. Insofar as the current research

demonstrates the feasibility of the same inference mechanism, namely, abduction in natural language processing, it is hoped that in the long run it may serve to integrate problem solving and language processing into a unified framework, as in humans.

5.0   REFERENCES

(1)   Ahuja S 85: An Artificial Intelligence Environment for the Analysis and Classification of Errors in Discrete Sequential Processes. University of Maryland.

(2)   Burton R R 76: Semantic Grammar: An Engineering Technique for Constructing Natural Language Understanding Systems. Report 3953, Bolt, Beranek and Newman, Cambridge, Mass.

(3)   Charniak E 83: Passing Markers: A Theory of Contextual Influence in Language Comprehension. In Cognitive Science, Vol. 7, No. 3.

(4)   Charniak E and McDermott D 85a: An Introduction to Artificial Intelligence. John Wiley. (In print). Chapter 8, Abduction, Uncertainty and Expert Systems.

(5)   Charniak E and McDermott D 85b: An Introduction to Artificial Intelligence. John Wiley. (In print). Chapter 10, Language Comprehension.

(6)   Charniak and Wilks 76: Computational Semantics. North-Holland.

(7)   Chu B 85: ABLOG/IC: A Programming Language Supporting Abductive Problem-Solving. TR-1526, Department of Computer Science, University of Maryland, College Park.

(8)   Grosz B 77: The Representation and Use of Focus in a System for Understanding Dialogs. Proceedings of the fifth IJCAI, Cambridge MA.

(9)   Harris M D 85: Natural Language Processing. Reston/-Prentice-Hall.

(10)   Litman D and Allen J 84: A Plan Recognition Model for Subdialogues in Conversations. TR-141, Department of Computer Science, University of Rochester, Rochester, NY 14627.

(11)   Peng Y 85: A General Theoretical Model for Abductive Diagnostic Expert Systems. Ph.D. Thesis, Department of Computer Science, University of Maryland, College Park. In preparation.

(12)   Peng Y and Reggia J A 86: A Probabilistic Causal Model for Diagnostic Problem Solving: Part One -

Integrating Symbolic Casual Inference with Numeric Probabilistic Inference. Submitted for publication.

(13) Pople H 73: On the Mechanization of Abductive Logic. IJCAI 73. pp. 147-152.

(14) Reggia J A, Nau D S and Wang P Y 83: Diagnostic Expert Systems based on a Set Covering Model. International Journal of Man-Machine Studies, 19, pp. 437-460.

(15) Reggia J A, Nau D S Wang P Y and Peng Y 85: A Formal Model of Diagnostic Inference. In Information Sciences, 37, 1985. pp. 227-285.

(16) Reggia J A 85: Abductive Inference. In Proceedings of Symposium on Expert Systems in Government. Karna K N (Ed). IEEE, McLean, VA. October 1985.

(17) Rieger C 79: Five Aspects of a Full-scale Story Comprehension Model. In ASSOCIATIVE NETWORKS Representation and Use of Knowledge by Computers, Pindler N (Ed). Academic Press.

(18) Rumelhart D E 75: Notes on a Schema for Stories. In Representation and Understanding - Studies in Cognitive Science. Bobrow D G and Collins A (Eds). Academic Press NY.

(19) Schank R C 73: Identification of Conceptualizations Underlying Natural Language. In Computer Models of Thought and Language. Schank R C and Colby K M (Eds). W. H. Freeman and Co., San Francisco.

(20) Schank R C and Colby K M 73: Computer Models of Thought and Language. W.H. Freeman and Co., San Francisco.

(21) Sidner C 78: The Use of Focus as a Tool for the Disambiguation of Definite Noun Phrases. In Proceedings of second TINLAP Workshop, University of Illinois. Urbana.

(22) Tennant H 81: Natural Language Processing - An Introduction to an Emerging Technology. Petrocelli Books, Inc., NY.

(23) Winograd T 72: Understanding Natural Language. Academic Press NY.

(24) Winograd T 83: Language as a Cognitive Language Process. Vol. 1 (Syntax). Addison-Wesley. Reading, Massachusetts.

QUESTION AND ANSWER PERIOD

Note: This presentation included recent work on the topic of the paper which was not included in the paper itself. Some of the questions during the question and answer session related to this material. It concentrated on details of what was presented in this paper. Concepts such as hypothesis construction from more than one hypothesis (which is a graph structure representing natural language concepts) and a notion of parsimony called specificity have been defined in the extra work presented. The following reference contains the details:

Dasigi V.R. 86: Discourse Processing: A Parsimonious Covering Model for Abductive Inference. TR-1657, Department of Computer Science, University of Maryland, College Park.

BOUDREAUX

The notion of abduction goes back to Peirce, the American logician, and he used it as a mechanism for discovering or eliciting scientific laws. It seems that what you've done is to attempt to supply a metric on your data set to allow you to decide questions of minimality, for example, and parsimony. Have you attempted to give a general definition of these rather horrendously difficult ideas like parsimony? What kind of metric do you have on this space of trees or graphs in terms of which you could define minimality as a kind of metric property?

DASIGI

So far we talked in the context of natural language processing. I do not have a unique definition to address all issues of language processing, but we expect it's going to be the winner. We do have, as I mentioned before, two criteria: one is minimality and the other is specificity, which are precisely defined. But in the context of diagnostic problem solving, which is where parsimonious covering was originally conceived, the notion of parsimony has been really extensively discussed and clearly defined and several interesting properties have been proved.

SLATER

Have you tried using graphs with length attributes assigned to handle some of the problems? Then you would have a sort of natural definition of parsimony by changing the length attributes you might be able to get.

DASIGI

If I understand you correctly, that amounts to incorporating some symbolic notion of probabilities, and one issue would be how to come up with the "length or weight attributes" in the first place. On a related, but slightly different note, what we are trying to do in the examples I've shown is to automatically have parsimonious covering handle the disambiguation problem. As most of you might have observed, there's no notion of syntax in the example that I've shown. I haven't yet built that in, but I am working on that currently. I have some examples where just extending these ideas with simple notions of syntax such as syntactic categories would greatly enhance the performance; for instance, "four red wings" is really a noun phrase. If you look at all those words as belonging together in a syntactical semantic category, that makes the processing much easier.

RELATING TWO KNOWLEDGE BASES:
THE ROLE OF IDENTITY AND PART-WHOLE

Roy Rada

National Library of Medicine
Bethesda, Maryland 20894

Lindley Darden

Institute for Advanced Computer Studies and
Committee on History and Philosophy of Science
University of Maryland
College Park, Maryland 20742

John Eng

University of Wisconsin Medical School
Madison, Wisconsin 53706

This paper presents the results of two sets of experiments about learning by relating two knowledge bases. In one experiment, subtrees from one hierarchical thesaurus for medicine are merged with another hierarchical thesaurus for medicine. In the other experiment, concepts from genetics and cytology are compared in the course of trying to recreate the discovery that genes are in chromosomes. Two types of relationships were explored: first, identity relationships in which two concepts are suspected to be identical and actions are then taken based on the identity assumption and second, part-whole relationships in which one concept or entity is hypothesized to be part of another entity. Compatible representations proved critical to successful knowledge refinement.

1.0 INTRODUCTION

In the development of AI systems three domains are frequently involved: representation, reasoning, and learning. Our study addresses all three. One learning (or discovery) strategy is to relate two previously unrelated bodies of knowledge and use information from one to learn new items in the other (and vice versa). This strategy builds on the view that learning from a tableau rasa is hopelessly inefficient (11). Learning is done in the contexts of large amounts of knowledge that already exist codified on machines so that the machine can use it in new ways. The way that knowledge is represented is critical to the success or failure of the reasoning and learning strategies that operate on that knowledge.

One of us (Rada) has been investigating using one knowledge base to augment another. The nature of the knowledge encoded and the overall structure of the knowledge base are crucial to the ability to transfer from one to the other. Terms that are the same are the easiest clue to a relationship. But sometimes terms that appear different may be analyzed at a lower level into component properties and thereby be shown to have a relation that facilitates transfer of knowledge. The other of us (Darden) has done work on how knowledge in one field of science can be related to knowledge in another field (4, 6), such that information from one can be used to gain knowledge in the other and vice versa. Thus, we have been pursuing collaborative work in representation of knowledge from different sources and the reasoning required to transfer from one to the other.

One strategy for using one body of knowledge to learn about another is reasoning by analogy. This has received attention in AI (1, 17). However, one of the numerous problems in doing analogical reasoning is locating a relevantly similar analog and then determining what properties to transfer from the analog to the target. If one could find relations that were stronger than analogy, then the transfer of knowledge would have a sounder basis.

A number of relations have been found to be important in inter-field connections in biological cases (4) that are stronger relations than mere analogy (5). These include identity, part-whole, structure-function, and cause. We have focused in this paper on the identity and part-whole relations between two concepts in two knowledge bases. By postulating a relation between two concepts in different knowledge bases, one can transfer knowledge from one to the other and test the adequacy of such transfer. If one knows, for instance, that high blood pressure and hypertension are identical, one can conclude that all properties of one are properties of the other and vice versa. That one can automatically conclude given the other three relations--part-whole, structure-function, and causal--is less clear. We discuss some analyses of part-whole below. Structure-function and causal relations are the subject of our future research.

In both our information retrieval and genetics work we have represented information in frame-like structures. For starters, in order to relate two knowledge bases it is necessary that the representations be compatible. Our research has alternated between refining representations and formulating general reasoning strategies to operate on hypothesized identity and part-whole relations. These relations guide the transfer of knowledge that can then be tested.

One of the key insights that we have about the relationships among representation, reasoning, and learning is that change should occur slowly. In general, no one knows how to achieve gradualness for machines that try to solve complex, knowledge-based problems. Some argue that digital computers (2), may be incapable of capturing the all-important gradualness of biological systems. Previous experiments by one of the authors have shown the importance of bringing knowledge to bear in the guiding of changes one makes in knowledge (1). The odds of a successful modification to a body of knowledge is increased if the unit of knowledge that is replaced is replaced by something similar to itself.

These experiments report on the beginning of an exploration of the role of identity, part-whole, and gradualness in knowledge refinement.

2.0   IDENTITY

2.1   An Information Retrieval Experiments

The National Library of Medicine (NLM) maintains the Medical Literature Analysis and Retrieval System (MEDLARS), one of the largest bibliographic retrieval systems (15). MEDLARS currently contains bibliographic information or about million articles from about 3000 biomedical periodicals. Much of MEDLARS can be accessed by remote terminal via telephone lines or network services. This part of MEDLARS is known as MEDLINE (MEDLARS online).

In addition to the usual bibliographic information (author, title, journal reference, etc.), each article stored in MEDLARS is also represented by a set of terms from the Medical Subject Headings (MeSH) list (16). MeSH is a classification system consisting of a defined set of approximately 14,000 indexing terms arranged in a hierarchical tree structure; in this form, MeSH is essentially an outline of medical knowledge. Before an article is stored in MEDLARS, a trained NLM indexer scans the article and chooses from MeSH a set of terms that together describe the contents of the article. This set of terms is stored along with the bibliographic data for each article. The process of encoding articles into MeSH terms is subject to specific guidelines set forth by NLM (10).

To retrieve an article from MEDLARS is to retrieve the article's bibliographic data. Articles can be retrieved from MEDLARS by specifying the author, title, date of publication, or other bibliographic information. Articles can also be retrieved by specifying a MeSH term, allowing the user to retrieve articles about a particular topic when no bibliographic information is known. Potentially, this is the most useful feature of MEDLARS. Queries to MEDLARS can also contain any combination of the above, separated by Boolean operators.

MeSH can be considered a knowledge base, with each term being a node, and each node connected in the MeSH hierarchy by links representing "is-a" relationships. In this way, MeSH represents the knowledge a trained NLM indexer possesses about the hierarchical organization of the medical literature. Presently, efficient use of MEDLARS requires the assistance of an experienced librarian (9), because non-bibliographic queries must contain only MeSH terms. General free-text queries are not meaningful to the system. Also, queries from inexperienced users are often too broad or too narrow; a librarian is required to help the user formulate queries of the proper depth.

Clearly, the automated utilization of MeSH as a knowledge base could ease the user's reliance on an experienced librarian, resulting in an overall improvement of MEDLARS. It is on this premise that research at NLM includes work on the development of knowledge bases, a research effort of which the this information retrieval experiment is a part.

2.1.1   Snomed Classification Structure

In the development of knowledge bases, a relevant research question is how knowledge bases can be augmented. In the present project, the Systematized Nomenclature of Medicine (SNOMED) was used to augment the MeSH tree structure. SNOMED was developed by the College of American Pathologists as a systematic nomenclature for use in hospital records (3). Much as MeSH terms are used to describe documents, SNOMED terms are used to describe patients.

SNOMED contains approximately 50,000 terms divided into 6 major categories: Topography, Morphology, Etiology, Function, Disease, and Procedure. Ideally, a physician can completely describe any patient by choosing one or more terms from each of the 6 categories. *Topography* terms describe what part of the patient is affected by the disease. *Morphology* terms describe what the disease looks like on both the gross and histological levels. *Etiology* terms describe the cause of the disease, if it is known. *Function* terms describe how the disease affects the patient's normal physiology. *Disease* terms describe the name given to the patient's particular constellation of signs and symptoms. *Procedure* terms describe what is being done to treat the disease.

SNOMED is an extremely detailed classification structure. For example, the Topography category contains two terms for most of the paired structures of the body, one term designating the left structure and one term designating the right structure. Where MeSH has about 10 terms dealing with blood group antigens and antibodies, SNOMED has 150 terms for the major and minor blood groups. SNOMED terms are grouped into a rough hierarchical tree structure, but this structure is much less explicit than it is in MeSH. Given the way SNOMED was designed to be used, it was not essential to have clear hierarchical organization beyond that of the 6 major categories. Despite its loose organization, SNOMED has been used as a knowledge base for the automatic indexing of pathology reports (7).

2.1.2 Augmentation Algorithm for Identity

Suppose knowledge base A (kb A) can be represented as a tree structure with nodes {A1, A2, ..., An}. Suppose we would like to augment knowledge base A with knowledge base B (kb B) which has nodes {B1, B2, ..., Bn}. (See Figures 1 and 2). A simple augmentation would be to identify any subtrees in kb B whose root is identical to a node in kb A. (This could be as simple as finding any nodes in kb B that are also in kb A.) The augmentation of kb A would then be accomplished by mapping the entire subtree identified from kb B into the node identified in kb A. For example, if A5 and B4 were identical terms (represented the same concept), the above augmentation scheme would result in the tree of Figure 3. In the present project, kb A is MeSH and kb B is SNOMED. Having defined an augmentation algorithm, SNOMED was analyzed for subtrees that could be automatically identified and augmented into the MeSH classification structure.

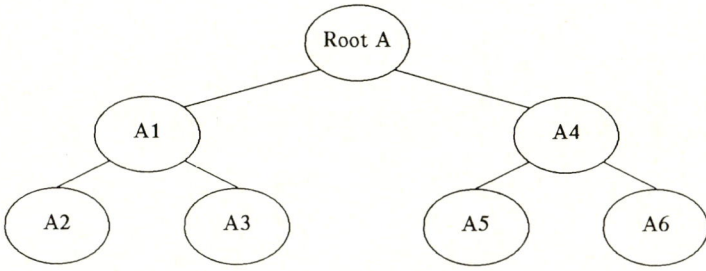

Figure 1

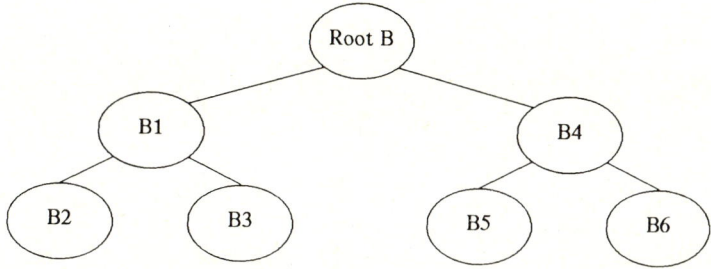

Figure 2

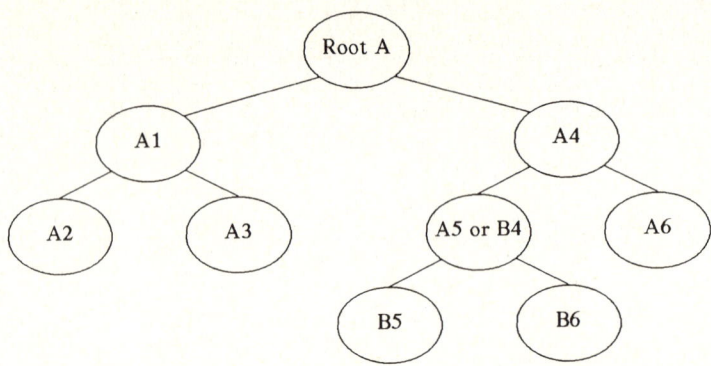

Figure 3

By the augmentation algorithm, any child of a SNOMED parent should also be a child of a MeSH parent if the same parent appears in both classification structures. Let us look at a particular example. In MeSH the term Rickettsia has 4 children (see Figure 4). In SNOMED Rickettsia has 10 children (see Figure 5). Applying the augmentation algorithm, MeSH would be given 6 new children from SNOMED.

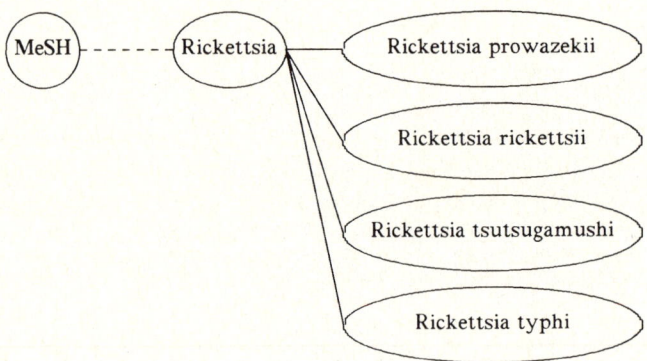

Figure 4

2.1.3   Evaluating the Augmentation

The purpose of augmenting knowledge bases is to "make them better." How would we know if a knowledge base was "better?" We needed a way to evaluate the quality of the knowledge base.

A logical method of evaluation is to use the knowledge base to perform a specified, hopefully useful task. In this project, the MeSH and augmented MeSH knowledge bases were used to automatically index titles of medical journal articles into the

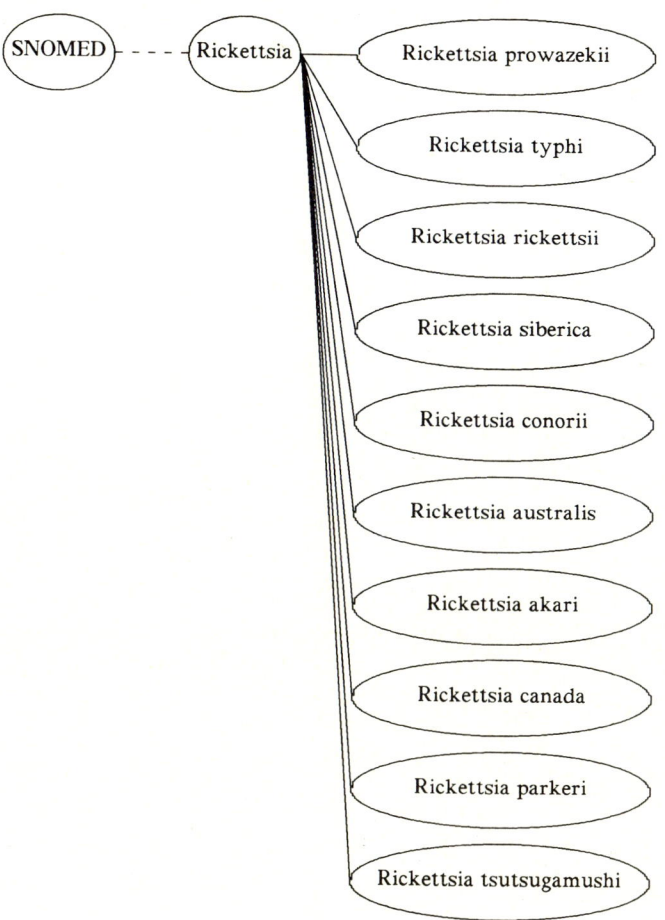

Figure 5

MeSH classification system. This was done by a computer program. The results of this program were then compared with how NLM's indexers (i.e., human experts) classified the same articles into the same MeSH system. For a given set of articles, if our automatic indexing program performed more like NLM indexers when the program used kb X than when it used kb Y, then kb X was judged as being a "better" knowledge base than kb Y. In our experiments, we first did computer indexing with kb Y, then tested Y against human indexers, then augmented Y to form kb X, and finally tested X against human indexers. Our automatic title indexer could have been a major undertaking in itself, since it was essentially a problem in natural language processing. Instead, a simple, if not simple-minded algorithm was used which had previously been developed by Rada (12).

2.1.4 Experimental Results

In building the required dictionaries, the System for Augmenting and Indexing (SAI) processed MeSH and SNOMED in their entirety. The unaugmented MeSH kb contained about 14,000 terms or concepts. Several thousand subtrees were extracted from SNOMED. The subtrees whose root terms matched MeSH terms led to the addition of several thousand terms to MeSH. From MEDLARS, 247 titles from the recent medical literature were chosen randomly. The titles were not constrained to any particular topic.

For each title, INDEXER (the indexing part of SAI) printed the MeSH terms assigned to the article by NLM indexers (set A) and the MeSH terms assigned by INDEXER (set B) according to the indexing algorithm explained previously. INDEXER also printed the number of agreements with the NLM staff indexers, i.e., how many terms are in the intersection of sets A and B. A term that is in both sets A and B is called a "hit." The average hit percentage (AHP) is calculated as the number of hits divided by the number of terms assigned by INDEXER (set B). Set B is used in the divisor instead of set A, since set A can contain terms not deducible from just the title. To summarize,

$$A = \{\text{terms assigned by NLM}\}$$

$$B = \{\text{terms assigned by INDEXER}\}$$

$$\text{Hits} = A \cap B$$

$$\text{AHP} = |A \cap B| \div |B|$$

where "$\cap$" is the symbol for set intersection and "$|x|$" denotes the cardinality (number of terms) of set x.

Our experiment used the same 247 randomly chosen titles (see Table 1). The third column of the Table is the total number of MeSH terms used by NLM indexers to represent the 247 titles. The fourth column is the total number of MeSH terms INDEXER proposed, employing its indexing algorithm. The other columns should be self-explanatory.

	TABLE	Experimental Results		
Experiment	Knowledge Base	Total NLM Terms	Total INDEXER Terms	Total Hits	AHP
1	Unaugmented	1929	524	255	49%
2	Augmented	1929	493	239	48%

Table 1

Experiment Results

INDEXER generated approximately one-fourth as many MeSH terms as NLM indexers used to classify the titles. This is a reasonable result since upon inspection of the 247 titles, it was noted that less than half of NLM's MeSH term assignments could be deduced from the title alone. This is not surprising since NLM indexers base their MeSH assignments on the entire contents of each document, not just the title.

The results of our experiments do not show that INDEXER benefited from the augmentation of MeSH with SNOMED. In fact, both the number of hits and the number of INDEXER-assigned terms decreased in the augmented runs. The augmentation algorithm seems eminently reasonable, yet no benefit was observed in these experiments. At least two explanations can be offered to explain the lack of improvement. First, perhaps our yardstick for the knowledge bases, namely, how they perform with INDEXER, is not sensitive enough. This could be addressed by improving the natural language processing aspects of INDEXER. Another possibility is that the choice of 247 random titles inadequately corresponded to the terms from SNOMED that were added to MeSH. For example in none of the titles was a species of Rickettsia mentioned, and the previously illustrated SNOMED Rickettsia subtree was thus unable to make any contribution to the indexing of the 247 titles.

Another, more intriguing explanation for the failure of the augmented MeSH to give better indexing would be related to the claim that the augmentation did not cause any real improvement of the knowledge base. A close inspection of SNOMED reveals many similarities between it and MeSH. For example, there is a strong correspondence between SNOMED's Topography category and MeSH's Anatomical Terms section. SNOMED's Etiology category closely corresponds to the Organisms and Chemicals sections in MeSH. There are many other sections of correspondence between the two knowledge bases; perhaps the augmentation failed because SNOMED offers MeSH few new conceptual pathways toward the root of the knowledge base (8).

2.1.5 Partial-Identity Match

Exact matches such as of Rickettsia to Rickettsia did not allow us to add terms and relationships to the knowledge base in a way which would allow us to demonstrate an increased utility to the kb. Accordingly, we explored the effect of connecting two terms that were "partial-identical". We did a small experiment by hand to test to what extent extra terms added through "partial-identity" MeSH would help indexing. For the documents which we considered the indexing accuracy dramatically increased.

An outline of the methodology for this experiment follows:

    (1) Documents were retrieved from MEDLINE under "blood transfusion".

    (2) Documents were encoded by our automatic method (with some augmentations to be described shortly) based on

MeSH and evaluated for their hit-rate on "blood transfusion"

(3) MeSH "blood transfusion" was augmented with children of "transfusion reaction" SNOMED.

(4) Documents were indexed by our algorithm via augmented MeSH.

We took the most recent 22 titles from a search about blood transfusion. Then we tested the extent to which the INDEXER, using MeSH alone, would produce the term "Blood Transfusion." Using the 22 titles we were able to encode 7 into "Blood Transfusion" based on MeSH alone.

Then we augmented MeSH with SNOMED by adding to the dictionary a part of SNOMED that included:

```
(TRANSFUSION REACTION)
(TRANSFUSION REACTION HEMOLYTIC)
(TRANSFUSION REACTION HEMOLYTIC IMMEDIATE)
(TRANSFUSION REACTION HEMOLYTIC DELAYED)
```

Upon repeat of the indexing procedure, none of the correctly identified titles were changed in their indexing. Of the 15 titles that previously were not encoded into "Blood Transfusion" an additional 5 are now correctly encoded. Of these 5, 3 had the words "delayed hemolytic transfusion reaction" which matched perfectly into a SNOMED term.

The addition of terms like "transfusion reaction" to "blood transfusion" helps indexing. "Transfusion reaction" is not an instance of "blood transfusion". We have, in these experiments, added terms to MeSH that were not instances of their new parents. A "transfusion reaction" is caused by "blood transfusion" but is not an instance of a blood transfusion. These other links led INDEXER to some excellent guesses about the content of the document. We would like to explore more fully the significance of this kind of result in the context both of machine learning and expectation-driven parsing.

2.2 Historical Case Experiment

In the history of scientific development, information in one scientific field has often been used to augment knowledge acquired using different techniques in another field. Although sometimes the same term might be the clue to interfield relationships, the situation in actual science is usually more complex. Thus, to capture the actual scientific knowledge, concepts as they were understood at a particular historical period are represented in frame-structures with properties and values. Then identity is hypothesized based on heuristic rules, and properties from one concept are used to add to the property list of another, or to change properties that do not match. The adequacy of the change is judged by whether it correctly matches the further historical developments that actually occurred. Thus, the history of science provides a framework for experiments in artificial intelligence, and a means of testing the adequacy of the outcome. However, it has the danger that we build into the representation and reasoning the ability to produce the expected results without fairly reflecting the historical state of the knowledge. One is continually struggling to both give the detail that confronted scientists in a particular case but also to give strategies which are general enough to apply to other cases.

The historical case to be examined is the relation between genetics and cytology in the early 20th century that resulted in the interfield connection establishing the relation between genes and chromosomes. The first task is to represent the two concepts in frame structures, using the knowledge from the time (4). Then to formulate a heuristic for testing to determine if the two concepts may plausibly be considered identical. Once one forms a hypothesis that the relation between genes and chromosomes is identity, then properties from one can be transferred to the other to form testable hypotheses about properties of the concepts. At this point, no means for automatically testing these hypotheses is part of the system; whether the hypothesis proved correct in the historical record is noted by the author.

2.2.1 Representation

We initially elaborated the following chromosome and gene concepts, which were meant to represent what scientists knew about these concepts in the early 20th century. The concepts are represented as LISP association structures (19). (See Boxes 1 and 2). The frame-like structures are headed by key concepts like chromosome and gene. Properties of a concept include problem, because concepts related to the same problem are likely to be related to each other.

Chromosome Concept

(setq chromosome '((problem heredity)
 (prop1 pure)
 (prop2 pairs-maternal+paternal)
 (prop3 maternal+paternal-pairs-not-mixed)
 (prop4 half-in-gametes)
 (prop5 number: few)))

Box 1

2.2.2 Reasoning

Our first level discovery method first checks for similarity of match. Given that greater than half the properties of two concepts are the same, the program then makes changes so as to

```
Gene Concept

(setq gene '((problem heredity)
    (prop1 pure)
    (prop2 pairs-maternal+paternal)
    (prop3 maternal+paternal-pairs-mixed)
    (prop4 half-in-gametes)
    (prop5 number: many)
```

Box 2

bring the two similar concepts even closer. The key function
in the identity resolver is called RESOLVER (see Box 3).
RESOLVER depends on two functions: DEGREE-MATCH and FIX-
THEORY. DEGREE-MATCH tests for the degree of match between two
concepts. FIX-THEORY chooses randomly among the dissimilar
parts of two concepts that have substantial match and makes the
two parts the same. We discussed but did not implement making
the changes non-randomly based on strength of belief in the
different properties.

```
(defun resolver (concept1 concept2)
    (cond ( (greaterp (degree-match concept1 concept2 ) (half-length concept1))
            (print "degree match is good") (terpr)
            (fix-theory concept1 concept2 concept2))
        (t (print "degree match is bad"))))
```

Box 3

2.2.3 Discovery

For the first representation of gene and chromosome, the
identity resolver finds 4 of 6 properties the same. Of the 2
which it might change, namely, prop3 and prop5, there are 4
ways that it can make the changes:

(1) Replace gene prop3 with chromosome prop3.
(2) Replace gene prop5 with chromosome prop5.
(3) Replace chromosome prop3 with gene prop3.
(4) Replace chromosome prop5 with gene prop5.

Only the 3rd of these is a correct change. This gives a 0.25
probability of improvement. The rule incorrectly changes the
number of one to be like the other. Since both were known to
be correct, the fact that there were more genes than chromosomes serves as a key to the formation of the hypothesis that
genes are parts of chromosomes.

3.0   PART-WHOLE

To extend our investigation in the light of the historical knowledge that the correct hypothesis is that genes are parts of chromosomes, we developed a rule for part-whole. For part-whole hypothesizing between two concepts x and y that are defined like the gene and chromosome above, we can readily use a rule with preconditions and actions (see Box 4).

When we applied the part-whole rule to the gene and chromosome concepts, the rule correctly concluded that genes are part of chromosomes. Yet, we readily recognize that there are many concepts on which this part-whole rule incorrectly operates. Accordingly, we launched a refinement of both the concepts (see Boxes 5 and 6) and the rule. We reasoned that parts and wholes should occupy some portion of the same space at the same time.

Rule for Part-Whole

Preconditions:
  1) Concept y has $number_y$ and concept x has $number_x$, where $number_x > number_y$.
  2) x and y have the majority of their properties in common.

Actions:
  Conclude x is a part of y.

Box 4

Beginning of Second Version of Chromosome Concept

(setq chromosome
 '((problem: heredity)
   (field: cytology)
   (location: nucleus of cell)
   (individuality: retained
       time: cell cycles
       space: cell nucleus)
   (relations to other chromosomes: pairs)
   (number: few)
   .
   .

Box 5

Our first rule for part-whole worked because of its harmony with our first representation. Our second rule operates on more primitive properties, namely, time and space, than we have

> Beginning of Second Version of Gene Concept
>
> (setq gene
> '((problem: heredity)
>   (field: genetics)
>   (location: in gametes and elsewhere)
>   (individuality: retained
>   time: through generations
>   space: somewhere in organism)
>   (relation to other genes: pairs)
>   (number: many)
>   .
>   .

Box 6

> Second Version of Part-Whole Rule
>
> Preconditions:
> 1) y is in space1 and x is in space1.
> 2) y is at time1 and x is at time1
> 3) y has $number_y$ and x has $number_x$, where $number_y < number_x$.
>
> Actions:
>   Conclude some x's are part of one y.

Box 7

been able to meaningfully incorporate into our representation of the chromosome and gene (see Box 7). The conceptual units of our chromosome and gene are not primitive enough to match the units of the second rule.

To try to better capture the complexity of the discovery that the gene was part of the chromosome, we

(1) made a part-whole hierarchy of cytological concepts related to the chromosome.

(2) connected the genetics field to the cytology field by noting that there was evidence that the gene was part of the germ cell but that the relationship was not as tight as one would want.

Noting the loose part-of link from gene to germ-cell, our new, more sophisticated reasoner then proceeds to traverse downward in the part-whole hierarchy of the germ-cell. As each unit within the germ-cell is encountered, its degree of match with

```
(setq germ-cell
   '((problem unknown)
    (part-of (value organism))
    (has-part (value nucleus cytoplasm membrane)))
)

(setq nucleus
   '( (problem unknown)
    (part-of (value germ-cell))
    (has-part (value chromosome nucleoplasm membrane))
    (individuality (retained through-cell-cycles)))
)
```

Box 8

the gene is checked. Two of the frames from this germ-cell part-whole hierarchy are here indicated (see Box 8).

At this point we had also elaborated the gene and chromosome concepts (see Box 9). While it is clear to a human's glance at the concepts, that the gene is closer to the chromosome than the nucleus or germ-cell, it is not clear that a computer algorithm would readily detect this.

One needs a way of directing the search for important matching properties within the part-whole hierarchy. If the gene is a functional concept and the chromosome is a structural concept (which in the early 20th century they were), then in looking for a relation between the descriptions of the two, the functional requirements of the gene guides the search for structures that can perform those functions. This will be a direction of our next reasoning strategy. The importance of these structure-function relations in guiding the search for properties to transfer in analogy matches is highlighted in the work of Winston *et. al.* (18), on learning physical descriptions from functional definitions.

4.0   DISCUSSION OF EXPERIMENTAL RESULTS

The information retrieval experiments depended on the identity relationship between two terms of MeSH and SNOMED. When such a match occurred the children of the SNOMED term were added to MeSH as children of the corresponding MeSH term. This augmentation strategy did not lead to improved power as measured by the performance of our indexing algorithm. Our hand experiments refined the representation by looking at parts of terms in MeSH and SNOMED. The reasoner then discovered matches based on other than identity relationships. These more sophisticated matches did allow the indexer to subsequently perform more robustly. However, we have not finished elaborating the representations upon which such reasonings can be made and,

```
(setq chromosome
  '((problem (value heredity))
    (part-of (value nucleus))
    (individuality (retained through-cell-cycles))
    (relations-to-other-chromosomes-in-the-same-nucleus
       (pairs
          (called homologues)
          (origin maternal-and-paternal)
          (appearance identical)
       )
       (sets-of-pairs
          (number (variability characteristic-of-species)
             (range 4-to-100))
       )
    ))
)

(setq gene
  '((problem (value heredity))
    (part-of (value germ-cell))
    (individuality (retained through-generations))
    (relation-to-other-genes
       (pairs
          (called alleles)
          (origin maternal-and-paternal)
          (types dominant-and-recessive)
          (appearance unknown)
       )
       (sets-of-pairs
          (number (variability characteristic-of-species)
             (range greater-than-100))
       )
    ))
)
```

Box 9

accordingly, have been unable to complete computer experiments with them.

The identity resolver for the genetics experiments was able to find a majority match among properties of gene and chromosome because of the way we carefully chose the representation. If the properties 1 through 5 given in an earlier figure were replaced by less well structured and more realistic knowledge, then our identity matcher would perform poorly. Furthermore, the random element of the program that changed the concepts ignored any guiding information that we know existed but was not available in the representation. We considered introducing probabilistic values as to the strengths of properties within the frames for gene and chromosome and then also modifying the reasoning strategy so as to weight more heavily hypotheses that

retained the properties that had the greatest strengths. We
don't believe, however, that the most incisive advances in
knowledge representation and automatic discovery will depend on
numeric manipulations. Accordingly, we turned next to the
study of part-whole relations.

In the development of rules for hypothesizing that a part-whole
relationship exists we again found that we could easily
contrive the representation of knowledge to correspond to a
simple rule for part-whole. On the other hand, the rule would
fail to hold in many, seemingly natural cases. The challenge
is to somehow naturally represent the genetics and cytology
information which led to the conclusion that the gene was part
of the chromosome and still be able to give a robust rule for
how that discovery was made.

As we extended the representation of the chromosome to one of
cytology more generally, we confronted several issues in the
definition of part-whole hierarchies and in how inheritance of
properties would occur among entities in a part-whole
hierarchy. If an entity is homogeneous in some property, then
all its parts have that property too. Other conditions for
inheritance are less apparent.

The matching that we though might be straightforward between
our most elaborated gene and chromosome concepts was not
straightforward. For instance, saying that the gene has
"individuality retained through generations" and that the
chromosome has "individuality retained through cell cycles" is
a significant match to a person who knows that cell cycles of a
chromosome correspond to generations of a gene, but to a
computer program that knowledge has to be explicitly stated and
referenced. There needs to be further decomposition of the
components of each concept so that connections between cell
cycles and generations can be made.

Trying to contrive our own knowledge-base of genetics and
cytology is a most demanding job. A better approach is to
borrow from others the knowledge that they have already
codified. To pursue this angle we considered the the *Medical
Subject Headings* (16). We extracted from the Medical Subject
Headings (MeSH) those parts which pertained most to our study.
About 10 per cent of those parts are presented in Boxes 10 and
11. As we studied these sections of MeSH we noted heterogene-
ity among the relations connecting terms. For instance,
Chromatin is a *part-of* the Cell Nucleus but Sex Chromatin is a
type-of Chromatin. Furthermore, there are a host of important
relationships among terms that MeSH makes no attempt to
represent. For instance, genes are linked and recombination is
an exception to linkage. If we were to use the vast MeSH
structure for reasoning we would either have to reason in ways
that were relatively insensitive to the many different kinds of
relationships that are subsumed under the category of broader-
than and narrower-than or would have to change the representation to encode those different relationships (13).

5.0 SUMMARY

In exploring criteria for connecting two knowledge bases we have focused on two experimental domains and two types of relations. In the information retrieval domain we have examined the role of identity relations in the augmentation of thesauri that also serve as the indexing language for a major document retrieval system. In the genetics domain we have used

---

A Part of MeSH Related to Cytology

A11.223 Cell Nucleus
A11.223.210 Cell Nucleolus
A11.223.349 Chromatin
A11.223.349.383 Heterochromatin
A11.223.349.625 Nucleosomes
A11.223.349.748 Sex Chromatin
A11.223.475 Chromosomes
A11.223.475.135 Centromere
A11.223.475.144 Chromatids
A11.223.475.190 Chromosomes Bacterial
A11.223.475.480 Chromosomes Human
A11.223.475.480.235 Chromosomes Human13
A11.223.475.480.280 Chromosomes Human45

Box 10

both identity and part-whole hypothesizing to try to simulate the discovery process that occurred in the early 20th century in genetics.

The information retrieval and gene history experiments show us the important role of hypothesis generation based on identity and part-whole relations. The existing library thesauri and past genetic literature are valuable guides to the representation and reasoning mechanisms that people use.

Computers now offer the opportunity to further make explicit and explore in greater detail strategies for the addition of relationships to a knowledge base.

The information retrieval experiments built on

   (1) the massive and important thesauri called MeSH and SNOMED and

   (2) the large textual database of hand-encoded documents at the National Library of Medicine.

By testing the ability of our thesauri to support an automatic indexing program, we were able to judge the success of our strategies to merge parts of SNOMED with MeSH. The experiments

to date show the difficulty and subtlety that must be
associated with these otherwise human operations of matching
concepts in thesauri.

We have taken representations of the gene and chromosome as
given in Darden and Maull (4). Although this representation
leaves many assumptions implicit, it serves as a useful
starting point. We placed the gene and chromosome concepts
into a frame system and manipulated them with a computer
program that embodied our first approximation of the identity-
driven hypothesis-generator. The program was able to correctly
change one property of the chromosome based on recognizing the

---

A Part of MeSH Related to Genetics

G5.275 Genes
G5.275.077 Alleles
G5.275.077.500 Immunoglobulin Allotypes
G5.275.180 DNA Insertion Elements
G5.275.201 Genes Bacterial
G5.275.304 Genes Dominant
G5.275.320 Genes Fungal
G5.275.348 Genes Immune Response
G5.275.359 Genes Lethal
G5.275.415 Genes Recessive
G5.275.470 Genes Regulator
G5.275.470.410 Enhancer Elements Genetics
G5.275.470.710 Promoter Regions Genetics
G5.275.470.810 Terminator Regions Genetics
G5.275.526 Genes Structural
G5.275.582 Genes Synthetic
G5.275.605 Genes Viral
G5.441 Genotype
G5.441.383 Heterozygote
G5.441.554 Homozygote
G5.568 Linkage
G5.735 Phenotype
G5.735.235 Dosage Compensation Genetics
G5.735.340 Epistasis Genetic
G5.735.450 Genetic Marker
G5.832 Recombination Genetic
G5.832.260 Crossing Over (Genetics)
G5.832.260.840 Sister Chromatid Exchange
G5.832.290 DNA Insertion Elements
G5.832.380 Gene Conversion
G5.832.401 Genetic Vectors

Box 11

---

matching property in the gene. However, the same program also
incorrectly concludes that the chromosome and gene are equal in
"number".

The property of number is connected to the part-whole relation which needs to be incorporated into the discovery process. Our second program specifies conditions under which the part-whole relation should be postulated and actions to be taken. The goal was to have this program determine that genes that are part of the same chromosome are linked to each other in inheritance, though the program has not achieved this goal. We are elaborating the reasoning algorithm and the representation of the concepts on which it works so that we better understand the conditions under which a given reasoning and representation pair work well together.

If we can detect that two frames or concepts participate in a relationship like identity or part-whole, we can then add that information to our knowledge-base. In this work on partial matching for the development of augmented thesauri in information retrieval and the theory of the gene we are focusing on two kinds of relationships, namely, identity and part-whole. These relationships are far from comprehensive, but they are important. A precise understanding of how to use them so as to augment a knowledge-base would be a step towards a more complete theory of knowledge representation and knowledge acquisition.

ACKNOWLEDGEMENTS

Much of this work was supported by NSF Grant ECS-84-U6683 through subcontract from Wayne State University to the Committee on the History and Philosophy of Science at the University of Maryland, College Park. Computer facilities were provided by the National Library of Medicine.

REFERENCES

1. Jaime Carbonell, "Learning by Analogy," in *Machine Learning*, ed. T Mitchell, pp. 137-161, Tioga Publishing, Palo, CA, 1983.

2. Michael Conrad, "On Design Principles for a Molecular Computer," *Communications Association Computing Machinery*, 28, 5, pp. 464-480, May 1985.

3. Roger Cote, *Systematized Nomenclature of Medicine*, College of American Pathologists, Skokie, Illinois, 1979.

4. Lindley Darden and Nancy Maull, "Interfield Theories," *Philosophy of Science*, 44, pp. 43-64, 1977.

5. Lindley Darden, "Theory Construction in Genetics," in *Scientific Discovery: Case Studies*, ed. T Nickles, pp. 151-170, Reidel, Dordrecht, Netherlands, 1980.

6. Lindley Darden, "Artificial Intelligence and Philosophy of Science: Reasoning by Analogy in Theory Construction," <u>PSA 1982</u>, V. 2, pp. 147-165, Philosophy of Science Association, East Lansing, MI, 1982.

7. G. Dunham, M. Pacak, and A. Pratt, "Automatic Indexing of Pathology Data," *Jr Amer Soc Inform Sc*, March 1978.

8. John Eng, "Augmentation and Evaluation of a Medical Knowledge Base," *Internal Report,* National Library of Medicine, August 1985.

9. Raya Fidel, "Online Searching Styles: Case-Study-Based Model of Searching Behavior," *Jr American Soc Inform Sc*, 35, 4, pp. 211-221, 1984.

10. National Library of Medicine, MEDLARS *Indexing Manual*, NLM Publication PB84-104829, Bethesda, MD, 1985.

11. Marvin Minsky and Seymour Papert, *Perceptions*, MIT Press, Massachusetts, 1969.

12. Roy Rada and Lynn Evans, "Automated Problem Encoding System for Ambulatory Care," *Computers and Biomedical Research*, 12, pp. 131-139, 1979.

13. Roy Rada, Susanne Humphrey, and Craig Coccia, "A Knowledge-base for Retrieval Evaluation," *Proc ACM '85*, pp. 360-367, Act 1985.

14. Roy Rada, "Gradualness Facilitates Knowledge Refinement," *IEEE Transactions on Pattern Analysis and Machine Intelligence*, 7, 5, pp. 523-530, September 1985.

15. Gerard Salton and Michael McGill, *Introduction to Modern Information Retrieval*, McGraw-Hill, New York, 1983.

16. Medical Subject Headings Section, *Medical Subject Headings, Annotated Alphabetical List, 1985*, National Library of Medicine, Bethesda, MD, 1984. Publication PB84-223156.

17. Patrick Winston, "Learning and Reasoning by Analogy," *Communications Association Computing Machinery*, 23, 12, December 1980.

18. Patrick Winston, Thomas Binford, Boris Katz, and Michael Lowry, "Learning Physical Descriptions from Functional Definitions, Examples, and Precedents," *Proc Nat'l Conf on Artificial Intelligence*, pp. 433-439, August 1983.

19. Patrick Winston and Berthold Horn, *LISP*, Addison-Wesley, Reading, MA, 1984.

FORMAL APPROACHES

ANALOGY IN PROGRAM DEVELOPMENT

Scott R. Dietzen and William L. Scherlis

Carnegie-Mellon University
Pittsburgh, Pennsylvania 15213

April 1986*

Consensus seems to be emerging concerning new process models for knowledge-based programming tools; surprisingly little progress has been made, however, in understanding the nature of the programming knowledge that is to be represented and organized in these tools. We approach this question by considering the role of past experience in programming, including immediate past experience, as applied to program modification, and more remote experience, as applied to new programming problems. It is necessary to represent this experience in a way that truly permits reuse of designs, without forcing direct reuse of code or even abstracted code. We suggest that this can be achieved by considering program derivations, which represent idealized program design histories. We illustrate how abstractions on this kind of structure can support a rich space of generalizations and analogies, and we speculate on how program derivations might be represented in a semantically based programming tool.

1.0   KNOWLEDGE, PROGRAMMING, AND ANALOGY

It is often stated that programming is a good candidate for mechanization into expert systems, and there are many good arguments to support this view. Consider: The results of the programming process are formal objects--programs--and the steps

---

*   This research was supported in part by the Office of Naval Research under contract N00014-84-K-0415 and in part by the Defense Advanced Research Projects Agency (DOD), ARPA Order No. 5404, monitored by the Office of Naval Research under the same contract. The views and conclusions contained in this document are those of the authors and should not be interpreted as representing the official policies, either expressed or implied, of DARPA or the U.S. Government.

along the way, especially when starting from formal specifications, seem to have a mechanizable character. Also, programming is highly conventionalized, so capturing a relatively small number of paradigms and techniques should suffice for prototype knowledge-based tools. And, further, we are all programmers, so we can avoid prolonged dealings with intractable domain experts and rely on introspection instead. Finally, there has emerged in the last three years a broadly based consensus (discussed below) concerning advanced tools for supporting the program development and maintenance process [Bauer85, Green83, Scherlis83].

In spite of these positive indications, it has become apparent that we are progressing all too slowly in developing any kind of understanding of or agreement on what is programming knowledge and on how it is to be organized and represented. The consensus on tools, for example, concerns models of the programming *process*. Interestingly enough, it has proven possible to work out these models in some detail while making only a few substantive assumptions concerning the nature of programming knowledge.

Similarly, the fact that we are all programmers has enabled us to build rudimentary "knowledge bases" for programming that, in fact, are largely case analyses for representing a few common data abstractions, such as lists, sets, graphs, and so on. The specificity of these rules allows for easily demonstrable results. But, when faced with the vast array of program structures and abstract objects that programmers really use as bases for conceptualization, such as editor buffers, process schedulers, windows, command parsers, tridiagonal matrices, sparse matrices, sorting algorithms, and the like, one can conclude that existing rule representations are too concrete to allow for substantial growth in functionality. Growth is inhibited by the flatness of the rule sets (*i.e.*, the absence of abstracted structure) and by the difficulty (because of the absence of structure) in maintaining consistency during growth.

We suggest in this paper an approach to the representation and use of programming knowledge that is based on a rich set of generalization (*i.e.*, abstraction) mechanisms in program *derivations*. This approach relies on a recognition of the need to represent past experience in a way that truly permits reuse of *designs*, without forcing direct reuse of code or even abstracted code. In addition to considering the issue of the *representation* of programming knowledge or experience, we must consider mechanisms by which the knowledge is *used*, particularly as a source of analogies and generalizations. This naturally leads to a number of ideas concerning user interaction with semantically based programming tools. Key to the acceptance of this approach is a recognition of the rich space of generalizations, which is illustrated with a number of simple examples from programming.

We start by reviewing some of the basic ideas concerning the nature and structure of program derivations. We then discuss the role of past experience in programming and examine a number of examples in order to expose the rich space of generalizations among programs and program derivations. It should be kept in mind that this is a speculative exercise. Significant experimentation must be done to substantiate the basic claims of mechanizability of the heuristic approach; theoretical work is required to help develop useful and powerful languages of generalizations; and, finally, we are only beginning to understand what is the nature of the basic program derivation steps.

Program Derivation. What are the real results of the program design process? If program *executions* were the sole results of interest, then it would be sufficient that the results of the design process be simply *programs*. But this is rarely the case in practical programming. Most programs undergo analysis, modification, and adaptation--even (*especially*, in fact) during their original development. The view has often been presented, by us and others, that in these cases delivering the *program* itself is simply not sufficient.

An indication is the experience of software maintainers, who (if statistics are to be believed) spend the bulk of their time just figuring out what existing code does. The problem, of course, is that there is knowledge about the programs being modified that is not explicitly represented in them. In other words, more knowledge has been brought to bear on the design and implementation of a program than is evident in the code alone. We have argued at length elsewhere that the knowledge is better presented in the form of an *account* or *derivation* of the program [Scherlis83]. That is, the designed objects must not be *programs*, but *program derivations*.

What is a program derivation? Very crudely, programming involves bridging two gaps: First, we must pass from an informal requirement description to a formal specification of *what* the problem is and, second, we must pass from the specification to an implementation, detailing *how* the problem is to be solved. One of the key insights represented by the new process models is that tools need not (and, indeed, should not) impose temporal constraints on these processes. Implementation activity, for example, can already be underway before the specification (and even the requirement description) is fully formulated.

Even if the formal specification is never actually expressed, it should be clear that there are two kinds of transitions being made, one from *informal* to *formal* and the other from *what* to *how*. Although it will probably continue to be a most problematic aspect of programming, we do not address here the first of these two transitions, turning directly to the second.

Specifications are distinguished from *implementations* by level of concreteness and commitment. It can be argued that a specification is simply an implementation with the details left out, but this does not reveal the real nature of the connection that must be made between them. Realizing a specification involves making commitments of various sorts, such as

representations of abstract objects, order of computation, and
so on, and optimizing on the basis of these commitments. We
view programming, in the ideal, as a process of specialization,
in which an aggregation of uses of general notions is transformed, introducing interdependencies and so replacing general
notions by more specific--and more efficient--ones. The
specialization, then, is not of the *functionality* of the
aggregate, but of its *structure*. The *cost* of the refinement
steps is a sacrifice of modularity and an introduction of
dependency--resulting in a loss of clarity and adaptability.
The *benefit* of the steps is better performance. (This idea is
presented in detail in [Scherlis83], which also raises a number
of related philosophical issues, and in [Scherlis81], which
presents a simple syntactic approach.)

Of course, there is no such thing as "programming in the
ideal." Programmers need to explore and backtrack, shifting
their attention from one aspect of a problem to another, in
order to make decisions that will be favorable in the larger
context. Semantically based programming tools, then, must not
require the programmer to conform to a methodology that demands
prescience, but one that allows attention to shift and, of
course, that enables productive use of past experience. We
thus distinguish the design results--program derivations--from
the design process--which we call inferential programming. It
is clear that the nature of objects designed must not be
confused with the structure of the design process itself; that
is, program derivations and inferential programming are
fundamentally different entities that must be conceptualized
independently.

The individual steps of a derivation are of two kinds--steps
that *establish* context for some general notion through choice
of representation or computation order, through proof of a
program property, or through some other means, and steps that
exploit context by means of simplification and transformation
rules. Together, these steps manifest *commitments* in program
development. A derivation is an *idealized* sequence (or, more
generally, a partially ordered set) of such steps. It is not
intended to represent a temporal history, with all the
backtracking, redesign, and shifting of attention that would be
entailed, but instead a "perfect" account of the program,
perhaps with annotations justifying decision points. Observe
that, because the individual steps record commitments,
derivations are *directional*. Of course, derivations can also
be read from implementation to specification as a record of
abstraction steps.

While program derivations, in theory, contain only the
idealized sequence of steps between specification and implementation, "practical" program derivations, as we expect they will
be represented in real programming tools, will be annotated
with all kinds of peripheral heuristic information. Although
we do not address below the question of exactly what sort of
information should decorate the bare derivations, it should be
clear that such information will be essential in controlling
search in a practical system.

Past Experience. Experience (the accumulation of which can be viewed as organizing into knowledge) has many manifestations and means of application in programming. Manifestations range from explicit existing code (a subroutine, abstract type, or module definition, for example) to idiomatic aggregations of program structures (as used by APL programmers or as represented as *idioms* in the Programmer's Apprentice database) to techniques for organizing computations (such as divide and conquer, memo functions, or dynamic programming) to specific program development techniques (such as frequency reduction, methods for introducing storage reuse, or methods for moving computations from data access points, for example, to less frequently evaluated data creation points) to very general techniques for developing programs (such as "find the hot spots and optimize there").

Further, experience can be applied at several levels simultaneously. Consider, for example, the process of program modification. Programmers spend the bulk of their time adapting existing code and so they are often making "fight-or-flight" decisions, choosing either to base a new development so closely on specific past experience that it is most easily reached by direct steps from existing code (*i.e.*, the results of that experience) or to start a fresh new development, making use, perhaps, of the *derivation* for the earlier implementation, but rejecting direct use of code as unproductive. But this decision itself is generally based on experience in similar situations!

The point, then, is that "past experience" exists, in programming, at multiple levels of abstraction and at multiple meta-levels. This strongly reinforces the need for meta-level representation mechanisms such as *chunking* [Laird85].

As an aside, it is interesting to note the parallel between chunking and certain program transformation techniques. It can be argued that the purpose of program transformation rules such as the specialization system or the unfold/fold system is simply to reorganize programs so program elements involved in some domain-dependent simplification become syntactically juxtaposed. Once such simplifications have been made, syntactic devices such as *expression procedures* [Scherlis81] are needed to represent the efficient derived methods. By viewing program *execution* as analogous to problem solving, expression procedures become analogous to chunks and, further, the derivation of expression procedures by transformations becomes analogous to the meta-level inference necessary to acquire new chunks. The problem solving associated with directing the transformation process thus works at this level and higher: Aggregations of low level transformations into higher level techniques, such as the aggregation of the composition, application, and abstraction rules into the specialization technique, are thus chunks at this, higher level. The point, then, is that our inferential programming activity cannot succeed without a capability to do serious work at a number of meta-levels simultaneously. Hence our views on the need for mechanisms such as embodied in Newell's Soar.

In this paper, we explore, in a tentative way, the structure of the space of programming experience, and suggest ways in which the experience can be represented and applied. In particular, we show that, while abstractions on programs go a long way [Barstow80, Dershowitz85, Rich81, Waters85], abstractions on program derivations are more useful.

Very roughly, the approach we are following is based on the use of a highly structured knowledge base accessed by a small number of distinct methods. Structure in the knowledge base is maintained through program derivation structure and through a hierarchy of generalizations (on programs and on program derivations). Generalized derivations and other facts in the knowledge base are applied (to the construction of new derivations) in three ways. The first and most obvious is *direct use* of an existing fact (for example, a known code fragment, idiom, or derivation). The second is application of an instance of an existing *generalization*, and the third is to use an existing fact or generalization (perhaps an inconsistent one--see below) *by analogy*. Use by analogy generally implies *recognition* (by either the system or a user) of the existence of a useful generalization, but the generalization does not play a direct role. It does not need to be expressed, nor, for that matter, does it even need to be expressible. In other words, generalization underlies all analogy, but analogy is nonetheless necessary because many useful generalizations are not easily expressible.

Generalization and Analogy. It should be clear, even at this level of discussion, that success of the approach depends on two factors. The first factor is the degree to which a knowledge base can be structured by means of abstraction (*i.e.*, generalization); this determines its versatility and adaptability and, ultimately, its power. The point is that the ability to *succinctly* articulate accumulated past experience is an indication, roughly, of the power of an expressive system. Succinctness is key because it reflects the degree to which abstraction can reduce detail. The second factor is the extent to which potential analogies can be detected in the absence of explicit generalizations. This, together with the extent to which the successful analogies yield useful new generalizations, predicts the ability of a system to assimilate new experience.

We illustrate these points in our examples below. With respect to the first factor, which is the power of abstraction, we demonstrate a number of kinds of abstraction in program development that go well beyond abstraction mechanisms for *programs* to abstraction mechanisms for *derivations*. We illustrate the second point by exploring several examples of analogies and showing how they can lead to "unjustified" generalizations and thence (perhaps) to justified generalizations.

Unlike many other candidate areas for expert system development, the objects of concern in programming are *formal*, with precisely defined syntax and meaning. As we learn more about the space of meanings of programs, the nature of program derivation steps, and the structure of program derivations, we correspondingly become better able to abstract and thus represent our programming knowledge, hitherto expressed only informally or indirectly.

This raises a common-sense point concerning use of programmers and other experts in building knowledge bases. It is clear that a command of technique does not imply mastery of meaning, nor, for that matter, does the converse necessarily hold. (Consider, for example, the respective abilities of a calculus student and a pure mathematician in solving integrals--or in expositing the meaning of differentials [Scherlis83].) This failure of linkage extends to **expression**: Mastery of technique may mean that rules are **used** but are hard wired and do not yield themselves to expression even on close introspection-- possibly because there is insufficient power in the language to express them. Mathematics students can perceive the connections between various algebraic systems without necessarily being able to **express** the connections in the language of category theory. This argues for use of analogy even in a context where a large range of generalizations is expressible. It might be preferable, for example, for a system to interact with a user by citing a prior example and indicating an analogy rather than yielding forth a full expression of a complex and deep generalization.

But the point here is somewhat different: Programming has been studied extensively, and there *is* a rich set of kinds of generalizations on programs and on program derivations. Programmers and algorithm designers make implicit use of many of these, hence gaining leverage from their prior experience. A significant portion of our task in building expert systems-- similar to the task of programming language theorists--is to develop precise **language** (*i.e.*, formal representation) to express (and reason about) these generalizations. Only by doing this will we be able to introduce adequate structure into our knowledge bases. It is better to have a few general principles with a large number of worked-out special cases than a flat database containing only a large number of independent special cases without supporting generalizations. Observe that the formal nature of programs makes this task much easier than in other domains! (A good example of this kind of structuring exercise in programming language theory is the Larch specification language [Guttag85].)

It is necessary to distinguish, in the realm of program derivations, consistent generalizations from inconsistent ones. Every instance of a **consistent** generalization of a program derivation is correct; that is, every instance is a legitimate derivation that needs no further verification. **Inconsistent** generalizations, on the other hand, need not produce correct or even meaningful instances.

Because of this lack of correctness of inconsistent generalizations, a working through of their instances is necessary whenever they are applied; here is where analogy has an essential role. But inconsistent generalizations provide an important mechanism for capturing certain kinds of knowledge in the absence of appropriate abstraction mechanisms--or for expressing initial approximations to consistent generalizations. (This reinforces our remark earlier concerning the continued need for analogy in the presence of powerful abstraction mechanisms.) These remarks notwithstanding, we expect that the exact roles of consistent and inconsistent generalizations in programming tools will most likely be determined by experiment.

2.0   AN INTRODUCTORY EXAMPLE

Let us start with an example program derivation--an extremely simple derivation involving the canonical example program, factorial. But even this simple derivation, which is carried out using the specialization system cited earlier, illustrates some points of importance in our discussion.

$$\text{fact}(n) \leftarrow \text{if } n = 0 \text{ then } 1 \text{ else } n * \text{fact}(n-1)$$

(Here, '←' denotes function definition.) The fault with the above program, from a performance standpoint, is that it makes implicit use of storage (in the form of the control stack) to store values of *n* on the way down the recursion, doing the multiplications on the way up the recursion.

The critical enabling observation for the derivation is that, because '*' is associative, we could just as well do the multiplications on the way *down* the recursion, *accumulating* a result and thus leaving no work to do on the way up the recursion--that is, leaving a tail-recursive definition that requires only a constant amount of implicit storage.

This plan is carried out by forming a procedure to calculate the value of accumulating expressions of the form $u * \textbf{\textit{fact(v)}}$ and simplifying.

$$u * \text{fact}(v) \leftarrow u * (\text{if } v = 0 \text{ then } 1 \text{ else } v * \text{fact}(v-1))$$

$$\leftarrow \text{if } v = 0 \text{ then } u \text{ else } u * (v * \text{fact}(v-1))$$

At this point we are able to make use of the associativity of '*', transferring the multiplication inside ***fact*** out to the accumulator. The resulting expression procedure is tail-recursive.

$$u * \text{fact}(v) \leftarrow \text{if } v = 0 \text{ then } u \text{ else } (u * v) * \text{fact}(v-1)$$

Finally, we abstract, in a conventional way, a subroutine definition from this procedure and, simultaneously, from the original definition of ***fact*** (introducing an identity value on the way).

$$\text{fact}(n) \leftarrow \text{fact}_1(1,n)$$

$$u * \text{fact}(v) \leftarrow \text{fact}_1(u,v)$$

$$\text{fact}_1(u,v) \leftarrow \text{if } v = 0 \text{ then } u \text{ else } (u * v) * \text{fact}(v-1)$$

As a final step, we unfold the tail-recursive call to the accumulating expression procedure and then eliminate it since there are no other calls.

$$\text{fact}(n) \leftarrow \text{fact}_1(1,n)$$

$$\text{fact}_1(u,v) \leftarrow \text{if } v = 0 \text{ then } u \text{ else } \text{fact}_1(u * v, v-1)$$

We now have the conventional "optimized" factorial, which requires only constant space (since it is tail-recursive). (Derivations similar to this one have appeared in a number of places; see [Scherlis83] for citations.)

Let us now consider a program similar to the original factorial definition, both in structure and in triteness, the list reversal function.

$$\text{rev}(\alpha) \leftarrow \text{if } \alpha = \text{nil then nil else } \text{rev}(tl(\alpha)) \bullet \text{cons}(hd(\alpha),\text{nil})$$

This function *appears* to be similar to *fact*, and indeed suffers from the same problem concerning implicit use of storage (in addition to the more serious problem of quadratic space used by *append*). How can we derive an efficient solution using our experience with *fact* as a guide?

The Key Issues. In any analogical reasoning paradigm, we must maintain a store of previously solved problems (in this case, *fact*) which contains an amount of additional information dependent on the paradigm. New problems are matched against old problems and, if they are sufficiently *close* by some metric, then we proceed to attempt development of a solution by analogy. The key design issues for us are, (1) how is the store of old problems to be represented and matched against new problems, and (2) what information should be retained relating to the previous solutions to facilitate development of solutions to new problems.

For the purpose of this first example, we make use of ordinary pattern matching of problem statements. In the cases of problems with complex specifications, this issue becomes more substantive. For our purposes, let us agree on an adequate solution in order that we can proceed directly to the second of the two design issues.

Matching. We suggest, following Huet and Lang, that matching between a new problem and a set of existing problems can be carried out using second order matching [Huet78]. We seek to find a second order *least general generalization* of the two definitions [Plotkin70]. Put simply, we (syntactically) generalize the first problem until the second is an instance. Generalization, in this case, refers to the syntactic generalization of uninterpreted terms. *Least general generalization* is, in a sense, a dual notion to most general unifier; a least general generalization of two patterns is a pattern that is general enough (in the sense of replacing subterms by variables) to have both the patterns as instances, but no more general. If this general pattern has sufficient structure, then our analogical solving would have a high enough chance of success (*i.e.*, performance advantage over direct solving) that it is worth the attempt. The following pattern generalizes both of the starting programs.

$$f(x) \leftarrow \text{if } x = a \text{ then } b \text{ else } g(f(h(x)),x)$$

(Here, *a*, *b*, *g*, and *h* are second-order variables.)

What Information Should Be Retained? Let us now consider use of two paradigms termed by Carbonell *transformational analogy* and *derivational analogy*, respectively, for making use of this evident analogy among the problems [Carbonell85].

The first of these, the transformational case, may be considered to involve use of a schematization of the solution of the first problem in order to point the direction to the solution to a second problem. The "solution" of the original problem, in the case of program derivations, is simply the last step. In generalized form (*i.e.*, with substitutions equal to those for the pattern above), we have,

$$f(x) \leftarrow f_1(b,x)$$
$$f_1(u,v) \leftarrow \text{if } v = a \text{ then } u \text{ else } f_1(g(u,v),h(v)).$$

We now instantiate the schema with the bindings from the new problem (for example, g is bound to $\lambda x,y.(\text{cons}(\text{hd}(y),\text{nil}) \bullet x))$, we obtain a *candidate* new solution.

$$\text{rev}(\alpha) \leftarrow \text{rev}_1(\text{nil},\alpha)$$
$$\text{rev}_1(u,v) \leftarrow \text{if } v = \text{nil then } u$$
$$\qquad\qquad \text{else } \text{rev}_1(\text{cons}(\text{hd}(v), \text{nil})\text{iu},\text{tl}(v))$$

The definition of rev_1 simplifies.

$$\text{rev}_1(u,v) \leftarrow \text{if } v = \text{nil then } u$$
$$\qquad\qquad \text{else } \text{rev}_1(\text{cons}(\text{hd}(v),u),\text{tl}(v))$$

We must now, according to the transformational paradigm, perturb this new solution until it conforms with the new problem requirements; that is, we must perturb it until it is *correct*. In this problem domain of programming, we suggest that there is, unfortunately, no easy way to do this. But, fortuitously, this new solution happens to be correct. It should be clear, however, that the naive "transformational analogy" is not viable in the domain of programming simply because of the overwhelming difficulty of verifying proposed solutions.

To reinforce this, consider the following problem, which also matches the pattern.

$$\text{diff}(\alpha) \leftarrow \text{if } \alpha = \text{nil then } 0 \text{ else } \text{hd}(\alpha) - \text{diff}(\text{tl}(\alpha))$$

Observe that, for example, *diff({4,2,5})* = 7, while the corresponding instance of the solution pattern yields -11.

What is wrong here is that the correctness of the schematized solution depends on the associativity of the accumulating function *g* (and on *b* being a left and right identity of *g*).

The problem with the transformational paradigm is that the generalized solution of the original problem simply does not carry enough information to make it a useful guide to a new solution. We consider now two more viable approaches to this problem of choosing what information to retain.

A Priori Generalization. The first and most obvious approach is simply to add annotations to the original solution indicating semantic constraints on the instances of the second-order variables, as determined in the original derivation. If there is mechanism to retain constraint information, then a derivation, once constructed, can be ***immediately*** generalized to a usefully abstract level (of course, the degree of abstraction depends on the expressiveness of the constraint language) with correctness of all instances guaranteed (*i.e.*, it is a consistent generalization). It is the ***generalized*** problem, preconditions, and solution that are then saved.

In this scenario, new problems are solved *not* by analogy, but by simple matching against a library of patterns (whose corresponding solution patterns are known to be correct by virtue of their derivations). The idea, then, is that reasoning by analogy can often be replaced by explicit *a priori* generalization, which is the translation of (overly) specific experiences into general principles.

Analogies Among Derivations. The second approach is to adopt, instead, a "derivational analogy" paradigm, in which we keep the ***entire*** old derivation and follow it as a guide to ***derive*** a solution for the new problem. This idea has already been used to advantage in developing (by hand) and presenting derivations of complex graph algorithms [Reif82]. Carbonell articulates the idea and examines it in a general way in [Carbonell85].

The value of this approach is that it is often easier to formulate heuristic methods than algorithmic ones. Analogy will have a role in solving problems that are similar, but whose similarity is not easily expressible. Further, common patterns of analogical reasoning can suggest candidate improvements to the language of generalizations. In short, expressiveness of the language of generalizations is crucial, but not ultimately limiting.

In the example above, the new ***rev*** program would have been derived by direct analogy with the original ***fact*** derivation, but the ***diff*** derivation would have failed as soon as associativity of '-' had been required. Consideration of these examples once again leads to the same conclusion just reached above (in the transformational analogy case), namely that it makes sense to consider ***a priori*** computation of generalizations--but this time of entire derivations. That is, once a derivation is created, we attempt to abstract on its structure as much as possible. We would thus have a *generalized derivation* connecting our problem schema and solution schema.

(The generalized fact derivation above provides a guide to deriving an efficient **diff**, but analogy must be employed. That is, if we take the generalized fact derivation and **forget** the constraints on associativity and so on, then the resulting (further) generalized derivation, while inconsistent, is a useful guide for analogically constructing a **diff** derivation.)

There are several important advantages to this hybrid paradigm. First, derivations can be used partially. If some part of a derivation or generalized derivation is relevant, it can match and be used *even if* the starting problem statements do not match. (That is, a new problem statement might match an intermediate step in an existing derivation.) Second, derivations provide a much richer basis for analogy. Since all the solution steps are spelled out, there is no need for the *a posteriori* verification process that was needed in the "transformational analogy" case. The derivation provides a guide to constructing a new derivation--which might indeed turn out to be a more general generalization of the original one. A final advantage is a technical one: It is often the case that preconditions for intermediate derivation steps do not easily translate themselves into preconditions expressed on the pattern variables in the initial step.

Returning to the example, the original derivation (generalized or not) relies on associativity of **g** and on **b** being a left and right identity for **g**. If we are presented with a problem that does not satisfy all the constraints imposed by our derivation schema, then the tactic would be to produce a new derivation by analogy with the original one. Since constraints relied on in the original generalized derivation must be **removed**, we attempt to rework it in the more general way. In this example, the added generalization in the original concrete derivation is straightforward to obtain; we omit the simplification of **u * 1** to **u** in the first step, and we avoid simultaneously abstracting the body of **fact** along with the body of **u * fact(v)**. (Instead, we unfold the expression procedure call in the original body of **fact**.) The result is somewhat more complicated, but has nearly identical performance.

```
fact(n) ← if n = 0 then 1 else fact_1(n,n-1)
fact_1(u,v) ← if v = 0 then u else fact_1(u * v,v-1)
```

This new concrete derivation leads to generalized derivation with a much broader range of applicability--requiring only associativity of **g** and no more. We thus have *two* levels of generalization above the lowly *fact* derivation. The first is the original one, which depends on associativity and identity (and is obtained by "dependency-directed" generalization), and the second is this new derivation (obtained by analogy) that depends only on associativity, but that yields a larger more complex program.

Structure, Learning, and Limitations. It should be clear that even from a small number of simple examples, a rich knowledge structure can be obtained fairly directly. It should also be clear that both (consistent) generalization and analogy are needed to access this rich knowledge structure and, more importantly, to enable new knowledge to be assimilated. The most obvious principle for access is the usual one, of seeking to match the most specialized case possible, since there is more context to be exploited.

The central role of learning in inferential programming tools cannot be overemphasized. Because of the high degree of structure obtained through the use of generalizations and derivations, we are pessimistic of any real success being obtained from programming knowledge bases that emphasize hard-wired knowledge rather than learned knowledge. On the other hand, we do expect that in the first generation of experimental systems, the language of derivations and ***consistently*** generalized derivations will be fixed (in contrast to the language of ***inconsistently*** generalized derivations and the mechanisms for applying such generalizations). That is, in the initial generation of systems we expect that learning will be primarily at the level of derivations and generalized derivations--and not at the level of the language of generalizations and techniques for generalizing.

The success of the initial approach, therefore, depends on the specific language of consistent generalizations. Because of the consistency requirement, the design of this language is a delicate matter, and the generalization techniques require *a priori* justification (as do the transformations linking individual derivation steps). The cost of this, of course, is that the system is, at least initially, nonadaptive with respect to the structure of derivations and consistently generalized derivations.

Let us summarize, then, the sources of adaptiveness. Most obviously, the system "learns" by storing consistent generalizations of derivations that get constructed through time. When new problems are presented, it is a relatively simple matter to detect if they or their subproblems are instances of known generalized problems. Inconsistent generalizations of derivations must also be stored, together with information concerning their success in application to instances. More subtle kinds of adaptiveness arise when the generalization mechanisms are themselves considered. First, mainstream heuristic techniques, such as [Mitchell86] (with derivations playing the role of explanations), can control the generation and use of inconsistent generalizations to drive the analogical reasoning process described above. Second, promising generalized notions, together with methods for generalizing to the level of the promising notions, can be submitted for manual or mechanical verification to establish that such generalizations are always ***consistent***.

3.0 EXAMPLES OF GENERALIZATIONS

As we have suggested, the success of the approach depends largely on the power of the language of consistent generalizations--that is, on the richness of the abstraction mechanisms in the languages of programs and program derivations. It should be clear from the prior discussion that a user need not be aware of the full power of the generalization facility embodied in a system. The system, in treating a new problem as an instance of a generalization derived from an older problem, could, in interacting with the user, make reference only to the previous problem--as if it were in fact working by analogy with that problem, even though there is no analogical reasoning going on. That is, the system can use analogical explanation to protect users from having to cope with very powerful abstraction mechanisms.

Let us turn to a new example to explore the difficulties of developing a suitable language of generalizations. The program below takes as input a binary tree and visits the nodes in preorder, calling the procedure *visit* at every node and leaf.

```
pre-walk(t) ←
        if isleaf(t) then visit(t)
            else begin
                    visit(t);
                    pre-walk(lson(t));
                    pre-walk(rson(t))
                 end
```

From this definition, one could easily imagine deriving a new program *pre-num* to number the nodes and leaves of a tree in preorder.

```
pre-num(t) ← pre-num₁(0,t)
pre-num₁(n,t)
   begin
     num(t) := n
     return
        if isleaf(t) then n + 1
            else pre-num₁(pre-num₁(n + 1, lson(t)),
                          rson(t))
   end
```

It is also easy to imagine generalizing this procedure to the case of simply *counting* the leaves and interior nodes of a tree.

```
count(t) ← pre-num₁(0,t)
count₁(n,t) ←
    if isleaf(t) then n + 1
        else count₁(count₁(n + 1, lson(t)), rson(t))
```

Armed with these derivations for the preorder case, let us now consider postorder walks. The initial walking procedure is straightforward, as before.

```
post-walk(t) ←
    if isleaf(t) then visit(t)
        else begin
            post-walk(lson(t));
            post-walk(rson(t));
            visit(t)
        end
```

We consider two questions. First, what sort of programs generalize **pre-walk** and **post-walk** and, second, how do we obtain corresponding postorder numbering and counting procedures using generalization and analogy.

A straightforward (uninterpreted) syntactic least-general generalization of **pre-walk** and **post-walk** is too general to be of interest. If, however, we allow a small degree of interpretation to the matching process, by adding a new binary operator '|' that indicates sequencing, but without commitment to the **direction** of sequencing, we obtain a useful definition.

```
tree-walk₁(t) ←
    if isleaf(t) then visit (t)
        else begin
            tree-walk₁(lson(t))  |
            tree-walk₁(rson(t))  |
            visit(t)
        end
```

We can interpret the '|' operator to mean a nondeterministic choice is made in choosing an ordering of evaluation of its arguments. (A technical assumption is also made, namely that **any** choice of ordering is acceptable.) This generalization of **pre-walk** enables us to rework the derivation of **count** for the more general case, because the new uncommitted sequencing operator is associative and commutative. Since addition is also associative and commutative, the **count** procedure is correct for any instance of **tree-walk**. This implies that a user seeking to derive a counting procedure from an **inorder** walk would be able to use this result directly, without any additional derivation work.

On the other hand, the **pre-num** derivation does not fully generalize, because the structure of the code is partly a consequence of the preorder commitment. This, then, is a case for mixed generalization and analogy in derivations. The essential first steps of the derivation carry over to the postorder case; it is just the final code simplification steps that prevent a full generalization. This is a more typical sort of sharing in programming, where the "basic idea" of a program carries over, but there is no direct syntactic correspondence. By preserving derivation structure, the "basic idea" has an explicit manifestation that can be used in other contexts. Generalization supports this kind of reusability; analogy often supports the remaining incompatible steps. In the case of postorder numbering, the following procedure can be obtained.

```
    post-num(t) ← post-num₁(t,0)

    post-num₁(t,n) ←
        if isleaf(t)
            then begin num(t) := n; return n + 1 end
            else let m = post-num₁
                 (post-num₁(n,lson(t)),rson(t)) in
                    begin
                        num(t) := m;
                        return m + 1
                    end
```

The space of generalizations becomes more interesting when we consider tree traversing programs that are further afield from preorder walk than the postorder or in order examples. Observe, first, that **tree-walk$_1$** above has an uncommitted strategy for walking the tree. An equally viable (but less general) generalization would provide access to information at individual nodes that could be used in choosing order of traversal. We indicate this commitment by using an **order** operator that takes a parameter indicating the ordering of evaluation to choose. (The notation is clearly inadequate; we have insufficient experience in designing languages to support rich abstraction mechanisms without regard for performance-- that is, languages for specifications.)

```
    tree-walk₂(t) ←
        if isleaf(t) then visit(t)
            else order h(t)
                    tree-walk₂(lson(t))  |
                    tree-walk₂(rson(t))  |
                    visit(t)
                end
```

Another level of generalization could lead us to a program that permits traversals that are parallel, random, and so on. For example, if *h* above is a constant function, then we obtain a tree walk of uniform strategy. These are less general than both **tree-walk$_1$** and **tree-walk$_2$**, but more general than preorder, postorder, inorder, and so on. The full range of examples illustrates how even a small amount of language support can sustain a rich collection of generalizations from a small set of concrete problems. As a final tree example, observe that tree **searching** algorithms (which do not visit every node) also share a useful generalization with the node visiting programs.

Analogies and Data Structures. The prior examples of generalizations have focused on control aspects of programs-- generalizing a particular sequence of actions to an unspecified sequencing, a nondeterministic sequencing, a sequencing in which some steps could be omitted, and so on. A similarly rich array of generalization steps exists in the case of data structures. These have been studied at length in the context of abstract data types specifications, and that research, particularly concerning type parameterization and abstraction mechanisms, is of great value in designing the language of generalized programs.

It is common wisdom, for example, that at the specification level, Lisp-style lists and queues are specializations of deques and that they are themselves incomparable. Clearly, then, any program that realizes an algorithm using lists will also work if deques are provided instead. On the other hand, it might be the case that a program on deques generalizes to a program on lists simply because of the restricted set of deque operations used.

The Larch *trait* provides a mechanism for abstracting properties of abstract type specifications. The extent to which a type is structured into traits or makes use of existing traits determines the extent to which sharing is possible among type-related derivation steps at the level of specifications. The Larch handbook (in [Guttag85]) provides a collection of examples that illustrate the extent of structuring in this domain.

Unfortunately, these traits are useful only when the matching occurs at a reasonably high level of abstraction. Once type *representations* are introduced, then specialization tends to obliterate structure, limiting the range of generalizations and obscuring the hierarchical structure of the specifications. For example, it can be the case that lists and queues can be viewed, at the representational level, as specializations of one another [Jorring86]. On the other hand, by recording how types evolve as specializations of other types, a rich structure can be built up that will facilitate reuse.

4.0 ANALOGIES IN PROGRAM DERIVATIONS

Generalizations on programs are an important part of the mechanism for relating present problems with past experience, but, as we have indicated, they by no means suffice. In fortuitous cases in which past and present problems are stated in similar terms at similar levels of abstraction, then it makes perfect sense to consider only first and last steps of derivations, and to probe the interior structure only when hot on the trail of a new analogically derived solution or when seeking a more general representation.

But in real problems, this is rarely the case. Consider our earliest example, involving *fact* and *rev*. A more realistic specification of *fact* might be in closed form.

$$fact(n) \leftarrow \prod_{i=1}^{n} i$$

Similarly, a specification of the list reversal function might make use of an ellipsis notation,

$$rev(nil) \leftarrow nil$$

$$rev([x_0, x_1, \ldots, x_{n-1}, x_n]) \leftarrow [x_n, x_{n-1}, \ldots, x_1, x_0]$$

The similarity between these two problems emerges only after certain commitments have been made in the respective derivations. Consider, for example, the original scenario of having an existing derivation of *fact*. One could imagine a system that maintained a discrimination net of known generalizations of *all* derivation steps and that, as soon as a user reached the stage in the *rev* derivation at which the commitment was made to reverse a list by iterating through its elements using *hd* and *tl*, the match with a (now) intermediate stage of the *fact* derivation would be made. At this point, the system would know how to solve the remainder of the problem, at least within a certain level of generality. (That is, further tuning that makes use of properties specific to *rev* could be carried on *after* the borrowed general derivation steps had been instantiated.)

It is interesting to observe that other similarities are more easily exposed at this more abstract level of presentation, such as the similarity between *rev* and *rev-all*.

$$\text{rev-all}(\text{nil}) \leftarrow \text{nil}$$

$$\text{rev-all}(x) \leftarrow x \qquad \text{if atom}(x)$$

$$\text{rev-all}([\alpha_0, \alpha_1, \ldots, \alpha_n]) \leftarrow$$
$$[\text{rev-all}(\alpha_n), \ldots, \text{rev-all}(\alpha_1), \text{rev-all}(\alpha_0)]$$

Programming Techniques. We hypothesize that most programming techniques (at the level of divide-and-conquer, conversion to tail-recursive form, reduction in strength, and so on) can be conceptualized as generalizations on sequences of program derivation steps. In this sense, the techniques developed to derive a tractable backtracking implementation of, say, the n-queens problem from a brute-force generate-and-test version could also be applied to developing better search implementations for, say, the knapsack problem or for propositional satisfiability.

In the case of n-queens, we could progress by a technique sometimes called *filter promotion* from a program that generates all board configurations containing n queens (and tests each) to more refined versions that generate configurations, say, that contain only a single queen in each row. Other techniques can also be used, eventually yielding a program that can test partial configurations for plausibility and, finally, the usual backtracking implementation. This is a common example, and an example derivation obtained with mechanical assistance is presented in detail in [Balzer81]. The intent is that the techniques (manifest as patterns of derivation steps), once worked out in this case, can be generalized and applied elsewhere. This can be demonstrated for small scale techniques, but, since there is not yet a well formulated language for derivations, we are not yet able to reach conclusions about the extent to which sequences of derivation steps can generalize in a productive way. There is clearly significant experimentation to be done before any of the hypotheses stated here can be substantiated.

5.0 CONCLUSIONS

The extent to which programming is considered an *engineering* activity acknowledges the importance of past experience and convention in program development. Experience is of such importance that modification of existing programs is often not possible except by those who developed the original code. But even in the case of new programs, the vast proportion of the development is carried on the basis of prior experience in similar situations.

We have observed that even if a collection of program texts turn out to have little in common, there can be similarities in the accounts or derivations of the programs that justify development by modification. Real program modification is ordinarily very difficult for programmers because, like *a posteriori* verification, it requires rediscovery of concepts used during development of the initial implementation. But by preserving the *derivation* of the initial program, it is often possible to pinpoint the design decision or commitment that must be altered, and carry over much of the remaining structure by generalization or by analogy. One point of our examples is that abstracted derivation structure provides a useful framework for expressing programming generalizations or, when failing to achieve this expression, for helping locate useful analogies. Another point made in the examples is that there is no special significance to the starting and ending points of derivations. We expect that in most real examples, generalizations and analogies will be exploited principally between sequences of intermediate steps. But, whatever our expectations, the hypotheses we have put forward here concerning the nature and use of programming knowledge representations still await experimental confirmation.

6.0 ACKNOWLEDGEMENTS

We thank David Steier for helpful comments and criticisms.

BIBLIOGRAPHY

[Angluin83]   Angluin, D. and C. H. Smith, *Inductive Inference: Theory and Methods.* Computing Surveys, vol. 15, no. 3, pp. 237-269, September 1983.

[Balzer81]   Balzer, R., *Transformational Implementation: An Example.* IEEE Transactions on Software Engineering, vol. SE-7, no. 1, pp. 3-14, January 1981.

[Balzer83]   Balzer, R., T. E Cheatham, Jr., and C. C. Green, *Software Technology in the 1990's: Using a New Paradigm.* IEEE Computer, vol. 16, no. 11, pp. 39-45, November 1983.

[Balzer85] Balzer, R., *A 15 Year Perspective on Automatic Programming*. IEEE Transactions on Software Engineering, vol. SE-11, no. 11, pp. 1257-1268, November 1985.

[Barstow80] Barstow, D. R., *The Roles of Knowledge and Deduction in Algorithm Creation*. Yale Research Report, 1980.

[Bauer85] Bauer, et al., *The Munich Project CIP*, Volume 1. Springer-Verlag, 1985.

[Carbonell81] Carbonell, J. G., *A Computational Model of Problem Solving by Analogy*. Seventh IJCAI Proceedings, pp. 147-152, 1981.

[Carbonell82] Carbonell, J. G., *Learning by Analogy: Formulating and Generalizing Plans from Past Experience. Machine Learning, an Artificial Intelligence Approach*, Edited by R. S. Michalski, J. G. Carbonell and T. M. Mitchell, Tioga Press, 1982.

[Carbonell85] Carbonell, J. G., *Derivational Analogy: A Theory of Reconstructive Problem Solving and Expertise Acquisition*. Carnegie-Mellon Technical Report, 1985.

[Dershowitz85] Dershowitz, Nachum, *Program Abstraction and Instantiation*. TOPLAS, vol. 7, no. 3, pp. 446-477, July 1985.

[Green78] Green, C. C. and D. R. Barstow, *On Program Synthesis Knowledge*. Artificial Intelligence, Vol. 10, p. 241, 1978.

[Green83] Green, C. C. et al, *Report on a Knowledge Based Software Assistant*. Kestrel Institute Report, 1983.

[Guttag85] Guttag, J. V., J. J. Horning, and J. M. Wing, *Larch in Five Easy Pieces*. DEC SRC Technical Report, 1985.

[Huet78] Huet, G. and B. Lang, *Proving and Applying Program Transformations Expressed with Second Order Patterns*. Acta Informatica, vol. 11, pp. 31-55, 1978.

[Jorring86] Jorring, U. and W. L. Scherlis, *Deriving and Using Destructive Data Types*. IFIP TC2 Working Conference on Program Specification and Transformation, North-Holland, 1986.

[Laird85]   Laird, J. E., P. S. Rosenbloom, and A. Newell, *Towards Chunking as a General Learning Mechanism* Carnegie-Mellon Technical Report, January 1985.

[Mitchell82] Mitchell, T. M., *Generalization as Search*, Artificial Intelligence, vol. 18, no. 2, pp. 203-226, March 1982.

[Mitchell86] Mitchell, T. M., *Explanation-Based Generalization: A Unifying View*, Machine Learning, vol. 1, no. 1, January 1986.

[Plotkin70] Plotkin, G. D., *A Note on Inductive Generalization*. Machine Intelligence 5, edited by Meltzer and Michie, pp. 153-163, 1970.

[Reif82]   Reif, J. and W. L. Scherlis, *Deriving Efficient Graph Algorithms*. Carnegie-Mellon Technical Report, 1982. To appear, TOPLAS.

[Rich81]   Rich, C., *A Formal Representation for Plans in the Programmer's Apprentice*. Seventh IJCAI Proceedings, pp. 1044-1052, 1981.

[Sacerdoti74] Sacerdoti, E. J., *Planning in a Hierarchy of Abstraction Spaces*. Artificial Intelligence, Vol. 5, 1974.

[Scherlis81] Scherlis, W. L., *Program Improvement by Internal Specialization*. Eighth POPL, pp. 41-49, 1981.

[Scherlis83] Scherlis, W. L. and D.S. Scott, *First Steps Towards Inferential Programming*. IFIP Congress 83, pp. 199-212, North-Holland, 1983.

[Scherlis83a] Scherlis, W. L., *Software Development and Inferential Programming*. In Program Transformation and Programming Environments, edited by P. Pepper, Springer-Verlag, pp. 341-346, 1983.

[Waters81]   Waters, R. C., *A Knowledge Based Program Editor*. Seventh IJCAI Proceedings, pp. 920-926, 1981.

[Waters85]   Waters, R. C., *The Programmer's Apprentice: A session with KBEmacs*. IEEE Transactions on Software Engineering, vol. SE-11, no. 11, pp. 1296-1320, November 1985.

QUESTION AND ANSWER PERIOD

BOUDREAUX

Are the analogies essentially algebraic properties of the program and the functions that are contained in it?

SCHERLIS

The issues are first, what are the generalized properties, and second, how are they to be expressed. For example, consider walking through a tree. What is the programming construct that generalizes both pre-order walks and post-order walks? There are all sorts of candidates, a few of which are enumerated in the paper. You could, for example, nondeterministically choose an order of evaluation at every node, or you could nondeterministically choose a fixed strategy at the start of the search and follow it at every node. The space of generalizations is clearly very rich. In order to make *a priori* generalization work, then, we have to come up with a collection of useful consistent generalizations that lets us operate at appropriate levels of generality. In the simpler examples in the paper, the generalizations are expressed using simple patterns together with certain additional constraints expressed as algebraic properties, as you indicate. But there is nothing in the method, such as there is a method, that requires any particular form of expression of the generalizations.

RADA

Do you consider yourself primarily interested in understanding analogical transformations or in how people build programs?

SCHERLIS

My interest is in building programming tools. This work was motivated by problems I encountered in building program derivations by hand. While deriving some hard graph algorithms, I found that the easiest way to derive the most complicated programs was to derive simpler programs and then make use of the resulting derivations, by analogy, to derive the more complicated programs. For example, a program to assign pre-order numbers in the depth-first search forest of a directed graph will share some design ideas with the much simpler program to number an ordinary tree. But, in the graph case, the tree is never concretely present as data structure; it is just a conceptualization that we impose on that program. So we cannot simply carry over our code from the tree case to the graph case. The similarity, then, is in the design, not necessarily in the code. I found that in the process of manually doing those derivations I was constantly making use of analogy -- and that the analogies were among derivations and not programs. The motivation for this work, then, is a desire to somehow rigorize this notion of analogy. This involves thinking seriously about representing generalized derivations and, ultimately, considering whether patterns of derivation steps can help in representing actual programming techniques.

GUIER

Every time I start thinking about generalizing, I always get into the subject of invention. Where is it, as kind of a straightforward generalization, that our real element of invention comes in? I'm not sure, but I think you're requiring some significant invention in some of those generalizations, aren't you?

SCHERLIS

The invention comes in a number of places. One obvious source is in the set of notions that are used to express the generalizations. If the set of notions is very simple, say simple first-order patterns, then the generalization process is algorithmic. You just compute the least generalization. (This is the dual notion of most general unifier.) But in more interesting cases, where some semantic richness is added to the language of generalizations, the problem of computing generalizations becomes very hard, and heuristic mechanisms are needed.

INTENSIONAL PROGRAMMING

A. A. Faustini[*]

Department of Computer Science
Arizona State University

W. W. Wadge[**]

Department of Computer Science
University of Victoria

2 March 1986

Imperative programming languages such as FORTRAN and Pascal have always played an important role in problem solving. In this paper we present a purely declarative programming language which we believe to be much more problem oriented than the conventional imperative languages. The language Lucid is based on intensional logic which is itself a relatively new branch of mathematical logic. Intensional logic is concerned with assertions and expressions whose meaning depend on an implicit context. Natural language abounds with these kind of assertions and we use natural language all the time for problem solving.

A number of Lucid programs that solve problems in the area of numerical analysis are included. In particular programs are included to solve two partial differential equations, namely Laplace's equation and the heat conduction equation.

1.0   INTRODUCTION

Computer scientists and logicians share a common interest in symbolic languages, though for different reasons. Logicians use formal languages to clarify basic foundational questions of

---

[*]   Supported by the National Science Foundation under grant DCR 84-15618

[**]   Supported by NSERC of Canada

mathematics. They are concerned primarily with discovering what can be stated or proved *in principle* - without regard to questions of efficiency. Computer scientists, on the other hand, use languages as practical tools: specification languages for stating problems in unambiguous terms, and programming languages for expressing mechanical solutions.

The languages of the logicians (such as the predicate calculus) certainly deserve the adjective "formal." They are powerful but extremely simple, and both syntax and semantics are precisely and unambiguously defined.

The languages of the Computer Scientists are, by the same criteria, rather less successful. The high level languages (beginning with FORTRAN) have indeed borrowed many important concepts from mathematical logic; but nevertheless they can hardly be considered as *formal systems*. Even the more modest languages (such as PASCAL) are extremely complex, and only the syntax is really clearly defined. The semantic definitions (language manuals) use informal, anthropomorphic terminology, and explain almost everything in terms of the actions of some (vaguely described) machine. The various language features are usually dealt with in isolation, and the results of many interactions are often completely unspecified (or even inconsistently specified). Under these circumstances it is extremely difficult to produce software that is correct and reliable, and impossible to prove such properties formally.

Computer scientists are well aware of this highly unsatisfactory state of affairs, and a series of efforts have been made to base programming languages more directly on the languages of mathematical logic. It is in fact possible to extend and adapt (say) the lambda calculus to produce a programming language which is at the same time a formal system. The language LISP (invented by McCarthy and others around 1960 [McCa-62]) was originally intended to be just such an adaptation of the lambda calculus, but it diverged in its treatment of variable binding and higher order functions. Shortly after, however, Peter Landin corrected the discrepancies in LISP and produced ISWIM, the first true functional language [Land-66].

These "logical" programming languages such as ISWIM are in many respects vastly superior to the more conventional ones. They are much simpler and better defined and yet at the same time more regular and more powerful. These languages are notationally closer to ordinary mathematics and are therefore much more problem-oriented. Finally, programs are still expressions in a formal system, and are still subject to the rules of the formal system. It is therefore much easier to reason formally about their correctness, or to apply meaning-preserving transformations. With these languages programming really is a respectable branch of applied mathematical logic.

Unfortunately, these logic based languages have proved to be difficult to implement efficiently. The problem is that they are not well suited to the sequential, storage based form of computation offered by conventional "von Neumann" machines.

As a result interest in declarative languages declined soon
after the promising initial work of McCarthy and Landin.

Recently, however, new advances in digital electronics (VLSI)
have made it possible to consider radically different architectures more suited to declarative (as opposed to imperative)
languages. This in turn has reawakened interest in declarative
languages, and brought about a series of new 'second generation' declarative languages, such as PROLOG [ClMe-84] and KRC
(recently renamed Miranda) [Turn-74].

In this paper we will discuss Lucid, one of these second
generation declarative languages. Lucid is based not so much
on the classical logical systems as on "intensional logic" -
itself a relatively new branch of logic [Thom-74] which reached
maturity during the period (1965-75) in which declarative
programming languages were in eclipse.

2.0   INTENSIONAL LOGIC

Intensional logic is concerned with assertions and other
expressions whose meaning depends on an implicit context.

This type of logic was originally developed to help understand
natural languages, in which such expressions abound. For
example, the expression

> *five degrees less than yesterday's temperature*

obviously denotes a numerical value. This value clearly depends
on a numerical quantity called *temperature*. It also depends on
the time of utterance, and on the place - even though there is
no explicit reference to either of these two parameters.

Stranger still is the way in which the value of the expression
depends on that of *temperature*. If we look outside and see
that the thermometer reads (say) 35, we cannot conclude that
the value referred to above is 30; in fact, we cannot conclude
anything about the value, because the value of the expression
on any given day depends on the value of temperature on the
previous day.

In other words, the expression quoted seems to correspond to a
mathematical expression of the form $y(t)-5$, where t is *temperature* and the function y corresponds to *yesterday's*. It is
obvious, however, that there is no function y, from integers to
integers which makes the value of the mathematical expression
correspond to that of the cited phrase. The expression in
question seems to violate the basic principle of *referential
transparency:* that the meaning of a whole expression depends
only on the meaning of its parts.

For many years examples such as these were considered by
logicians to be simply further evidence of the nonmathematical
and illogical nature of natural languages. It was recognized
that expressions like the one given could be translated into a

"respectable" language like the predicate calculus, but only by
introducing variables which refer explicitly to those factors
(such as place and time) which implicitly determine the meaning
of the natural language expression.

It is only comparatively recently that logicians discovered a
more direct and natural way to capture formally these 'context-
sensitive' operators and expressions. The solution to this
long-standing puzzle is based on the distinction between what
is called the *extension* and the *intension* of expressions
[Thom-74].

The *extension* of an expression is the value in a given context;
for example, a truth value (as with the first example above),
or an integer (as with the second). A natural language
expression can obviously have different extensions in different
contexts. The *intension* gathers all these different extensions
together, and captures the way in which the extensions depend
on the contexts. In other words, the intension is the function
which assigns to each context the value of the expression in
that context.

The various paradoxes disappearance we realize that the intension is the true meaning of a natural language expression.
Consider again the temperature example cited earlier. The
intension of *temperature* is essentially a table giving the
temperature on each day in question; part of the table might
look like this:

..	..	..	..
30	Dec	84	23
31	Dec	84	21
1	Jan	85	25
2	Jan	85	23
3	Jan	85	19
..	..	..	..

The intension of *five degrees less than yesterday's temperature*
is a similar table, which might look in part like the next
table. It is now easy to see that the meaning of *five degrees
... really does depend on the meaning of *temperature*, if we
take the intensions to be these meanings. In fact we can
obtain the intension of the former from that of the latter by

..	..	..	..
31	Dec	84	18
1	Jan	85	16
2	Jan	85	20
3	Jan	85	18
4	Jan	85	14
..	..	..	..

- subtracting 5 from all the temperatures in the right-hand column

- advancing all the dates in the left hand column by one day.

We can even find a mathematically respectable function *y* which accurately captures the meaning of the phrase *yesterday's*. The function *y*, which maps intensions to intensions, simply increases all the dates by one day.

It is possible, of course, to formalise these ideas in a conventional, extensional logical system in which variables and expressions denote context-to-value functions. We could declare these objects to be the real extensions, thereby restore referential transparency, and dispose of the notion of intension. In practice, however, this approach is unnatural and impractical. Intensions are complicated mathematical objects. No one in their right mind would think of *temperature* as denoting some vast infinite table; nor would they consider statements about the temperature to be assertions about infinite tables. Furthermore, assertions involving a hidden context have a logic of their own which is in itself quite simple but which cannot be studied in a purely extensional system without ugly explicit context 'indices.'

Programmers very often think intensionally about programs in conventional languages. For example, when examining the body of a procedure declaration, we cannot know exactly what values they have - that depends on an implicit parameter, the 'call' of the procedure in question. In the same way, the variables in the body can have many possible values - depending on another hidden parameter, namely the iteration index of the loop in question (and the indices of the enclosing loops).

We would not, however, characterize these languages as being "intensional." They lack intensional operations - operations which, like *yesterday's*, give the programmer access to extensions in contexts other than the current one. In PASCAL, for example, there is no operator which yields the value an expression had on the *previous* iteration. Nor is there an operator which, in a procedure body, gives the value an expression had in the 'environment' from which the procedure was called.

It would be possible to extend PASCAL with intensional operators like those just described; but it would probably not be a good idea. The new operators might be useful but they would interact in complicated ways with other features, such as side effects and aliasing. The extended language would have intensional "features," but it would not be based on intensional logic.

By "Intensional Programming" we mean programming in a language which is at the same time a formal system based on intensional semantics. Intensional programmers should be encouraged to think intensionally (when appropriate), and should be provided

with 'context switching' operators which allow values from
different contexts to be combined without explicit context
manipulation. We now turn our attention to Lucid, which is
just such a language.

3.0   THE INTENSIONAL LANGUAGE LUCID

Lucid is a data flow programming language invented by E.A.
Ashcroft and W.W. Wadge [WaAs-85]. Lucid was originally
intended to be a purely declarative (nonprocedural) language in
which iterative algorithms could be expressed easily and
naturally. It was soon realized, however, that the language
was well suited for expressing algorithms based on a dataflow
view of computation - one in which dataflows through a network
of asynchronously operating processing stations.

The development of Lucid began in 1974, and at that time it was
widely believed that declarative languages were inherently
incapable of describing dynamic activity in any very natural
way. The problem, so it seemed, was that logical languages
dealt only with unchanging extensions, whereas iteration
requires values which are constantly changing.

The paradox was resolved by basing the language on an intensional logic in which the values (extensions) of expressions
and variables depend on an implicit natural number time
parameter. Lucid programmers do not manipulate time indices
explicitly; instead, they use intensional operators such as
next and **fby** (pronounced **followed by**). Lucid otherwise looks
very much like a functional programming language, and its **where**
construct is copied almost directly from Landin's ISWIM. The
inventors of Lucid first became aware of the relationship
between intensional logic and Lucid after reading [HuCr-72].

Here is a Lucid program which calculates the partial sums of
the series $1 + x + \frac{x^2}{2!} + \frac{x^3}{3!} + \cdots$ for the number e.

```
        sum (term)
         where
          term = 1 fby term/(i+1);
          i = 0 fby i+1;
          sum (a) = s where s = a fby s + next a; end;
        end;
```

The Lucid program is obviously nothing like the program one
might produce if one formulated the same algorithm in PASCAL.
Nevertheless, its meaning should be clear enough once the
significance of the special Lucid operators is understood. The
operator **next** takes us one moment ahead in time; the value of
next **X** at a given point in time is the value **X** has at the next
point in time. In the same way, **fby** takes us back one moment
in time. The value of **A fby B** is the value **B** had on the
previous instant - unless the time is 0, in which case the
value of **A fby B** is the current (time 0) value of **A**. Now

consider the equation $i = 0$ **fby** $i+1$. Like all equations in a program, it is taken to be true at all points in time. This means that the value of i at any point in time is that of 0 **fby** $i+1$. In other words, the value of i at any point in time is the value of $i+1$ at the previous instant or 0, if the time is currently 0. We can rephrase this as follows: i is initially 0, and the value at the next point in time is 1 plus the current value. We can therefore imagine that the values of i are produced by a computation in which i is initially assigned the value 0 and then repeatedly incremented by 1. This is the sense in which Lucid programs can describe iterative algorithms.

The computational meaning of the definition of **term** should now be clear as well. It is initially assigned the value 1, and repeatedly updated by dividing its current value by the current value of $i+1$. Note that the definition could have been written

    term = *1* **fby** term / **next** i;

because **next** i is always $i+1$.

To finally understand the whole program, we need only understand the function **sum**. This function is defined by the user (in the program itself), but it is nevertheless an intensional one. It should not be hard to see that **sum** 'accumulates' the values of its arguments; the value of **sum(a)** at any point in time is the sum of the values (extensions) of **a** for all time points up to and including the present one.

The meaning of the program as a whole is the value of the expression **sum(term)** with **sum** and **term** as defined. The extension of the program at a given point in time is therefore the sum of the extensions of **term** for time points up to and including the present one. In other words, we can imagine that the program is computing the partial sums one by one. In Lucid the output values are defined to be its extensions. The program therefore outputs the sequence of partial sums of the series for e.

Of course we could still forget about intensional logic and consider the above to be an ordinary Iswim program in which the data objects are infinite sequences. In this view the operator **next**, given a sequence $<x_0, x_1,...>$ returns the sequence $<x_1, x_2,...>$. The operator **+** adds sequences component wise, even numerals like *1* denote infinite sequences (such as $<1,1,1,...>$) whose components are all the same. This approach is mathematically correct but in practice is extremely confusing and misleading. It is our experience that people who understand Lucid from this purely extensional point of view find it difficult if not impossible to write even simple programs.

It is somewhat paradoxical that people should reject a form of thinking (namely, intensional thinking) which forms the basis for their natural language and of the way they think about problems.

The Lucid approach to iteration can to some extent be mimicked in the newer functional languages, such as Turner's Miranda. These languages, however, are purely extensional and consequently do not encourage problem solving in a context-dependent manner.

4.0   FIELD LUCID

Intensional reasoning arises naturally in many problems and usually involves contexts other than (or in addition to) time. Consider, for example, a classic problem in engineering: heat transfer in a solid. Suppose that we have a long thin metal rod which is initially cool (temperature 0) but whose left-hand end touches a heat source (temperature 100). The heat will gradually diffuse through the rod, with parts nearer the heat source at first warming more quickly than those further away. The problem is to determine the temperature in various parts of the rod after a given interval.

We can compute an approximate solution to the problem by thinking of the rod as a sequence of small slices each of which at any point in time has a uniform temperature. We then apply the basic law of heat transfer, which says that the flow of heat between two bodies is proportional to the temperature difference. Let T_1 be the temperature of one of the slices (at some given point in time) and let T_0 and T_2 be the temperatures of the slices on the left and right, respectively (in general $T_0 > T_1 > T_2$). In any small interval of time the middle slice will gain an amount of heat proportional to T_0-T_1, and lose an amount of heat proportional to T_1-T_2. The new temperature of the middle slice will therefore be *(k*T_0 - (1-2*k)*T_1 + k*T_2)* for some small constant *k* depending on the length of the time interval and the properties of the metal.

Using this formula we can repeatedly 'sweep' the rod and determine the heat distribution at successive time instants. In so doing, we are really using a simple discrete (forward) difference approximation to solve the partial differential equation

$$\frac{\partial T}{\partial t} - a^2 \frac{\partial^2 T}{\partial s^2} = 0$$

This problem and the solution described involves an intension (temperature again) which varies in space (1-dimensional in this case) and time. Can our solution reflect this intensional point of view?

The solution to the heat flow problem expressed in a conventional language such as FORTRAN might use a pair of arrays, say T and NEWT. The T array would initially hold information about the heat source and the cold rod. The program would repeatedly

execute a main loop which counts time instants. Nested inside
the main loop we would find another loop which sweeps through
the array in space, executing the assignment statement

NEWT(I+1)=K*T(I)+(1-2*K)*T(I+1)+k*T(I+2)

To mimic this in Lucid we could always extend the simple
numerical Lucid described earlier by allowing extensions to be
entire vectors or matrices. This would not be particularly
difficult - the existing pLucid interpreter already supports
streams (intensions) whose values (at a given point in time)
can be arbitrarily complex LISP-like data structures. This
approach would not, however, allow us to think and write
intensionally about space. Our language would be significantly
less problem-oriented.

The authors and E.A. Ashcroft have recently taken an alternate
approach, and have extended the language (and its interpreter)
to allow intensions to vary in space as well as time. If we
need only one dimension of space (as in the present example),
it is enough to define our intensions as functions of two
natural number parameters t and s.

We can solve the current problems with only two primitive
spatial intensional operators, *right* and *sby* (pronounced
succeeded by), which correspond more or less to *next* and *fby*.
The value of *right X* at a given spacepoint is the value of *X* at
the spacepoint immediately to the right. The value of *A sby B*
at a given spacepoint is the value of *B* at the spacepoint
immediately to the left if there is such a point; otherwise it
is the value of *A* at the origin. More formally,

- $(\text{right } X)_t^s = X_t^{s+1}$

- $(X \text{ sby } Y)_t^s = \begin{cases} X_t^0 & \text{if } s=0; \\ Y_t^{s-1} & \text{otherwise} \end{cases}$

The following equation formalises the above FORTRAN solution:

T = 1 *sby* (0 *fby* (k*T - (1-2*k)*(*right* T) + k*(*right right* T));

Thus at any time *t* and space point *s*, $T^{s,t}$ is the temperature
of slice *s* at time step *t*.

To illustrate the problem oriented nature of Lucid let us
derive a program from the mathematics (the heat transfer
equation). As before, we can use user defined intensional
operators to present the same solution in a form very close to
the original statement. The differential equation given above
can be integrated in time to give

$$T = c + \int \frac{\partial^2 T}{\partial s^2} dt$$

We already have a time integration function (the sum program
in section 3); we need another operator which gives us (an
approximation to) the second space derivative. This is quite

easy, if we think intensionally. Suppose we have a quantity X varying in space, and that X_1 is the value at a particular spacepoint, and that X_0 and X_2 are the values of the points to either side. The ratio

$$\frac{X_1 - X_0}{ds}$$

is the derivative one-half step to the left, and

$$\frac{X_2 - X_1}{ds}$$

is the derivative one-half step to the right (**ds** is the spatial step size). It follows easily that the following is (approximately) the second derivative at the middle spacepoint:

$$\frac{\frac{X_2 - X_1}{ds} - \frac{X_1 - X_0}{ds}}{ds}$$

this in turn reduces to

$$\frac{X_2 - 2*X_1 + X_0}{ds^2}$$

From this we are led to the definition

Ds2(X) = *0 sby (X - 2*(right X) + right right X)*/ds**2;

Then for some appropriate constant c we can rewrite the definition of T as

```
     T    = 1 sby I(0,Ds2(T))
It(c,v)   = w where w = c fby w+dt*v; end;
 Ds2(F)   = 0 sby (F-2*right F+right right F)/ds ** 2;
```

The heat transfer problem just presented dealt only with a 1-dimensional rod and we were able to solve it by adding two primitive spatial intensional operators. In practice problems of this nature usually involve at least two or three dimensions. To deal with these more general cases the language allows arbitrary numbers of space dimensions. This extended version of the language is called **Field Lucid** and an interpreter already exists for the language. The name Field Lucid was chosen because the language is well suited to problem solving over an n-dimensional space that changes with time.

In solving the heat transfer problem we used a forward difference technique for computing an approximation to the second space derivative [IsKe-66]. We could also have used a central or backward difference method in which the definition of **Ds2(F)** would be

Ds2(F) = *0 sby (left F-2*F+right F)*/ds ** 2;

for the central difference method and

Ds2(F) = *0 sby (left left F-2*left F+ F)*/ds ** 2;

for the backward difference method. Note that the backward
difference method assumes that we have negative space co-ordinates since the intensional expression *left left F* requires the
value of space co-ordinate -1 to compute the value at space coordinate +1. Indeed the language does support negative space
and time co-ordinates. The negative space co-ordinates permits
intensional programming using a full Euclidean space. The
negative time co-ordinates are extremely useful for placing
initial conditions used in the main computation (or main inductive definition). Without this these initial conditions would
have to be placed in the first few points in time which is
sometimes counter intuitive. These additional features are
defined by intensional operators that we have not defined in
this paper.

Our next example is a solution to Laplace's equation using the
usual *relaxation* method [IsKe-66]. This program was originally
written by E.A. Ashcroft [Ashc-85] and we present it here in a
slightly modified form. The relaxation method is well suited
to the intensional paradigm as the value of a point in space is
determined by the average value of its four immediate spatial
neighbours at the previous point in time. The following is an
outline of a program that solves Laplace's equation over a two-
dimensional space *M*.

```
    s
      where
        s = if ELECTRODE then POTENTIAL else 0 fby avg(s) fi;
        avg(M) =(left M + right M + up M + down M)/4;
      end
```

ELECTRODE is true in a region of the plane, and at any point at
which *ELECTRODE* is true *POTENTIAL* is the potential of the electrode at that point. The initial potential at all other points
in the rectangle is 0. This forms the basis for the relaxation
method, in which points outside the electrode area undergo the
averaging process described above. Successive approximations
occur until the process settles down inside some region of
interest.

Note that this solution to Laplace's equation in 2-dimensions
would work equally well in 3-dimensions by simply changing the
definition of the average function to:

avg(M)=(*left* M+*right* M+*up* M+*down* M+*front* M+*rear* M)/6;

where *front* and *rear* are similar to *left* and *right* but in the
3rd space dimension.

5.0   THE ROLE OF EXTENSIONAL THINKING

In Lucid, programmers are (as we have already seen) more or
less forced to think intensionally about time. In our experience, it is usually not a good idea to think of Lucid variables
as giant immortal extensions. We therefore chose names such as
"next" and "whenever" which strongly suggest an intensional
interpretation.

In Field Lucid, variables vary in space as well as time, and we have already seen examples in which spatial intensional thinking was natural and reflected the original problem statement. On the other hand, it seems that sometimes a 'global,' non-intensional view of space-varying entities is also appropriate.

Perhaps we should not be surprised that time and space differ in this fundamental way. After all, in the real world we are more or less forced to experience time moment-by-moment. Sometimes we experience space in the same way: we are immediately aware only of the local region of space which we are occupying: the room we are in, the street where we live, the city we are visiting. Sometimes, however, we are able to perceive whole regions of space at once: a floor plan of a building, a whole city seen from an airplane, a highway map of a state or province. We should therefore expect to be able to use both global and local (intensional) concepts in stating and solving problems involving space.

Consider, for example, the problem of enumerating the prime numbers using the 'sieve' method of Eratosthenes. We can formalize this algorithm as a simple Field Lucid iteration, but one in which the variable being repeatedly 'updated' denotes an infinite sequence of natural numbers - a different sequence on each step of the iteration.

The iteration begins with the sequence of all natural numbers greater than 1. We chose the first item of this sequence, 2, as the first prime; then we remove all multiples of 2 from the sequence. On the second step of the iteration, the sequence enumerates the odd numbers. The first item in the sequence is 3, which we take as the second prime number. Then we remove from the sequence all numbers which are divisible by 3.

On the third step of the iteration the sequence therefore begins <5,7,11,13,17,19,23,25,29,...>

Its first element, 5, is the third prime, and we proceed to the fourth step of the iteration by removing all multiples of 5 from the sequence. In general, then on the nth step of the iteration the sequence enumerates those numbers (>1) which are not divisible by the first n-1 primes.

The next program is the Field Lucid program for the sieve.

```
p
where
        p  = side D;
        D  = N2 fby (D wherever (D mod p ne 0));
        N2 = 2 sby N2+1;
end;
```

It is not hard to see that the program given corresponds closely to the informal description of the algorithm. The infix operator **wherever** passes on only those extensions on its left that have a corresponding right argument (always a predicate) that is true. The operator *side* is used to select the space 0 value at each point in time.

6.0 CONCLUSION

Intensional Programming languages like Lucid are very useful tools in problem solving. Indeed programs written in these languages are indeed problem oriented. Another way of viewing this is that programs in a language like Lucid are executable specifications [Turn-74].

Intensional programming languages bring with them new problems of implementation and of course new solutions. In the case of Lucid a novel model of parallel computation called *eduction* has been developed [Faus-86]. This model of parallel computation is the basis for a parallel architecture being developed jointly by the authors and E.A. Ashcroft at SRI International.

Lucid is by no means the only computer science example of an application of intensional logic. Another example is in the context of a tree oriented file system such as is found in UNIX. In such a system moving from a lower directory to a higher one can be accomplished by the command *cd ../...* This type of a command is indeed intensional, in this case the implicit context is not a hidden time or space parameter, rather it is an implicit tree structure. On does not need to know where one is when issuing the above command all one need know is that it will move you two levels up the tree.

We recommend that those interested in this approach to problem solving write to Arizona State University for a copy of the Field Lucid Interpreter which runs under the UNIX operating system (all requests should be accompanied by a small magnetic tape).

REFERENCES

[Ashc-85] E.A. Ashcroft, "Massive Parallelism in Lucid," *Proceedings of the Phoenix Conference on Computers and Communications*, 1985, pp. 16-20.

[ClMe-84] W.F. Clocks in and C.S. Mellish, *Programming in Prolog*, Springer-Verlag, Berlin, 2nd Edition, 1984.

[Faus-86] A.A. Faustini and W.W. Wadge, "An Eductive Interpreter for pLucid," Technical Report TR-004-86, Department of Computer Science, Arizona State University, 1986.

[HuCr-72] G.F. Hughes and M.J. Creswell, *An Introduction to Modal Logic*, Methuen and Co. Ltd., London, 1972.

[IsKe-66] E. Issacson and H. Keller, *Analysis of Numerical Analysis*, Wiley, New York, 1966.

[Land-66] P.J. Landin, "The next 700 Programming Languages," Comm. ACM, Vol. 9, No. 3, Mar. 1966, pp. 157-166.

[McCa-62] John McCarthy et al, LISP 1.5 *Programmer's Manual*, MIT Press, Cambridge, Mass., 1962.

[Thom-74] R. Thomason, editor, *Formal Philosophy, Selected Papers of R. Montague*, Yale University Press, New Haven, Conn., 1974.

[Turn-74] D.A. Turner, "Functional Programs as Executable Specifications," Phil. Trans. R. Soc. London, A312, 1984, pp. 363-388.

[WaAs-85] W.W. Wadge and E.A. Ashcroft, *Lucid, the Dataflow Programming Language*, Academic Press U.K., 1985.1

COMPUTATIONAL ONTOLOGY

J. C. Boudreaux

Center for Manufacturing Engineering
National Bureau of Standards

In order to automate tasks which bring about actual modifications of the physical universe, systems must have access to representations of common sense knowledge and to inferential rules which allow this knowledge to be applied to specific situations. But common sense knowledge has proven to be highly resistant to algorithmic analysis. An important reason for this is the fact that common sense knowledge presupposes an elaborate theory of mid-sized (macroscopic) objects. This topic is a very important theme of an ancient philosophic discipline called ontology. This paper adopts the ontological methods of Carnap by reducing questions about the general structure of common sense knowledge to more readily answerable questions about the structure of linguistic frameworks. Though these issues are inherently abstract, requiring thorough acquaintance with the formal techniques of mathematical logic, the main contribution of this paper will be the presentation of linguistic frameworks as executable models in FranzLISP.

1.0   INTRODUCTION

Simulated by the pioneering efforts of McCarthy /11/ and McCarthy and Hayes /12/, there has been a recent upsurge of interest in formalizing what has come to be called commonsense knowledge. The main outlines of this emerging discipline may be discerned in the following remark of Jerry Hobbs:

> We are capable of intelligent action, in part, because we know a great deal. If intelligent programs, or robots, are to be constructed, they too must have a great deal of knowledge. In most artificial intelligence (AI) systems, some knowledge of particular problem domains has been encoded, but most of the work has been too specific to be of much use to the field in general. There is a certain minimum of "core knowledge," however, that any reasonably sophisticated intelligent agent must have to make its way in the

> world. This is not knowledge of the world as science perceives it, but the "commonsense theories" of the world that ordinary people have--their everyday beliefs about what the world is like /10/, xi.

Hobbs' distinction between "scientific" and the "commonsense" theories is problematic, especially since the history of the modern epoch may be interpreted as a series of accommodations of the latter to the former. What could be more obviously a part of our present commonsense view of the world than the fact of the Earth's motion, which a few centuries ago was a disturbing, indeed revolutionary, scientific hypothesis!

Since this modest relativism is a familiar theme, I presume that the disputed point is not that common sense is somehow radically different from scientific knowledge, but rather that, during any historical epoch, common sense is what is immediately and commonly available to all competent cognitive agents. However, it should be a sobering thought that for well over two thousand years, philosophers of all schools have justified their often baroque constructions by maintaining that they are needed to explain the deliverances of common sense. The conclusion that should be drawn is that the business of charting human common sense is much more difficult than we imagine.

One theme of this paper is that a useful account of common sense knowledge requires techniques of conceptual analysis which presuppose the logico-mathematical methods developed by the intellectual descendants of Gottlob Frege. Though there have been many important contributions, one of the most important is Tarski's model theoretic analysis of the notion of truth in formalized languages. Tarski's achievement may be taken as convincing evidence that difficult philosophical speculation can on occasion be replaced by formal construction, which is as precise a summary of the main theme as I can manage!

In addition to specific technical results, the descendants of Frege have also developed a rich and powerful philosophical vocabulary. Of direct concern to us is the cluster which introduces two pairs of distinctions: the distinction between universals, such as the general notion "man," and the particulars which instantiate them, such as "Caesar"; and also the distinction between particulars and individuals. These distinctions mark ontological differences, that is, differences which separate one kind of entity from another.

One way to distinguish kinds of entities is by examining the syntactic structure of linguistic expressions by which they are introduced. Though we may believe that language, especially formal language, is ontologically neutral, this view can be maintained only so long as it is used as an uninterpreted calculus. Once a semantic interpretation is supplied, then the resultant ontological commitment may be associated with the values over which the language's variables range:

> If we use variables that we construe as having
> entities of any given kind as values, we acknowledge
> that there are such entities. In using variables that
> have individuals as values we are acknowledging that
> there are individuals -- and acknowledgement we are
> not likely to be able or to want to avoid. If we also
> use variables that call for classes as values, we
> acknowledge that there are classes. /8/, 34.

We may on occasion use variables ranging over sets or classes without explicitly undertaking an ontological commitment to their existence, but only if our use of such variables amounts to no more than a certain manner of speaking. This condition requires us to describe a mechanism for translating all sentences containing such variables into sentences which lack them.

Predication has been taken as an important indicator of ontological status. That is, the entities tied together by predication differ in kind. Entities which are predicated of others are traditionally called **universals**:

1. *Caesar is a Roman*

may be construed as a sentence in which the expression "*is a Roman*" is predicated of "*Caesar*." This verb phrase introduces a universal which may in turn be predicated of other entities:

2. *Cicero is a Roman*

Sentence (2) says the same thing about Cicero as (1) said about Caesar.

Entities which are not predicated of others are traditionally called **particulars**. In the preceding examples both "*Caesar*" and "*Cicero*" introduce particulars. At first glance, the following sentence seems to be a counter example to this claim:

3a. *Caesar is Cicero*

but as Frege noted, the resemblance between the first two examples and sentence (3a) is only superficial. Natural language here disguises a significant difference in logical form. (3a) is an identity statement, albeit a false one, whose logical form is more perspicuously rendered by the following:

3b. *Whatever may be truly predicated of Caesar may be truly predicated of Cicero, and conversely.*

This version contains explicit quantification over predicates, and thus (3a) makes a more complicated statement than either of the first two examples.

Nothing requires that only one particular be introduced in a sentence, for example:

4. *Caesar is older than Brutus*

is a sentence in which a complicated web of predicative links are being mutually exchanged. Specifically, "*is older than Brutus*" is being predicated of "*Caesar*"; "*Caesar is older than*" is being predicated of "*Brutus*"; and the predicate "*is older than*" is being predicated of "*Caesar*" and "*Brutus*," in that order. In the third case, the predicate is said to be dyadic, or two-placed, because it introduces a relation between two particulars.

Predication seems to presuppose the prior notion of an indicative sentence, at least in the sense that the procedure for generating predicates is to delete noun phrases from such sentences. The linguistic substrate upon which this procedure is based should be understood as providing a notation for universals in much the same way that a system of numerals provides a notation for numbers.

Since classical antiquity, ontology has occasioned elaborate, and often fanciful, attempts to distinguish the kinds of things that are ultimately real from those that are real in a derivative, secondary sense. Often a school of thought will be identified not by the kinds of things it accepts but by the kinds of things it rejects. For example, nominalism may be defined as the rejection of such abstract entities as properties, relations, and classes. The contemporary nominalist Nelson Goodman describes his position quite clearly:

> Nominalism, then, consists of the refusal to countenance any entities other than individuals. Its opposite, platonism, recognizes at least some non-individuals. The nominalist's language contains no names, variable or constant, for entities other than individuals. /8/, 37.

This passage shows the emphasis that Goodman and almost all contemporary ontologist place on the role of language.

The distinction between individuals and such non-individuals as classes is not based on some intrinsic characteristics of the entities in question. In Goodman's view, anything can be taken as an individual. Whether an ontology "recognizes classes as well as individuals depends upon how it makes up entities out of others" /8/, 47. Thus, if we begin with precisely three primitive entities, say *A*, *B* and *C*, then a system is nominalistic if it permits the construction of at most seven distinct individuals:

$$A, B, C, AB, AC, BC, ABC$$

where concatenation represents the sum or fusion of the concatenated entities, i.e., "*AB*" is the individual whose parts are the parts of *A* or the parts of *B*. If a platonistic system begins with the same supply of primitives, then there is no upper bound on the number of entities that can be constructed:

$$A, \{A\}, \{A\{A\}\}, \{A\{A\}\{A\}\}\}, \ldots$$

This sequence has been constructed according to the following rule: the $(N+1)$'th member is the class whose members are precisely the preceding N members of the sequence. This is an example of the prodigious explosion of constructed entities that Goodman refuses to countenance. Unlike the platonist, he is unable to recognize any significant differences between the members of this infinite sequence of classes, i.e., the content of each member of the sequence is the individual A itself -- and nothing more!

Though the ontological frugality of Goodman's approach appeals to one's sense of good order and discipline, his sparse system suffers from a fatal weakness. Much of what we ordinarily want to say is difficult, even impossible, to translate into the language of individuals. This weakness, which Goodman himself admits (/8/, 45 et seq.), suggests that the naive, untutored ontology of common sense far outstrips the expressive capacity of the language of individuals. For this reason, it seems reasonable to base our present studies on Carnap's principle of ontological toleration:

> Are there properties, classes, numbers, propositions? In order to understand more clearly the nature of these and related problems, it is above all necessary to recognize a fundamental distinction between two kinds of questions concerning the existence or reality of entities. If someone wishes to speak in his language about a new kind of entities, he has to introduce a system of new ways of speaking, subject to new rules; we shall call this procedure the construction of a linguistic framework for the new entities in question. And now we must distinguish two kinds of questions of existence; first, questions of the existence of certain entities of the new kind with the framework; we call them internal questions; and second, questions concerning to existence or reality of the system of entities as a whole, called external questions. /6/, 206.

No doubt the nominalist would object to Carnap's permissiveness; after all, the root complaint of nominalists is that classes are unintelligible. But our purpose is not to reform common sense, but to provide a linguistic framework within which common sense can be best approximated. Hence, our approach will be to examine linguistic frameworks as structural hypotheses, useful if they shed light on some obscure corner that strikes our fancy, but always subject to revision and even wholesale change.

The remainder of the paper will be thoroughly Carnapian in spirit and technique. I shall be investigating linguistic frameworks which I believe are central to the analysis of naive physics /9/. In the next two sections, I will present a general overview of two paradigms for linguistic frameworks, namely, the first order paradigm and the higher order paradigm. Both of these sections will concentrate on the realm of predicates and relations, which are Platonistically interpreted as universals. In the concluding sections, I will examine ontological primitives which belong to the metalanguage of what Carnap calls the thing-language: "the simplest kind of entities dealt with in the everyday language: the spatio-temporally ordered system of observable things and events" /6/, 206-207. Though the discussion of these issues will be rather abstract, a crucial methodological component of this paper is the presentation of executable models. These models will be constructed in FranzLISP. For a crisp introduction to this language, see Wilensky /17/; and for an explanation of the choice of this language in this context, see Boudreaux /5/.

2.0   THE FIRST-ORDER PARADIGM

Predication is an example of a more general syntactic notion, called application. With respect to the general techniques of decomposition, application is very much like predication, except that it does not presuppose the notion of indicative sentences. Thus, the arithmetic expression "1+2" is clearly not a sentence, but it does represent the number obtained by applying the function "+" to the numbers 1 and 2. If we agree to use functions to designate the class of entities which may be applied to other entities, then it is apparently the case that every function may be roughly categorized by noting number and respective categories of its proper arguments, and also the category of the resulting value. This implies that predicates are simply special kinds of functions, specifically, functions which yield truth-values when applied to the appropriate number of arguments. In this section we will be looking at the simplest and best known theory which arises from an exact analysis of application, namely first-order logic. The first-order paradigm is based upon a simple yet remarkably powerful conception of the collection of **well-formed formulas** (**wffs**).

The set of all wffs is defined by recursion. The first step is the definition of atomic wffs. Atomic wffs are expressions obtained by applying N-adic predicates to sequences of precisely N terms. A term is either a constant symbol, a variable symbol, or an expression obtained by applying an N-adic function with a sequence of N terms.

Molecular wffs are constructed from atomic wffs by repeated applications of lexical items which may be called logical constants. Unlike the constituents of atomic wffs, the distribution of logical constants in a wff determines its inferential properties, at least in the field of classical logic. The classical logical constants can be divided into two families: sentential connectives, such as negation and implication; and variable-binding operators, like universal and particular quantifiers.

In classical logic, each sentential connective has one and only one adicy. Once the adicy of the connective is known, then the expression obtained by applying the connective to the correct number of wffs is itself a wff. If "*p*" and "*q*" are wffs, then "(*p* -> *q*)" and "-*p*" may be used to symbolize the implication

and negation wffs. In the first case, "*p*" is called the
antecedent and "*q*" the consequent of the implication. These
molecular wffs may also be written in a LISP-style notation
"(*if p q*)" and "(*not p*)" without modifying any logically
important properties. In the sequel, the distinction between
executable functions in FranzLISP and wffs written in the
LISP-style will be obvious in context.

In addition to such classical sentential connectives as "*and*,"
"*or*," "*if and only if (iff)*," "*exclusive or (xor)*," "*stroke*,"
and so on, there are many non-classical connectives, including
modal connectives "*possibly*" and "*necessarily*," and epistemic
connectives "A knows that..." and "A believes that...". Though
interesting in their own right, non-classical logics have as
yet not shown their practical utility in knowledge representation, though some workers expect important breakthroughs in the
near future.

Variable-binding operators are usually composed of an initial
sign, say "*all*," "*some*," or "*lambda*," which is associated with
a variable. Thus, "*all x*" or such notationally equivalent
spellings as "(*x*)," or the LISP-style variant "(*all (x)...*),"
are all instances of the universal quantifier containing an
occurrence of the variable "*x*." The syntactic structure of
variable-binding operations is to generate new wffs when
applied to existing wffs, and to bind otherwise free occurrences of variables. The existing wff is called the scope of
the operator. That is, an occurrence of a variable is free if
and only if it is not within the scope of a variable-binding
operator which also contains an occurrence of the same variable. If an occurrence of a variable is not a free occurrence,
then it is said to be a bound occurrence. Every variable-
binding operator binds all occurrences of its component
variable which lies within its scope.

Let *p* be a wff which contains zero or more free occurrences of
the variable *x* and let *t* be any term, then the wff obtained by
substituting *t* for *x* in *p*, symbolically, "(*subst x t p*)," is
identical to *p* except that it has a free occurrence of *t*
wherever *p* has a free occurrence of *x*. Thus, if *p* contains no
free occurrence of *x*, or if one of the free occurrences of *x* is
in the scope of a quantifier which contains an occurrence of a
variable which also has an occurrence in the term *t*, then
(*subst x t p*) is identical to *p*.

In addition to syntactic simplicity, the first-order paradigm
also has an elegant theory of meaning, or semantics. It is
this second attribute which workers in this field value above
all others. After the pioneering investigations of the
logician Alfred Tarski, the first stage is the identification
of a domain of discourse. Now any unempty set will do; that
is, there is no reason save usage to choose one collection of
entities over another. Once the selection of a domain has been
accomplished, then we begin the task of providing each
syntactic item with an interpretation with in that domain.

Since constant terms are like proper names, function symbols like functions, and predicate symbols like relations, a natural way to correlate the language with the domain of discourse is by introducing an interpretation function which preserves the syntactic structure of each lexical item. That is, any reasonable interpretation function should map constants onto single elements of the domain of discourse; N-adic predicates onto subsets of the N'th product of the domain; and N-adic functions onto functions from the N'th product of domain into the domain itself.

A Tarskian model, or *possible world*, may be defined as an unempty domain with an interpretation function.

The next step in the development of this semantic theory is to describe a method for mapping all terms, including variables and functional terms, into Tarskian models. Unlike constants, variables are not like proper names, their closest analogues in natural languages are pronouns. Any association of world elements with variables can only be achieved by arbitrary assignment. The corresponding set-theoretical operation is to define the set of all functions which map variables into the domain of discourse. Appropriately enough, these functions are called assignment functions. Once a particular assignment function is selected, then every term can be associated with one and only one world element.

Since the referent of every term is uniquely determined by the selection of a Tarskian model and one of the many assignment functions, the central semantic notion of satisfaction can be defined as a kind of table look-up. In keeping with the intuitive notion that the primary role of atomic wffs is to reflect, however imperfectly, the factual or empirical structure of a possible world, the following point defines the conditions under which an atomic wff is satisfied:

   5. *Atomic Wff*: a model satisfies an atomic wff with respect to a given assignment function iff the ordered N-tuple of the referents of the argument terms of the wff is an element of the N-adic relation which interprets the predicate symbol.

If a model satisfies an atomic wff under all assignment functions, then the atomic wff is said to be true in that model. On the other hand, if a model does not satisfy an atomic wff no matter what assignment function is selected, then the atomic wff is said to be false in the model. Since variables are analogous to indefinite pronouns, atomic wffs containing variables may be neither true nor false in a given model, i.e., they may be satisfied by some assignment functions but not by others.

Tarski's analysis can now be extended to molecular wffs by describing the manner in which logical constants affect the satisfiability of wffs containing them. This can be done by adding one new clause to the previous definition of satisfaction for each way of forming molecular wffs; that is, if *M* is an arbitrary possible world and *f* is an assignment function with respect to *M*, then:

6. **Negation**: {*M,f*} satisfies (*not p*) iff {*M,f*} does not satisfy *p*.

   Implication: {*M,f*} satisfies (*if p q*) iff {*M,f*} either does not satisfy *p* or does satisfy *q*.

   Universal Quantifier: {*M,f*} satisfies (*all (x) p*) iff for every assignment function *f**, differing from *f* at most in the value assigned to *x*, {*M,f**} satisfies *p*.

The remaining sentential connectives and quantifiers of classical logic may be introduced as definitional abbreviations of those already mentioned, and thus do not constitute essentially new cases. This is not true for modal connectives, like "*possibly*" and "*necessarily*," which are not reducible to boolean-valued functions. From a purely syntactic point of view, "*possibly*" and "*necessarily*" are adverbs which, when applied to statements, yield statements. In this respect they are analogous to negation. But if one considers the available supply of monadic truth functions in the classical theory, one notes that there are only four possible functions: negation, affirmation, "all-false," and "all-true." None of these functions are plausible interpretations for either modal connective. There are many alternatives for providing the semantics of non-classical operators, including the introduction of more truth values than the two classical values "true" and "false," or by adopting even more radical approaches.

A wff is true in a model if and only if it is satisfied by all assignment functions. A wff is false in a model if it is satisfied by no assignment functions. A wff may be neither true nor false in a model, but this is possible only if the wff contains at least one occurrence of a free variable.

Some wffs have the same truth-value in all models. Wffs which are true in all models are said to be logically true, and wffs which are false in all models are said to be logically false. Other wffs are true in some models and false in others. These wffs are said to be factual.

Logically true wffs are true by virtue of their syntactic structure alone. The proof of this observation is the main burden of the Soundness and Completeness theorems of classical logic. They express universal properties of models, that is, properties which models must possess in order to be accepted as logically coherent. For this reason, the informational content of logically true wffs is precisely empty. As Wittgenstein so aptly remarks, "I know nothing about the weather when I know that it is either raining or not raining." To be genuinely informative, a true wff must be at least potentially vulnerable to falsification. All and only factually true wffs are vulnerable in this sense. That a factual wff is true in a model says that the model has a property which it could conceivably not have had.

3.0 THE HIGHER-ORDER PARADIGM

The first-order paradigm has had a very powerful influence on the manner in which theories have been presented for formal analysis. Even though this paradigm is rich enough to support all of the customary axiomatizations of set theory, and hence all axiomatizations in classical mathematics, there are still many ordinary sentences whose first-order analysis is very difficult to produce. Consider, for example: "**Bonaparte had all of the properties of a great general**." We think we understand this statement -- until we have to provide an account of its logical form! Sentences which admit quantifiers over predicates, i.e., quantifiers whose range are universals, will be said to conform to the higher-order paradigm.

In most natural languages there is a process, called abstractive nominalization, in which predicates are transformed into abstract nouns. For example, by the usual methods of decomposition, the sentence

7a. *That book is heavy*

yields the predicate "*is heavy*." But what is the relation between "*is heavy*" and the abstract noun "*heaviness*"? The supposition that there is some connection may be in part explained by the apparent tie between (7a) and the next sentence:

7b. *That book has heaviness*

This sentence suggests an analogy between "*having heaviness*" and "*having a penny*," which has led many to suspect that abstractive nominals like "*heaviness*" are correctly interpreted as proper names for the universal introduced by the predicate "*is heavy*." But one needn't be a Goodmanian nominalist to view this move with alarm. After all, the appropriateness of considering universals to be the kinds of things introduced in the same way as particulars can hardly be said to be obvious!

A more prudent alternative is to invent a notational device for such nominalizations, i.e., "[*is heavy*]" to designate any abstractive nominalization of "*is heavy*." This notation permits the construction of English sentences in which abstract nouns occur as arguments:

8a. *Heaviness is a physical property*

may be rewritten as

8b. [*is heavy*] *is a physical property*

which seems marginally less likely to encourage extreme Platonism. McCarthy /13/ suggests that such concepts be represented in first-order paradigm as special kinds of proper names. To do this, we must construct possible worlds in which the interpretation functions map expressions like [*is heavy*] onto some element of the domain of individuals. If successful, this proposal would mark a significant economy in the need for additional linguistic frameworks, but I must admit to a feeling of uneasiness.

Even if we avoid paradoxical consequences by having two or more sorts of individual variables, say one run of variables for "regular" individuals and another for abstractives, we would still have to provide for a convincing analysis to explain the intuitive validity of the following argument:

9. *That book is heavy;*
   [is heavy] is a physical property;
   therefore, that book has some physical property.

The logical form of (9) is not immediately apparent, but I think that it depends in part on the equivalence of (7a) and (7b). The validity of (9) implies a close connection between "*is heavy*" in the first premiss and the expression [*is heavy*] in the second. Though it may indeed be possible, I don't see how to define this connection if we assume that [*is heavy*] is a particular. Of course one could formally specify the connection by extra-logical axioms, but this has two unacceptable consequences. First, since any inference can be validated if one is prepared to introduce suitable extra-logical axioms, the need for them to explain the validity of (9) effectively defeats the intuitively correct claim that (9) is logically valid, a claim that I am not prepared easily to forgo. Second, the axioms themselves could not be first order wffs, because they would require at least one argument to be the predicate "*is heavy*", which destroys the primary inducement for even considering this proposal!

One alternative is to use the "*lambda*" variable-binding operator to represent abstractive nominals. Suppose that *p* is a wff containing two and only two free variables, say *x* and *y*, then the expression

(lambda (x y) p)

is a dyadic predicate, and according to the rules of lambda-conversion, the result of applying the *lambda* expression to a pair of arguments is equivalent to the result obtained by performing simultaneous substitutions in the *lambda* expression's body, that is:

((lambda (x y) p) A B)

is equivalent to

(subst x A (subst y B p))

What I now want to suggest is that [*is heavy*] should be identified with *(lambda (x) (x is heavy))*, and thus that both expressions should be interpreted as predicates, which means that they should be mapped by the interpretation function onto sets of domain elements. Even though "*is heavy*" and "*is a physical property*" are both monadic predicates, there is a clear distinction between them. Specifically, "*is heavy*" may be significantly applied to particulars but "*is a physical property*" may be significantly applied only to predicates. This distinction marks the fundamental insight of the theory of types, proposed by Russell in 1908 and used in the *Principia Mathematica*, written in collaboration with A. N. Whitehead. The version of the theory of types to be described here is due to the British logician Frank Ramsey. The basic idea of Ramsey's theory is that the type of any expression is unambiguously determined by specifying the order and types of the expression's arguments. This idea yields an infinite hierarchy of types. The lowest component of the hierarchy, called the 0'th order, consists of the collection of all particulars, i.e., expressions predicated of nothing; and the *(K+1)*'th order consists of the collection of all predicates, at least one of whose arguments is a *K'th* order expression, and none of whose arguments is higher than the *K'th* order. If we agree that variables are indexed by types, then it is a simple matter to extend this type definition to *lambda* expressions.

The main difference between first order and higher order consists in the syntactic structure of atomic wffs. In fact, the inferential rules of the simple theory of types are the same as those for first order logic, except that the rules for variable-binding operators must be adjusted to reflect type restrictions on the substitution operation: if *Y* is any (typed) variable and *T* any term, then *(subst Y T p)* exists if and only if both *Y* and *T* belong to the same type, in which case *(subst Y T p)* differs from *p* only in having a free occurrence of *T* wherever *p* has a free occurrence of *Y*. But to do the job that Russell and Whitehead had in mind, i.e., to be a foundational system for the entire corpus of classical mathematics, the theory of types has to be extended by the addition of axiom schemata of *Extensionality* and *Comprehension*. Though not sufficient (to do any serious work one also needs axioms of *Infinity* and *Choice*), these two schemata are regulative principles which impose strict conditions on the minimal complexity of typed universes of all possible worlds.

The *Extensionality* schema is a regulative principle which specifies the conditions under which predicates are to be judged to be equal:

    10.   *(all (PHI PSI)*
           (if (all (x..y) (iff (PHI x..y) (PSI x..y)))
           (equal PHI PSI)))

Given the conventions of type theory, it must be the case that *PHI* and *PSI* belong to the same type. What *Extensionality* says, is that if *PHI* and *PSI* may be truly predicated of precisely the same set of arguments, then *PHI* and *PSI* are to be considered equal. The dyadic relation "*equal*" is defined in the style of Leibniz, i.e., entities are said to be equal just in case they have the same properties:

    11.   *(all (PHI PSI) (iff (equal PHI PSI)*
                  (all (rho)
                      (iff (rho PHI)(rho PSI)))))

Even though the ideas introduced by *Extensionality* are very familiar, there are many difficult issues involved. For example, we have already mentioned that a wff is logically true if and only if it is true in all possible worlds, but it is a simple matter to show that there are some possible worlds in which *Extensionality* is false. Imagine a world of colored polygons in which all polygons are red if and only if they are square, that is, in this world "is red" and "is square" are truly predicated of the same particulars. But "is red" is a color property and "is square" is not, which implies that "is red" is not equal to "is square" in the sense of Leibniz -- thereby falsifying *Extensionality!* Though it is true that the polygon world suffers from a radical insufficiency of particulars, which could be cured by adding just one non-red square polygon or one non-square red polygon, still the underlying point is unchanged: if *Extensionality* is a logical truth, then its status is very different than that of the inferential rules inherited from first-order; see Boudreaux /4/.

The fate of *Extensionality* suggests that *Comprehension* is unlikely to have a smooth course. To avoid unhelpful complexity, let's first consider a subschema of *Comprehension* which permits the introduction of monadic predicates:

    12a. *(some (PHI) (all (x) (iff (PHI x) (wff-in-x))))*

Subschema (12a) may be construed as follows: let "**wff-in-x**" stand for any wff whose free variables include the variable "**x**" and which contains no occurrences of the predicate variable *PHI*, then there is a predicate *PHI*, which is truly predicated of all and only those values which, when assigned to the variable "**x**" in **wff-in-x**, yield a true statement. The set-theoretical content of this schema is obvious. Once we have established a semantic interpretation for **wff-in-x**, this wff can be used to define a class of entities:

    {x : wff-in-x}

Comprehension requires there to be at least one (and by *Extensionality*, at most one) predicate which is truly predicated of all and only the members of this class. Thus, to falsify *Comprehension* one need only omit one of these predicates from the appropriately typed universe; see Boudreaux /3/ for details.

The restriction that *PHI* be a monadic predicate may be lifted by replacing "**x**" with a list of (everywhere distinct) variables. Also that if **wff-in-x** has free variables other than *x*, then these are assumed to be bound by a prefixed universal quantifier:

    12b. *(all (y..z)*
            (some (PHI)
                  (all (x) (iff (PHI x) (wff-in-x-y..z)))))

This strengthens *Comprehension* since it says that given any assignment of values to the variables in the list *y..z*, there is at least one predicate *PHI* which is truly predicated of all and only those values which, when assigned to *x*, cause **wff-in-x-y..z** to be true. By applying a Skolemization procedure, this version of *Comprehension* can be readily seen to be permitting the introduction of higher order functions on predicate terms. For example, the following instance of (12b) can be used to introduce a familiar set-theoretic operator:

    13.   *(all (X Y)*
           (some (PHI)
              (all (x) (iff (PHI x) (or (X x) (Y x))))))

During Skolemization, the most obvious name to choose for the function to replace *PHI* is "union," i.e., for all possible values of *X* and *Y*, "*(union X Y)*" is the predicate whose existence is guaranteed by (13).

There is a close connection between *Comprehension* and **lambda** abstraction. Suppose **wff-in-x** is any expression satisfying the conditions on (12a), then according to the rules of **lambda** conversion:

    14a. *(iff ((lambda (x) (wff-in-x)) x)*
           (subst x x wff-in-x))

Since (14a) depends on no hypothesis, familiar inferential rules inherited from first order allow us to bind all free occurrences of *x* in (14a) by a prefix universal quantifier:

    14b. *(all (x)*
           (iff ((lambda (x) (wff-in-x) x)
             (subst x x wff-in-x)))

In order to obtain (12a), what we would now like to do is to apply the existential quantifier introduction rule to (14b). Though this may seem like an obvious move, in the view of many contemporary logicians, especially Quine, it is precisely this move which forces an ontological commitment to *lambda* expressions as bona fide entities in the universe of discourse. In retrospect, the very ease with which we fall into Platonism shows how really difficult Goodman's project is!

The distinction between first-order and higher-order logic is based primarily on the syntactic structure of atomic wffs. The practical consequence of this distinction on the construction of possible worlds is that instead of a single undifferentiated domain of individuals, higher-order possible worlds consist of many domains, i.e., a different domain for each type. The construction proceeds by induction: if M is any unempty set, then M may be taken as the domain of 0'th order individuals; and if a domain has been defined for all *K*'th order types, then the domain for each *(K+1)*'th order type is the set of all functions from the Cartesian product of the domains of its component types into the set of truth values. Thus, the Tarskian semantics of higher-order logic differs from first-order only in the sense that (5) has to be revised to include more complicated atomic wffs, and also the last clause of (6) pertaining to universal quantifiers has to be restated so that the substitutions on the variable x are confined to those whose type is the same type as that of the variable of quantification.

At this point the story gets a bit more complicated. If one defines logical truth for higher order theories as true in all higher-order possible worlds in the sense just given, then it is a simple exercise to prove that both *comprehension* and *extensionality* are logically true, thereby contradicting the arguments mentioned above. In fact, Goedel's incompleteness theorem shows that the situation is even worse: the set of higher-order logical truths is not recursively enumerable, which means that higher-order logical truth is radically incomplete and cannot be completely characterized by the addition of any finite set of axioms or axiom schemata.

This unpleasant situation was at least partially rectified by Leon Henkin, who proved a version of the completeness theorem for higher-order logic in 1949. Henkin's idea was to dramatically increase the number of possible worlds by allowing those whose typed domains contained fewer, but not noticeably fewer, than all possible functions of the appropriate type. From Henkin's perspective, the earlier negative result was an indication that too much emphasis had been placed on the need for each type domain to contain all appropriately typed functions. This restriction, which yields the class of so-called standard worlds, results in collection of worlds which is too small and too lacking in essential diversity. Henkin's crucial insight is that each standard world is surrounded by a vast penumbra of non-standard worlds, each of whose typed domains is a subset of the identically typed domain of the "core" standard model. It is an interesting fact, first proven in Boudreaux /3/, that the set of higher-order wffs true in all of these worlds is precisely the set whose proof-theoretic validity reduces to that of first-order.

To construct a notion of logical truth that is intermediate between the first notion of standard logical truth and the second more permissive notion of truth in all non-standard worlds, we need to discover "natural" restrictions on the set of non-standard worlds. If this is done cleverly, we can introduce completeness theorems for many higher-order theories, including the very useful theory based on both *Extensionality* and *Comprehension*. In this case, the relevant restriction is that the higher-order domains of non-standard worlds are atomic boolean algebras, and that there are characteristic homomorphisms between certain typed domains. These results are fully stated and proven in Boudreaux /3/ and /4/.

The preceding sections have shown the inner structure of the realm of predicates, including those which conform to the first-order paradigm and those which conform to the higher-order paradigm. Though some issues have been resolved, it would be inaccurate and misleading to suggest that we now understand this structure in anything like adequate depth. In my opinion, an adequate theory of predication has yet to be written. In the next section, we will consider the ontology of those entities which may only occur as the subjects of predication, namely, individuals and particulars.

4.0 PARTICULAR = INDIVIDUAL + STRUCTURE

The notion of "universal individualhood" is considered and rejected in Hayes /9/ as follows:

> An important general point is that we do not want anything like universal individualhood. Common sense is prolix -- many kinds of entities -- but also very conservative -- very few entities of each type. This contrast with more "universal" schemes such as nominalism, in which any piece of spacetime can be an individual, allowing such things as the sphere of radius 20 meters centered on my left thumbnail now, during the month of August 1980 (say).

Though this reaction is understandable, I think that the barely concealed horror at the sheer multiplicity of individuals really flows from a confusion between the notion of an individual and that of a particular. This ontological distinction, and its many ramifications, will concern us for the rest of this paper.

Though the terms "individual" (literally, "un-divisible") and "particular" (literally, "little part") are far from ideal, their common usage forbids any replacement. Hence, we may begin with a blunt, but useful, definition: an individual is any one of a collection of entities that satisfy the axioms of the calculus of individuals. These axioms say that the domain of individuals is closed under a dyadic "*part of*" relation and under a generalized fusion operation. The "*part of*" relation is a partial ordering such that any pair of individuals has a *l.u.b.*, that is, the "sum" or "fused" individual whose parts are precisely the parts of one or the other; and every individual has at least one part, i.e., there is no "null" individual. Suppose C is a non-empty collection of individuals, then generalized fusion guarantees that there is at least one individual, called "*Klass(C)*," such that every part of every member of C is a part of *Klass(C)*, and every part of *Klass(C)* has a part which is part of some member of C. Thus, *Klass(C)* is that individual which consists of the results of fusing the members of that collection.

Individuals are identical if and only if they have the same parts, i.e., every part of one is a part of the other, and conversely. This criterion of identity does not take spatial or temporal dispersion into consideration. Thus, the fact that an individual is "scattered" or widely dispersed does not affect its status as a single individual.

An atom is an individual which is identical to any of its parts, i.e., whatever is a part of an atom is identical to that atom in the sense just defined. A calculus of individuals is atomistic if and only if every individual is a *Klass* of atoms.

A calculus of individuals is non-atomistic if and only if there are no atoms. That is, every individual has at least one proper part. In the non-atomistic calculus, there can be infinitely descending chains formed by "part of" relation.

The "equation" in the title of this section tells us that particulars are structured individuals. To make the slogan a bit more precise, let's consider the notion of a sortal predicate.

Sortal predicates satisfy the following necessary, but perhaps not sufficient condition: if an individual is an instance of a sortal predicate, then no proper part of that individual instantiates the predicate, and no individual of which the original individual is a proper part instantiates the predicate. For example, if an individual instantiates "*man*," then no proper part of that individual is a man nor is any individual of which that individual is a proper part. Sortals supply segmentation criteria which are often needed in such simple algorithms as those involved in counting instances. Since counting algorithms require that each instance be processed once and only once, the fact that a monadic predicate supports this activity is a sure sign that it is a sortal.

Not all monadic predicates are sortals. Consider, the monadic predicate "*is white*." Suppose that there is a white sheet of paper on a desk top, and that our instructions are to count all white things on the desk. Then one seemingly plausible approach would be to assign the next numeral to the white sheet and then to move on to another instance of "*white*." But this would not fully comply with the instructions. Both the top half and the bottom half of the sheet are also white and have not yet been counted, which means that both halves must be separately counted. Since this "*halving*" operation can be repeated indefinitely, we must conclude that "*white*" does not provide an adequate basis for the counting algorithm, and hence that it is not a sortal.

The systematic analysis of sortals is a subtle and difficult task, whose main outlines are at best imperfectly grasped. One important point is the need to represent the specialized inferential properties of sortals. For example, identifying an individual as a man provides information about that individual's structural organization, i.e., a mammalian body plan, a pelvis and spinal column design to support a vertical posture, a gripping mechanism which includes an opposable thumb, and so on. Such information may be formulated as probable inferences:

    15. *Caesar is a man;*
         therefore, Caesar probably has a kidney.

This inference seems intuitively correct, i.e., there is something about being human which makes the possession of a kidney more likely than not. But the conclusion of (15) cannot be strengthened; it is logically possible, even factually possible, for there to be a kidney-less human. Though these observations are banal, we quickly encounter more difficult problems. For example, would the following be a reasonable formulation of (15)?

16. *There is an individual K such that K is part of Caesar and K is a kidney.*

However plausible it may appear to be, the unacceptability of (16) is obvious once we see that (16) would have been true had Caesar had no kidney of his own, but had just finished dining on Pompey's! This simple example shows that logic of sortals demands close attention to detail. In a related discussion, Hayes /9/ remarks that sortals seem to form bundles or clusters, which is certainly correct. What I would ultimately like to do is to invent a formal mechanism for resolving sortal clusters into their fundamental components. An interesting step in this direction has been taken in Sowa /15/, especially Chapter 3.

Particulars do not satisfy the criterion of part-identity. That is, we routinely re-identify an individual as the same man even though the individual now available has many parts that that earlier individual did not, and conversely. If we assume the persistence of the ultimate "stuff," then that same individual still exists as a "scattered" *Klass*. Thus, assuming the persistence of ultimate "stuff" is tantamount to assuming the eternality of individuals, which implies the seemingly odd result that one and the same particular successively coincides with different individuals.

Suppose that we accept an atomistic calculus of individuals, then every particular at every time is a *Klass* of atoms. Since each collection of atoms defines one and only one *Klass* individual, we must say that this self-same individual persists through all time. But the particular man gains new parts and loses others, which means that the particular, which is also persistent, coincides which different individuals throughout its history. Thus, the identity of particulars is not and cannot be reducible to part-identity of individuals.

There are many different species of particulars, but one species -- bodies -- are especially important. Bodies are spatio-temporally definite particulars, that is, each may be spatially and temporally localized. Moreover, bodies persist through time, that is, it must be possible to re-identify a body as the same body as the one previously encountered. This is a logical possibility, and not necessarily a practical one. Human perceptual recognition seems to be strongly biased toward the recognition of such human features as (human-like?) faces, which allow us to re-identify members of our own kind. It is very difficult to store sufficient information about non-human, and especially non-animate, bodies to be able to re-identify them. This point goes a bit deeper than one might suppose. Suppose we have a fixed collection of bodies, and suppose that our job is to record enough information to be able to re-identify each member of this collection from all of the others. This is in principle possible, though it is very difficult to determine that the job has been completely done.

But the underlying assumption here is that the bodies in the collection do not alter significantly during the process, for if they did change shape or were crushed or broken, then the information requirements of this task would be enormous.

5.0 THE BEAD WORLD

In order to make this paper reasonably self-contained, I will here introduce enough information about FranzLISP to allow the reader to follow the examples given in the remainder of the section. As an initial focus, I will take examples several FranzLISP functions which suggest a method for representing sets as LISP objects. The following explanations are adapted from Boudreaux /5/.

FranzLISP recognizes only two kinds of objects: atoms and lists. Atoms include such scalar values as integers (fixnums), floating point reals (flonums), symbols, and strings. A list is an object that may always be resolved into a head component which may either an atom or a list, and a tail component which must be a list. The accepted notation for lists is to enclose their components within mated parentheses. The list which has no components is called the null list and may be represented by the empty-nest expression "()" or by the constant symbol "**nil**."

The only other class of entities recognized by FranzLISP are functions. In order to signal the FranzLISP interpreter that a particular function is to be applied to a (possibly empty) sequence of arguments, the programmer simply presents the interpreter with a list object whose head is the symbolic name of the function and whose tail is the list of the expressions to be passed to the function as arguments. Though there are important exceptions, FranzLISP functions usually have a fixed number of arguments which is identical to the number of components, or length, of the argument list.

FranzLISP programmers work in programming environments that are already supplied with pre-defined FranzLISP functions. In fact, one FranzLISP dialect will differ from another in both the variety and complexity of the pre-defined functions that it makes available. Two functions, **car** and **cdr**, are used to select the components of any list; in particular, **car** selects the head component and **cdr** selects the tail. The primitive constructor function for lists is **cons**, which when applied to two arguments, returns a list whose head is equal to the first argument and whose tail is equal to the second.

Another function, **cond**, which expresses the primitive conditional test method in FranzLISP, may have any finite number of arguments. Each argument is a list, called a conditional clause. The interpreter processes each clause in order until one is discovered whose **car** is non-**nil**. Then the **cdr** of the successful clause is interpreted, that is, all of the components of the **cdr** of this clause are processed and the value returned by the **cond** function is the final result obtained.

All LISP systems share the characteristic that programmers are encouraged to construct new application-specific functions. These functions have the same status as the functions supplied by the LISP system. Since we are interested in the representation of sets in FranzLISP, an important function is the set-theoretic membership relation, which may be called "**epsilon**":

```
(def epsilon (lambda (x y)
    (cond
        ((null y) nil)
        ((equalset x (car y)) t)
        (t (epsilon x (cdr y))))))
```

This recursive definition may be read as follows:

> *x epsilon y is*
> *nil (i.e., false), if y is the null list;*
> *t (i.e., true), if x is set-theoretically equal*
> *to the car of y;*
> *otherwise, it has the same truth-value as*
> *x epsilon the cdr of y.*

The lambda expression creates a nested environment in which all **lambda** bound variables are set to the argument values, then the inner expression is evaluated in the usual way until some resulting value emerges. Once this value has been obtained, the nested environment is deleted and the resulting value is returned in place. The definition of *epsilon* depends on the prior understanding of the function "**equalset**," that is, set-theoretic equality. In keeping with normal mathematical practice, we may define **equalset** as follows:

```
(def equalset (lambda (x y)
    (cond
        ((and (atom x) (atom y)) (equal x y))
        ((and (listp x) (listp y))
            (and (subset x y)(subset y x)))
        (t nil))))
(def subset (lambda (x y)
    (cond
        ((and (null x) (null y)) t)
        ((null x) t)
        ((null y) nil)
        ((epsilon (car x) y) (subset (cdr x) y))
        (t nil))))
```

These definitions are woefully inefficient, but the main point that we can approximate set theory in FranzLISP. The complexity of **equalset** is apparent when we consider that set-theoretic equality is not violated by element repetition or by any permutation which does not cross boundaries. For example, the next pair of lists, though very different as lists, are set-theoretically equal:

((this is) ((one) case))

((case case (one one)) (is is this))

Though this representation of sets is more comprehensive than those usually presented, at least in the sense that it permits sets to have arbitrarily complicated structure, it is not really as useful as we would like it to be. First, there has been no provision made for recursive infinite sets, which play a vital role in the foundational aspects of set theory. But second, the domain of sets is static and eternal, and what we are really interested in is the representing the domain of spatio-temporal objects. To do this, I will now invent a game -- especially, a (glass) bead game! Though the name is borrowed from Herman Hesse, the idea of building a game-world to explore the issues of this section is due to Barwise /1/, and Barwise and Perry /2/.

Imagine a world consisting of beads, each of which has a left and a right "hook." Imagine that beads can be created and deleted at will, and that the main activity in this world is stringing beads together by gluing the left-hook of one bead to the right-hook of another. Once connected, beads can be disconnected by ungluing them. To represent this in FranzLISP, we should first introduce the notion of a property list. Control over property lists is obtained through the functions **putprop** and **get**, the first assigns a value to a property and the second accesses that value. Thus, to express the fact that Abraham has the property of being the father of Isaac, we would write

```
(putprop 'isaac 'abraham 'father)
```

To retrieve the value of a property, we would write

```
(get 'isaac 'father)
```

The symbol **bead-world** will be used as a global record of all existing beads. In the beginning, the variable **bead-world** is set to **nil** by the pre-defined FranzLISP function **setq**:

```
(setq bead-world nil)
```

Bead-world may be modified by **make-bead** which creates a new bead, and **del-bead**, which deletes an already existing bead:

```
(def make-bead (lambda (one)
  (cond
    ((memq one bead-world) (princ "ERROR: bead used"))
    (t (setq bead-world (cons one bead-world))))))

(def del-bead (lambda (one)
  (cond ((memq one bead-world)
         (sever-bead one)

    (setq bead-world (remove one bead-world)))
    (t (princ "ERROR: no bead")))))
```

When a bead is deleted, some care must be exercised to ensure that the bead is really annihilated and that no ghostly traces of it are visible by some round-about mechanism. Annihilation is guaranteed by **sever-bead**:

```
(def sever-bead (lambda (one)
    (cond ((right one) (unglue one (right one))))
    (cond ((left one) (unglue (left one) one)))))
```

The following transcript of a session with the FranzLISP interpreter will show what's been done so far:

```
-> (make-bead 'this)
(this)

-> (make-bead 'that)
(that this)

-> (make-bead 'them)
(them that this)

-> (make-bead 'those)
(those them that this)

-> (del-bead 'that)
(those them this)
```

Each bead has a left- and a right-hook and multi-bead entities, called **necklaces**, may be formed by gluing the left-hook of one bead with right-hook of another. Before defining these operations, let's introduce three auxiliary functions whose intended interpretation should be clear:

```
(def isbead (lambda (one)
    (cond ((memq one bead-world) t)
          (t nil))))

(def left (lambda (one) (get one 'left-hook)))

(def right (lambda (one) (get one 'right-hook)))
```

The representation of gluing is defined by **putprop**-ing onto the appropriate bead the name of its companion under either the left-hook or right-hook attribute. The representation of ungluing is defined by **putprop**-ing **nil** to the right-hook of the first argument and the left-hook of the second.

```
(def glue (lambda (one two)
    (cond ((and (isbead one)
                (isbead two)
                (null (right one))
                (null (left two)))
           (putprop one two 'right-hook)
           (putprop two one 'left-hook)
           t)
          (t (princ "ERROR:  no glue.")
             (terpr)))))
```

```
(def unglue (lambda (one two)
   (cond ((equal (right one) two)
          (putprop one nil 'right-hook)
          (putprop two nil 'left-hook)
          t)
         (t (princ "ERROR:  no unglue.")
            (terpr)))))
```

The following session shows the application of **glue** and **unglue**:

```
-> bead-world
(those them this)
-> (glue 'them 'this)
t

-> (glue 'those 'this)
ERROR:  no glue

-> (left 'this)
them

-> (left 'them)
nil

-> (right 'them)
this

-> (unglue 'them 'this)
t
```

The next functions interrogate a bead to see if it is the leftmost or the rightmost bead of a necklace:

```
(def left-end (lambda (one)
   (cond ((and (null (left one))(right one))
          t)
         (t nil))))

(def right-end (lambda (one)
   (cond ((and (null (right one))(left one))
          t)
         (t nil))))
```

Some necklaces have no left- and right-end beads. Consider the following interaction:

```
-> (make-bead "stop)
stop

-> (glue 'stop 'stop)
t

-> (left-end 'stop)
nil

-> (right-end 'stop)
nil
```

```
-> (left 'stop)
stop

-> (right 'stop)
stop
```

In this example, the left-hook of bead stop is attached to the right-hook of the same bead. This operation violates none of the rules of the bead world. But once such a necklace has been constructed, it can participate in no other gluing episodes.

Since bodies are spatio-temporal continuants, each body may be paired with its own unique spatio-temporal trace, to be called a *tube*. Cross-sections of tubes are spatial locations during small temporal intervals, or instants. The natural clock in **bead-world** may be defined by a simple operation counter, e.g., the incrementation of a global variable, say **tic**, whenever any modification is made to **bead-world** entities. If we introduce an explicit clock function:

```
(def bead-clock (lambda ()
    (setq tic (plus tic 1))))
```

and if we initialize **tic** to 1, then the only question to be decided is which of the preceding functions to add **bead-clock** to. Though there is little apparent reason for selecting one answer rather than another, let's add **bead-clock** to **make-bead**, **del-bead**, **glue** and **unglue**. If we do this, then **sever-bead** will always take two tics and **del-bead** three and the auxiliary functions take no time at all. In this respect, the auxiliary functions are the same as the underlying FranzLISP functions.

The spatial structure of **bead-world** is a bit more difficult to determine. Once two beads have been glued together, then we know where each of them is:

```
-> bead-world
(stop those them this)
-> (glue 'them 'that)
t
-> (left 'that)
them
-> (right 'them)
that
```

What we are unable to determine is the relative location of beads and necklaces which are not glued together. E.g., where is the bead "those"? For that matter, where is "stop"? As a closed necklace, "stop" is to the left and again to the right of itself, which is certainly an unhappy result. Though the present spatial structure of bead-world does seem unusual, this is because it has a local, as opposed to global, structure. If we impose a global spatial structure on **bead-world**, then there are two questions that have to be answered. First, how may one compute the spatial properties of unconnected beads and necklaces? Second, how may one compute the spatial properties of beads within the same necklace. Though there is no one correct way to answer either of these questions, there are constraints that have to be satisfied. For example, we would expect that the global location of a necklace's beads is functionally related to the global location of the necklace itself, and conversely. We would also expect for the beads in the same necklace to be near one another. But these expectations jointly force us either to impose some spatial constraints on the legality of gluing and ungluing, or to allow very odd instantaneous motions.

Particulars have history and individuals do not. This is again a seemingly paradoxical statement, but it is an immediate corollary of everything that has been said so far. Unless we are prepared to admit the construction and destruction of atoms or to appeal to a notion of identity which is quite different from part-identity, then we have to be prepared to admit that the total supply of individuals is given in advance. Not so the particulars. Particulars can come into being (generation) and pass away (corruption). As a first approximation, what we would expect a history to contain is a list of all of the time-consuming, operations which have taken place. The easiest way to do this is to modify each of the operations to have side-effects on **history**. But where to put this **history**? I suppose the best place is as an attribute of the symbol **bead-world** itself, which means that the side-effects would be accomplished by **putprop-ing** the modified history onto **bead-world** under the attribute "history". A clause to do this has to be added to all historic operations, but for now let's look at the clause to be added to **glue**:

```
(putprop 'bead-world
         (cons (list 'glue one two)
               (get 'bead-world 'history))
         'history)
```

Once this clause has been added, every time the command to glue two beads together is executed, that very same command, or better, a FranzLISP object which identically represents it, is entered in **history**.

6.0   WHAT'S NEXT?

Having come this far, I am keenly aware of the enormity of the task that lies ahead. Let me conclude this paper with a brief overview of some of the more pressing projects that need to be attended to.

The bead world is admittedly a "toy" domain, but in a different sense than those that Hayes rightly complains about in /9/. That is, it's small in size, i.e., in the number of primitive functions, but not in the number or the diversity of the constructions that it permits. In this respect, the bead world is analogous to set theory, which is based entirely on the epsilon of set membership, but which is expressive enough to support all of classical mathematics. If this analogy is correct, the first line of attack should be to investigate the bead world more deeply.

Another line of attack which is particularly important is the one which explores the logical analysis of particulars. Recall that particulars have been identified as structured individuals. Though the example given above is based on the spatial organization of particulars, i.e., the relation between Caesar and Caesar's kidney, sortals also support inferences about the temporal organization of particulars by supporting law-like generalizations concerning their development or evolutionary potential in much the same sense as grammatical rules govern the temporal development of an English utterance. This analogy suggests that the bead world may be modified by introducing "context-sensitive" rules which limit or restrict the formation of necklaces by controlling the manner in which necklaced beads may be glued and unglued.

Finally, computational ontology offers us the opportunity to study notions which for milennia have been matters for philosophical speculation. Though there is little hope that such questions can be resolved, it would be significant progress if such speculations become less the preoccupation of solitary workers and more the shared work of an intellectual community. This ideal is not new. Its origin may be traced to the beginnings of the modern epoch, as is clearly seen in the remarks of Leibniz:

> If one could find characteristics or signs appropriate for expressing all our thoughts as clearly and exactly as arithmetic expresses numbers or analytic geometry expresses lines, we could in all subjects in so far as they are amenable to reasoning, accomplish what is done in arithmetic and geometry. Moreover we should be able to convince the world of what we had found or concluded since it would be easy to verify that calculation, either by doing it over again or by trying tests similar to that of casting out nines in arithmetic. And if someone doubted my results I should say to him: "Let us calculate Sir," and taking pen and ink we should soon settle the question.

BIBLIOGRAPHY

1. Barwise, J. "Scenes and other situations," *The Journal of Philosophy*, vol 78 (1981), 369 - 397.

2. Barwise, J. and J. Perry "Situations and attitudes," *The Journal of Philosophy*, vol 78 (1981), 668 - 691.

3. Boudreaux, J.C. "Defining General Structures," *Notre Dame Journal of Formal Logic*, vol 20 (1979), 465-488.

4. Boudreaux, J.C. "Frames versus Minimally Restricted Structures," *Notre Dame Journal of Formal Logic*, vol 21 (1980), 251-262.

5. Boudreaux, J.C. "Problem Solving and the Evolution of Programming Languages," in R. Jernigan, B.W. Hamill, and D.W. Weintraub, *The Role of Language in Problem Solving-I*, North-Holland, 1985; 103-126.

6. Carnap, R. *Meaning and Necessity: A Study in Semantics and Modal Logic*, University of Chicago Press, 1956.

7. De Kleer, J. and Brown, J.S. "A Qualitative Physics Based on Confluence," *Artificial Intelligence*, vol 24 (1984), 7-84.

8. Goodman, N. *The Structure of Appearance*. Bobbs-Merrill, 1966.

9. Hayes, P.J. "The Second Naive Physics Manifesto," in Hobbs and Moore.

10. Hobbs, J.R. and Moore, R.C. (eds.) *Formal Theories of the Commonsense World*, Ablex; Norwood, NJ, 1985.

11. McCarthy, J. "Programs with Common Sense," *Semantic Information Processing*, ed. M. Minsky, MIT Press; 1968; pp. 403-417.

12. McCarthy, J. and P.J. Hayes "Some Philosophical Problems from the Standpoint of Artificial Intelligence," in B. Meltzer and D. Michie, *Machine Intelligence* vol 4, Edinburgh University Press, 1969.

13. McCarthy, J. "First Order Theories of Individual Concepts and Propositions," in J.E. Hayes, D. Michie, L.I. Mikulick (eds), *Machine Intelligence*, Ellis Horwood, 1979; 129-147.

14. Salmon, N.U. *Reference and Essence*, Princeton University Press; Princeton, NJ, 1981.

15. Sowa, J.F. *Conceptual Structures: Information Processing in Mind and Machine*, Addison-Wesley; Reading, MA, 1984.

16. Wittgenstein, L. *Tractatus Logico-Philosophicus*, Routledge and Kegan Paul; London, 1961.

17. Wilensky, R. *LISPcraft*, W.W. Norton; New York, 1984.

QUESTION AND ANSWERS

SLATER

One of the problems I find with developing something along these lines is that until you get well up into the analytic hierarchy, and even high up in the analytic hierarchy, unless you get into things like measurable sets, you're very unlikely to have uniqueness of models.

BOUDREAUX

You never have uniqueness of models.

A CONSTRUCTIVE APPROACH TO VALIDATION *

Guillermo Arango and Peter Freeman

Department of Information and Computer Science
University of California
Irvine, California 92717, USA

1.0 INTRODUCTION

We are exploring a transformational paradigm for software construction which is based on the formal representation of knowledge about classes of application. Within this paradigm the validation of an *application domain* is an important issue. A domain will be defined as a structure which embodies the knowledge for some range of applications. There is no effective procedure to validate an arbitrary formal domain definition against applications which are part of a (non-formal) "real-world." This paper discusses some steps toward the development of *practical effective* procedures for domain validation. The approach is based on the idea of "pushing" the edge of the formal-informal boundary towards the real-world by rigorously recording factual and deep domain knowledge acquired from experts. Factual knowledge constitutes the base on which a *validation scaffolding* incorporating domain-specific knowledge is built. The validation scaffolding, in turn, supports the conceptual structure that constitutes the theory of the domain. An underlying assumption is that the validation process may be pushed arbitrarily far in order to satisfy our belief in the validity of a domain definition.

2.0 A DOMAIN-BASED PARADIGM FOR SOFTWARE CONSTRUCTION

2.1 The Draco Paradigm - The Draco Tool

Our research on the capture, representation and reuse of knowledge in the process of software construction has lead to the development of a paradigm for the construction and maintenance of software systems [Neighbors 84a, Neighbors 84b, Arango 86b]. The Draco paradigm is a method for constructing software systems from libraries of software components capturing domain-

---

* Support for this research has been provided by National Science Foundation grant MCS-83-04439, by Aluminum Company of America and the University of California MICRO grant 85-131 and by the Organization of American States fellowship 83607.

specific knowledge. The notion of a domain is fundamental to
the Draco paradigm. Informally, *a Draco-domain is an area of
captured expertise.* For example, we could consider separate
domains for arithmetic, relational databases, graphics, etc. A
slightly more explicit statement of this notion is: a Draco-
domain is a machine processable representation for the purpose
of software construction capturing our understanding of a
problem area.

The notion of a Draco-domain is that of a particular type of
representation of a slice of reality. This representation
captures a domain analyst's *understanding* for a slice of
reality in such way that a computer-based agent can use it for
some *purpose*. Thus, the representation must provide a conceptual structure rich enough to capture the common structures
from a class of problems as required for the implementation of
software systems from problem oriented specifications.

The Draco paradigm is an instance of a more general class of
transformational approaches to software construction[1]. The
Draco paradigm presumes that one will construct a number of
similar software programs. These programs share the property
that they operate on objects from one (or usually more) Draco-
domains. We use the expression *range of applications* or *application area* to stress our belief that *reuse* of captured knowledge would be (economically) effective only if it could be
applied to rather large *classes of similar problems* - or applications in the software engineering sense. That is, domain
analysis is not concerned with the capture of knowledge about a
particular problem e.g., the database system needed for the
Inventory Control System of company X. Rather, domain analysis
would address a more comprehensive class of application, e.g.,
the class of relational databases.

A *machine processable representation* of the Draco-domains must
be available to the Draco system prior to program construction.
These representations are currently constructed by hand. The
power of the software construction paradigm depends on having a
computer-based agent manage and perform the transformation of
problem-oriented specifications into executable code. The
description of a Draco-domain for the Draco system [Neighbors
84a] includes:

- a domain language describing a formal external notation for problem specification (a concession to human
  engineering);

- an abstract graph schema which provides a formal
  internal representation for the notation in terms of
  the domain semantics;

---

[1] Readers unfamiliar with the transformational approach to
programming should refer to [Partsch 83] for a broad
overview of transformation systems.

- domain parser which maps sentences from the domain language to the graph schema; a pretty printer mechanism provides the reverse mapping;

- domain semantics expressed as an (informal) set of concepts composed of objects, operators and relations;

- a set of refinements which map individual abstract concepts in the domain to configurations of concepts in *other* domains closer to a target implementation; and,

- a set of transformations, which map internal representations in a domain to equivalent internal representations in that *same* domain, generally used to effect optimizations.

The domains required to develop software for a given application area, and their relationships in terms of refinements can be viewed as constituting a "domain structure graph". A node in the graph represents a Draco-domain. Arcs in the graph indicate the existence of refinements from one Draco-domain to another. Such a graph indicate the refinement paths from high-level specification domains to low-level implementation domains. Thus, the semantics of a concept in a Draco-domain are defined through a *reductionistic process of abstraction substitution*, until a "ground-level", executable Draco-domain is reached. The concepts in the executable domain (i.e., programming languages) are in turn defined by the semantic interpretation of the underlying processing mechanisms. This paradigm provides a fully operational definition of a domain semantics.

2.2   Application Area, Domain or Micro-World?

We have briefly discussed the notion of application area/domain in the context of Draco. Similar notions have been developed by others within the field of software engineering, (see for example, [Balzer 85], [Borgida 85], [Barstow 85], [Fickas 85]). Furthermore, different communities have evolved different notions of what constitutes a *domain*. Software engineering, database and artificial intelligence share the following perspective for domain. Given,

- a loosely specified but not completely unspecified *range of applications*, and

- a *problem solving task* (requiring some kind of knowledge about that range of applications),

a domain is

- a set of interrelated *concepts* (a conceptual structure in Sowa's terminology [Sowa 84], which can generate a variety of empirical claims about the range of applications),

- which is cast in a *machine processable representation* (to support problem-solving by a computer-based agent).

This common perspective is grounded on two fundamental assumptions.

1. Reality can be objectively captured and represented in a machine processable form (i.e., as a bounded set of discrete facts, relationships, etc.); and

2. we can effectively map an *open* world into a *closed* world in which a machine could succeed in problem solving without human intervention.

In his critical examination of the underlying assumptions of Artificial Intelligence, H. Dreyfus [Dreyfus 79] offers refutations to such "universalist" claims. However, in appropriately qualified situations, *practical competence* can be achieved by a computer-based agent operating on a context-free model of a slice of reality. Success stories in the field of Expert Systems are proofs by existence that such goal a can be reached. There also seems to be consensus that we can successfully model a given situation in terms of a discrete set of facts *for a specific purpose*. Again, this conjecture is confirmed by experience - by the effectiveness of database systems and of some diagnosis expert systems or program generators. It is appropriate to re-emphasize here that our research is primarily concerned with the very specific purpose of generation of software systems.

2.3   A Definition of Domain

In this section we will present an informal definition of domain as an extension of the notion of domain in logic. We will also provide definitions, borrowed from logic, for concepts such as theory, interpretation, model, consistency, etc. The reader must be reminded that such definitions restrict (and sometimes conflict with) the informal meaning of those terms in everyday use. However, we believe that it would be inappropriate to re-invent existing well-established terminology.

In logic the notion of domain is related to the notion of *interpretation*. In propositional logic, an interpretation is an assignment of truth value to each of a set of propositional symbols in a sentence. The truth value of the sentence is then found through the application of a set of semantic rules (e.g., not, if-then, and, etc.). In predicate logic, the sentences involve terms; thus, an interpretation must include a set of objects, a *domain of individuals*, that provide meaning for those terms. An interpretation for a sentence must assign meaning to each of the sentence's symbols. It must assign domain elements to the constants and free variables, functions (over the domain) to the function symbols, and relations (over the domain) to the predicate symbols [Suppes 64],(in computer science, the concept of **binding** is a close analogue). Using this notion of interpretation the following definitions are standard in logic:

- a sentence is **universally valid** if and only if every interpretation of it in every non-empty domain of individuals is true.

- a formula Q **logically follows** from a formula P if and only if in every non-empty domain of individuals every interpretation which makes P true also makes Q true.

- a formula is **consistent** if and only if it has at least one true interpretation in some non-empty domain of individuals.

Definition: (The view held in logic and mathematics is that) a **theory** is a set of sentences in a well-defined linguistic system.

Definition: A set of individuals D is said to be a **model** of a theory T if there exists such a consistent interpretation of entities and operators of T by means of objects, relations and functions of D, so that all theorems of T describe facts observed in D.

It must be noted that we could define an arbitrary number of interpretation maps between a given theory and one (or more) sets of individuals. The set in the range of the interpretation map may be a model of the theory or not depending on whether **all** theorems (or sentences) of the theory correspond to facts in D.

Tarski's definition: "possible realization in which all valid sentences of a theory T are satisfied is called a model of T" assumes that a model is a non-linguistic[2] entity in which a theory is satisfied [Tarski 53].

J. Sneed [Sneed 76] has proposed a view of theories strongly based on the models of those theories rather than on the linguistic entities traditionally used to characterize the

---

[2] The literature in mathematics and physics is very rich in examples of **set-theoretic models**. For example, a model of the theory of groups can be any non-empty set *G* with a binary operation closed in *G*, associative with inverse and identity. Suppes [Suppes 61] argues that to define a model formally as a set-theoretical entity which is a certain kind of ordered tuple consisting of a set of objects and relations and operations on these objects is not to rule out the physical model of the kind which is appealing to the physicist, for the physical model may be simply taken to define the set of objects in the set-theoretical model.

models. Different formalisms could be adopted to represent the models, for example, first order logic, informal or formal set theory[3].

We share Sneed's view of considering the linguistic components *and* the models as a parts of a whole. In our definition of domain we capture those elements that we have previously incorporated in the informal notion.

Definition: A domain is the aggregation of

- a conceptual structure - sometimes called the *theory of the domain*, the theoretical component of the domain.

- a range of applications, (the non-theoretical component or anchor in some reality -- referred to as the set of *models of the domain*. The models of the domain may be represented either in a set-theoretical or logical form for the purpose of formal manipulation, *but consensus must exist on a map between them and a physical realization*).

- the interpretation map defining the semantics of the theoretical elements in terms of the models, i.e., the empirical claim of the theory.

A more detailed definition of the domain architecture is given in [Arango 86b]. Let us examine now the problem of domain validation.

3.0 THE PROBLEM OF DOMAIN VALIDATION

3.1 How Do We Validate Computer Software

At the risk of oversimplifying, we may view the software development process as a generic problem solving activity consisting of two major phases: problem definition and solution construction, or formalization and implementation using Barstow's terminology [Barstow 85]. In the context of Draco, the problem definition stage can be further split into two phases: domain construction and concrete-problem definition using the domain-specific notation. We may then speak of two major validation steps: we must first make sure that we are working on the *right problem* (in Draco terms, that we have a valid Draco-domain for the range of application sat hand), and only then, that we are *solving it right*.

---

[3] We will not dwell on representations here. In our research we are exploring the use of variations of Sowa's [Sowa 84] conceptual graphs, which can be shown equivalent to FOL propositions, and can be extended to incorporate higher order and model logic operators.

In the software engineering community there has been growing concern about the first validation phase. The adequacy of the requirements for a software product, i.e., their correctness, completeness and consistency must be thoroughly analyzed. Vague or untestable requirements leave the validity of the delivered product in doubt. Late discovery of requirements inadequacies is often very costly. Thus tools, formal notations, and informal techniques have been developed to provide a disciplined framework for expressing and evaluating requirements. Similar developments have been aimed at the solution design and construction stages [Freeman 84, Gehani 85].

Besides the work on tools and techniques for helping to produce problem definitions and solutions that meet some quality attributes, considerable research has been done in the field of verification and testing. The literature on software validation, [Deutsch 82, Hausen 84], discusses validation, verification, and testing techniques as a means to improve the "quality" of software. The term quality refers to a hierarchy of attributes including: reliability (adequacy -- correctness, completeness, consistency, robustness), testability (understandability, measurability), usability, efficiency, transportability, maintainability, etc. [Adrion 82]. The definition of some of these qualitative attributes is still a matter of controversy. Adrion *et al* [Adrion 82] offer a comprehensive survey of this "most discouraging area of research". Why discouraging?

There is an irremediable validation problem in the first stage of the problem solving process. To validate software requirements means to establish a map between an non-formal world and a formal object (the statement of requirements), and there is no formal procedure for achieving this.

Even if we have a formal definition of an arbitrary problem, there is no algorithm to find a formal proof of the validity of a given solution (as Church proved for FOL), or to find a reliable, valid and complete test criteria [Howden 76].

Some of the difficulties for testing software have been blamed on an insufficient theoretical basis from which to relate the behavior of software to verification. Should start asking, are structural attributes the appropriate raw materials for software validation? If what we wish to validate is how well a piece of software captures knowledge about slice of reality and how this knowledge determines its behavior, the actual (implemented) structure of software might turn out to be a hindrance. Since the days of fastidious binary coding, the history of software engineering shows a consistent trend towards improved abstraction and notational mechanism to support problem solving. We should start looking at software validation at a different conceptual level than the structural properties of implemented software.

Besides, some of these techniques have either high customization or application costs (e.g., simulation and symbolic execution), or unproved applicability in practice (proof of correctness) [*Adrion 82*]. Freeman [Freeman 83] has long advocated the explicit capture and reuse of product **as well as** process information in SE. It is time to consider validation knowledge, not as disposable matter, but as a very valuable resource that can be **reused** on instances of similar problems (i.e., belonging to the same domain). The notion of domain as defined above offers a promising context for supporting this type of reusability. It is interesting to note that Adrion *et al.* conclude from their survey that the most successful among the many techniques used to validate software, have been the **manual** techniques, such as walk-throughs, reviews and inspections, applied to all stages of the software life cycle. Furthermore, they acknowledge the irremediable non-formal-formal gap in requirements analysis by recognizing that disciplined manual techniques will continue to be the key verification technique. The term "manual" is being used as an euphemism for "done by a human". The paradox here is that its success depends precisely on the fact that there is very little manual manipulation in those techniques. Rather, the key element is **human interpretation**, an essentially intellectual activity. This motivates our note in the definition of a domain, in the sense that the physical realization of formal models should be "obvious" to the community of users of the domain. Finally, there seems to be growing consensus on integration of validation with software development. Although we will not explore this point here, let us note that the approach to validation we propose is intimately related to the process of domain construction [Arango 86b].

3.2 From the Non-formal to the Formal

The lack of effective procedures to bridge the non-formal-formal gap may lead us to ask, "Is the situation hopeless?" We contend it is not. The effectiveness of disciplined "manual" inspection techniques show that humans can do it rather well. The key could be to provide humans with adequate support for the validation task - appropriate abstractions and notations to improve understanding and enforce discipline.

When confronted with the task of validation we could start by asking ourselves, "what kind of a problem is this? Are there solutions for this kind of problem? If so, does the type of the problem suggest the type of the solution?"

We identify validation as an instance of a "derivation problem" [Amarel 71]. Derivation problems are characterized by problem conditions in the form of properties that the solution **boundaries** must satisfy. The construction of a solution proceeds by "anchoring" the solution path on the given boundaries and extending it piece wise to meet the other boundaries or path segments that develop from them.

> We are given specific problem conditions in the form of **parts** of a solution description, and we are asked to complete the description by using given rules for solution construction -- in such a manner that the

initially given parts will be well integrated in the
solution structure. [Amarel 71, p. 414]

Polya suggests that this is typical of deductive reasoning
problems within formal systems.

> When we have to prove or disprove a mathematical prop-
> osition stated in the most usual form, the hypothesis
> and the conclusions of the proposition are appropri-
> ately called the **principal parts** of our problem. In
> fact, these principal parts deserve our special atten-
> tion. To prove a proposition we should discover a
> binding logical link between the principal parts
> ...[Polya 81, Vol. I, p. 121]

Within the context of domain validation, we may ask, "what are
the principal parts in the validation task? Which kind of
solutions are we expected to produce?" We can reformulate the
validation problem as: show that a domain theory is relevant
by discovering interpretation links between its parts and the
real-world oriented description of reality. That is, *given*:

1. existing data about the application domain, as
   perceived by a community of users represented in
   some formal notation (in practice the **knowledge
   sources** could be many: expert problem solvers,
   existing software systems or documentation of
   software systems, textbooks, research papers,
   etc.).

2. some conceptualization of the knowledge in the
   domain acquired from domain experts -- i.e., we
   will not be concerned, at this point, with issues
   of concept or theory formation.

develop an explicit interpretation map linking the data to the
conceptual knowledge acquired from the domain experts.

What does it mean for a domain theory to be "appropriate"? In
the empirical sciences the two major purposes of a theory are:
to describe phenomena in the world of our experience and to
establish general principles by means of which phenomena can be
explained and predicted. The power to predict is the essential
attribute by which empirical theories are judged as scientific.

What is the analogue of prediction for the case of domain theories? That the software systems specified and constructed
using the domain theory behave according to user expectations
in the application domain. This agrees exactly with the informal sense of "validation" as used in software engineering.

"Testing" a domain theory is out of the question. It would
require an indefinite number of programs in executable form,
descriptions of their expected behavior, means for observing
each program's behavior, and methods for determining whether
the observed behavior corresponds to the expected behavior. We
need some assurance of the effectiveness of the theory

"intensionally" as opposed to "extensionally." In other words, we need a way of constructing the interpretation map rigorously and explicitly, so that experts and users may *believe* in the theory and be ready to cope with future anomalies through a systematic approach to domain evolution.

4.0   AN ARCHITECTURE FOR VALIDATION

In this section we will propose a general architecture for representing the principal parts of the validation problem.

C. Hempel [Hempel 62] likens a scientific theory to a complex spatial network: its terms are represented by knots, while the threads connecting them correspond in part to definitions and, in part, to the fundamental and derivative hypotheses included in the theory. The whole systems floats, as it were, above the plane of observation and is anchored to it by rules of interpretation. Hempel's metaphor helps to illustrate our proposal: the concepts in a domain theory form a complex system which is anchored to a rigorous representation (the "observation language" in traditional scientific parlance) of the domain data through "interpretation strings". These strings are not part of the theory, but of the interpretation and constitute what we will call the *validation scaffolding*. Concepts in the theory are linked to observational data by virtue of those interpretive validating connections. We can ascend from the data to the theory, proceed (through the conceptual structure to other points in the theory from which another interpretive string permits us to descend to the plane of observation.

As mentioned in the previous section, we view a domain as a whole composed of a rigorous representation of data from a range of applications, a conceptual structure (imposed on that data), and a validation scaffolding which uses the data as foundation to support the conceptual structure.

4.1   The Domain Data

The data of the application domain corresponds to *evidential knowledge* shared by the domain experts and the community of users. Let us assume for example that we are interested in validating a "traffic-control domain" for the construction of traffic control software. In this context, evidential knowledge could be expressed by sentences such as: there are cars, cars come in different sizes, there are green lights, cars are driven by people who ride in the cars (i.e., no remote controlled cars!), cars may crash at intersections, red is a color, streets are divided into lanes, etc. which my be relevant for the purpose of developing a theory of traffic control or not (e.g., some cars have license plates from other states, there is a newspaper stand on the corner of Campus Dr. and Verano Rd., signal posts are either wood or steel pipe, etc.). The domain data provides a sketch of the set of potential models of the domain theory. It provides us with a rough definition of this slice of reality.

By constraining the non-theoretical vocabulary to that representable using a given formalism, we are in effect establishing the standards of an "observational language". This is the case for the empirical sciences [Hempel 62].

The evidential quality of the domain data is a key issue. By stipulating that everybody agrees on the meaning of those non-theoretical statements we are in effect "closing" an otherwise open world. Closing the domain at this level provides a direct anchor for the shared semantics of non-theoretical terms. This helps (although it is not sufficient) to avoid the infinite-regression problem[4] triggered by explanation seeking questions, such as, "Why is concept *X* an adequate concept in our domain theory?"

The definition of the set of factual (non-theoretical) elements in the domain pushes the formal edge of the informal-formal gap to the point where bridging the gap can be accomplished best by people.

4.2 The Conceptual Structure

Problem solvers in a given application area develop a sort of conceptual map. They impose (or elicit) a conceptual framework on the mass of factual evidence available to them. Facts do not dictate the outcome of the problem solver's choice of explanatory frameworks. However, this choice is not arbitrary. It is strongly restricted by pragmatic concerns -- the ability to predict and control. A result of the concept selection process (we do not make any claims at this point on how it occurs) is the emergence of theoretical language. Let us take, for example, a possible sentence in the domain theory for traffic:

> When a *vehicle* arrives at an *intersection* if the *corresponding traffic-light* is *red* the vehicle may *request permission* to proceed by stopping at the *corresponding request position*.

Such a simple rule is loaded with theoretical terms, which are the product of a complex conceptualization process. For example, take the term "vehicle". It stands for a generalization of a the notion of car, truck, bus, van, etc. and excludes other vehicles on the basis of world knowledge (e.g., planes do not ride on streets) or of hidden technological assumptions (e.g., bicycles are so light that they cannot effect changes on the pressure sensors in the pavement - ad hoc buttons are provided for cyclists). The term "red" in the rule, plays quite a different role than in non-theoretical descriptions. The issue here is red opposed to green or yellow. Shades of red, brightness, size, shape of the light, are not relevant as long as the

---

[4] N. Rescher, on The problem of Explanatory Ultimates, pp. 140-145, [Rescher 70].

light is visible and differentiable from the yellow and green lights.

4.3 The Validation Scaffolding

To validate such a sentence requires us to construct an interpretation map linking each of the terms in the sentence to models in the domain data set. The validation scaffolding makes this mapping explicit. The scaffolding enables us to examine, both the validity of the theory and the meaning of the theoretical terms.

Let us take for example the concept of **corresponding request position.** Briefly, a request position is a sector of the traffic lane close to street intersection where slabs of pavement have pressure sensors attached. The traffic-control node at the intersection can thus detect the presence of a car waiting to cross and acknowledge the request for permission to cross by setting the traffic-lights appropriately. This informal definition appeals in turn to deeper knowledge. For example, the term "corresponding" indicates that there could be many such request positions but that only one is appropriate.

Different kinds of knowledge are explicitly incorporated in the validation scaffolding:

- Domain-specific *factual* knowledge for example: "only two streets meet at intersections" -- a good street map of the city is sufficient to corroborate this. The threshold for the granularity of this type of knowledge is entirely subjective and related to the notion of "evidence".

- Some knowledge is the result of **logic inferences** from factual knowledge or the results of other inferences. For example, "there are at least four different groups of request positions at any given intersection", can be derived from the premises: "only two streets meet at each intersection" and "each street has two ways with at least one lane in each" and "there is one request position for each lane" and some knowledge of elementary geometry, which points to the next class.

- Some concepts appeal to **underlying theories**, for example, a simple theory of control loops. By stopping at the "corresponding" request position, the driver-car entity is acting as the **agent** in a control loop that requires of an agent to effect a request of service on a control node (by means of a sensor connected to the node) and to be able to recognize the acknowledgment of the request by reading some signal. Note that this brief account mixes elements of a physical model (e.g., assuming physical connections between sensor, node and signal, power sources, etc.) and functional (the role of agent, the request-permission cycle, etc.).

- There are also *domain-specific assumptions*. For example, driving consistently on one lane derives from a regulation - which, although it is enforced by the police does not guarantee actual behavior. Thus, "corresponding" in "corresponding request position" has the meaning of "the lane on which the car was riding".

This grouping corresponds roughly with the classes proposed by Clancey [Clancey 84] in his taxonomy of MYCIN's rules - world fact and identification rules, domain fact rules and causal rules. This correspondence is not accidental, the validation scaffolding is meant to behave like a knowledge base in the expert system sense. We expect we could to move up and down the interpretation map between the domain theory and its models by searching the scaffolding knowledge in a forward or backward chaining manner, collecting along the way all pertinent definitions, assumptions, constraints, etc. about particular concepts in the theory or models of the theory. This process is similar to the notion of justification implemented in rule-based expert systems for diagnosis [Buchanan 84] [Davis 82]. Research done on the Integrated Diagnostic Model by Fink *et al*. [Fink 85] show the feasibility of incorporating in a single framework a similar combination of "shallow" and "deep" knowledge to support explanation.

5.0   TOWARDS A PRACTICAL EFFECTIVE PROCEDURE

A domain theory is a conceptual structure that we somewhat arbitrarily impose on some perceived slice of reality. The purpose of the validation scaffolding is to reveal how the imposed conceptual structure relates to the data set through a web of inferences augmented with (extra logical) domain-specific knowledge. It has been shown by A. Church and R. Carnap [Suppes 64, Carnap 62] that even if we could treat the factual knowledge in a domain as a set of *premises*, and the conceptual structures as a hypothesis to be shown to be true, there do not exist effective procedures to develop the proofs. In the context of deductive logic it must be noted that the rules of deduction are rules of permission and of prohibition. These do not support any type of prescription for how to prove implication. In the context of inductive logic, *c* the degree of confirmation is not a computable function in general - quantitative inductive logic is useful only in restricted domains where statistical methods are used for the description of distributions of certain properties, in those cases, inductive inferences take the form of statistical inferences.

Since our pragmatic goal is to realize some effective procedure for domain validation, we will assume that the intelligent agents that were responsible for the process of concept formation could also produce supporting evidence of the relevancy and accuracy of the concepts produced, - the prime matter for constructing the validation scaffolding. Under this assumption, to validate is to make the supporting evidence explicit, in order to induce a broader community into holding the domain theory. The validation question can than be re-formulated in logical terms for a deductive context as: given E, h and an alleged proof that E implies h, find an answer to the question whether the alleged proof is really a proof [Carnap 62]. In an inductive context: Given: E, h and r and an alleged proof that $c(h,E) = r$, find an answer to the question whether the alleged proof is correct.

In the deductive case, a proof of implication requires either: that a sequence of sentences leading from E to h be constructed according to the rules of deduction, or that a proof in the metalanguage leading to "E implies h" be produced.

In both cases each step in the sequence must consist of the application of a single rule. This is not the case in practice. In the strictest sense, the method for testing proofs is not effective. However, these procedures may be considered *practically effective*. The person testing a proof, if not satisfied with an implication may ask the author to split the implication into simpler ones. This method is fraught with dangers as De Millo *et al*. have shown in [DeMillo 79]. In the inductive cases we can approach the problem in the same way. The notion of justification as implemented, for example, in MYCIN-class diagnosis expert systems is an instance of the first approach. The user is shown a trace of the sequence of rules that fired and together with some (probabilistic) confidence or confirmation weights associated to each fired rule, from E to h. Proofs of the second type tend to be more satisfying. They employ natural language as the metalanguage and subjected to the same practical problems as in the deductive case.

In summary, we view the validation process as a domain-centered activity based on human-interpretation. We assume a formal representation for domain data and domain theory. We propose to facilitate validation by:

- pushing the non-formal/formal border until consensus on the semantics of the non-theoretical terms is reached among the user community;

- constructing a validation scaffolding following rules of logical deduction or induction (depending on the availability of conclusive or only supporting evidence) augmented with domain-specific annotations to enhance the understandability of the atomic validation steps (beams in the scaffolding);

- if a validation step is not clear enough for someone inspecting the scaffolding (yes, a very subjective notion!), the step should be refined into a sub-steps until the validation step becomes clear. These refinements substitute the original step and must be recorded accordingly.

6.0 ON RELATED WORK

It was mentioned above that validation should be considered as an integral part of the process of software development. In our view, the validation of a domain is a process that cannot be separated from its construction. Our approach to domain construction [Arango 86b] is driven by a model of domain-specific facts and causal relations together with a theory of how acquired knowledge can be shown valid. Our current research is aimed at generating practical effective procedures for identifying and capturing concepts in the domain theory, and to help define their semantics and semantic constraints based on an explicit validation scaffolding. There - construction of a domain theory go hand in hand with its validation. There is a strong parallel between our research goals and those of the MORE system [Kahn 85]. The MORE project is focused on the automation of knowledge acquisition for building domain models to be used in diagnosis.

In contrast, our domain models are to be used for software specification and implementation. The model driving the process of construction is intended to persuade the constructor and the intended user community of the validity of the domain and its graceful evolution.

One way of "testing" the adequacy of a domain theory is to observe the actual behavior of software derived from the theory. The Draco paradigm for software construction provides us with the mechanism for deriving executable implementations from software specifications defined using the domain notations. The paradigm is an instance of a pure operational-specification approach in which the semantics of a concept in a domain are defined by (refined into) concepts in underlying domains and ultimately in terms of some processor's instruction set. Where do the specifications for each refinement come from?

The evidential knowledge formally represented as the domain data and the domain-specific knowledge available from the validation scaffolding capture the semantics of the domain concepts and are thus the basis for the specification of the refinements. Furthermore, the appeal to underlying theories during the validation of a given domain theory is reflected in the introduction of subsidiary Draco-domains in the Draco-domain graph structure required for software construction. For example, in the graph structure for the Draco-domain *Traffic-Control* there would be a subsidiary Draco-domain *Control-Loops* capturing knowledge for the implementation of the functional aspects of control loops.

Evolution is an important issue in theory construction in general. There are several sources of change that may affect the domain theory: changes in the set of domain data, in the domain users' relevance criteria, or in the users' knowledge (e.g., they have learned something new). Evolution includes validation over time. Evolution is a key issue in theory construction in general and this is being recognized in software engineering as well. As R. Balzer [Balzer 85] puts it, enhancement, not initial development, is the central software engineering activity. A fundamental reason for keeping an explicit validation scaffolding is to be able to allow for a graceful evolution of the domain over time. This view has been also explored in the context of the Explainable Expert Systems approach by Neches *et al*. [Neches 85]. Imagine, for example, that after having the computer controlled traffic-control system operating, the city pedestrians complain of a very serious oversight in the requirements analysis: they have no means for resetting traffic lights and sometimes cannot "legally" walk across intersections. The validation scaffolding of the *Traffic-Control* domain, by making explicit the conceptual connections between the operation of the lights, request positions, function of control loops, etc. allows the "domain maintainer" to bring the domain from its current stable state (invalidated by the pedestrian's complaint) into a new stable state valid to the extent that the pedestrian's requirements are also satisfied. The new validation scaffolding reveals for example, a new type of agent in the traffic system (in addition to heavy-vehicles and cyclists) which defines new relations with the existent agents and objects and new theoretical constraints.

It must be noted that we have already explored this type of support for evolution in the field of software implementation [Arango 86a]. In that context, the software specification behaves as a theory, and all the possible implementations as possible models of the theory. The Draco paradigm defines an inverted "implementation scaffolding" in which each beam corresponds to the refinement (or implementation) of a concept.

Maintenance of an implementation can be done by regenerating the application using a transformed implementation scaffolding (i.e., using a different set of components or implementation design decisions).

7.0 SUMMARY

We are exploring a transformational paradigm for software construction which is based on the formal representation of knowledge about classes of applications. Within this paradigm the validation of an **application domain** is an important issue. A domain is a formal object which embodies the knowledge for some range of applications. There is no effective procedure to validate an arbitrary formal domain definition against applications which are part of an informal real-world. We have discussed some steps toward the development of practical effective procedures for domain validation under the assumption that validation steps can be carried arbitrarily far, both in terms of pushing the formal boundary towards the informal real-world and in terms of the granularity of the explanation steps uncovering deeper domain knowledge. We have put emphasis on the need for keeping a rigorous and explicit record of the validation scaffolding supporting our belief in a domain theory. Ultimately, belief in the knowledge recorded in the scaffolding is a state as subjective as belief in a mathematical proof.

It could be argued that the cost of developing the scaffolding of a domain theory could be very high. We can offer two answers to this objection: the scaffolding is a supporting mechanism and direct by-product of the process of domain construction. It is expensive in the same sense that documenting the results of systems analysis and software design is expensive. Secondly, domain construction is in itself an expensive job, which is justified by the assumption of its intensive reuse in the specification and implementation of software for a certain range of applications. By keeping a rigorous record of the validation scaffolding we preserve a valuable asset for future reuse.

Our current research is focused on the integration of the notion of validation within the domain construction and domain evolution processes. Some of the ideas are being tested on toy problem domains before attempting to tackle interesting real-world ones. We believe that current developments in artificial intelligence-related technologies, such as knowledge representations, belief maintenance systems [Barr 82, Doyle 79], and rule-based systems will provide the necessary leverage to mechanize many of the clerical aspects of the validation process.

BIBLIOGRAPHY

[Adrion 82] Adrion W., Branstad M., and Cherniavsky J., "Validation, Verification and Testing of Computer Software", *ACM Comp. Surveys*, Vol. 14, No. 2, pp. 159-192.

[Arango 86a] G. Arango, I. Baxter, P. Freeman and C. Pidgeon, "A Transformation-based Paradigm of Software Maintenance", *IEEE Software*, Vol. 3, No. 5, May 1986.

[Arango 86b] G. Arango, *Domain In Software Engineering*, Dept. of Information and Computer Science, U. of California, Irvine, 1986.

[Amarel 71] Amarel S., "Representation and Modelling in Problems of Program Formation", in *Machine Intelligence* 6, (eds. Meltzer Michie), pp. 411-466, American Elsevier, 1971.

[Balzer 85] R. Balzer, "Automated Enhancement of Knowledge Representations", *Procs. IJCAI 85*, pp. 203-207, 1985.

[Barr 82] A. Barr, E. Feigenbaum, *The Handbook of Artificial Intelligence*, Vol. 2, W. Kaufman, Inc., Los Altos, CA, 1982.

[Barstow 85] D. Barstow, "Domain-Specific Automatic Programming", *IEEE Trans. on Softw. Eng.*, Vol. SE-11, No. 11, Nov. 1985, pp. 1321-1336.

[Borgida 85]   A. Borgida, "Features of Languages for the Development of Information Systems at the Conceptual Level", *IEEE Software*, Vol. 2, No. 1, pp. 63-73, Jan. 1985.

[Buchanan 84]   B. Buchanan, E. Shortliffe, Eds., *Rule-Based Expert Systems*, Addison-Wesley, Reading, MA, 1984.

[Carnap 62]   Carnap R., *Logic Foundations of Probability*, The University of Chicago Press, 1962.

[Clancey 84]   W. Clancey, "Extensions to Rules for Explanation and Tutoring", in *Rule-Based Expert Systems*, (Eds.), B. Buchanan and E. Shortliffe, Addison-Wesley, Reading, MA, 1984, pp. 531-570.

[Davis 82]   R. Davis, "Teiresias, Applications of Meta-Level Knowledge", in "Knowledge-Based Systems in Artificial Intelligence", (Eds.), R. Davis and D. Lenat, McGraw Hill, New York, 1982.

[DeMillo 79]   R. De Millo, R. Lipton and A. Perlis, "Social Processes and Proofs of Theorems and Programs", *Communications of the ACM*, Vol. 22, No. 5, pp. 271-280, May 1979.

[Deutsch 82]   M. Deutsch, *Software Verification and Validation - Realistic Project Approaches*, Prentice-Hall Inc., Englewood Cliffs, NJ, 1982.

[Doyle 79]   J. Doyle, "A Truth Maintenance System", *Artificial Intelligence*, Vol. 12, No. 3, 1979, pp. 231-272.

[Dreyfus 79]   H. Dreyfus, *What Computers Can't Do - The Limits of Artificial Intelligence*, Harper and Row, New York, 1979.

[Fickas 85]   S. Fickas, "Automating the Transformational Development of Software", *IEEE Trans. on Softw. Eng.*, Vol. SE-11, No. 11, Nov. 1985, pp. 1268-1277.

[Fink 85]   P. Fink, J. Lusth and J. Duran, "A General Expert System Design for Diagnostic Problem Solving", *IEEE Trans. on Pattern Analysis and Machine Intelligence*, Vol. PAMI-7, No. 5, Sep. 85, pp. 553-560.

[Freeman 83]   P. Freeman, "Reusable Software Engineering - Concepts and Research Directions" *Proc. ITT Workshop on Reusability in Programming*, Newport, RI, 1983, pp. 2-16.

[Freeman 84]   P. Freeman and A. Wasserman, (Eds.), *IEEE Tutorial on Software Design Techniques*, IEEE Computer Society Press, Silver Spring, MD, 1984.

[Gehani 85]   N. Gehani and A. McGettrick, (Eds.), *Software Specification Techniques*, Addison-Wesley, Reading, MA, 1985

[Hempel 62]   C. Hempel, *Fundamentals of Concept Formation in Empirical Science*, The University of Chicago Press, 1962.

[Hausen 84]   H-L. Hausen (Ed.), Procs. of the Symposium on Software Validation, Darmstadt, FRG, Sep. 1983. *Software Validation*, North-Holland, New York, 1984.

[Howden 76]   W. Howden, "Reliability of the path testing strategy", *IEEE Trans. on Softw. Eng.*, Vol. SE-2, No. 3, 1976.

[Kahn 85]   G. Kahn, S. Nowlan and J. McDermott, "Strategies for Knowledge Acquisition", *IEEE Trans. on Pattern Analysis and Machine Intelligence*, Vol. PAMI-7, No. 5, Sep. 1985, pp. 511-522.

[Neches 85]   R. Neches, W. Swartout and J. Moore, "Enhanced Maintenance and Explanation of Expert Systems Through Explicit Models of Their Development", *IEEE Trans. on Softw. Eng.*, Vol. SE-11, No. 11, Nov. 1985, pp. 1337-1350.

[Neighbors 84a]   J. Neighbors, "The Draco Approach to Constructing Software from Reusable Components', *IEEE Trans. Software Eng.*, Vol. SE-10, pp. 564-573, Sep. 1984.

[Neighbors 84b]   J. Neighbors, G. Arango and J. C. Leite, *Draco 1.3 Users Manual*, Tech. Report No. 130, Dept. of Information and Computer Science, U. of California, Irvine, CA., 1984.

[Partsch 83]   H. Partsch and R. Steinbruggen, "Program Transformation Systems", *ACM Computing Surveys*, pp. 199--236, Vol. 15, No.3, September 1983.

[Polya 81]   G. Polya, *Mathematical Discovery*, J. Wiley and Sons, Vol. I, p. 118, 1981.

[Rescher 70]   N. Rescher, *Scientific Explanation*, The Free Press, New York, 1970.

[Sneed 76]   J. Sneed, "Philosophical Problems in the Empirical Science of Science: A Formal Approach", *Erkenntnis*, D. Reidel Publ., Vol. 10, No. 3, Oct. 1976, pp. 115-146.

[Sowa 84]   J. Sowa, *Conceptual Structures*, Addison-Wesley, Reading, MA, 1984.

[Suppes 61]   P. Suppes, "A Comparison of the Meaning and Uses of Models in Mathematics and the Empirical Sciences", in *The Concept and Role of the Model in Mathematics and the Social Sciences*, (Ed.) H. Freudenthal, D. Reidel, Dordrecht, Holland, 1961, pp. 163-267.

[Suppes 64]   P. Suppes, *Introduction to Logic*, D. Van Nostrand Co., New York, 1964.

[Tarski 53]   A. Tarski, A. Mostowski, and R. M. Robinson (Eds.), *Undecidable Theories*, Amsterdam, North-Holland Publishing Co., 1953.

QUESTION AND ANSWER PERIOD

BOUDREAUX

Do you have any idea as to how one could elicit domain knowledge? One of the problems that I'm having in getting people to tell me the truth is not that they lie, but that they really haven't a thought about how to express answers to the questions which I'm formulating for them. I can get the obvious truths about a manufacturing domain easily, but those are almost never what I want. It's the exceptions and the qualifications that turn out to be interesting to me. Have you thought about how to elicit that kind of information?

ARANGO

In the talk I said that it was a tough problem we are currently working on. (That means we don't have the answers.) I can tell you which directions we are following. When I said I consider a domain to be a scientific theory, I implied that the model that guides our process of knowledge acquisition is that of scientific explanation. There is a rich tradition of studies in what scientific explanation is. What we're trying to do right now is to put together a model that would guide the knowledge engineer into keeping the expert honest in his account of the problem. That's why we're trying to include facts, domain-specific assumptions that could be hidden in the problem solving process. We try to identify laws and the way in which laws are applied over several applications to formalize subtheories that people can be using. We also acknowledge the fact that scientific explanation, or explanation in general, is a pragmatic process that has a meaning in a particular context and depends on the purpose of the questioner and the answerer. That's why the human is always going to be in the loop. For example, there is this old anecdote about the minister asking Billy Sutton, the bank robber (in jail), "But Billy, why do you rob banks?" And Billy answering, "Well, that's where the money is." What is the point here? The point is that when you ask a question like "Why do you rob banks," you may be putting emphasis on banks, or on the word robbing. The minister was asking why do you rob as opposed to doing some decent work. Billy Sutton was thinking of why do you rob banks as opposed to, say, book stores or laundromats. In the studies of scientific explanation a lot of work has been done on these types of problems. We have, for example, the notion of contrast spaces, so in the particular case of that question, you have a contrast space associated with robbing, that is, robbing as opposed to other activities, and another with banks as opposed to other institutions or businesses. We're trying to compile a methodology for knowledge acquisition based on a formal treatment of scientific explanation.

SLATER

One of the reasons it's hard to get domain-specific knowledge out of users is that they don't know what they are doing. I think that none of us knows what we're doing when we're programming; I know that I have fewer bugs when I listen to Mozart when I'm programming than if I listen to Beethoven.

ARANGO

As I said before I acknowledge the fact that we don't have the final answers. I think that that's precisely the challenge. In a way, what we haven't done in Software Engineering yet is to make explicit the knowledge we are applying in our everyday tasks. In other engineering disciplines people have <u>formalized</u> and <u>reuse</u> a body of knowledge. That is the main theme of our work.

LANGUAGE AND REASONING: SORTING OUT SOCIOPRAGMATIC
AND PSYCHOPRAGMATIC FACTORS

Marcelo Dascal

Tel Aviv University
currently at the
Netherlands Institute for Advanced Study
Meyboomlaan 1, 2242 PR Wassenaar, The Netherlands

1. Reasoning, in the form of some sort of inferential process, seems to be at the core of problem solving. The most natural hypothesis to account for this fact is to assume that people employ a system of logic to perform such inferential processes. Yet, this supposed logical competence has proven to be quite elusive when one attempts to trace it experimentally. Instead of reasoning "logically," subjects in reasoning experiments persistently incur "errors" and stubbornly stick to their "wrong" ways, even when the fallacious nature of their reasoning is pointed out to them.

There are roughly two ways to explain this fact: 1) the logic in peoples' heads is not the logic of logic textbooks, but rather some "natural logic" with quite different rules. 2) The standard logical competence is there in peoples' heads, but it is not fully manifested in behaviour because of the interference of "disturbing" factors.

I think the first possibility is almost certainly true. For one, logicians, following Frege's lead, have insisted in the anti-psychologistic nature of their enterprise. The rules they describe are not the so-called "laws of thought" but rather abstract rules of an axiomatic system, which at best correspond to an ideal form of rationality, not necessarily having any psychological counterpart. Secondly, logicians themselves have become increasingly unsatisfied with "standard" logic and have developed systems of alternative logics, e.g., the so-called relevance logics or the more recent para-consistent logics, which differ significantly from traditional standard logic. Nevertheless, it would seem natural to suppose that even without assuming a necessary correspondence between logic and psychology, at least some basic rules, extremely intuitive in their nature, guide peoples' behaviour in some kinds of tasks. Among these rules we might mention, Modus Ponens, Modus Tollens, Double Negation, etc. Furthermore, such rules are usually kept as a part of any of all but the more "revolutionary" systems of logic. They should, therefore, be considered to be the core of any logical "competence" that people might eventually possess. And yet, performance in some reasoning tasks is found to be significantly inconsistent even with these basic rules. Of course, one could deny, on the basis of such inconsistency, that people actually have a general logical competence at all, and go on to characterize their reasoning performance in terms of ad hoc strategies of various kinds adapted for the nature of specific tasks - a position indeed adopted by some researchers.

Instead of pursuing this line of inquiry, in this paper I want rather to explore the second - usually favored - alternative, for it brings into sharp focus the issue of the role of language in reasoning and in problem solving. My purpose is mainly to point out implicit assumptions in current theorizing and research about this problem and to suggest some conceptual distinctions that may help to clarify the issues, to reinterpret the results of some experiments, and to suggest further empirical research. For reasons of space I will restrict my remarks to a consideration of deductive reasoning, though the distinctions here proposed would apply as well to a discussion of other forms of reasoning, notably to some kinds of bias found in inductive reasoning and well-known through the work of Tversky and Kahneman (e.g., 1974).

2. In considering "disturbing" factors that affect performance in reasoning tasks, two non-exclusive possibilities have been much discussed in the literature. One of them consists in attributing these factors to temporary lapses, distractions, and undue influence of the content rather than the form of the problem (see Henle, 1962). This view assumes a distinction between competence and performance - a distinction well-known in the work of linguists of the Chomskyan school - and describes the disturbing factors as performance factors that do not indicate the absence of a logical competence, but affect the overall behaviour in specific ways. The other possibility stresses rather the influence of contextual factors such as the task environment, the subject's expectations as well as problems arising in connection with the interpretation of the formulation of the problem and of the instructions given by the experimenter.

It is within this second possibility that the role of language in reasoning is usually highlighted, and it is brought in by way of what is usually called the "pragmatic" aspects of language use. Thus, Fillenbaum (1975) has shown that so-called pragmatic inferences or implicatures (Grice, 1975) play a role in performance in reasoning tasks involving conditional sentences. Along similar lines, Geiss and Zwicky (1971) suggested that the use of a conditional sentence in certain contexts invites its interpretation not as a conditional but as a biconditional, and hence induces certain reasoning "errors." Similarly, Wason (1965) has shown the role of the context in the interpretation of negation and, more recently, the role of background knowledge and other pragmatic factors in the understanding of such sentences as "no head injury is too trivial to be ignored" (Wason, 1981). The ability to understand implicatures, to take into account the background, to rely upon one's expectations, etc., is clearly, from a linguistic point of view, not a marginal or disturbing factor - a factor to be ascribed to performance - but rather a central element in our ability to understand language. Therefore, most linguists would agree that a pragmatic component should be included in the description of linguistic competence. Yet, from a logical point of view, from the point of view of performing a reasoning task, such factors might eventually be considered along with distractions, lapses and so on, as a disturbing performance factor. Let us consider a few examples of these so-called pragmatic effects.

a. Sentence Verification and Negation

Verification tasks have been widely used to test the effect of negation in the understanding and processing of information. The task consists of presenting a sentence (affirmative or negative) and a picture and asking the subject to say whether they match or not. According to Evans (1982, p. 30) "the one undisputed result that all these experiments (and similar subsequent ones) have in common is that negatives are reliably more difficult to process than affirmatives." Yet, Wason, who conducted himself the earliest experiments of this kind, realized later that the effect of negation was not due to mere syntactic complexity (i.e., to the presence of a negative morpheme), but was also the result of semantic and perhaps pragmatic factors. He hypothesized that negative sentences were sometimes harder to assess, not only because of their syntactic complexity, but because they involved the existence (in the context) of some prior presupposition that was denied by the negative sentence (Wason, 1965). Furthermore, he discovered that by varying the context in which a negative sentence was presented, the higher latency of response for such sentences would in fact be cancelled out. For example, if subjects were shown a display of numbered coloured lights in which seven were red and one was blue, it was found that a negative of the form "nr. 3 is not red" was more readily verified than a sentence of the form "nr. 5 is not blue." Wason conjectured that this was so because in that particular context the former was more "natural" than the latter. But this is just another way of saying that the readiness with which a sentence is interpreted is a joint function of the sentence (including its syntactic and semantic structure) and of the context of utterance or presentation, i.e., of syntactic-semantic *and* pragmatic factors.

b. Validity of Syllogisms and the Atmosphere Effect

Woodworth and Sells (1935) suggested that one explanation for subjects' evaluations of invalid syllogisms as valid was that the global impression of the (linguistic) form of the premises created an "atmosphere" effect that predisposed the subject to accept conclusions in accordance with that global impression. For example, syllogisms whose premises were both affirmative and universal, would tend to be viewed as having also an affirmative and universal conclusion, irrespectively of whether the disposition of the subject and predicate terms in the premises would logically warrant such a conclusion. The principles of this effect have been made explicit by Begg and Denny (1969) as follows: 1) whenever at least one premise is negative, the most frequently accepted conclusion will be negative, and 2) whenever at least one premise contains the quantifier *some* the most frequently accepted conclusion will contain it too (I quote from Johnson-Laird and Wason (eds.), 1977, p. 84). Notice that, on this hypothesis, the relevant contextual influence is in fact co-textual. That is to say, the preceding text, consisting in the two premises, creates the co-text in which the conclusion is to be inserted, and thereby determines a preferential interpretation of the "right" conclusion to draw. (On the parallels between the roles of co-text and context in interpretation, see Dascal and Weizman, forthcoming.) In reviewing evidence pro and con the atmosphere effect hypothesis, Evans (1982, p. 89-90) concludes that the hypothesis fits most of the data except for those cases that could be accounted for in terms of misinterpretation of one of the premises. In either case, we have an effect of context and/or of co-text that generates a pragmatic problem of interpretation.

c. Linguistic Factors in Conditional Reasoning

Here I refer to reasoning tasks involving conditionals of the form "if p then q." It has been observed that although such a form is logically equivalent to the form "p only if q," subjects will treat these forms differentially and will have more or less difficulty in drawing correct inferences from them, according to the content of the conditional used. For example, they will more readily understand, accept and use a sentence like "if it rains on Tuesday, then I shall go swimming," than the logically equivalent sentence "it will rain on Tuesday only if I go swimming." But the situation would be exactly the opposite in the case of the pair of sentences "the match will take place only if the weather has improved" and "if the match takes place then the weather has improved." Here, the relevant pragmatic factor is one's background knowledge of the temporal order of the events or one's expectation of such a temporal order.

Evidence of these kinds could be and has actually been used in order to criticize models that do not display sufficient pragmatic sensitivity. This includes information processing models such as Clark's (1969), or Chapman and Chapman's (1959), which postulate a fixed set of operations of representation, index inversion, conversion, comparison, etc. These are models which, although able to predict results in certain experiments are excessively paradigm-specific and non-generalizable to other tasks. (The same kind of criticism could be addressed to models that assume some form of "naturalness" in the representation of information, such as Hunter's (1957) and Osgood's (1980), whose model has not been so far related to problem solving but is relevant to the issue of sentence comprehension in general.) Consider for example the case of one of Clark's principles, namely, the principle of lexical marking, which states that "the nominal sense of *good* - the sense found in noncommittal *how good*? questions - is stored in a less complex and more available form that the contrastive sense of *good* and

bad" (Clark, 1969, p. 101). In slightly modified experimental conditions, the effect of this principle, which had been detected in Clark's own experiments, disappears (Potts and Scholz, 1975). Nevertheless, there is nothing in a model such as Clark's which prevents its expansion to include a pragmatic component, which will endow it with the required sensitivity. In fact, this is the line taken by Clark himself, whose 1977 model of sentence comprehension includes an additional pragmatic stage of interpretation. The same is true of models such as Osgood's that assume some sort of naturalness principle: data and behaviour that do not appear to conform to the postulate of naturalness are accounted for in terms of such additional constructs as a "psycho-logic" and a forthcoming, additional "pragmatic" component of the theory. (For discussion of Clark's extended model see Dascal, 1983, and of Osgood's, see Dascal et al., 1985.)

3. The essential idea of all the above examples of "pragmatic" effects as well as of the extension of the non-pragmatic models in order to include pragmatic sensitivity is that contextual and co-textual factors should be acknowledged as being able to influence the easiness of decoding, i.e., interpreting or understanding sentences, and thus might eventually override semantic and logical factors in the determination of behaviour. The effect of pragmatics is thus seen to belong basically to the stage of interpretation of the linguistic material. It was not explicitly hypothesized, at least as far as I know, that once such an effect and concomitant difficulties were overcome and the sentences properly understood and interpreted, their processing for further deductive or other problem solving tasks would still be liable to - eventually different - "pragmatic" effects. The assumption was that what prevented such further linguistic effects was the fact that processing was to take place in some sort of an abstract medium which, though "propositional" in nature, was purely semantic and hence "language-free." Among other things, such a "purely semantic" medium would display such characteristics as lack of ambiguity, a clear logical structure, etc.

On this view, language would be relevant to the substantive processes involved in reasoning and other forms of thought only at its semantic/logic level, namely, at that level which is perhaps the less "linguistic" of all. All remaining linguistic influence - including all of its putative "pragmatic" influences - should be considered to be external to thought processes themselves, and should be confined to the stages of decoding a linguistic input or producing a linguistic output. The best formulation of these underlying assumptions, if only one could add to it the pragmatic dimension, remains therefore that of Newell and Simon (1972, p. 66):

> "The position implicit in the analysis of this book can be summed up as follows: (1) the generation or processing of symbol structures that are isomorphic with the strings of natural language or with their surface structures (in the linguist's meaning of that

> phrase) is inessential to human problem solving of the
> kinds we examine. (2) The internal symbol structures
> that represent problems and information about problems
> are synonymous with the linguist's deep structure. If
> "language" means deep structure, then language is
> essential to thinking and problem solving. In sum,
> paraphrasing Dewey: (1) The surface structure of
> language and language strings are the garb or clothing
> of thought necessary not for thought but only for
> conveying it. (2) While linguistic deep structure is
> not thought, it is necessary for thinking."

Of course, this immediately raises a large number of questions, especially the question of how "deep" deep structures are and to what extent they are or are not linguistic (see Dascal, 1973), and the question of the nature of the mental representations used in thought processes, i.e., of the nature of what Fodor has called "the language of thought." Important as they are, I don't think these questions can be properly addressed unless one overcomes the false dilemma embedded in the above assumption, and takes due notice of an alternative that has not been so far explicitly considered. The false dilemma is this: having acknowledged that linguistic factors influence performance in reasoning tasks, one must say either that such an influence is located in the stages of interpretation of linguistic input and production of linguistic output, or else that the reasoning process itself is essentially linguistic in nature. The latter alternative, namely the one according to which language is constitutive of thought, if adopted in its strong form, would clash with observations about people that think in a non-linguistic way, about the role of visual imagery in thought, etc. Hence - the argument would go - the only alternative left is the first one, which means that one must somehow squeeze all the influence of language in reasoning in the two "external" stages of interpretation and production, a task in which pragmatics would be, presumably, of much help.

4. Such a view of the role of pragmatics corresponds in fact to the generally accepted characterization of this discipline as being a theory of the communicative, i.e., "external" use of language. No doubt the communicative use of language is overwhelmingly important and may even have been at the origin of the first development of language by human societies. Also it is no doubt true that the main achievements of pragmatics to this day have been in elucidating different aspects of the communicative use of language. Nevertheless, the equation of pragmatics with a theory of this particular use of language is unduly restricted. For it is necessary to admit that language - as well as other semiotic systems - has (nowadays, if not from origin) another fundamental type of use, which might be loosely described as "mental." Language and other semiotic systems are not only instruments of communication but also instruments of our own thought. Linguistic and non-linguistic signs play an essential role in our mental processes, particularly in higher level cognitive processes and states. One such non-communicative use of language is what Harman (1977, p.418), following Hobbes and Leibniz, calls the "calculative" use:

> "There are symbol systems that are primarily for communication, e.g. Morse code. But there are others that are used mainly for calculation, e.g. the special notations of mathematics. Language surely has both uses, and the second is as important as the first. We use language to help solve our theoretical and practical problems. By stating our ideas in words, we make them precise; we are able to calculate their consequences, to test them, and to improve them - and this is an essential aspect of language. A system used for communication, like Morse code, is not a language."

If pragmatics is a theory of the use of language, the investigation of the calculative, as well as other mental uses of language, belongs *de jure* to its domain. I have proposed to call this subdomain of pragmatics "psychopragmatics," to distinguish it from its other main subdomain, namely "sociopragmatics," which is concerned with the communicative use of language. (See Dascal, 1979, 1983.)

5. Of course, *de jure* right to existence is not enough to justify the introduction of a point of view, if not of an entirely new subdiscipline. Some supporting argument, as well as a clear demonstration of the empirical implications of such a move, especially if one wants to claim that it is relevant to cognitive psychology, are required. I have provided such arguments elsewhere (see Dascal, 1983, 1985, 1986), and I trust that the discussion, in the next section, of one significant puzzle in the theory of deductive reasoning will further support the claim that such a move is useful. But it will be convenient right now to provide some further clarification of the distinction just proposed.

First of all, we must recall that our lives are so communication-oriented that it is hard to come by clear-cut examples of purely non-communicative uses of language, let alone to observe them. Nevertheless, ideally, a psychopragmatic use of language should not be connected in any direct way either to the interpretation of speech input or to the production of speech output. It should be a use of language performed by, say, "a solitary thinker" with no immediate intention of communicating his or her thoughts. More mundanely, one should be able to isolate a stage in, say, a reasoning task, which is performed after interpretation has been achieved and before the problem of verbalizing the solution is engaged, and to inquire whether at this hypothetical stage language has a role to play. Admittedly, this is a difficult task, and except for a few suggestions below, I shall have to leave it to the ingenuity of cognitive psychologists to devise the means to perform it.

Secondly, psychopragmatics does not arise, in my view, as a consequence of the fact pointed out by Wittgenstein, that any mental representation, whether pictorial, propositional or of any other sort, is unable to solve the problem of interpretation, because no interpretation whatsoever is self-interpreting. (On the non-self-interpretive character of pictures, see, for example, Kolers and Brison, 1984.) Assuming this Wittgensteinian claim to be true, it would follow that, after a stage of interpretation of linguistic input, there would arise the problem of the further interpretation of the "mental representation" reached in that stage, and one might think that this stage would be in some sense psychopragmatic rather than sociopragmatic, insofar as it is not anymore directly connected to communication, but has to do with internal mental processes. Yet, though there is much to be said in favor of Wittgenstein's cautions concerning the fiction of self-interpreting representations, if one accepted his position in its full force, one would be led to the elimination *tout court* of the idea of mental representation and, with it, to the elimination of psychopragmatics as well as of sociopragmatics. Since I don't want to accept such a conclusion, I don't propose to define the main task of psychopragmatics as being analogous to that of sociopragmatics, namely as being a matter of providing systems of rules and other devices for the interpretation of mental representations of whatever sort.

The distinction between sociopragmatics and psychopragmatics I have in mind is rather a distinction between the "external" pragmatic factors that have to do with the perception of linguistic input and its interpretation as well as with the production of appropriate linguistic output in a given situation, and the "internal" pragmatic factors that are operative in the performance of the cognitive operations themselves, and that in some way involve language. Such pragmatic factors, however, have a peculiar nature. Their external counterparts are such that they take language as input and rely upon it and contextual information in order to produce a non-linguistic representation as output, or else they are directed to the generation of a "target" linguistic output, which they endeavour to make appropriate to a given situation. The internal pragmatic factors, however, run in the "opposite" direction. From this point of view, language in this respect is one of the "environmental" factors, that is to say, one of the factors that affect the performance and outcome of the cognitive operations themselves, regardless of their "external" manifestation or motivation. In this sense, psychopragmatics is a theory of the way in which the "linguistic environment" of thought influences thought, whereas sociopragmatics is a theory of the ways in which the "non-linguistic environment" (which includes both thought and situation) affects language interpretation and production. In essence then, talk of psychopragmatics is talk of viewing language not as relying upon context, using context, etc., but as being itself contextual.

These inverted orientations should not be seen as parallel to the different orientations of comprehension and production of speech, whereby in comprehension the linguistic input is given and serves as a trigger to one's seeking the non-linguistic pieces and bits that will help one to interpret it, and in production the linguistic element is not the input but rather the target, functioning thus, in a sense, also as an "environment" of thought. The reason is that the latter possibility does not exhaust the possible ways in which a linguistic environment can function both as a tool and as a background for the thought process itself, though speech production can certainly be conceived as one particular case of such a kind of functioning (see Dascal, 1983, pp. 153-7, on what I call "the formulating strategy").

Such an inversion of perspective has important - because potentially leading to testable prediction - consequences. When one interprets a piece of discourse, the piece of discourse is "given" in the sense that it occupies a focal position in one's field of attention. But the context used in the interpretation is also in some sense given, though it occupies a less focal position in one's field of attention. One might say that the context lies at the "horizon" or that it is "in the offing." Thus, in some important sense, the contextual factors are not explicit in the linguistic utterance, but they are rather essentially implicit, especially if they have a pragmatic nature (on this point see Dascal, 1983, pp. 85-91). Now, when language in turn functions as context in its psychopragmatic uses, it is reasonable to expect that its presence is implicit rather than explicit.

In speech production, this implicit, contextual role of language is well attested by such things as the TOT (tip-of-the-tongue) phenomenon and priming. Kubovy (1977) reports interesting results concerning the latter. When subjects were unexpectedly asked to write down or report "the first digit that comes to mind," the most frequent choice was 7 (28.4%), followed by 3 (13.3%). When the request was "Give me the first one-digit number that comes to mind," however, the most frequent response was 1 (18.0%), and only 12.1% of the subjects chose 7. This was explained in terms of priming, i.e., of the availability of 1 in short-term memory, due to its presence in the formulation of the request. But his results also suggest the need for distinguishing between different modes of availability. For, when the request had the form "write down the first number that comes to mind between 0 and 9, excluding fractions, and using only whole numbers like 1," the priming effect was considerably smaller; the frequency of 1 as a choice dropped to 5.4%. According to Kubovy, the difference is due to the fact that in one case 1 is unobtrusively **used** in the request, whereas in the other it is **mentioned**. One might as well say that the reason why 1 is not chosen in the last case is that, having been given as an example, it "doesn't count" as an appropriate response. Whatever the explanation, Kubovy's evidence suggests that the linguistic elements that play a role in production are not simply "available," but that they may be available in different capacities and ways: topically or non-topically, focally or non-focally, more or less implicitly, etc., just as the various contextual elements required for the interpretation of an utterance are "present" to the mind in a differentiated and stratified way. What remains to be done is to obtain evidence of this kind - possibly employing priming techniques too - for psychopragmatic uses of language that are not immediately related to speech production.

6. With this admittedly sketchy characterization of my proposed conceptual distinction, let me now turn to the examination of a puzzle in the account of the influence of linguistic factors in reasoning tasks.

A most robust finding in many studies of conditional reasoning, especially those concerned with Wason's well-known selection task, is a certain effect, usually known as the "matching bias." The subjects in this task are given a conditional sentence and a set of four cards, and they are requested to say which cards they would have to turn in order to tell whether the sentence is true or false. The matching bias consists in the fact that subjects tend to view a given card as relevant to the task, i.e., as either falsifying or confirming the conditional statement, if its items match those named in the conditional sentence itself. More specifically, a double match occurs when an instance matches both values named in the conditional. For example, given the conditional "if the letter is A then the number is 7," the instance (i.e., the card) having on one side "A" and on the other side "7," is a double match. Logically, it corresponds to a case in which both antecedent and consequent are true (TT) and thus it verifies the conditional rule. If the conditional is "if the letter is not A then the number is 7" the same instance, namely, "A7" is also a double match. But now it corresponds logically to the combination FT, which neither falsifies nor verifies the conditional. What has been found is that people have a preference for double matches, regardless of whether they are relevant to falsifying or verifying the conditional statement (see Evans, 1982, pp. 140-144). This bias is extreme in young children, "who tend to classify all matching cases as "true" and all other cases as "false," irrespective of the linguistic form of the rules presented" (Paris, 1973, quoted in Evans, 1982, p. 142). Wason suggested that when adults behave similarly in reasoning tasks, they are showing a regression to a childhood pattern of thought. Evans takes such an effect as evidence of the existence of a "non-logical" component in conditional reasoning, and as supporting his two-factor theory of reasoning, according to which behaviour in such tasks is determined simultaneously by two independent factors, a logical and a non-logical one. According to him,

> "the 'logical' component reflects the degree to which subjects' responses are related to the logical structure of the task - such responses need *not* be 'logical' in the sense of logically correct. The non-logical component reflects the extent to which subjects respond to logically irrelevant features of the problem. ... The logical component is thought to arise from the subject's attempt to solve the task as instructed. The non-logical component is thought to reflect response biases, attention to logically irrelevant features or application of inappropriate heuristics." (Evans, 1982, p. 125)

According to this, one would expect that the matching bias, since it involves reliance upon features - such as what is actually named in the conditional - which are irrelevant to the logical structure of the task, should be viewed as belonging to the non-logical factor, which is indeed what Evans claims. Yet, to our surprise, he goes on to lump together the logical and the linguistic factors, going as far as almost to identify them. For example, he says: "One way in which the two-factor theory is testable is in its assumption that linguistic factors affect only the logical component of performance, whereas non-logical biases arise from specific operational requirements of the task." (p. 126) Furthermore, he views linguistic influences as reducible to interpretational factors (Evans, 1972) and finally suggests that the logical component should rather be called the "interpretational" component:

> "In this section the term *interpretational* rather than logical component will be preferred. It will be assumed that any effects of syntactic or semantic linguistic factors are orthogonal to the non-logical effects ... This means that even if only affirmative rules are used, any shift in, say, the rate of MT (= modus tollens) inference, occasioned by manipulations of linguistic content, will be assumed to be mediated by the interpretational component." (p. 144)

We have thus a paradoxical situation in which a detectable, clearly linguistic, influence on reasoning, namely the matching bias, is ascribed to the non-logical component, which in turn is characterized as being essentially unrelated to linguistic influence, the latter being rather characteristic or almost definitory of the logical factor.

The paradox becomes even more explicit in the revised and expanded version of the theory, the so-called "revised dual-process theory," in which processes underlying reasoning tasks are described as belonging to two types, one of them (type 1) being non-verbal and the other (type 2), verbal. To be sure, this theory is proposed in order to account for the discrepancies between subjects' verbalizations and their actual behavioral performance in the tasks in question, and it is important to register here Evans' qualifications: "this does not mean that type 2 processes consist of words, but merely that their function is to generate verbal responses. Because such verbalizations appear to be independent of aspects of decision processes, it is assumed that type 1 processes are non-verbal." (Evans, 1982, p. 240). Nevertheless, the two types of processes are connected to the two factors mentioned above, and the explicit claim is made that "type 1 processes are considered to underly the non-logical response processes, such as matching bias, but are *not* seen as responsible for the logical/interpretational component of performance. This is attributed instead to type 2 processes." (Ibid.)

It seems to me that, in the light of my proposals in the previous section, the solution to this apparent paradox is rather straightforward. Instead of lumping together all the kinds of linguistic influence in reasoning under a single label, namely "interpretational" factors, one should rather distinguish between the interpretational, i.e., sociopragmatic, effects of language and the non-interpretational ones, namely the psychopragmatic factors. This "solution" of the paradox is not a purely terminological one and I don't think that the problem faced by Evans' theory is of a terminological nature. It is rather a conceptual problem which the distinctions here proposed might help to solve. Furthermore, in the light of this suggestion, one could take effects such as the matching bias as evidence for a particular kind of linguistic influence upon thought, distinct in nature from the better known sociopragmatic effects.

7. It is impossible to generalize from one single example. In fact, one must be careful not to infer from that example that psychopragmatic effects of language upon thought have always certain specific characteristics typical of the example in question. For example, matching bias is indeed a "disturbing" factor in this particular case, if one takes logical correctness as a criterion. There might be other cases in which the psychopragmatic influence of language has a facilitating effect. On the other hand, there is a characteristic of this particular case, briefly considered and then abandoned by Evans, that deserves perhaps to be taken as typical, at least to some extent, of psychopragmatic effects in general. In an earlier version of the dual-process theory, Wason and Evans (1975) have emphasized the fact that type 1 processes are inaccessible to introspection, whereas type 2 processes are introspectible, being in fact responsible for the generation of reports of introspection. In the revised version, this distinction is abandoned on the grounds that both processes are unconscious or non-introspectible, since type 2 processes underly so-called introspective reports, but are not themselves reportable (Evans, 1982, p. 240). Though this is certainly true, still there might be a difference in accessibility to introspection of the two kinds of processes. In our terms, insofar as the two kinds of processes are related to the different forms of influence of language upon cognitive processes, this would support the observation previously made about the different orientations and different (contextual vs. non-contextual) status of language in its psycho- and sociopragmatic roles.

How can one detect psychopragmatic effects in general, is a question to which I have no definite answer at this point. There are a number of techniques that might be exploited for this purpose. The already mentioned case of priming, in which language is influential in thought, though in a form which is inaccessible to recall, is one of them. Another might be based on an application of Potts and Scholz's (1975) technique of postponing the presentation of the problem-question until one is sure the subject has properly understood (i.e., "interpreted") the data and the requirements. Such a technique might presumably be able to separate between the sociopragmatic factors involved in interpretation and, at the latter stage of working out the solution, the possible psychopragmatic effects of language. In order to avoid possible interference with sociopragmatic effects related to the production of verbal

output, the tasks should be designed in such a way as not to
require a verbal response. It is significant, in this respect,
that Potts and Scholz have found that the effect of the
marked/unmarked distinction postulated by Clark disappeared in
their experimental setting.

However difficult it may seem to be, at the present stage of
research, to indicate ways of sorting out psychopragmatic and
sociopragmatic influences of language upon reasoning and other
cognitive processes, it seems to me that the pay-off of
attempting to do this may be well worth taking the trouble, for
it will certainly help to clarify, both empirically and conceptually, the intricate issue of the relationships between language and thought.[1]

REFERENCES

Begg, I. and Denny, P. J. (1969), "Empirical reconciliation of
   atmosphere and conversion interpretations of syllogistic
   reasoning errors." *Journal of Experimental Psychology* 81.
   351-354.

Chapman, L. J. and Chapman, J. P. (1959), "Atmosphere effect
   reexamined." *Journal of Experimental Psychology* 58. 220-
   226.

Clark, H. H. (1969), "Linguistic processes in deductive reasoning." *Psychological Review* 76. 387-404. Reprinted in
   Johnson-Laird and Wason (eds.), pp. 98-113.

Clark, H. H. and Clark E. V. (1977), *Psychology and language:
   an introduction to psycholinguistics*. New York: Harcourt
   Brace Jovanovich.

Dascal, M. (1973), "Are 'semantic structures' really 'deeper'
   than 'deep structures'?." *Semiotica* 8. 163-192.

Dascal, M. (1979), "Towards psychopragmatics." Paper presented
   at the second congress of the International Association of
   Semiotic Studies, Vienna, August 1979.

Dascal, M. (1983), *Pragmatics and the philosophy of mind,
   volume I: thought in language*. Amsterdam/Philadelphia:
   John Benjamins.

Dascal, M. (1985), "Language use in jokes and dreams: sociopragmatics vs. psychopragmatics." *Language and Communication* 5. 95-106.

1 I wish to thank the N.I.A.S. for providing the quiet,
   relaxed, and yet intellectually rewarding environment where
   I was able to write this paper. I thank in particular
   Professor Johannes Engelkamp for stimulating conversations
   on the topics discussed in this paper, and Mrs. Marina
   Voerman for the typing.

Dascal, M., Borges Neto, J., and Francozo, E. (1985), "Modeling the psycholinguistic mold." *Journal of Pragmatics* 9. 345-376.

Dascal, M. and Weizman, E. (forthcoming), "Contextual exploitation of interpretation clues in text understanding: an integrated model."

Evans, J. St. B. T. (1972), "On the problems of interpreting reasoning data: logical and psychological approaches." *Cognition* 1. 373-384.

Evans, J. St. B. T. (1982), *The psychology of deductive reasoning*. London: Routledge and Kegan Paul.

Fillenbaum, S. (1975), "If: some uses." *Psychological Research* 37. 245-260.

Fillenbaum, S. (1976), "Inducements: on phrasing and logic of conditional promises, threats and warnings. *Psychological Research* 38. 231-250.

Geiss, M. C. and Zwicky, A. M. (1971), "On invited inferences." *Linguistic Inquiry* 2. 561-566.

Grice, H. P. (1975), "Logic and conversation." In P. Cole and J. L. Morgan (eds.), *Syntax and semantics 3: speech acts*. New York: Academic Press, 41-58.

Harman, G. (1977), "Review of J. Bennett's Linguistic Behavior." *Language* 53. 417-424.

Henle, M. (1962), "On the relation between logic and thinking." *Psychological Review* 86. 376-382.

Hunter, I. M. L. (1957), "The solving of three-term series problems." *British Journal of Psychology* 48. 286-298.

Johnson-Laird, P. N. and Wason, P. C. (eds.) (1977), *Thinking: readings in cognitive science*. Cambridge: Cambridge University Press.

Kolers, P. A. and Brison, S. J. (1984), "On pictures, words, and their mental representation." *Journal of Verbal Learning and Verbal Behavior* 23. 105-113.

Kubovy, M. (1977), "Response availability and the apparent spontaneity of numerical choices." *Journal of Experimental Psychology: Human Perception and Performance* 3. 359-364.

Osgood, C. E. (1980), *Lectures on language performance*. Berlin: Springer.

Newell, A. and Simon, H. A. (1972), *Human problem solving*. Englewood Cliffs: Prentice-Hall.

Paris, S. G. (1973), "Comprehension of language connectives and propositional logical relationships." *Journal of Experimental Child Psychology* 16. 278-291.

Potts, G. R. and Scholz, K. W. (1975), "The internal representation of three-term series problems." *Journal of Verbal Learning and Verbal Behavior* 14. 439-452.

Tversky, A. and Kahneman, D. (1974), "Judgment under uncertainty: heuristics and biases." *Science* 185. 1124-1131. Reprinted in Johnson-Laird and Wason (eds.), pp. 326-337.

Wason, P. C. (1965), "The contexts of plausible denial." *Journal of Verbal Learning and Verbal Behavior* 4. 7-11.

Wason, P. C. (1981), "Understanding and the limits of formal thinking." In H. Parret and J. Bouveresse (eds.), *Meaning and understanding*. Berlin: De Gruyter, pp. 411-421.

Wason, P. C. and Evans, J. St. B. T (1975), "Dual processes in reasoning?" *Cognition* 3. 141-154.

Woodworth, R. S. and Sells, S. B. (1935), "An atmosphere effect in syllogistic reasoning." *Journal of Experimental Psychology* 18. 451-460.

PANEL:
THEORETICAL AND
EMPIRICAL APPROACHES

PANEL SESSION: THEORETICAL AND EMPIRICAL APPROACHES

             Panel Chairman: R. P. Rich
             Panel Members: V. R. Dasigi
                              S. L. Epstein
                              B. W. Hamill
                              W. L. Scherlis
                              B. Shneiderman

RICH

The title of this panel is Theoretical and Empirical Approaches, which leaves us quite a bit of freedom. It doesn't, for example, say approaches to what. I'd like to take just a minute at the beginning to try and narrow that down a little bit. I think it probably means theoretical and empirical approaches to use of language in problem solving, and I'm personally going to proceed on that assumption. But I don't want to impose any restrictions on the rest of the panel.

One of my serious discomforts with this topic is that in the use of computers, generally, it's sometimes hard to tell the difference between theoretical and empirical approaches. The theoreticians that I know tend to spend about as much time tapping the keys of their terminals as the empirical persons, and the empirical persons are willing, over the third beer, to spend as much time talking theory as their theoretical colleagues. I thought it might help all of us to have a real black and white example of theory, as opposed to practice, at the beginning. I therefore went to great trouble and expense preparing a viewgraph which will show an example, not from this intellectual area, of a theory and a practice. I hope that example will be familiar enough to all of you that it won't take very much of our time.

$$\frac{\lambda}{\sigma} = \frac{V^2}{GD}$$

This is the theory. Let me just say a word about it. Suppose that I'm riding a bicycle and I lean lambda degrees to the right and I turn the handlebars sigma degrees to the right, and I'm pedalling at a velocity "V", on a planet whose acceleration of gravity is "G", on a bicycle, the distance between whose axles is "D". If I satisfy this equation, then I will not fall over. If I do not satisfy this equation, then I <u>will</u> fall over. I should say to the theorists present that I have made the usual small angle approximations, so I assume that the tangent of lambda is lambda and that twice the sine of sigma over 2 is sigma. My feeling is that unless you've ridden on a bicycle more recently than I, if you depart from the angle for which these approximations are appropriate, you'll probably be in trouble anyway.

I have not prepared any specific example of the practice in this case...I assume that everyone here has learned to ride a bicycle, or has tried to teach a five-year-old the same thing, so I don't have to spend a lot of time arguing that in this particular area of activity, the theory does not notably inform and facilitate the practice, and so far as I know, the practice has not strongly driven the theory.

This is an extreme example, and I hope a clear one, of a theory and a practice which live quite happily, independently. What we'd like to do this afternoon is to depart from this paradigm and illustrate ways in which the theory can assist the practice and the practice can inform and drive the theory. And each of the panelists has agreed, at least in principle, to try and illustrate such points as this.

HAMILL

I'd like to address some cognitive aspects of representation for problem solving. One of the driving forces behind this symposium in its origination was to find ways in which language and the underpinnings of language, going back to human cognition and the representation of problems in the human mind and in the computer, could facilitate one another. In particular, I'm interested in finding ways in which computer systems can be designed to help people solve the problems that face them. So let me focus a little bit on some ways in which modern cognitive science, I think, can contribute to theorizing and applications in the development of representational formalisms and in the development and design of languages for problem solving.

Modern cognitive science, including cognitive psychology, artificial intelligence, computer science, linguistics, and a number of other contributing sciences, is essentially trying to characterize how humans perform higher brain functions in explicit and testable terms. Very often these testable terms take the form of computer programs. Cognitive scientists are seeking ways in which to map problem-solving processes onto theoretical structures so that they can be exercised and tested against other mappings onto alternative theoretical structures. To my knowledge, there has not, thus far, been a lot of comparative work done in this direction, except for a recently published study in AI Magazine by Niwa, Sasaki, and Ihara, who looked at the relative effectiveness of four different representational formalisms on performance in a particular problem-solving task. There is, however, lots of theoretical work on the computer science frontier, which, in fact, is founded in earlier psychological investigations, to develop formalisms intended to characterize human performance data concerning the handling of concepts or ideas in the mind. About fifteen years ago, for example, Quillian (1969) and Collins and Quillian (1972) published some seminal papers that dealt with semantic networks, or associative networks, and the idea of spreading activation as a means of representing in a formal way, in a computer system, mental behavior in the course of problem solving. This has since been picked up and extended by John Anderson (e.g., 1983) at Carnegie-Mellon.

Another example is hierarchical structures; they could be strict hierarchies, which are used to represent certain kinds of structured domains of knowledge like animal taxonomies and plant taxonomies, or they might be tangled hierarchies, in which concepts don't fit into strict hierarchies, where concepts are apt to be represented at more than one level in a given structure. There are also inheritance hierarchies in which features can be inherited from a given higher level node down to all of its lower level nodes.

Another example is the schema or frame representation, which harks back to work in psychology as early as the 1920s and 1930s by Jean Piaget (e.g., 1928; 1963), where a number of these ideas came from. These constitute representations of sets of knowledge about things in the world about which we know. They are ways to capture essential properties of concepts, including expected values of features or properties that might not be explicitly represented in the problem-solving process, and they also provide triggers for procedures that might be needed in conjunction with concept activation.

Another formalism which has been addressed extensively here this morning is that of logical structures and frameworks, which may be applicable in certain circumstances. Certainly in science and engineering problem solving, they may very often be the methods or representations of choice, but in many real world circumstances, there may be places where logical formalisms are not quite so applicable. Logical deduction and formal mathematical calculation have not yet been shown adequate, for example, to solve problems involving common kinds of things that we all do: noticing relevant or irrelevant facts with respect to a problem at hand, spotting patterns in data of whatever sort, noticing similarities between current and past observations that had hitherto not been connected, and even having new ideas and old memories, whether relevant or not, occur spontaneously while thinking about something else.

Also, how do we explain learning phenomena in a logical framework? Rule-bound formulations found in logical deduction and formal rigorous calculation may carry us some distance along the way in understanding how people think, how they make decisions, and how they solve problems, but there's certainly more to it. A recent assertion by Donald MacKay (1986) is illustrative. He suggests that rule-governed thinking may constitute the special case, and that intuitive cognition founded in some other structures and processes may be the norm.

One major problem that we have to face is that all these representational formalisms, together with others not mentioned here, are part of each of us. We use whichever ones we need for the problem at hand, either separately or in some conjunction. Notice that this implies a good bit of task specificity for matching representations to problems. This is a fundamental observation in psychological investigations which needs to be recognized in the conceptualization and design of tools intended to help people solve problems, including the design of languages and notations, programming environments, work stations, and other computer-based artifacts which are intended to help people, whether they be ordinary folks or high-powered experts, to perform the tasks that they have before them.

Of course, these representational formalisms are intended as a means of capturing the structure and related processes involved in certain problem-solving performance...or let us call it thinking. That is, they are intended to reflect what goes on inside people's heads. But there's another layer to consider. The ideas that are contained in these representational structures often have to be conveyed or transmitted from the originator to someone else. And it might be from the originator through a computer system. There is a consequent need for some vehicle through which to convey those ideas in a veridical manner.

This is where language comes into play. In ordinary souls, like those not present at this symposium, this vehicle is what we might call natural language, our mother tongue. For me, it's English. For you, it might be English or some other natural language, or even two or more natural languages. And those of you who are multi-lingual might even get involved in the Sapir-Whorf hypothesis (see, e.g., Whorf, 1956), whether we can express the same idea equally well in each language, or whether language somehow influences the way in which we think.

In extraordinary souls, like those of us gathered here at this symposium, the vehicle for expressing and conveying our ideas may be somewhat more specialized. We like to think we are concerned with a smaller piece of the action than the whole of thought--for example, how to think about and solve problems in some subset of logical operations like theorem proving or searching through databases; or perhaps how to facilitate the formulation and solution of problems related to the design of experiments in some specific field, say molecular biology; or how to enable naive users to use computers in a manner they consider natural to them, so that the computer responds in accordance with their expectations. But it may turn out that objectives like these will actually require us to understand more about thought as a complete entity, together with all of its structures and processes and other baggage!

If we have as at least one goal the development of natural ways for language or languages, in the sense of computer languages, to be designed and used in the service of various kinds of problem solving, perhaps we ought to recognize explicitly a multiplicity of tasks to be supported and, consequently, a multiplicity of natural idioms, languages, notations, and other mechanisms that we need to create for different people to use to solve different kinds of problems. Perhaps what we really need is a complete set of tools of various kinds for use in problem solving in various domains. Would you, for example, use a screw driver to drive a nail? Well, you might if it were small enough. Would you use a hammer to drive a screw? Well, you could, but that might nullify the effectiveness of the threads on the screw. Analogously, problem solving may require task- and domain-specific representational "tools".

Design and development of languages for problem solving must include consideration of theory and data from the cognitive sciences. In particular, understanding how people solve

problems in the domain in question seems to me to be a
prerequisite to the design of effective tools in support of
problem solving in that domain. If we're given the goal either
to design tools to aid thought, in the sense that Allen Newell
suggests, or to design what David Woods and Emily Roth of
Westinghouse call "joint person-machine cognitive systems,"
then the more we know about how humans process information in
the structural representations they have in their heads for
formulating and solving problems, the better we can expect to
become at designing and developing tools, including languages,
to facilitate that process.

References

Anderson, J.R., The Architecture of Cognition, Cambridge, MA:
    Harvard University Press, 1983.

Collins, A.M., and Quillian, M.R., Experiments on Semantic
    Memory and Language Comprehension. In L.W. Gregg (Ed.),
    Cognition in Learning and Memory, New York: Wiley, 1972.

MacKay, D.M., Private Communication, 1986.

Niwa, K., Sasaki, K., and Ihara, H., An Experimental Comparison
    of Knowledge Representation Schemes. AI Magazine, 1984, 5,
    No. 2, 29-36.

Piaget, J. Judgement and Reasoning in the Child, New York:
    Harcourt Brace, 1928.

Piaget, J. The Origins of Intelligence in Children. New
    York: W. W. Horton, 1963.

Quillian, M.R., The Teachable Language Comprehender: A
    Simulation Program and Theory of Language. Communications
    of the ACM, 1969, 12, 459-476.

Whorf, B.L. Language, Thought, and Reality. Cambridge, MA:
    MIT Press, 1956.

EPSTEIN

It seems to me that good languages for problem solving do not
spring forth full-grown from the foreheads of their creators.
Rather, they appear to be the outcome of perpetual revision
based on actual attempts to use them, either by hand or by
machine.

The issues I'm particularly aware of center around expressive
adequacy, computational performance and extensibility. By
expressive adequacy, I mean the ability of the problem-solving
language to describe the problem conditions and the solution in
a useful manner. By computational performance, I mean the
ability of the problem-solving language to search efficiently
and appropriately. Finally, by extensibility I mean the
ability of the problem-solving language to assimilate concepts,
either concepts that have been discovered or concepts that have

been learned, when they lie outside the original vocabulary of the system.

I'm going to use three examples to illustrate these ideas. The first one is a classic study in the computational performance of problem-solving languages, Saul Amarel's 1968 paper on the missionaries and cannibals problem. The general case of this problem was that there could be any number of missionaries and any number of cannibals, as long as they were equal to each other; that they could start in any location, either on the left or the right bank of the river; and that the boat capacity was fixed. There must be at least three missionaries and three cannibals and a boat capacity of at least two.

In a sequence of six languages, Amarel began with natural language as a formulation and eventually arrived at a compact production system with an efficient planning space. This last language, which he called F6, was particularly interesting, because not only could it achieve optimal solutions, but it could also derive them very rapidly. Now, here's a fine example, I think, of computational performance. Each of Amarel's languages was adequate to find and express the solution, but search became more efficient as the languages evolved. The transitions from one of these languages to the next was motivated by the discovery of regularities, both in the problem conditions and in trial solutions which were carefully observed and examined. These regularities were then used to revise the current problem-solving language. The languages form a spectrum. As the changes removed irrelevancies, they shifted the focus of the search and of the language to what appears to be the "core" of the problem.

The moral of this story, for those of us who are designing problem-solving languages, appears to be, "find the regularities and exploit them." This raises the following questions. What makes a regularity useful as a constraint on a solution language? Do you seek such regularities by hand or by machine? Do you revise your language once you've found the regularities by hand or by machine? Are there domain-independent principles for such detection or such revision?

In reply I'm going to describe two incidents in the search for regularities. Both of them deal with the other two issues that I raised earlier, expressive adequacy and extensibility. The first case occurred when Paul Utgoff and Tom Mitchell were working on LEX. LEX is an automated system for learning problem-solving heuristics in the domain of symbolic integration. LEX begins with a list of valid calculus integration rules, many of which may be applicable to any given problem at any point in time. The trick, as any calculus student will tell you, is to decide which rule you're supposed to use to eliminate the integral sign. LEX solves integration problems like the one in Figure 1. From such a solution it attempts to extrapolate heuristics for the application of integration rules to other problems. The sample technique in Figure 1 only is applicable when the exponent of the cosine is an odd integer. LEX tried this problem with 7 as the exponent of the cosine and

solved it successfully. Then LEX replaced the 7 with a 5 and
solved that problem successfully. Next LEX tried the problem
with a 6 and found that the technique would not solve the
problem. LEX understood and was able to come up with optimal
solutions for $\cos^7 x$ and $\cos^5 x$, but what LEX lacked was the
vocabulary to describe just what regularity distinguished 7 and
5 from 6.

$$\int \cos^7 x \, dx$$
$$\text{Let } u = \sin x$$
$$\cos^2 x = 1 - \sin^2 x$$
$$\cos^7 x = (\cos^6 x)(\cos x) = (\cos^2 x)^3 (\cos x)$$

$$\int \cos^7 x \, dx = \int (1 - u^2)^3 \, du$$
$$= \int (1 - 3u^2 + 3u^4 - u^6) \, du$$
$$= u - u^3 + 3/5 \, u^5 - 1/7 \, u^7 + c$$

Figure 1

A Calculus Problem

This lack of expressive adequacy did not prevent the efficient,
and even the optimal, solution of the integration problem, but
LEX's task, remember, was to construct heuristics for rule
application. Few of us would be very pleased to encounter a
rule which began "if the exponent is a 5 or a 7 but it's not a
6...." Can such failures be anticipated? Should they even be
prevented? Utgoff and Mitchell found that a language extension
to accommodate such a new concept need not even be unique. In
fact, when they attempted to automate such extensions, it
raised difficult issues about the terminology already in LEX's
vocabulary. And, once the new concept was developed, its
correct assimilation into LEX's hierarchically arranged
vocabulary was problematic.

My other example comes from my own work on problem-solving
languages for graph theory. Again, I want to focus on
extensibility and assimilation. Imagine, if you will, a
machine which performs original mathematical research in graph
theory, a fairly open-ended form of problem solving.
Researchers regularly invent and/or incorporate into their
knowledge bases new concepts. How might a representation
accommodate new concepts? What regularities in mathematics
might be capitalized upon to construct such a representation?
My approach was to assume that interesting graph theory
concepts were expressible in terms of properties of graphs.
Thus, a theorem such as "Every tree is acyclic" could be
rewritten as "If a graph has property 'tree' then it has
property 'acyclic'." Now that's not a terribly informative way
to rephrase the theorem, but it gave me some ideas as to how I

might go about doing research with graph properties. I assumed that a graph property was just a symbol for the class of graphs that had that property. For example, the property of being a tree denotes merely membership in the set labelled as "trees."

These classes frequently turn out to be infinite. How would you go about representing a class like that? Presumably, and this is a large presumption, some mathematical regularity does exist within the class. (That presumption is based upon the fact that some mathematician found that class interesting to begin with.) Perhaps each of the members of this class "trees" might be in some way related to the other members. One idea that I hit upon for trying to find this regularity was structural deformation, the expectation that any individual tree might be deformed so that it guaranteed the creation of another tree.

I sought, therefore, a set of controlled deformations and a language to describe them which would capture the unknown regularities which pervade such a class. At first, I experimented with very simple deformations and tried to express a variety of graph properties. For example, $B_{xy}^{*}(K_1)$ where $x \varepsilon V, y \not\varepsilon V$ is the expression for tree. Essentially it says that you begin with a single vertex, the graph K_1, and you branch from any vertex x in the graph to any vertex y which is not in the graph. The process will create any tree. This expression is a concise description; when I couldn't puzzle out a property with my current set of deformations, I simply added the ones that appeared necessary. This pragmatic method produces very interesting results. At the moment I've been able to represent more than 40 graph properties spanning most interesting, popular graph theory topics. The graph property languages so developed form a partially ordered set based on the deformations they permit.

Problems do arise. Although the representation has been employed and extended successfully in so many cases, there is no proof that it is complete for all of graph theory. Part of the problem is that graph theory isn't finished being discovered yet. Is such a proof required? And if so, what must be the structure of an argument for the expressibility of concepts yet to be discovered either by people or by machines? Unlike LEX, this graph theory representation has shown a remarkable ability to formulate hierarchies of concepts and to assimilate new ones. Similarities between property notations have enabled me both to generate conjectures about appropriate insertion points in a hierarchy and to construct effective algorithms for testing subset relationships. Once again, there's no proof that the technique is perfect. And my question is, is empirical success ever evidence enough?

DASIGI

I want to address theoretical and empirical approaches to problem solving. In most areas of scientific endeavor, theory guides experiments and experiments verify and thereby enrich theory. I want to concentrate on two ways of problem solving: problem solving by humans and automated problem solving by computers.

Concerning problem solving by humans, I want to mention something about Nilsson's metaphor of heuristic search for the kind of mutual interaction that exists between theory and experimentation [Nilsson 80]. For instance, we can compare the nodes, operators, goal conditions, and heuristics of the heuristic search process to the theory existing in human problem solving and in heuristic search. The process of expanding a node may be compared to performing an experiment. What kind of experiment is to be performed is usually guided by theory the same way the heuristics in the heuristic search process decide which node to select, which node to expand next. And the series of experiments that lead to a new discovery is analogous to the solution in the heuristic search paradigm. With this analogy in mind, we can say that blind experimentation is like blind search, and it suffers from combinatorial explosion. The mutual reinforcement that exists between theory and experimentation may also be compared with the mutual interaction between the theoretical knowledge and the process of expanding a node in the case of heuristic search, in that if we have good heuristic knowledge, we focus much faster towards a solution, and a successful solution increases our confidence in the heuristics that we have.

Next, I want to digress a little into the work I'm doing, and I'll try to convince you that I'm not really digressing. The second aspect that I mentioned before is problem solving by computers. I have two purposes in talking about abductive inference viewed as a hypothesize-and-test process. The first is that there exists a clear analogy between abductive problem solving and the way theory and experimentation interact in scientific endeavor. The other purpose is to look at some useful ideas for automation of problem solving.

These examples of inference most of you saw this morning in my presentation on diagnostic problem solving and natural language processing. Let me give a quick review of what I said about diagnostic problem solving.

What I have in mind in mentioning this as an example for the problem here is to account for the presence of a symptom by hypothesizing the presence of a disorder which could possibly be causing this manifestation. In fact, there could be more than one manifestation which needs to be accounted for. The way one could start solving this problem is first to take a set of all disorders which could possibly cause the first symptom or manifestation that is known, and then test any element of the set to see if it actually accounts for the remaining symptoms also. So, first we hypothesize that one particular disorder could be causing the symptom and then we test that, and if the test fails we go ahead and take another element of the same set and apply the same test again, and finally after this process of hypothesizing and testing, we hope to arrive at an explanation. So we start with some knowledge, which is like theory, and we build hypotheses, test them, and then revise them if necessary, and finally have a confirmed hypothesis that forms the theory. All these aspects of abductive inference, a number of these key features of abductive inference, can be captured by the parsimonious covering model, which should be distinguished from abductive inference. These two are different in that abductive inference is an imprecise notion while parsimonious covering is a well defined model of abductive inference that can be implemented or applied on computers towards problem solving.

But there is an important point that is missing in all this; the problem is how to choose, how to design experiments automatically. That is an open problem which is not yet resolved to my knowledge; that is, you come up with a possible hypothesis automatically when you attempt to solve the problem using the computer, come up with a hypothesis and then attempt to test it. In human problem solving it is possible: we do choose a proper test, we design a proper experiment to verify the hypothesis or refute the hypothesis. But how can we do the same thing automatically on a computer? That, I think, is an open problem.

Reference

Nilsson, N. J. 80: The Interplay between Experimental and Theoretical Methods in Artificial Intelligence. In Cognition and Brain Theory, 1980, 4(1), 69-74.

SHNEIDERMAN

I'm pleased to be here to talk about the topic of theory and empirical approaches. I'd like to bend your ear a little and maybe bend your thinking a little bit to lean more in the direction of thinking about the human side of the use of computers. I see a similarity in some of the work presented here and some of the work presented last year, but I have my concerns, because many times strong claims are made about the way people think, what is natural, whether natural language is the ultimately desirable way of interacting with the computer, or whether some programming environment is effective. I would like to promote attention to theoretical underpinnings and the kind of empirical studies that have been suggested by Bruce Hamill and by Venu Dasigi. It seems to me that that is the route to rapid progress.

I was very strongly influenced by an article by John Platt in Science magazine in 1964 (October 10, p. 347). He relates the history of primary disciplines in the 20th century, molecular biology and particle physics. He recounts how the laboratories of researchers would have on their bulletin boards or blackboards tree structures of experiments. The outcome of each experiment would determine the next experiment--very clear delineation of research plans. Yet, much of the work I see today is just an exploration, without a formal basis, without a rigorous underpinning, without a theory of human behavior, and without a commitment to an empirical approach which is based on human factors studies about how people really use different systems. I think once we move in that direction and get beyond the arguments about "my language is more user friendly than your language" and "my system is more natural than your system" -- whenever you hear the speakers in the next two days saying "better", "natural", "more understandable", try to ask them what they mean, what are the metrics--and only when we get to measurement do we begin to really talk about science.

How do we evaluate the products of our work; that's the central thesis. And I'm concerned because I see so much of the promotion of the notions of artificial intelligence, rule-based expert systems, without a thoughtful evaluation to the outcome of the work. I think we risk being perceived by not only the general population but our colleagues and other scientific disciplines as being so much the snake oil salesmen. We may discover some tool or idea which works well for one domain, maybe it cures some people of headaches sometimes, but then we promote it as if it's the cure-all for everything. I hope for a much more rigorous and diligent approach to address what Bruce referred to as the multiplicity of tasks that users have to accomplish and the diversity of users. For me that's been the greatest encounter in becoming 20% of an experimental psychologist, in discovering how very differently individuals behave from each other and how very different they are from myself. It's a great struggle to overcome the egocentric approach that many people take towards design and to open our minds, to find out how other people work. Is predicate calculus really a natural language for many people or is it a great struggle for them to use it, as a number of studies have tried to show?

And so maybe that's the right note to pass on to Bill Scherlis. Why does he really think that predicate calculus is a natural language and for whom and for what tasks? With that, let me just restate my point: I think we can sharpen our thinking by having clearer theories about human cognition, and we can provide support for them from controlled, psychologically oriented studies.

SCHERLIS

Let me focus the issue at hand, which is contrasting empirical and theoretical approaches, into my particular research world, which is the design of programming tools. While it can be argued that any researcher must work in both empirically driven and theoretically driven modes, it is certainly the case that individual workers tend to favor one mode or another, for example, by relying on theoretical work as a principal source of inspiration, or by developing theories mainly to support existing data. This point is pretty obvious. It has been observed, in the case of computer science, that there is a certain tendency towards polarization in the community. What I would like to do here is illustrate the adverse effect of this polarization in the area of knowledge-based programming tools.

At the beginning of my paper with Dietzen (in this volume), we consider some existing approaches that have been taken to developing knowledge-based programming tools. These approaches have, in general, tended to be strongly empirical, relying on psychological data gained through protocol analysis, introspection, or whatever means. I suggest that there is a potential weakness in this approach. Unlike many other expert areas, programmers have not yet developed precise language for describing the program design process. This reflects the fact that, even though we have a well developed understanding of programming language notions, there is still much conceptualization to be done about program DESIGN concepts. The results of this poverty of conceptualization are fuzzy concepts cloaked in formal clothes in our programming knowledge bases. The knowledge bases tend to have little structure and are difficult to enhance.

The point is that the knowledge representation problem, in this case, is not simply one of codifying formally a well developed set of conventions. There are still very challenging conceptual problems that must be cracked before genuine progress can be made in designing advanced programming tools and automatic programming systems.

What is the evidence for this? If we look at existing programming knowledge bases, we find that they can work well in well defined domains, but they are difficult to extend and generalize. These systems (again, there are exceptions) generally do not assimilate experience. It is, of course, an ability to reckon with past experience that is necessary, for example, to successfully apply the systems to program modification. But my paper addresses this issue at length, so let me return to the issue at hand.

The difficulty here is mostly a result of the (persistently underestimated) difficulty of the programming problem, but a definite contributing factor is the lack of communication between those taking empirical approaches and those pursuing the question theoretically. The empiricists need help from the theorists, and the theorists need to know more about what the real practical problems are.

What sort of help can the theorists provide in this case? Theory is a source of concepts, a source of language for expressing those concepts, and a source of methods for reasoning about those concepts. We have, for example, a fairly good understanding, both theoretical and practical, of sequential programs, as compared, say, with our lack of understanding in areas such as parallel programs. We do not understand very well how to develop or reason about parallel programs. The old empirical fallback, testing, fails in this case, simply because several runs of a program with identical data can produce several different answers. Another area of difficulty is specifications. We are simply very used to thinking operationally, and, as programmers, we have to consciously will ourselves to avoid unnecessary commitment when writing down specifications.

Theory helps us by providing a lens through which we can see the inherent structural characteristics of a problem.

If we are to succeed in building knowledge-based programming tools, then we will have to see a blending of ideas. Since the ultimate users of the tools are human, it is essential that the concepts embodied in the tools have some intuitive correspondence. It must be stressed, however, that this does NOT require the intuitive notions to exist *a priori*; they can be learned. This brings me back to my earlier point, about the impact of empirical results. I suggest that it is entirely possible -- indeed, probable -- that the notions that will underlie the next generation of tools are now unfamiliar to us and are unlikely to show up in current psychologically oriented investigations of the programming process. Concepts such as recursion, information hiding, and higher order functions were, at some point in the past, unfamiliar to most programmers, but today they are part of the general folklore. These notions are all difficult to assimilate, but they are powerful conceptual tools, once grasped. I ask the empiricists this question: How, given such a notion, can we determine its ultimate intuitive appeal and ease of applicability, once it has been assimilated?

RICH

With the panel's permission, I will open it up to discussion from the floor.

GUIER

I would like to address the analogy with the older days in particle physics and so on, partly because I'm pretty old by now and that was my heyday of graduate school. I think what you said is quite valid. Speaking from some memories and experience, when the experimentalists first achieved 300 million-electron-volt accelerators and one could start probing the nucleus at those energies, those were very precious instruments, very expensive instruments, and you planned those experiments very carefully a long way ahead of time. You did make sure that even if you got no answer, it was a useful no answer. The cost of the experimentation was very high, both in money and in time and access and so on. The theoreticians were absolutely in concert with the experimentalists in the sense that they knew how expensive it was, and if they were developing a nuclear theory, they worked very hard at finding a critical experiment that they'd take to the experimentalists and say, "Look, this looks like a great theory; if you do this it'll say yes or no." And there was a lot of very thoughtful collaborative work going on. Maybe an insight. In my own personal work with computers it is not so methodical; you sit at a terminal and you work on a computer and you're kind of by yourself. It is also awfully easy to get fascinated with a small, relatively inexpensive trivial experiment. I would suggest that one of the reasons we're not doing as much theory and competent experimental design is that it's just such a great toy, we don't ever get ourselves disciplined enough to do it.

BLUM

Concerning the difference of computers, Marr, in talking about AI theories, talks about two levels of theories, one which can be explicitly stated, and the second which can only be stated in a complex system which itself works, which sort of says that the product itself becomes the theory. I think that's one of the things that happens in software. There's a very close bond between the developer and the product that he develops. We really haven't trained our people, because culturally we came from a mathematical discipline, and so when we talk about theoretical, we really mean mathematical, logical, provable, sort of bottom-up kind of thing. The kinds of things that Ben is talking about are really external in terms of user interaction. There are no golden rules for that; we have relatively poor metrics, we have relatively small samples, and we don't really train our people. Ben, thank goodness, is on the forefront of making people aware of the fact that this is a tremendous void.

But if we're going to talk about languages and problem solving, we really can't talk about a language that we stick into the computer and some AI something-or-other grinds it out and does the problem solving for us. We really have to talk in terms of the human interaction, how we can measure it, how we can worry about the variability, and so on. Maybe people in the panel might like to comment on some of those comments. How specifically can we measure impact of language?

SHNEIDERMAN

It is not easy. I guess to answer it, I want to clarify the term "empirical." I see two meanings here. One is that empirical programming seems to be hacking around, or you try it and explore and you build it and you see what happens, and I guess we could get into talking about that. I'm talking about another meaning which involves studies of groups of people performing specific tasks using computers, and looking for the ways to make them more effective at performing that task. I'm talking about more psychologically oriented experiments; my own preference is more for controlled experiments and hypothesis-testing designs that some people mentioned here earlier. That definition is important to me.

Now, how do we do those kind of studies? It takes a lot of time and effort, and I think we look at small problems one at a time. For example, a currently interesting issue is about the impact of response time on human performance with computers. We have about 30 studies that have been done and the issue is beginning to be clarified. People change their performance as a function of response time; the profile of commands is different, and the time it takes for them to initiate the next command changes as a fairly linear function. As the response time grows longer, people take more time to think. In part, they're sort of picking up the pace; when it's faster they work more quickly. But when it's slower they're more cautious; the cost of making an error is great because it takes longer to recover.

So we're beginning to understand a little bit about how people's behavior changes, and some surprising things come out. It turns out that people in some situations make more mistakes when the response time is shorter because they work more quickly and they make mistakes. Now, if there's no problem with recovering from a mistake and if the machine captures it, throughput increases. However, if the errors are costly in terms of human life, say air traffic control or medical systems, there's an argument which says that based on these studies we ought to think about sometimes slowing the users down, or at least educating them to think more cautiously in some cases. Here's one narrow area, this area of response time, which has many dimensions, many tasks, many kinds of users, and it's going to take us 20 years to understand that. We have lots of other interesting issues: design of command languages, design of menu structures, design of visual graphics-oriented direct manipulation systems that I talk about. We've got a whole lifetime of fascinating work, and the sooner we get to it, and the more ready we are to deal with doing those tough experiments, the more rapidly we'll get there in understanding these questions.

HAMILL

I agree with Ben. I was trained in the experimental design paradigm, where you generate hypotheses and you test them under careful, controlled conditions. I certainly recognize the value of that approach.

More and more I'm also recognizing the value of an alternative empirical approach which has to do with capturing the best representation of the problem solving space, or whatever it might be, in software, testing it, revising it, and testing it again against human problem-solving performance. It's an iterative kind of development which I think in this kind of a domain has a realistic place in addition to the standard experimental design.

SLATER

I'd like to raise a very basic question here. I heard some comparisons with physics in the 1950s, and one of the things that physics in the 1950s had going for it was 5500 years of playing around with the concepts and blind exploring. I may be off a year or two, but that's about it. They knew what questions they were looking at. I don't think we can get an agreement here about what the questions of computer science are; and so rigorous, controlled experiments have the disadvantage that while they're very good at answering questions, they're not, in my opinion, that good at finding questions. Chemistry would never have progressed if loads of people hadn't tried mixing all types of things together to try to make gold

and noted down all types of wild results that theoreticians
could then play with.

Then you get the theoretical-empirical controversy; the question is are we ready yet for the theoretical-empirical controversy in all of computer science, or do we have to first find
out what computer science is, at least in some areas? I'm not
saying the theoretical-empirical controversy is totally
meaningless. I'm saying that maybe we're in a dark room with
the light in a small area of it, and in that small area of
light we can start using these techniques; but let's also turn
on the lights in the rest of the room and just blindly grope
around and play with our computers as we've been doing in
physics for 5500 years. Then we can start doing meaningful
work.

SHNEIDERMAN

I've heard that one before. And I won't buy the all-or-nothing
approach. I was careful when I started to say I want to bend
your ear a little bit, I want to lean in the direction of being
more thoughtful about evaluations. I'm not saying only
controlled experiments; there are lots of places where informal
kinds of experiments are appropriate, but I'm not prepared to
wait 5500 years for the evolution that's been going on in
physics. I think we can do it more rapidly if we get down to
the hard work in trying to understand these issues. Now, I
can't prove that to you; that's an informal hypothesis, but I
think there's ample evidence that in the places where you get
down to work, you do find solutions. I don't want to spend
hundreds of millions or hundreds of billions of dollars of
taxpayer money to give people chemistry sets, if you will, to
play around and hack around; I want to see greater productivity
for the research that's being supported. I won't say only
controlled experiments, but I would like to see for every
research project, that in the proposal there's an explicit
statement about the way the project will be evaluated, the way
the outcome will be evaluated.

SLATER

I think that has killed many scientists, and I think many
research proposals should have it. But I think many research
proposals should not; many research proposals should just look
around in the dark and see if they can find anything else out
there.

SHNEIDERMAN

I would again partialize it and agree; I would grant that to
those who have demonstrated, in their past performance, high
productivity.

WEINTRAUB

Bit of a shotgun shell here; there are several small points.
First of all, Ben, I had presumed your comment about learning

was in response to Bob Rich's original viewgraph. To take the comment just made about designing the experiments, several thoughts came to mind at once, primarily on something I saw about the Jackson methodology (I believe) that was just advertised by ACM's Washington chapter. One of the claims for the greatness of this methodology was that given the same problem specification and 500 different programmers, they would all come up with exactly the same program in exactly the same language, and this was stated as a proof that this was a wonderful methodology. My point is that the problem is not just a question of designing the experiment, but also a question of designing what you want the answer to be, that is, what you expect would be a good answer; we're still getting burned.

There is an excellent experimental facility out there which is working very well, and that is the marketplace, specifically what's happening with PCs. This is not original to me; the comment was made, I believe, by Ben last year, that the marketplace sees lots of things come out, and those that work will sell, and (unless your name is IBM) those that won't work will not sell. We end up stuck with a lot of programmers designing huge systems which then get used, and if you'd just stopped for a minute and thought about what was going on, it would have been quite clear that the approach to the problem was inappropriate; however, it sold. There are a lot of charlatans in this business, and some of them are very, very successful. And so you have methodologies being sold, and really these methodologies are experiments. Just as we learned today that officially the waterfall model is just now being dropped as being inappropriate, we also will probably see in 20 years that a lot of concepts that were driving the industry are still there. On the other hand, I would point out that there are experiments which have gloriously failed which are still very much being funded. For example, COBOL--it's going on and on, but in a sense that in itself is an experiment; you have millions of people spending billions of dollars, probably, developing programs. I have a friend who was hired by Nabisco, and the first thing he had to do was write an interactive calculator system in COBOL. It took him a lot longer than it would have taken him to do it in BASIC but they had COBOL on the machine and that's what the company wanted the system to be written in.

As to the analogy with physics and the development in chemistry, etc., I would mention "The Ascent of Man," specifically the beautiful episode Bronowski had on the materials in the Japanese Samurai sword. Here was a technology that was available in one part of the world; it was kept very secret, but certainly worked, and still works, and yet the process was reduced to ritual by trial and error, because people couldn't understand what was going on microchemically, micromaterialistically, or microphysically. We see the same things in computers: There are certain things that work and there are certain ones that don't work; every time a person approaches a screen, that's an experiment. The problem is: How do you measure the experiments? How do you determine whether or not the results were good?

I would close with a comment made by Bill Ace. At APL, we have this huge database, as every "industrial facility" has, of what has not worked around here, and there ought to be some way to analyze this and at least understand where the so-called "industrial state" of our techniques is falling on its face.

RADA

I have a comment related to Bruce Hamill's talk about representations and the need to investigate which representations are good for which task. I want to point out two articles to which he didn't allude. One was done by James Reggia, advisor of one of the panelists, who was studying a rule-based approach versus a more geometric approach, building an expert system in a particular domain, with conclusions about which representation worked better, and why. Another was a study by Ruven Brooks, exploring how different software support systems for developing expert systems would be happily used by different people and concluded that it was somewhat independent of the representational form; it depended more on the user-friendly interface and the documentation that was provided.

On the issue of experimentation, I am curious to what extent Bill Scherlis' and Venu Dasigi's bodies of work are experimental. For the work they reported on, what were the hypotheses and what were the tests of those hypotheses?

HAMILL

I thank Roy for those references. I certainly don't think that the Japanese study that I alluded to is the only comparative study of these formalisms, and I'd be happy to learn of more. I'm sure that I'm heartened and that Ben is heartened that there is more experimentation being done in this area.

DASIGI

I was not referring to any specific experiment. What I had in mind when I talked about hypothesizing and testing is how basically we go about doing it. When I mentioned abductive hypothesizing and testing, I was referring to the automatic generation and testing of hypotheses for problem solving.

RADA

Maybe you're not addressing my question. You talked about abductive inference as something you were studying, and I understood you had a method and you tried it on a few examples and you showed it to us and it seemed reasonable. And the other paper on derivations looked at some examples and showed how you could reason by analogy, and the example seemed to work.

DASIGI

You are referring to the paper I presented about the work done with Jim Reggia. Our initial hypothesis was that parsimonious covering can model the abductive inference underlying natural language processing. While this hypothesis presupposes that abduction actually underlies language processing by humans, it is agreed upon by some other researchers, too. A preliminary prototype described in the paper demonstrates that abduction actually underlies natural language processing. Many examples can be cited. It soon became clear to us, however, that the initial hypothesis should be revised to include the fact that parsimonious covering as it is formulated so far needs to be extended to handle complications such as word order and the inherent structure of concepts.

The hypothesis itself is derived in a way similar to what you describe in a recent paper of yours, co-authored by Lindley Darden, where you start with some horizontal relations between two areas or entities and postulate a hypothesis based on some vertical relations (Darden and Rada 85).

Experiments involve working out examples to focus the hypothesis in order to characterize the exact modifications needed and testing the hypothesis, which could possibly be further revised, using a prototype computer implementation. Part of the refinement is under way. The hypothesis can be called a theory only after it is proved or confirmed by appropriate experimentation.

Reference

Darden, L. and Rada, R. 85: Hypothesis Formation via Interrelations. In Proceedings of Analogica '85, Computer Science Department, Rutgers University.

SCHERLIS

The question is, what is the empirical part of my work with Scott Dietzen on analogy? We are addressing two very broad questions concerning, on the one hand, the structure of program derivations, and, more specifically in the paper, the structure of an accumulation of derivations. We are further along in our work on the first of these two questions, so I will answer in that context. At the moment, I view the question as primarily a theoretical one, in that we are trying to formulate good hypothetical structures and not to bind ourselves too closely to present practice.

We must consider, however, how to test the hypothetical structures that we develop. At the moment, we have been doing it by building derivations by hand. The various complex examples that were alluded to in the talk are a part of the corpus of examples that we have worked up over the years. Now, there is clearly no quantitative technique that can be used to measure the degree of success of applying a particular approach to deriving a particular algorithm. We cannot know, yet, if at

some point a better technique will be developed (and there is
clearly a theoretical question lurking here). The only way we
can measure success now is to see if particular derivations
have intuitive value for others. If somebody decides that use
of a derivation is a nice way to teach an algorithm, then that
is an indication, for us, of success with respect to
"naturalness" of the approach.

There is a certain comfort to be gained from quantitative
approaches but I do not think we will soon see such approaches
here. Quantitative approaches to software productivity, for
example, are of value only as crude approximations. Relying on
them in experimental work, simply because nothing better is
around, is dangerous. Software engineering has always been
plagued by an inability to produce meaningful productivity
data.

The other approach we are taking to experimentation is to
construct a mechanized system and experiment with that
system. That will allow us to try many examples and, more
importantly, it will allow other people besides the developers
to try examples. But I do think that, although we are a great
distance from being able to apply quantitative techniques to
help assess our hypotheses, we should not let this prevent us
from approaching the problem and making progress, even if it is
measured in a crude fashion.

JERNIGAN

There seems to have crept in here some kind of equating of
experimentation with empiricism. I don't think that's what you
intended, and if it is, say so, so we can argue about it. I
don't think, also, that there is an either/or situation with
regard to the theoretical and empirical approaches. We have
had several mentions today of the first-order predicate
calculus; do we need to examine, empirically, whether or not
that is a valid theory? That's kind of absurd on the
surface. Or on the other hand, we might want to consider, in
our own actions of how we go about solving problems ourselves,
whether or not we as problem solvers can arrive at solutions by
using first-order predicate calculus, and that is an empirical
question.

DREILING

We've been going for a language-independent attitude in this
whole symposium so far, and I've done some wondering about the
empirical and theoretical practices of language in problem
solving. We say that problems can be solved in any language,
or that we can solve them, and yet we know that there are some
problems we'd rather solve in some languages than others, and
that people react differently to languages. The constructs of
language influence the way people think about them, and indeed,
that's the whole question of how is problem solving affected by
the elements of or the ability to express in languages.
Expressive adequacy--there's a question that languages are
different and their constructs are different, and yet we're not

coming up with theory or practice that leads further along those lines.

EPSTEIN

I want to come back to regularities. It seems to me that a great deal of the experimentation in computer science is a search for regularities. Once these regularities are discovered, if we take them back and incorporate them into the theory, and therefore into the problem-solving language, it would seem to me that we are making progress. I think it's extremely difficult to define a metric on a concept like discovery. As the domain becomes more ill-defined, a metric gets more and more difficult to quantify. The alternative that I have used in my work is to establish human behavior as a benchmark. When I took, for example, three graph theory textbooks that were considered by mathematicians to be reasonably complete and to cover the field fairly well, I measured expressive adequacy by whether or not I could describe most of what was in those books. I believe that is the only kind of measure we can put on an ill-defined domain. If there are any suggestions, I'd be delighted to hear them.

DREILING

The only thing I'd add in response is that different people solve problems differently, and that, unfortunately, affects this whole process. When you come up with a language which solves one domain, you can take a whole range of people and you'll get different results because of their ability to express themselves in that language to solve that problem.

LOCKER

Comparison has been made to two types of theory, physics on the one hand, psychology on the other hand. In both cases, we have existing behavior: We've tried to build exploratory systems and to generate hypotheses to test out those theories. On the other hand, if I tried to analyze what is being said today in any literature, the computer vehicle is valid for testing those truths, so I don't see theory in terms of those things.

KLERER

I'd like to ask Ben Shneiderman to elaborate on two things which he mentioned. I think he said he posed a question as to how one goes about evaluating the products of our works, measuring collectively, I assume, and particularly, what sort of metric one should use. What would he recommend as a metric? For myself, it seems to me in most cases I've looked at, the obvious metric is simply to measure the time that it takes to get a solution. If one's a programmer, how long does it take to program? I don't go about counting the number of operators and number of arguments to program; I don't think that's valid from Mr. Shneiderman's point of view. That's one question.

The other thing he raised was that there is a large diversity among users, or I think he put it in the context of their psychological framework--I hope I'm not misinterpreting him-- and he also mentioned the necessity to do well-controlled experiments. I'd like him to elaborate on what I see as an apparent contradiction. If, indeed, it's true, and I happen to think it's very true, that there is a large diversity in the psychological orientation of users and, particularly, even larger diversity in the capability to program, I think there's a tremendous variability in programming ability. How does one go about doing a controlled scientific experiment when most statistical designs I'm aware of assume that the variance is controllable? I think these are rather profound questions.

SHNEIDERMAN

Wonderful. Thank you for the opportunity. I'll try not to be too long, but I think we're exactly dealing with these issues. Let's follow up one of the examples. Scherlis suggested that his way of evaluating a concept he generated was whether it was well received by what he called the social process of science. In fact, I like what he's doing, but how much stronger would his case be, if we took a group of students who were learning programming, and conducted a controlled experiment. Half would get the previous method of learning, and half the Scherlis approach, and we could ask them to perform some tasks. We might measure the time it takes, or the rate of errors, or work with subjective impressions, as well. So, depending on the situation, we measure typically five categories, the time to learn something, the speed of performance on benchmark tasks, the rate of errors, subjective satisfaction by a set of scales, usually 1 to 7 scales, and then their retention over time. If, for example, their performance or retention over time were better for one method, that would indicate some advantage.

One of the issues he mentioned earlier was exactly something students of mine are doing. He said, "Recursion...Once you've got it, you've got it." That to me is not a very scientific statement. It doesn't help me understand how to teach recursion or whether recursion is more appropriate than iteration. Now why is it? What is the strange phenomenon underlying recursion that gives it the impression of being difficult at first, but once you've got it, you've got it. I think that it would be interesting if we could understand a little better why recursion has this remarkable pull for many people and disapproval from other people. We might trace it to individual differences; possibly it has to do with background training. Maybe if they'd been trained, as suggested, in Fortran first, they'd never learn recursion, but maybe it has to do with other aspects of their background.

It's not simple to do controlled studies, but I think we can return to the analogy with physics. A skeptic might say, how could you possibly study the electrical conductivity of metals, because there are so many kinds of metals, and of course, the metals sometimes are hot and sometimes are cold and sometimes there are impurities? Well, we have to follow it through. We have to look at particular communities of users for particular tasks, and then begin to broaden out, generalize, and we will, I believe, find theories that will accommodate larger cases. I liken each of these experiments to a tile in a mosaic. By itself it's small, and you know one tile won't give you the whole picture, but with hundreds and thousands of experiments we will be getting a theory, an image of human performance which will be predictive in the future.

We begin to see it now for certain domains, such as the study of menus. There have been about 40 or 50 experiments in the last few years about the design of menus. The one issue I'll just ask you about is menu tree width or breadth. Would you think the performance improves as the breadth of menu tree increases, or as the depth increases? There were arguments on both sides, and it's quite interesting that a priori, it might be difficult to guess. Once I tell you the answer, you'll say, Oh yeah, sure, sure, sure. But many people were stuck in the design of menus as to whether to make it a broader, shallower tree, or a deeper, narrower tree, and the evidence seems to be that the intervening factor that cluttered people's attention was the display rate of the systems. If you have rapid display rates and reasonable size screens, then, in general, it turns out that broader, shallower trees are extremely more productive in their performance. Yet in the current issue of Datamation there is someone who recommends making narrower trees.

So it's not obvious until I tell you, and after we see a half dozen experiments supporting the same general notion with different users and different tasks, we begin to get useful theories that predict performance. I think we're getting there, and I'm excited to see all that happening. I'd like to encourage further attention in that direction. I don't want to eliminate the other things. I want exploration, I want different kinds of ventures to be put forth. Controlled experiment is not the only way, but I do see it as an important paradigm of research, which is why I wanted to bring it forward and to provoke the kind of discussion I've seen here. I thank you for your questions, and I appreciate your differences, as well.

DESIGN ISSUES

ISSUES IN THE DESIGN OF MARKER-PASSING SYSTEMS

James Hendler

Department of Computer Science
University of Maryland
College Park Maryland

Recent work in Artificial Intelligence has focused on the presence of a spreading-activation, or marker-passing, mechanism. Our goal in this paper is to describe such mechanisms, to provide a vocabulary for discussing such programs, and examine the set of common issues such systems must address. We present a methodical examination of many of the issues involved in the design and implementation of marker-passing systems.

1.0   INTRODUCTION

Recent work in natural language processing (cf. Charniak, 1982, forthcoming; Norvig, forthcoming; Granger 1984; Alterman, 1985) and problem-solving (Hendler, 1986) has revived interest in algorithms that perform marker-passing. While not a new idea--the first such system was proposed by Quillian 20 years ago (Quillian, 1966)--it is only with the recent interest in parallelism that marker-passing has gained prominence. The goal of this paper is to examine such systems and describe the issues that the designers of such systems should be aware of.

Marker-passing systems, also called spreading activation systems, work by passing activation markers and information through an associative network. To better understand this idea consider an associative network as a bunch of hockey pucks connected to one another by springs hanging in midair. If one of these hockey pucks is struck it will start to vibrate. This in turn will start the hockey pucks next to it vibrating, and so on and so on and so on. Because of friction, each puck would vibrate a little less than the puck before until we reached some limit where the vibrations were relatively imperceptible. Assume that at this point we struck another hockey puck elsewhere in the entangled web. This puck would also start a set of pucks vibrating. At some point, a hockey puck already vibrating from the first node might be shaken from the second. The collection of those pucks vibrating from both nodes forms a set with an interesting property: informally, it is the set of all nodes for which some path connects the two first nodes. The paths through these nodes therefore contain a set of connections which, in a network in which the links (or springs in our hockey puck system) carry information, can be examined for semantic content.

The first computational model of a spreading activation mechanism is M. Ross Quillian's (1966) *semantic memory* model. This work attempted to make a cognitive model of several memory processes concerned with word definitions and language tasks. Quillian's model kept word senses in an associative network form, and thus was able to compare and contrast meanings by expanding out a set of *activation tags* from each concept. Using this scheme Quillian was able to generate a set of paths found by intersecting word concepts. Quillian is probably better known for a later work derived from this earlier one. His Teachable Language Comprehender, TLC (Quillian, 1969) was designed to handle natural language comprehension using this activation approach.

Although Quillian's model gained wide attention among cognitive psychologists it was less well received by the computer science community. This was primarily due to issues relating to the complexity of the computations involved and the lack of specificity in the design of the knowledge representation. It was with the work of Fahlman (1979) that the idea started to reemerge in its present form.

Fahlman's NETL system was designed as a hardware implementation of a marker-passing scheme (actually simulated in software). The network memory was similar to that of Quillian, but was realized quite differently. Each node in memory was replaced by a simple hardware device called a *node unit*, and each link became a hardware *link unit*. These devices were able to propagate a set of markers in parallel throughout the network. The system's goal was to deal quickly with certain types of knowledge-base issues: those concerning type hierarchies and property inheritance. NETL worked by passing markers throughout the system via a parallel architecture containing various types of processors. The system propagated marks through the network and used a controller process to query nodes to find how they've been marked.

An approach more like Quillian's original approach was taken by Charniak (1982) in a natural language processing system. The idea was to take stories such as:

>   Jack wanted to commit suicide. He found a rope.

and pass markers on each word as it came in. Paths found between words were examined by the deductive component, a *path checker*, which would check to see if they proposed a consistent context for the story. In this case a path such as:

>   Suicide -> Kill -> Hang -> Noose -> Rope.

would be found and the context "hang" would be used. Hirst (1983) used Charniak's approach for doing word sense disambiguation in his *Polaroid Words* system.

More recent work by Charniak (forthcoming) attempts to provide a uniform treatment of natural language analysis based in marker-passing. A syntactic parser breaks sentences down into constituent pieces, which are then put together by the marker-passer. Charniak contends that the act of connecting these pieces into the semantic representation, via the marker-passer, subsumes many of the traditionally difficult parts of language processing.

Other work in natural language processing has also involved marker-passing schemes. This work has included research into the use of marker-passing for the recovery of intended inferences from text (Norvig, 1986), examined the use of marker-passing for the parallel control a system doing both syntactic and semantic analysis (Granger, Eiselt, Holbrook, 1984), and have examined procedural logic implementations of marker-passing (Alterman, 1985).

Riesbeck and Martin (1985) take a somewhat different approach to the use of marker-passing in natural language. Their direct-memory access parsing system, DMAP-0, is based on Quillian's model, but builds form tests directly into the marker-passing algorithm. In this system, marker-passing isn't a simple "dumb" spreading-activation mechanism: the marker-passer uses information found at the nodes to determine how activation is to be spread. DMAP-0 used two types of markers: *activation* markers and *prediction* markers. It has a complex algorithm for how each type of marker is placed and how they can be removed.

Another use of marker-passing was suggested in (Hendler, 1986). In this work we show that such algorithms can be used by planning systems for making more efficient choices and to avoid certain pitfalls. Marker-passing was used to avoid paths for which necessary participants were unavailable, to suggest the use of paths where needed objects were available, to avoid certain types of negative interactions within plans, and to do demon-invocation at an early stage of planning.

This recent resurgence of interest in activation-spreading systems leads to a need for a method of categorizing the behaviour of such systems and a methodical analysis of the issues involved in the design of such systems. In this paper we develop such a categorization and provide such an analysis.

2.0   DESIGN ISSUES

Marker-passing systems can be categorized in terms of three design decisions: what is returned, the correctness of this return, and whether the processing is based on a parallel or serial model. In this section we will describe these issues.

2.1   What is Returned

One decision to be made by the designer of a marker-passer is what it is to return. Should it, like Quillian's program, return a set of paths linking nodes of origin? Or should it return a set of nodes representing the intersections of the origins, as Fahlman's system did?

If the marker-passer is viewed as a system which "answers a specific question", returning a set of nodes may be all that is necessary. If, on the other hand, the marker-passer is viewed as returning inference paths between concepts, a set of nodes is insufficient. We need to examine the whole path, not just the node of intersection.

Keeping track of the paths has a cost in terms of computation time. For a marker-passer to return only the nodes of intersection requires a marking time solely proportional to the number of nodes marked. In a concurrent formulation this time becomes proportional to the length of the longest path found, usually a far smaller number. If paths are to be returned, then as each node of intersection is found the return path must be computed. The time for the marker-passer to run is thus increased by a time proportional to the product of the number of paths found and their lengths.

2.2 Correctness

Since performance can degrade quickly as the number of paths increases, it is incumbent upon the designer of the marker-passing system to keep the number of paths returned by the marker-passer small. Ideally, only paths useful to the system using the marker-passer would be returned. One way of achieving this is to make the system take advantage of features of the underlying representation scheme--to have the marking differ depending on the links between nodes.

The changing of marks and marking procedures based on the links traversed is sometimes called "smart" marker-passing. The goal of a smart marker-passing scheme is to make sure that the system returns only correct information. If we're returning a set of nodes, each element of the set will be, in essence, a correct answer to the question that invokes marker-passing. When the smart marker-passer returns paths, these paths should all be of use to whatever mechanism is evaluating them--many other paths are considered to be an error.

In contrast to this is a technique in which the marker-passing algorithm does not take into consideration the semantics of the nodes being traversed--this is the classical marker-passing paradigm described by Quillian. Such systems are often called "dumb" marker-passers in contrast to the "smart" marker-passers described above. In a dumb marker-passing scheme the links being traversed have little or no effect on the algorithm. This type of marker-passer will find all paths between the nodes being marked, regardless of how meaningful they are.

The decision between "smart" and "dumb" is not deciding between two poles, but rather picking a point on a spectrum. At one end are the very dumb marker-passers which return a large number of nodes or paths, many of them incorrect; at the other end are systems which return small sets of correct paths.

2.3   Parallel vs. Serial

Since Fahlman's work, marker-passing has generally been viewed as a parallel process--Quillian's model is too computationally inefficient to run on a traditional serial machine. This does not, however, have to be the case. Some marking programs, for example Riesbeck and Martin's DMAP-0, have a different and often serial formulation. In these models marks pass outwards in more or less discrete steps, and the order of these marks is important. In other models it is important that paths of length N be found before paths of length N+1. Both of these designs impose some serial constraints on the marker-passing algorithms.

The most parallel formulation of marker-passing views activation spreading as a massively parallel process. The programs for marking a node are formulated to be "local" algorithms-- algorithms that can be performed by a fairly simple processor located at the node and knowing only of itself and its connection to its neighbors. This imposes a severe constraint on the marker-passing algorithm: it may not take into account "global" effects. For example, if a smart marker-passer had a rule saying to mark the node "circus elephant" only if the nodes for both "elephant" and "performer" were already marked, it would be very difficult to implement as a local computation, since nodes would need to query other nodes which might not be neighbors.

Adding parallelism to the marker-passer affects the design decision mentioned above. The gain in efficiency from parallelism can make up for some of the extra time needed to return paths or to make the algorithm smarter. A smart, serial marker-passer returning paths would be the slowest formulation but the one needing the least post-processing (by a path evaluator or the like). A massively parallel, dumb algorithm which returned only nodes would be the most efficient, but also the least concise.

3.0   MARKER-PASSING ISSUES

Whatever formulation of marker-passing is used there are common issues which must be attended to. In this section we will discuss these issues.

3.1   Attenuation

The most important issue involved in marker-passing is attenuation of the marking. Consider of our hockey pucks vibrating with no frictional damping. If we strike one puck the entire network starts to move--we activate all the concepts in our net. If we now strike another puck the set of nodes vibrating from both is still the whole network. Clearly this is not useful and we must limit the marker-passer somehow.

One type of limitation is simply to use a smart marker-passing algorithm. In this case we do not pass to all the neighbors of each node marked, but rather only to some distinguished ones. The NETL system, for example, marked all the nodes in the direct IS A hierarchy above a selected node, but only under certain conditions were the other nodes this node was linked to marked. Thus NETL had no explicit attenuation mechanism, since the algorithm was designed so as not to need it.

In a dumber marker-passer the attenuation mechanism can be built into the algorithm in the form of a length limitation. In a complex network all the nodes are connected to each other. Some of these paths are long and tortuous--they require that a large number of inferences hold true. If one holds the breadth of activation spreading to a set limit these long paths can be avoided. Quillian's system, and most of the systems based on it, use such a limitation.

A limitation on length is not enough, however, since many paths that add no information are quite short. Charniak (1983) suggested dealing with this problem by checking the outbranching of nodes during marker-passing. Those "promiscuous" nodes which have an outbranching greater than a certain constant will not propagate marks. They can be marked, but they cannot pass marks through. The length and promiscuity limitations have a serious, failing. When we use such limitations our marking becomes very dependent on the form of the knowledge we are representing, not on the meaning.

Ideally an attenuation mechanism should combine information about length and promiscuity so that longer paths are allowed if they involve little outbranching, and short paths that go through some what promiscuous nodes are also allowed. One such attenuation mechanism was proposed in our earlier work (Hendler, 1986). This attenuation mechanism was designed to limit both length and branchout of the paths found without violating the locality constraints needed for massively parallel computing. This was done by using a numerical constant, called *zorch*, to start marker-passing and dividing it by outbranching as we proceed. If we start at a highly branching node, it and all its first set of descendants can be marked, but the zorch runs out quickly. If, however, we hit such a promiscuous node late in processing, its descendants are not marked since we do not have enough zorch left.

3.2   Marks

Another decision to be made is how much information to leave on a mark. The simplest form of mark is a tag bit on a node, set to 1 if the node is marked. This type of marker tells us if a node has been marked but not anything about when it was marked or from what origin. Other schemes use very complicated marks which include more information at the cost of space. A list of the types of information a mark can contain follows:

(1) *Point of origin*. We may wish to record a pointer to the node of origin for a set of marking. This enables

us to tell, upon encountering a node already marked, the source of that marking. This is essential in a marker-passer that returns paths.

(2) **A pointer to preceding nodes**. If the marker-passer is to return a path it must be able to follow back pointers to the node of origin. To do this a mark must contain a pointer to the immediately preceding node.

(3) **Path Information**. If the marker-passer in question is to return paths as opposed to just nodes of intersection, it is useful to keep track of the links which are traversed.

(4) **Weight**. Some schemes entail an activation which decays overtime. Others involve being able to compute a strength of a path to be returned. In these cases we need to encode information about the strength of marking.

(5) **Time and date**. Later in this chapter we will discuss several schemes for avoiding marker-passing problems that require information about when a mark occurs. We'll use the term "time" to refer to a property corresponding to an actual system clock time or any other means of making available to parallel processors uniquely identified, monotonically increasing time units. A property that is set by the system on all marks in a given set of mark propagations will be called a "date."

3.3 Link Types

One simple form of "smarts" that can be added to a marker-passer is the ability to handle some types of links differently from others.

One way the marker-passer can be limited is by treating certain links in the network as "one-way links"--markers can be passed over them in only one direction. As an example consider the marking of IS A links. A node like MAMMAL will have a very large set of nodes connected via IS A links (cat, dog, moose, platypus, *etc., etc.*. If we mark one of these exemplars we'd like to mark MAMMAL and also to mark the properties of MAMMAL that might be important during inferencing (lactates, live-bearing, *etc.*. We would probably not, however, like to mark all the other exemplars, since this would require marking many nodes.

This type of thing cannot be handled simply by our attenuation mechanism. A node like MAMMAL is likely to be tagged as a promiscuous node (or to have a high enough outbranching that zorch cannot flow through). We will therefore not mark any of its neighbors. To be able to mark the appropriate "important" properties we need to eliminate the alternate exemplars from the nodes considered during marker-passing.

Another way to influence the behavior of the marker-passer is to give each link in our network a different weight. When marks are passed those nodes having greater weight get activated "more." This method only works either in the presence of an attenuation mechanism such as the zorch scheme or when the paths returned by the marker-passer are ordered by strength.

There are two ways that such weights can be assigned: each link can have its own weight, or each type of link can be given a value. For the former we could say, for example, (IS A A B) has weight X while (IS A C D) has weight Y. For the latter we would say all IS A links have weight X. Whichever way is used, the marker-passer takes advantage of this information during marker-passing and spreads activation accordingly.

One possible use for weighted links would be to add "learning" to a marker-passing scheme. In such a system, each time a path returned by the marker-passer was used by the rest of the program the links in that path would be given slightly greater weight. The more often such a path was used, the more preferred it would become. While a system like this is relatively easy to implement, it is difficult to predict its learning behavior over time. The issue is further complicated by decisions as to what happens to weights over time, how the unused links are to be treated, and how the weights are to be set.

The primary problem with using weighted links is finding a way to assign the values--one hopes to be able to assign these links in something other than an *ad hoc* manner, and yet finding a rational basis is difficult.

3.4 Loops and Multiple Paths

When markers are passed over an associative net, the network structure of the representation causes a difficulty. Wherever a loop occurs the marker-passer can have problematic behaviors which we discuss in this section.

3.4.1 Loops During Marking

Consider the network of Figure 1, which represents the following facts:

```
(FRAME: ANIMAL
 ...
SLOTS: (HEAD-OF (HEAD))    ;the head of an animal is some
)                          ;type of head

(FRAME: ELEPHANT
 ISA: ANIMAL
SLOTS: (HEAD-OF (ELEPHANT-HEAD)) ;an elephant has a specific
)                                ; kind of head

(FRAME: ELEPHANT-HEAD
 ISA: HEAD
SLOTS: (NOSE-OF (TRUNK))   ;an elephant's nose is a trunk
)
```

Consider what happens when we pass marks starting at ELEPHANT.
The first nodes marked from ELEPHANT are ANIMAL (via the IS A
link) and ELEPHANT-HEAD (via the slot restriction). Marks then
flow from ANIMAL to HEAD, from ELEPHANT-HEAD to HEAD, and from
ELEPHANT-HEAD to TRUNK. We continue to pass markers and mark
ANIMAL and ELEPHANT-HEAD from HEAD.

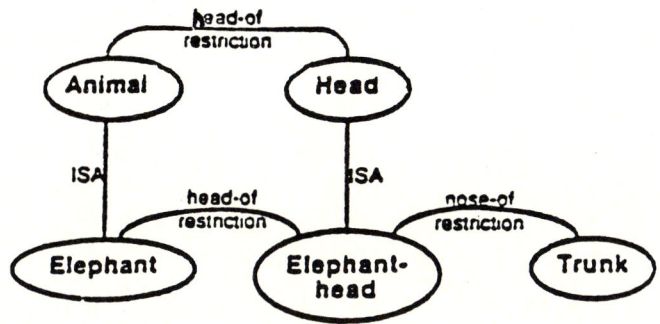

Figure 1

A network with a loop

The next step then marks ELEPHANT from both ANIMAL and
ELEPHANT-HEAD. If marking now continues we repeat this whole
process, since we are starting at ELEPHANT once again. This
continues until we reach the attenuation limit and stop. We
need a scheme to eliminate this redundant work.

The traditional way of handling this (*a la* Quillian (1967)) is
to leave a trace of each origin; if we come to a node marked
from the same origin, we stop marking. Thus, in the example
above we would not mark ELEPHANT-HEAD from HEAD since it has
already been marked from ELEPHANT.

While this method eliminates loops that occur during marking,
it can cause problems in systems in which the marker-passer
returns multiple paths. This issue is discussed in the
following section.

3.4.2   MULTIPLE PATHS

Consider what happens in the example above when an activation
from another origin encounters one of the nodes we have marked
during looping. If an intersection were found at the node
TRUNK, say, the set of paths returned would be:

(1)   ELEPHANT -> ELEPHANT-HEAD -> TRUNK

(2)   ELEPHANT -> ANIMAL -> HEAD -> ELEPHANT-HEAD -> TRUNK

(3)   ELEPHANT -> ELEPHANT-HEAD -> HEAD -> ANIMAL ->
       ELEPHANT -> <Path 1>

(4) ELEPHANT -> ELEPHANT-HEAD -> HEAD -> ANIMAL ->
     ELEPHANT -> <Path 2>

(5) ELEPHANT -> ELEPHANT-HEAD -> HEAD -> ANIMAL ->
     ELEPHANT -> ELEPHANT-HEAD -> HEAD -> ANIMAL ->
     ELEPHANT -> (<Path 1> or <path 2>).

and so on--the set of paths being returned has grown large.

If we use the scheme discussed in the previous section, we will eliminate all but the first path. However, path 2 provides certain information that path 1 does not, and this information may be important to the system invoking the marker-passer. We have thus eliminated the looping paths (3 and on) at the cost of losing a path we need. To avoid this a more complex mechanism must be designed.

In one such mechanism, each mark keeps track of its origin as before. This time, however, when we encounter a node marked from the same origin we do not stop; instead, we update the information found at that node to allow two backtraces. Thus, if ELEPHANT-HEAD is asked to report a path back to ELEPHANT it will report both subpaths. These subpaths are then combined by the path return mechanism.

This solution works in the situation above, but is not fully general in a parallel environment, since path 1 maybe reported before the mark from HEAD reaches ELEPHANT-HEAD. In this case the new information is updated on ELEPHANT-HEAD but the marking then stops. Nothing now encounters TRUNK again, and therefore path 2 is not returned. The set of paths returned is thus determined by the exact characteristics of the parallel system, in some we would get path 2, in some we wouldn't--a race condition decides.

A solution for this problem is to use a scheme in which an extra property is put on each node. Each time a path through a node is found, a time stamp is put on this property of the node. When we mark a node for a second time from the same origin we check to see if a path has come through at an earlier time. If it has not, we add the back pointer to the set of marks and pass no more marks from this node. If a path has come through, we allow marker-passing to continue.

To see how this works, consider our example once again. First, consider the case in which we find the path from TRUNK to ELEPHANT before the marking of ELEPHANT-HEAD from HEAD. As the path is found we set the property on ELEPHANT-HEAD to show that a path came through at time T1. We now come to mark from HEAD. Since the path property is already set, we know that we must continue marker-passing. The markers propagate once again and TRUNK is marked. We now follow the path back from trunk to ELEPHANT. Since ELEPHANT-HEAD contains two paths back to ELEPHANT, both paths can be found.

If, instead, we had reached TRUNK after the second marking of ELEPHANT-HEAD, the situation would be different. In this case the mark from HEAD comes to ELEPHANT-HEAD but the path property has not been set. We therefore mark ELEPHANT-HEAD with information leading back to both origins and mark no further. (so as to eliminate loops in marking--see previous section). At a later time the path from TRUNK to ELEPHANT is computed, and since both paths are recorded at ELEPHANT-HEAD paths 1 and 2 are both reported.

The scheme as outlined so far has one remaining bug: when the TRUNK node was found before the second marking of ELEPHANT-HEAD, path 1 was returned twice. This is solved by using the time stamp associated with the property. If a time stamp is associated with each mark on a node we need only report paths through marks that came later in time than the last path through. In this way we would mark ELEPHANT-HEAD from ELEPHANT at time T_i, put a path property on ELEPHANT-HEAD at time T_j, and mark ELEPHANT-HEAD from HEAD at time T_k (where $i<j<k$). When we once again compute a path from TRUNK we would report only those paths containing nodes marked later than T_j and thus do not not report the redundant information.

3.4.3   Follow-on

Another problem that arises during marker-passing that of "follow-on." What do we do when we encounter a node marked from a different origin? We certainly wish to report the path found, but do we continue marking? Consider the example in the previous section: when we mark TRUNK from ELEPHANT-HEAD, do we continue marking? If so, we may find redundant paths, since TRUNK may have been marked from some other origin, say NOSE. In this case the first path reported would be:

(6)   ELEPHANT -> ELEPHANT-HEAD -> TRUNK -> NOSE

If marks continued the next marker-pass would activate NOSE from TRUNK. Since this is already marked a path would be returned. This path, however, would be the same as path 6. If the path from NOSE to TRUNK involved intermediate nodes, path 6 would be reported as each one was marked. Eliminating redundant paths from the return would keep the path evaluator (or whatever program calls the marker-passer) from needing to examine them, but the time necessary merely to compute them can easily swamp the marker-passing.

Again, an apparently simple solution is just to stop marker-passing at the point at which a path is returned. Certain aberrant conditions, however, can occur in an attenuating system. Consider the case shown in Figure 2. Let us assume that we start marking from A and that B is the last point marked (due to attenuation. If we now start marking from C we will reach B and report the path from A. Consider, however, that we may still have activation energy left. If we stop marking (since a path has been found), we will not try to mark node D. It may be the case, however, that D has been marked (either from A or some other origin) and a legal path, perhaps a necessary one, will not be reported.

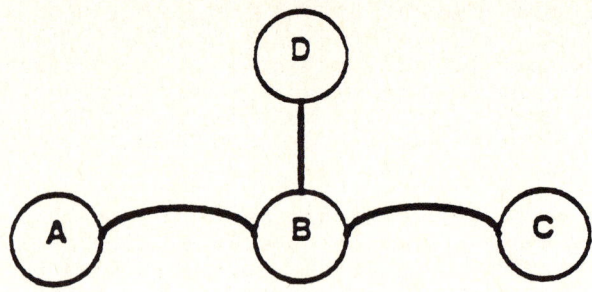

Figure 2

Some nodes

A solution to this is to extend the time stamps used as a solution to the loop detection problem. Instead of just noting a time, we also keep track of where the back path originated. Follow-on is now allowed, thus avoiding the problem of missing paths. To keep from reporting redundant paths we have the marker-passer check the path property of a node before a path meeting at that node is reported. If the path would be redundant it is not reported.

Let us make this clearer by once again using the example in Figure 2. We mark starting at A and proceed to mark B. The attenuation limit is reached so we stop marking. We now start marking at C and reach B, finding the mark from A. A path is computed and the marker-passer adds

    A -> B -> C

to the list of paths to return. As this path is computed A, B, and C are stamped with path properties reporting a connection between A and C. We now continue the marking and both A and D are checked.

At this point we find the information that A has already been marked (from itself) and therefore we check by, looking at A's path property, to see if a path should be reported. Since we have already reported a path from C to A, no new path is reported.

If, on the other hand, D had been marked (either from A or a different origin) no path property would be found. When it is marked from C the check for such a property fails and the system reports the new path. This would update the path property on B to include the earlier path to A and the new path to D. If yet another node were to come along and wish to mark B, both of these nodes are listed, so as to prevent redundant paths back to each of these nodes.

3.4.4 Loops in Paths

One other type of loop occurs in marker-passing systems, this kind during path reporting when two nodes mark each other from the same origin. As an example of this, consider what happens if we add a link from A to D in Figure 2. If we pass marks from A, both B and D will be marked at the first step. At the second step B is marked from D and D is marked from B, both with origin A. C is also marked from B.

If C had previously been marked from another origin a problem would now arise. As the path-reporting algorithm tries to find all paths from C to A, it follows the link from B to D and adds to the subpath found so far all paths back to the origin A. Unfortunately, one of the paths from D back to A is through B. Thus a loop arises as B goes to D and D goes to B -- our path-finder never stops.

This sort of loop is easy to detect, however. If the same node occurs twice in a path we know that some sort of loop has occurred. We simply have the path-checking algorithm check whether the node it is presently examining is an element of the path found so far. If it is, the path-finder is in a loop and can terminate this path.

3.5 Erasing Marks

If the marker-passer is used by another system, or several other systems for that matter, it will eventually get full of marks. The issue of erasing the marks thus arises.

There are essentially two ways of doing mark erasure: erasing them all and having marks degrade. In a system where the marker-passer is called for the solution of a specific problem, we can define discrete marker-passing "events." At the end of one of these, we can erase all previous marks begin a new round of marking. Thus, erasing marks requires no more than a message broadcast to all nodes asking that marks be removed.

More interesting is the case where a system uses the marker-passer continuously. In this situation the marks in the system must be erase dover time. Charniak (forthcoming) and Norvig (1986) use a time stamping system and exponential decay of marks. Each mark includes a number representing the present weight of that mark. As time passes this weight is decreased, and when it falls below a certain threshold the mark is removed.

3.6 Path Ordering

When the return from the marker-passer is to be processed by another program, it is useful to have some heuristics for judging the strength of a path. In one model, the second program rates the returns of the marker-passer, ordering the paths returned. In a second model the marker-passer judges the paths and orders its own return using some heuristic evaluation.

Past systems (*e.g.* Hirst (1983), Norvig (1986)) have used two heuristics for judging the strength of paths returned by the marker-passer: path length and the number of connections through the nodes. Shorter paths are preferred, as are paths which have the smallest number of outbranching links. The exact combination, however, has been left to be decided by experimentation and *post hoc* comparison and generally involves heuristics formulated so that a path strength can be computed using some combination of these factors.

In the second model paths are given a strength rating according to properties of the nodes and links traversed during marker-passing. If this rating falls below a certain threshold the path is not returned. Paths with strength above this threshold are ordered by strength so that the evaluator examines "better" paths first. Path strength is not equivalent to equal semantic utility: it is quite possible for a strong path to be returned in which, for example, variables would not unify or an IS A plateau is encountered. Path strength does, however, correlate well with semantic use, since stronger paths will usually require fewer inferences for realization.

4.0   CONCLUSIONS

Marker-passing algorithms are clearly of interest to the community at large. They have been shown useful in several different AI domains and have generated much discussion at recent conferences. Our goal in this paper was, in part, to provide a vocabulary for such discussions and examine the set of common issues such papers must address.

We have presented a methodical examination of many of the issues involved in the design and implementation of marker-passing systems. It is unclear, however, whether we have defined either a necessary or sufficient set. Rather, we have tried to examine the details of implementing such a system and have described some of the programming techniques and data structures that can be used for such tasks.

5.0   ACKNOWLEDGEMENTS

Dr. Eugene Charniak of Brown University and Dr. Doug Wong of Union College were both involved in the work that led to this paper and have both contributed to the ideas found herein.

6.0 REFERENCES

Alterman, R., A dictionary based on concept coherence *Artificial Intelligence*, 25(*2*), *1985, 153-186*.

Charniak, E., Passing markers: A theory of contextual influence in language comprehension *Cognitive Science*, 7(*3*), 1983, *171-190*.

Charniak, E., *A Single-Semantic-Process Theory of Parsing*, (forthcoming).

Charniak, E., Gavin, M. K. and Hendler, J. A. *The FRAIL/NASL reference manual*, Computer Science Department, Brown University, Technical Report CS-83-06, 1983.

Fahlman, S. E., *NETL: A System for Representing and Using Real World Knowledge*, MIT Press, Massachusetts, 1979.

Fahlman, S. E., Representing implicit knowledge *Parallel Models in Associative Memory*, (ed.) Hinton, G. E. and Anderson, J. A., Lawrence Erlbaum Associates, New Jersey, 1981.

Fahlman, S. E., Hinton, G. E. and Sejnowski, T. J., Massively parallel architectures for AI: NETL, Thistle, and Boltzmann machines *Proceedings of the National Conference on Artificial Intelligence*, 1983, *109-113*.

Granger, R. H., Eiselt, K. P. and Holbrook, J. K., *Parsing with Parallelism: A Spreading-Activation Model of Inference Processing During Text Understanding* Artificial Intelligence Project, University of California, Irvine Technical Report #228, Sept. 1984.

Hendler, J. A. *Integrating Marker-Passing and Problem-Solving: A spreading-activation approach to improved choice in planning* Doctoral Dissertation, Department of Computer Science, Brown University (available as Technical Report CS-86-01), 1986.

Hirst, G. J. *Semantic Interpretation Against Ambiguity* Doctoral Dissertation, Department of Computer Science, Brown University, (available as Technical Report CS-83-25), 1983.

Hirst, G. J. *Semantic Interpretation and the Resolution of Ambiguity* Cambridge University Press, Cambridge, England, 1986.

Hirst, G. J. and Charniak, E., Word sense and case slot disambiguation *Proceedings of the National Conference on Artificial Intelligence*, 1982, *95-98*.

Norvig, P. *Recovering Intended Inferences from Text*, Doctoral Dissertation, Computer Science Department, University of California at Berkeley, (forthcoming).

Quillian, M. R. *Semantic Memory*, Doctoral Dissertation, Carnegie Institute of Technology (Carnegie-Mellon University), 1966. Published as Report 2, Project 8668, Bolt, Beranek, and Newman Inc., 1966.

Quillian, M. R., The Teachable Language Comprehender: A simulation program and theory of language *Communications of the ACM*, 12, 1969, *459-476*.

Riesbeck, C. K. and Martin, C. E. *Direct Memory Access Parsing*, Computer Science Department, Yale University, Research Report #354, 1985.

QUESTION AND ANSWER PERIOD

SLATER

Does your path evaluator ever unmark a node, as in the example, the astronomer married the star?

HENDLER

At the moment, it doesn't. The whole issue of marking turns out to be a very difficult issue. What we generally use is exponential decay. The problem is, you really want to keep around the wrong meaning of star. I can show you the situation in planning where you want to keep around the mark on something that was not the one your path evaluator picked. Now in language, the marks on the wordstream tend to use weak marks that decay quickly.

THE AUTOMATED PROGRAMMER SYSTEM: LANGUAGE DESIGN ISSUES FOR SCIENTIFIC-MATHEMATICAL-ENGINEERING APPLICATIONS PROGRAMMING

Melvin Klerer

Department of Electrical Engineering and Computer Science
Polytechnic University
333 Jay Street
Brooklyn, New York 11201

Fred Grossman

School of Computer Science and Information Systems
Pace University
Pace Plaza
New York, New York 10038

Robert Klerer

Department of Computer Science
Long Island University
University Plaza
Brooklyn, New York 11201

A discussion of issues and motivations relating to the design of the language features of The Automated Programmer System (TAPS) is given. The language of TAPS is oriented toward scientific-engineering-mathematical applications programming and permits complex two-dimensional representation of mathematical formulas embedded in a linguistic structure which is multi-phrase, multi-line in form, with a flexible syntax which permits alternative forms and control structures. Minimization of the difference between the representation of the problem specification in a notation that is conventional to the application area and the representation of the corresponding executable program is a major goal, as is the goal of a self-documenting program. Ambiguity resolution is accomplished by contextual analysis, reliance upon a cognitive model of the user, and immediate feedback to the user of the system's interpretation of the input program. To ease language learning, the linguistic goals emphasize minimization of explicit programming rules and minimization of many programming requirements such as explicit declarations for storage allocation and data type. Programming output formatting is designed to be highly user oriented. Because of specific program representations in TAPS, verification between specification and program is facilitated. TAPS has been designed as a translator to optimize portability between different computers and to be an "automated programmer" in a variety of conventional programming languages. TAPS output programs will interface, in a user-oriented manner, with program libraries existing in the user's current programming languages.

INTRODUCTION

The purpose of this paper is to outline the language design issues involved in constructing a system for scientific-engineering-mathematical application programming. The Automated Programmer System (TAPS) is such a programming language system, currently under development, whose goal is to minimize the linguistic difference between the problem-solver's specification of a scientific or engineering application problem solution and an equivalent executable program. Ideally, the user's problem specification should be executable. Thus, we have chosen the representations of the programming language to be rooted in conventional mathematical syntax, i.e., its two-dimensional notational forms, with supporting vocabulary and forms that mimic technical English. If the problem specification is already expressed in representations which are similar or identical to those of the programming language, then the linguistic difference between specification and program is minimal. It is generally acknowledged that the initial representation of a problem specification can be crucial in formulating a solution [8]. We transpose this notion to the executable program by decreasing the differences in the representations. This point of view was implicit in the Klerer-May language [1], and TAPS attempts to expand this concept for the current programming environment. Figure 1 contrasts a problem specification to the corresponding executable program. Figure 2 is a similar executable program which represents a different specification of the problem solution.

Minimizing the difference between the expression of the application specification and the corresponding concrete program virtually removes the need of constructing a separate requirements document for the purpose of future maintenance of the specification [9]. It also avoids an approach which attempts to use a "natural", i.e., non-mathematical language specification [11] for an application area which is intrinsically oriented toward mathematical notation.

for sets of linear algebraic equations of the form $\sum_{k=1}^{n} A_{ik} X_k = C_i$
where $i = 1, 2, ..., n$ *and* A_{ik}, C_i *are given for* $n \leq 20$, *compute*

① $\alpha_{ij} = A_{ij} - \sum_{k=1}^{j-1} \alpha_{ik} \alpha_{kj}$ $(i \geq j)$

② $\alpha_{ij} = \dfrac{A_{ij} - \sum_{k=1}^{i-1} \alpha_{ik} \alpha_{kj}}{\alpha_{ii}}$ $(i < j)$

③ $\gamma_i = \dfrac{C_i - \sum_{k=1}^{i-1} \alpha_{ik} \gamma_k}{\alpha_{ii}}$ *then determine* $X_n, X_{n-1}, ..., X_1$

from the computation ④ $X_i = \gamma_i - \sum_{k=i+1}^{n} \alpha_{ik} X_k$

DIMENSION A=(20,20), C=20, γ=20, X=20, α=(20,20).

READ n.

READ A_{ij} FROM j=1 TO n AND i=1 TO n.

READ C_i FROM i=1 TO n.

FROM j=1 TO n AND i=1 TO n IF i>j THEN $\alpha_{ij} = A_{ij} - \sum_{k=1}^{j-1} \alpha_{ik}\alpha_{kj}$ OTHERWISE $\alpha_{ij} = \dfrac{A_{ij} - \sum_{k=1}^{i-1} \alpha_{ik}\alpha_{kj}}{\alpha_{ii}}$.

FROM i=1 TO n COMPUTE $\gamma_i = \dfrac{C_i - \sum_{k=1}^{i-1} \alpha_{ik}\gamma_k}{\alpha_{ii}}$.

FROM i=n BY -1 UNTIL i<1 COMPUTE $X_i = \gamma_i - \sum_{k=i+1}^{n} \alpha_{ik} X_k$.

PRINT 1(2), X_i FOR i=1, 2, ..., n.   FINISH.

Figure 1

The Upper Text is a Problem Specification in a Conventional
   Representation. The Lower Text is a TAPS Program

MAXIMUM n=50.

READ n.

{ READ THE COEFFICIENT MATRIX ROW BY ROW }

FOR i=1 TO n AND j=1 TO n READ $W_{i,j}$.

{ READ RIGHT HAND SIDE }

FOR i=1 TO n READ $W_{i,n+1}$.

{ INITIALIZE PIVOT VECTOR } $P_i = 1$ FOR i=1,...,n.

FOR i=1,...,n COMPUTE $D_i = \max_{1 \leq j \leq n} |W_{i,j}|$,

   IF $D_i = 0$ PRINT MESSAGE MATRIX NOT INVERTIBLE AND EXIT.

FOR k=1,...,n-1, COLMAX = $\max_{k \leq l \leq n} \left| \frac{W_{P_l k}}{D_{P_l}} \right|$

   (IF COLMAX = 0 MESSAGE MATRIX NOT INVERTIBLE AND EXIT)

   { INTERCHANGE P_l AND P_k WHERE l IS THE INDEX OF THE MAXIMUM COLMAX }

   $PT = P_l$, $P_l = P_k$, $P_k = PT$,

   FOR i=k+1,...,n AND j=k+1,...,n+1, $W_{P_i j} = W_{P_i j} - \frac{W_{P_i k}}{W_{P_k k}} W_{P_k j}$.

IF $W_{P_n n} = 0$ PRINT MESSAGE MATRIX NOT INVERTIBLE AND EXIT.

{ SOLVE FOR UNKNOWNS BY FORWARD AND BACKWARD SUBSTITUTION }

$$x_k = \frac{W_{P_k, n+1} - \sum_{j=k+1}^{n} W_{P_k j} x_j}{W_{P_k k}} \quad \text{FOR } k=n, n-1, \ldots, 1.$$

{ OUTPUT THE RESULTS } FOR k=1 TO n PRINT x_k.   FINISH.

Figure 2

A TAPS Program Representing a Different Solution
to The Problem Illustrated in Figure 1.

LINGUISTIC CHARACTERISTICS

The characteristics of TAPS can be summarized as:

1. The program is represented in terms of structures and notations normal to the application domain.

2. The syntax is flexible and provides alternative forms and control structures.

3. The linguistic structure is a multi-phrase, multi-line sentence.

4. Synonymous keywords, imitative of conventional usage, are provided.

5. Notation which is unconventional or idiosyncratic in the application domain is purposefully avoided in the language design.

6. Ambiguity resolution strategy is based on (a) contextual analysis, (b) a cognitive model of the user, and (c) feedback of the system's interpretation of the input program.

7. Explicit "programming" requirements are minimal, virtually eliminating the need for user training in the use of the system.

8. The executable program should be self-documenting.

9. Program editing techniques are highly user-oriented and functionally obvious.

10. Conditioning the user to unnatural or overly rigid linguistic forms is unnecessary, and the underlying strategy for ambiguity resolution may change as a function of experience.

11. Program verification is facilitated due to the consistency of representation between the executable program and the original problem statement.

12. Since the program representation is intelligible to other practitioners in the application domain, verification, maintenance, modification and extension are facilitated.

13. A rich selection of output format choices ranging from highly structured reports to "pictures" is available.

14. TAPS permits interfacing with program libraries in the user's current programming language since the target output of the translation may be equivalent programs in such commonly used programming languages as Fortran, Basic, Ada, etc.

DESIGN ISSUES

Language characteristics 1 through 5 are motivated by considerations having to do with the evolution of linguistic expression in specific scientific and technical fields. While the underlying linguistic framework has traditionally been a particular natural language, the international nature of technical communication has been characterized by notation, vocabulary and syntactical structure which are specific to the particular scientific/technical area. Thus, while technical communication exceeds the boundaries of natural language, it is limited to a specific knowledge domain. Programming has evolved as a discipline that seeks to translate problem formulations and their solution specifications, expressed in conventional forms, into an equivalent representation which is computer executable. However, experience in software development has made it clear that this translation process is expensive in terms of human effort, and that proof of program correctness even for a moderately complex program is a goal that has not yet been achieved. Also, conventional programming languages are considered to be obscure by the user who is not a professional programmer and whose goal is to produce reliable, verifiable computable specifications rather than cleverly or elegantly designed computer code.

For us, the principal language design issue is whether it is possible to adopt linguistic forms traditionally used for the representation of problem specifications and demonstrate that these forms, or psychologically acceptable variants, are directly executable without the need for user coding. TAPS has been designed to demonstrate the feasibility of this design goal specifically for scientific-engineering-mathematical computational applications. We emphasize that variants of conventional forms must be psychologically acceptable to the user in that they are recognized as being consistent with his normal mode of expression. The reader of a TAPS program should be able to understand the meaning of the program if he is mathematically literate and familiar with the application, but only superficially acquainted with TAPS. To illustrate this, we note that the formula has always been central to scientific-engineering-mathematical applications [2]. Figure 3 illustrates a program fragment which is self-explanatory to those with minimal mathematical literacy and which is directly executable in TAPS. Of course, more general specifications require a richer vocabulary and more complex syntactical forms for the representation of an executable specification. TAPS is designed to accommodate these problems without requiring arcane and possibly error-prone language constructs. Intuitively, the intent is to reduce the programming process to that of copying a well-formulated problem specification. If, indeed, individual programming performance is specific to the application area [20], then an executable representation that mirrors the application specification should have positive effects. Certain categories of problem specifications may not be well-formulated or may not be expressed in directly executable notation or structure. Here, the intent is to minimize the user's need to translate the original specification representation to one executable by TAPS.

FOR $\beta=2(2)n$ AND $\alpha=2$ TO n^2-2 WITHIN $n=3$ BY 3 TO 9 READ r,γ,μ, IF $\frac{\gamma}{n} < \beta$ THEN COMPUTE

$$\theta_{\alpha\beta} = \int_2^n \int_3^{\sqrt{\frac{y}{n}}} \frac{\frac{e^{-\mu x}}{y+n} \sum_{i,j=1}^{n} \left\{ \text{COS } y + \frac{\text{SIN}^{i+j} x}{(i+j)x} \right\}}{\frac{\text{LOG}_r\, x + \text{TAN}^{-1} \frac{x^n}{y^{n-1}}}{\sqrt{\frac{\alpha}{\beta + \frac{\gamma}{y}} + \frac{\alpha + \frac{y}{\beta}}{x}}} + \prod_{k=1}^{n^2-\alpha} \left[\frac{\beta^k}{k} + \sqrt{(x+y)^{-k}} \right]} \, dx\, dy,$$

AND PRINT $\alpha,\beta,n,\theta_{\alpha\beta}$ OTHERWISE $y=e^z z^3 - \text{SIN}^2 z \text{ COS } z + 1 - \frac{\text{TAN}^{-1} z}{1-|z|}$,

IF $\frac{\text{SIN } \alpha z \text{ COS } z}{z^2-\beta^\gamma} \leq y < \beta^n \text{ LN } \frac{(\beta+z)^2}{\alpha^2-\gamma z^2}$ PRINT α,β,y,z ELSE PRINT α,β,γ.

FROM $t=2$ TO 5 AND $\theta=4$ TO 6 COMPUTE $\lambda_t = \int_1^t \frac{\text{COSH}^{-1} \frac{x+\theta}{2}}{e^{tx} + \frac{\sqrt{x}}{2}} \, dx$,

$\delta_t = \sum_{j=1}^{t} \left\{ \frac{\text{COS } j^2\theta \text{ SIN}(j\theta + \frac{\pi}{2})}{1 + \sum_{k=1}^{\theta} \frac{\text{COS } k}{k}} \right\}$, $\epsilon_t = \prod_{i=1}^{t} \text{SIN } \frac{\theta}{t}$ AND PRINT $t,\lambda_t,\delta_t,\epsilon_t$. FINISH.

Figure 3

An Illustration of The Two-Dimensional Nature of TAPS Programs

Thus, TAPS is designed to accept conventional mathematical notation: subscripts, superscripts, implied multiplication, fractions nested to any level expressed in their normal numerator over-denominator form, symbols such as Σ, Π, $\sqrt{\ }$, [,],{,} to any size necessary for textual clarity, and other user-definable operators. Minimizing the user's translation from the problem specification to the executable program is facilitated by providing acceptable control structures which permit syntactic flexibility and alternative forms. Figure 4 illustrates some of the possible forms for repetitive computation. In the specific context, FOR, FROM, AND and a comma(,) function as equivalent language tokens designating an

FOR N=1,3,...,k, j=N(-3)k and i=j BY N to M PRINT i,j,N.

FOR N=1(2)k AND j=N BY -3 TO k AND i=j,j+N,...,M PRINT i,j,N.

PRINT i,j,N FOR N=1 BY 2 TO k, FOR j=N,N-3,...,k, i=j(N)M.

PRINT i,j,N FOR N=1,3,5,...,k AND j=N,N-3,...,k AND FOR i=j,j+N,...,M.

FOR N=1(2)k, j=N(-3)k, i=j(N)M PRINT i,j,N.

    (a) Iterations may be written in a variety of styles and need not appear at the beginning of the controlled sentence. All of the above formulations are equivalent.

FOR i=a+2b, a-2b, π(.02)2π, C BY D-1 TO E, r,r+1, F(G)H, z,...,w-a, L,M TO N, p-α PRINT i,2i,3i.

FOR i=a+2b, a-2b PRINT i,2i,3i.
FOR i=π(.02)2π PRINT i,2i,3i.
FOR i=C BY D-1 TO E PRINT i,2i,3i.
FOR i=r,r+1 PRINT i,2i.3i. FOR i=F(G)H PRINT i,2i,3i.
FOR i=z BY z-H TO w-a PRINT i,2i,3i.
i=L, PRINT i,2i,3i. FOR i=M TO N PRINT i,2i,3i.
i=p-α PRINT i,2i,3i.

(FOR i=a+2b, a-2b PRINT i,2i,3i), (FOR i=π(.02)2π PRINT i,2i,3i), (FOR i=C BY D-1 TO E PRINT i,2i,3i), (FOR i=r,r+1 PRINT i,2i.3i), (FOR i=F(G)H PRINT i,2i,3i), (FOR i=z BY z-H TO w-a PRINT i,2i,3i), i=L, PRINT i,2i,3i (FOR i=M TO N PRINT i,2i,3i), i=p-α PRINT i,2i,3i.

    (b) Flexibility in writing the loop parameters permits iteration representations which are easier to formulate and easier to understand, as can be seen in the first of the three equivalent formulations above.

Figure 4

Examples of Variants of Syntactic Forms For Repetition of Computations

iteration. Furthermore, such iterative phrases control the
entire sentence unless the range of control is otherwise
delimited by parentheses. Parentheses may also be used to
explicitly delimit the scope of WHILE/UNTIL phrases. FOR
phrases, or their synonymous forms, may appear other than at
the beginning of a sentence if clarity of semantics is
enhanced.

Our attempt to introduce syntactic flexibility into our
language design is grounded in the notion that doing so reduces
cognitive complexity. Learning the necessary rules and
notations of the language system is eased because the representation of the underlying grammatical rules can be minimized.
There is some experimental evidence that supports this conclusion [17]. Providing a choice of keyword synonyms and language
constructs compatible with the user's problem specification
language and notation system gives him the ability to vary his
expressive style. The justification here is psychological
rather than technical [4].

For those who advocate a more conventional viewpoint, this may
appear to be a drawback since computationally equivalent programs may have different representations. Figure 5 illustrates
three different program representations of the same problem
specification. Indeed, this would be a drawback if it were
customary to formulate all problem specifications for a given
application area in a single representational style. In
reality, this is not the case. Therefore, since diversity in
specification representation is an acknowledged fact, and since
imposition of a uniform representation style is unlikely,
flexibility in program representation is desirable because it
minimizes programming effort.

One cognitive model of programming uses the process of "chunking" [18]. The program segment pattern

```
          S=0
          DO 10 I=1,N
     10   S=S+X(I)
```

would be chunked into the concept "calculate the sum of the 1st
to Nth elements of the array X" by an experienced programmer.
The collection of operators, operands, and other tokens of the
three-line program segment above is replaced by the single
cognitive entity given in quotes. The program segment is
actually a rather low-level coded representation of the much
higher-level problem-oriented concept. TAPS enhances this
model of programming by the availability, for the example in
the above case, of the equivalent expression

$$S = \sum_{I=1}^{N} X_I$$

and by providing other more complex syntactical structures at
the conceptual level of the problem specification.

To avoid the arcane use of tokens or punctuation [6] and to
preserve similitude to the specification, symbols and language

```
MAXIMUM n=20.           DIMENSION x=20, y=20.              MAXIMUM W=20.
READ n.                 α=0, READ ω.                       READ W.   ρ=0.
READ A₁, B₁ FROM 1=0 TO n.   FORMULA 1.   READ xα, yα.    FROM X=0 TO W READ uₓ, vₓ.
                        α=α+1. IF α≤ω GO TO FORMULA 1.    DO FORMULA 3 FROM X=0 TO W.
X = Σ{A₁ Π B_j A_j}.    S=α=0. STATEMENT 1. β=α, P=1.     σ=1.
                        STATEMENT 2. P=Px_β y_β, β=β+1.   FROM Y=X TO W COMPUTE σ=σu_Y v_Y.
PRINT X.   FINISH.      IF β≤ω THEN GO TO STATEMENT 2.    ρ=ρ+uₓσ.
                        S=S+Pxα AND α=α+1.                FORMULA 3.   PRINT ρ.
                        IF ω>α GO TO STATEMENT 1.         END OF PROGRAM.
                        PRINT S.   END OF PROGRAM.
```

Figure 5

Alternate Representations of Computationally Equivalent Programs

constructs may have more than one meaning which is resolvable in context. An obvious example is the use of the symbol "=" for either assignment, relational equality, definition, or equivalence. This minimizes the language learning effort and those programming errors which arise in conventional languages due to the use of artificially created symbolism in an attempt to avoid ambiguity when the actual meaning is clear from the local context. We placed strong emphasis on the avoidance of the baroque possibilities of language design which may occur in programs written in such languages as Ada. Also, the linguistic structure of TAPS excludes such arcane constructions as ++X used by the C programming language to specify that X is to be incremented by 1.

In many instances, any apparent ambiguity arising from the use of the flexible syntactic structure, synonyms, or symbols with non-unique meaning may be definitely resolved by analysis of context [13,14]. Other instances may fall into the category of a logically incomplete specification, and either a default choice is made by TAPS on an empirical basis founded upon prior user experience, or the program fragment may be inherently ambiguous and the user is so informed. In this sense, TAPS incorporates a simple cognitive model of the user, justified only by empirical experience, and which is subject to change. The purpose of the cognitive model is to reduce the probability that TAPS interpretations will differ from the semantic intentions of the user [10]. However, what enhances the viability of the TAPS approach is the immediate feedback of the interpretation given to the user's program. Emphasis is given to those fragments in which the system has made explicit what the user stated implicitly. A simple example would be the system's interpretation of the expression AB+C. If the user had not explicitly or implicitly defined AB to be a multi-character identifier, and TAPS, in its scan of the program, had inferred that it was the user's intention to use implied multiplication, then the system would indicate its interpretation by visually emphasizing that A*B was meant at the position in the program text where AB had originally appeared. However, if the program contained the assignment AB=5, even without any declaration that AB is an identifier, TAPS would infer that AB was a multi-character name and treat it as such both in the displayed interpretation feedback and in other occurrences of this string throughout the program.

The small number of explicit programming rules permits the use of a brief user manual. The feasibility of this approach was demonstrated by the successful use of a one-sheet manual for the Klerer-May system [1,3]. To be effective, this concept assumes "hidden rules", i.e., rules not necessarily known to the user. This is based on a model of the user which assumes that because of his implicit conditioning in the specific application environment, the probability is high that he will either produce certain constructs without explicit rule prompting, or will avoid certain bizarre constructions that are possible in a logical sense, but improbable from psychological considerations. The test of the success of this technique is always immediate via the operational mode of feedback of system interpretation to the user.

TAPS minimizes the necessity for storage or type declaration which can be inferred from a scan of the program. Implicit to this point of view are the assumptions (a) that the possibility of error detection through mandatory declaration of storage and type is outweighed by programming ease when the system can reliably make these determinations, and (b) that the probability of certain pathological errors not consistent with a realistic cognitive model of the user is small. For example, Knuth [2] has pointed out the impracticality of the use of complex techniques to optimize code generation for long Fortran assignment statements. As he discovered by empirical study, Fortran programs, overwhelmingly, contain very short assignments. Long assignments are pathological to Fortran programming practice, but not to the specification of formulas in the scientific-engineering-mathematical applications domain.

Output format is an area that has been historically neglected in programming language design, e.g., Algol 60 and Pascal. Even when format specification is an integral part of the language design, as in Fortran, Cobol, PL/1. etc., specifying the format is a programming task often relying on trial and error attempts to get output to look right. In the current programming environment, this difficulty has been eased by the availability of fourth-generation systems for report generation, and by the development of integrated software systems which provide for the presentation of intermixed text, computed results and graphics. TAPS offers a simple approach designed to make the output specification intuitively obvious. The format statement is either a linear string of literal characters or a two-dimensional "image" which is a graphic structure whose components are alphanumeric characters or substructures composed of interlocking characters. Embedded within these formats are arbitrarily positioned value "placeholder" symbols. Ordered sequences of computed values are inserted in the connected strings of place-holders using a left-to-right sequential precedence, and, in the case of the two-dimensional image, a top-down precedence at each horizontal position. That is, a command PRINT IMAGE n V1, V2, V3,... will cause the computed value of V1 to be appropriately scaled and inserted at the point in the format IMAGE n where the first string, in precedence order, of place-holders occurs. The scaled value of V2 will be inserted where the second string of place-holders occurs. If two or more strings of place-holders are aligned vertically, then precedence is given to the topmost string. Scaling is controlled by the length of the place-holder string and explicit embedding of decimal point, plus-minus sign and floating point exponent specifiers into the place-holder string. The major significance of this language technique is that the linear or two-dimensionally structured output result is an exact replica of the program fragment that controls output format, with the actual computed values, properly scaled, replacing the place-holder symbols. In this case, verification of output format has been reduced to simple proofreading. Figure 6 illustrates a program utilizing the IMAGE format and the corresponding two-dimensional output.

In recognition of the widespread reluctance of users to learn and integrate a new programming language into their computing milieu, TAPS has been designed as a translator to optimize portability between different computers and to output programs in a variety of conventional programming languages. Since Fortran is still the most widely used language for scientific-engineering-mathematical computations, and probably will remain so in the foreseeable future, the initial implementation of TAPS will be an "automated Fortran programmer". This Fortran target code may be immediately executed without any user intervention, or it can be treated as if it were written by a human programmer. Subsequent updates of TAPS will have other target language back-ends as befits the current programming environment.

Another characteristic of the scientific-engineering- mathematical application domain is the huge investment in extensive application program libraries, particularly those coded in Fortran. TAPS has been designed to interface with these libraries in ways which support the user-oriented approach.

THE ANTHROPOMORPHIC PROBLEM

Perlman [15] argues for a "natural artificial language" which he defines as a well-designed artificial language that people find easy to learn and use. Our language design viewpoint differs somewhat from the criteria detailed by him, and also considers different issues. In the restricted linguistic domain of mathematically-oriented expressions, we are not actually using "natural" language [5,16]. Rather, we are employing "natural" notational systems and forms so that the translation from specification to executable program can be automated to the highest degree possible. Our linguistic model is based essentially on empirical observation and attempts to anticipate correct resolution of syntactic and semantic ambiguity. But, the naive user may identify with the system and

FROM $i=2$ TO 5 SLEW 5, PRINT IMAGE 1,i,i,i, $A_i = \int_0^i \frac{e^{-iz}\,\text{SINH}^{-1}\frac{z}{2}}{z^5+\frac{1}{2}}dz$, i,i,i, $B_i = \sum_{r=1}^{i} r^i$, i, $k=i^2+1$, $\sqrt{k}$.

IMAGE 1

$$A_x = \int_0^x \frac{e^{-xz}\,\text{SINH}^{-1}\frac{z}{2}}{z^5+\frac{1}{2}}\,dz = .xxxxx \qquad B_x = \sum_{i=1}^{x} i^x = xxxx \qquad C_x = \sqrt{xx} = y. \quad \text{FINISH.}$$

$$A_2 = \int_0^2 \frac{e^{-2z}\,\text{SINH}^{-1}\frac{z}{2}}{z^5+\frac{1}{2}}\,dz = .12922 \qquad B_2 = \sum_{i=1}^{2} i^2 = 5 \qquad C_2 = \sqrt{5} = .223606798 \;\; 1$$

$$A_3 = \int_0^3 \frac{e^{-3z}\,\text{SINH}^{-1}\frac{z}{2}}{z^5+\frac{1}{2}}\,dz = .07884 \qquad B_3 = \sum_{i=1}^{3} i^3 = 36 \qquad C_3 = \sqrt{10} = .316227766 \;\; 1$$

$$A_4 = \int_0^4 \frac{e^{-4z}\,\text{SINH}^{-1}\frac{z}{2}}{z^5+\frac{1}{2}}\,dz = .05161 \qquad B_4 = \sum_{i=1}^{4} i^4 = 354 \qquad C_4 = \sqrt{17} = .412310562 \;\; 1$$

$$A_5 = \int_0^5 \frac{e^{-5z}\,\text{SINH}^{-1}\frac{z}{2}}{z^5+\frac{1}{2}}\,dz = .03577 \qquad B_5 = \sum_{i=1}^{5} i^5 = 4425 \qquad C_5 = \sqrt{26} = .509901951 \;\; 1$$

Figure 6

A Two-Dimensional Image Format and Corresponding Output

attribute to it an "intelligence" and linguistic flexibility for which it was not designed. This kind of anthropomorphism or reification can be countered by disclaimers of "naturalness" and by emphasizing that there are explicit linguistic rules, albeit flexible in form, and by giving the user immediate feedback of system interpretation including rejection of inadmissible structures. While the psychological aspects of reification that occur with so-called natural language systems are, in general, to be seriously considered [7], experience with the Klerer-May system has convinced us that this is a controllable aspect for a system such as TAPS. In any case, the final judgment on this point will be determined by empirical observation.

FUTURE EXTENSIONS

The current version of TAPS is oriented toward numerical computation. Future versions will be enhanced to include:

1. symbolic and algebraic processing,
2. generic (unsubscripted) array representations and matrix and vector operations,
3. user-oriented word processing and typesetting of mathematical text, and
4. expansion of non-procedural representations, e.g., a system of equations in conventional textbook form subject to the command SOLVE.

REFERENCES

[1] Melvin Klerer and Jack May, "An Experiment in a User-Oriented Computer System", Comm. ACM, Vol. 7, No. 5, May 1964, pp. 290-294; _____, "Two-Dimensional Programming", Proc. Fall Joint Computer Conference, AFIPS, 1965, Vol. 27, Part 2, pp. 63-75.

[2] Donald E. Knuth, "An Empirical Study of Fortran Programs", Software-Practice and Experience, Vol. 1, 1971, pp. 105-133.

[3] Melvin Klerer, "The Economics. Politics, and Sociology of Two-Dimensional Systems", ACM SIGPLAN Notices, Vol. 7 No. 10, October 1972, pp. 11-22.

[4] M.I. Good, J.A. Whiteside, D.R. Wixon, and S.J. Jones, "Building a User-Derived Interface", Comm. ACM, Vol. 27, No. 10, October 1984, pp. 1032-1043.

[5] Robert Wilensky, Yigal Arens, and David Chin, "Talking To UNIX in English", Comm. ACM, Vol. 27, No. 6, June 1984, pp. 574-593.

[6] Richard Rubinstein and Harry Hersh, <u>The Human Factor</u>, Digital Press, Boston, 1984.

[7] Phyllis Reisner, "Use of Psychological Experimentation as an Aid To Development of a Query Language", IEEE Trans. Software Engineering, Vol. 3, No. 3, May 1977.

[8] Peter Naur, "Programming Languages, Natural Languages, and Mathematics", Comm. ACM. Vol, 18, No. 12, December 1975, pp. 676-684.

[9] David S. Wile, "Program Developments: Formal Explanations of Implementations", Comm. ACM, Vol. 26, No. 11, November 1983. pp. 902-910.

[10] Elliot Soloway, Jeffrey Bonar, and Kate Ehrlich, "Cognitive Strategic and Looping Constructs: An Empirical Study Comm. ACM, Vol. 26, No. 11, November 1983, pp. 853-860.

[11]   Bertrand Meyer, "On Formalism in Specifications", IEEE Software, January 1985, pp. 6-26.

[12]   Jerry R. Hobbs, "What the Nature of Natural Language Tells Us About How to Make Natural-Language-Like Programming Language More Natural", SIGPLAN Notices. Vol. 12, No. 8, August 1977, pp. 85-93.

[13]   Melvin Klerer and Jack May. "Automatic Dimensioning", Comm. ACM, Vol. 10, No. 3, March 1967, pp. 165-166.

[14]   J. T. Schwartz, "Automatic Data Structure Choice in a Language of Very High Level", Comm. ACM, Vol. 18, No. 12, December 1975, pp. 722-728.

[15]   Gary Perlman. "Natural Artificial Languages: Low Level Processes", Int. J. Man-Machine Studies, Vol. 20, 1984, pp. 373-419.

[16]   Ben Shneiderman, <u>Software Psychology: Human Factors in Computer and Information Systems</u>, Little Brown, Boston, 1980.

[17]   Phyllis Reisner, "Formal Grammar and Human Factors Design of an Interactive Graphics System", IEEE Trans. Software Engineering, Vol. 7, 1981, pp. 229-240.

[18]   B. Curtis, I. Forman, R. Brooks, E. Soloway and K. Ehrlich, "Psychological Perspectives For Software Science", Information Processing and Management, Vol. 20, No. 1-2, 1984, pp. 81-96.

[19]   Bill Curtis, "A Review of Human Factors Research on Programming Languages and Specifications", Proceedings Human Factors in Computer Systems, ACM, March 1982, pp. 212-218.

[20]   R. Brooks, "Toward a Theoretical Model of the Comprehension of Computer Programs", Int. J. Man-Machine Studies, Vol. 17, 1983.

QUESTION AND ANSWER PERIOD

TAYLOR

In mathematics, much of the symbolism is dependent upon the fact that we did all these things because we had no computers. McCluhan often said that we go into the future looking into the rearview mirror, that is, our implementation in a new medium really is prone to look back to the old medium. And I wonder in our use of problem solving techniques, generally, if we are probably not doing the same thing. I wonder how much of this symbolism would somehow be changed if we wanted to represent the process in a way that we would deal with it in the computer, rather than the way in which we've always dealt with this sort of thing mathematically. Are there alternatives which might better be represented symbolically some other way, if they're going to be done on the computer?

GROSSMAN

I'm not sure if there is new mathematical symbolism that is replacing the old. But, if that is the case, and it becomes the traditional symbolism, then a system should adopt that as well. Our basic philosophy is that you shouldn't have to code. You're already coding by writing in this symbolism. But if this is your normal way of problem solving, and you think of your problem in a particular frame and use this notational system, then this notational system is what you should tell the computer. "Natural language" is a term that's been overused. I think "natural notation" is preferable. So if the notation changes, then the systems which support that computation should change accordingly. I don't see any problem with that.

JERNIGAN

Do you find this useful primarily as a teaching tool or as a tool for practicing physicists? Is this a way of teaching a physicist to write programs so that he can compare the results of what is in here with the results that are produced in Fortran or the target language, or would a practicing physicist use this as is?

GROSSMAN

Our belief is that a practicing physicist would use this as is. In fact, we are constantly being told, as we discuss this approach with practicing scientific computing users, that they spend up to, or maybe even more than, half of the time working on their Fortran programs--or whatever language it may be, and typically, it's Fortran--not on their problem. To me that's horrible. They admit it's horrible, but they go ahead and do it anyway. So a physicist, I'd like to think, presented with a system similar to this would naturally want to use it. That's what we found when we had a similar system in production use in the '60's. Even though Fortran and other languages were available to both scientists and programmers in our laboratory at the time, they all naturally gravitated toward our system. It just seemed like an obvious thing to do.

LANGUAGES FOR PROBLEM SOLVING IN GRAPH THEORY[*]

S. L. Epstein

Hunter College of the
City University of New York

The traditional representation of knowledge in a predicate calculus format has proved reasonably effective for theorem proving. There are, however, other ways to manipulate knowledge besides proving truths. A recursive formulation for graph properties is described as the foundation of a knowledge-based system for graph theory. Emphasis here is on the applications such a representation affords. Benefits include the automatic construction of related algorithms and conjecture testing, as well as theorem proving. The subsumption, equivalence and merger of graph properties is discussed, with heuristic principles for their automation.

1.0   INTRODUCTION

An undergraduate class encounters graph theory for the first time. "A graph," opines the instructor, "is an ordered pair of sets <V,E>, where V is a finite set of elements called **vertices** and E is any set of pairs of elements of V." Eyes glaze. "An example of a graph is G = <{1,2,3,4,5},{12,23,34,45,51}>." There is rustling and the occasional sound of a diligent pencil. "One way to think about a graph might be to draw a picture of it, like this:" (See Figure 1.) Aha! The more visually alert are intrigued now. "Why did you draw it that way?" asks one Inquiring Mind (henceforth IM). "Why not as a pentagon?" (See Figure 2.)

Why not indeed?[1] Why draw a picture at all? Although graph theory is about sets, mathematicians reading and writing and thinking about graph theory, and students learning about graph theory, regularly consider examples and draw these diagrams. When graphs are displayed as pictures, people find them more accessible, easier to examine and manipulate.[2] It is important to remember, however, that such a picture is only an alternative representation for a graph.

This paper describes recent work in knowledge representation for both problem solving and theorem proving in graph theory. Although extensive exploration and hand tracing has provided

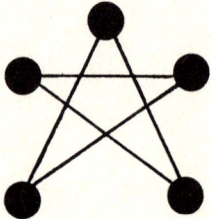

Figure 1

A Graph

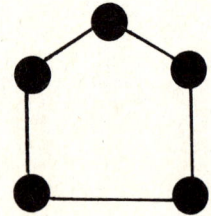

Figure 2

Another Graph?

ample support for its performance, the representation has not yet been implemented.

IM is not a computer program, but a model for that facet of intelligence which applies concepts to tasks, and it is IM's facility which the representation is designed to capture. IM is expected to:
- conjecture
- create new concepts
- detect natural hierarchies
- construct algorithms from definitions
- adapt knowledge to a new environment
- prove theorems[3]

With such requirements, IM will need (and presume) a natural language processor to interface between its knowledge representation and outside stimuli. The representation described here is intended not only to enable the execution of such tasks, but to simulate their execution environment as well. In other words, easy tasks should have simple, rapid solutions, unencumbered by the (possibly vast) scope of the data available. More difficult tasks will be recognized as such and may take longer.

The remainder of this paper is organized into eight sections:
- the origins and definition of the representation
- constructing recognition algorithms from definitions
- detecting natural hierarchies
- creating new concepts
- exploring
- adaptation
- scope, limitations and future work
- conclusions

An aside on what this paper is *not* about seems appropriate here. There is no statement of strong formal results in this paper. The representation has been judged successful because it meets the goals cited above. A goal is deemed to be met when at least one procedure for achieving it is formally delineated and successfully hand-tested on a variety of examples. Such testing, by hand or machine, cannot be exhaustive. The results described here are the requisite procedures and a sample of the highly successful testing, but they cannot guarantee a flawless representation. In a logic-based representational system, an expression containing unbound variables is said to be *satisfiable* if there exists some binding for the variables which makes the expression true. In this paper, procedures may construct or attempt to construct expressions which are unsatisfiable. Satisfiability is not a concern because the non-existence of such objects is often of interest to mathematicians. Finally, because this representation not only tolerates but encourages redundancy, complexity is not an immediate concern. Additional details and a more formal presentation are available in [Eps].

2.0 THE ORIGINS AND DEFINITIONS OF R-LANGUAGES

There have been, thus far, two primary representations for mathematics in knowledge-based systems: predicate calculus and frames. Symbolic logic focuses on the syntax of descriptive statements, rather than their semantics. In particular, a predicate calculus representation for mathematical knowledge provides a variety of valid argument forms, each of which guarantees that any conclusion it draws will be correct. However, when predicate calculus is used to represent a large database of facts in some mathematical domain, some of the organization natural to the information is likely to be obscured. (For example, hierarchies may not be transparent, and examples may not be cited as extremal.) The most successful theorem provers (e.g., those working in ternary boolean algebra and equivalential calculus [Wos]) therefore rely heavily on heuristics, domain-dependent techniques to organize data and direct search.

Frames were used by Lenat in AM [Len] to represent an initial database of concepts in set theory. From these concepts AM was able to conjecture quite a reputable amount of mathematics. Frames, however, lack the deductive power of formal logic; AM does not prove theorems, it infers them from generated examples. The example generators are not guaranteed (or even likely) to be complete or correct.

The languages described here attempt to capture both the deductive power of predicate calculus and the inductive power of a semantic network of frames. Such an immodest ambition must at least be restricted in its domain of application; it is limited here to graph theory.

The evolving body of mathematical knowledge known as graph theory includes definitions, examples, theorems, algorithms, conjectures and proofs. The definition taken here for graph theory is that formulated by experts, as represented in three general texts. One [Ore] is a classical development in elegant mathematical fashion. The second [Har] encompasses a broader range of topics, presented as definitions and theorems. The third [Bon] takes an algorithmic approach. Together, these texts are the benchmark; their contents are assumed to be *graph theory* and their contents "of interest" to graph theorists.

Among the many representations for graph theory, graph grammars (see, for example [Ros]) are probably best known. Their approach emphasizes the derivation of a graph through productions, similar to those for classical string grammars. Based in category theory, these grammars focus on an individual graph, and do not readily lend themselves to the applications highlighted in Section 1. (A detailed discussion of operational graph rewriting systems is available in [Dor].)

Graph theory is primarily *about* graph properties and their relationships. Conjectures and theorems in graph theory are frequently of the form:

        Type 1: If a graph has property p, then it has property q.
        Type 2: A graph has property p if and only if it has property q.
        Type 3: It is not possible for a graph to have both property p and property q.

This observation led to the development of the alternative representation described here, whose focus is graph properties. Let a *graph property* p be a (possibly infinite) set of graphs P. A graph G is said to have the property p (or be a graph with property p) if and only if G is in P.[4] The alternative representation is a family of languages based upon recursion, hence their designation as *R-languages*.[5]
Recursion is by no means a new representation; Pascal [Pas] and

Poincare [Poi,Poi2] recognized its significance long ago. The results cited here are interesting because they are able to harness the power of recursion in a variety of ways.

In an R-language, the expression representing a graph property p is a concise statement whose semantic interpretation is a specialized algorithm. That algorithm is describable as an automaton (a *p-generator*) intended to generate precisely the set P. A p-generator is said to be *correct* if and only if every graph output by the p-generator is in P. A p-generator is said to be *complete* if and only if, for each graph G in P there exists a finite sequence of iterations of the p-generator whose final output is G. When a property p is expressed in an R-language, the p-generator so defined must be shown both correct and complete with respect to P.

An R-language is a language triple $<F,L,\Sigma>$. A specific *R-expression* is written as $<f,S,\sigma>$ where f is a terminal F-expression, S a terminal L-expression, and σ a terminal Σ-expression. There are many possible choices for the languages F, L and Σ. (Some particularly effective ones are detailed in [Eps].) A language F in $<F,L,\Sigma>$ constructs composite operators from a set of primitive operators (such as those in Table 1) by adding or multiplying the primitive operators. For primitive operators $\pi_1, \pi_2, \ldots, \pi_n$, the grammar for F is

$$I \rightarrow I + I \mid II$$
$$I \rightarrow \pi_1 \mid \pi_2 \mid \ldots \mid \pi_n$$

A language L in $<F,L,\Sigma>$ is any language which precisely specifies a set of graphs, even another R-language. A language Σ in $<F,L,\Sigma>$ has a formal grammar which generates descriptions of the properties of vertices and edges within a graph. Terminal Σ-expressions are sequences of statements such as "x ϵ V," "xy = wz" and "degree (v) > 2."

Take the property of being a cycle as an example.[6] In an
R-language, that property could be represented by the
expression:

$$\text{CYCLE:} \quad S^*_{xvy}(K_3) \text{ where } x,y \in V,\ v \notin V,\ xy \in E$$

Each R-language expression has three parts:

- an operator
- a seed set
- a selector

The **seed set** is one or more "minimal" graphs, each of which has the property in question. A seed set is described in the language L. The seed set in the example contains only a single graph, K_3, the complete graph[7] on three vertices, shown as the first graph in Figure 3. The **operator** in the expression describes the way a graph with the given property may be deformed to construct another graph with the same property. Operators are described in the language F.[8] In the example, the operator is S_{xvy}, which means "subdivide the edge xy into the edges xv and vy." Finally, the **selector** describes the restrictions for binding the variables appearing in the operator. The selector language is Σ. In the example, "where $x,y \in V,\ v \notin V,\ xy \in E$" is the selector.

It remains to produce the algorithm which is the semantic interpretation of such a triple. The p-generator is started by the input of any graph from the seed set S. (CYCLE would require K_3.) The p-generator then iterates an undetermined number of times. On each iteration the selector σ chooses one or more vertices and/or edges with respect to the current graph G, and then the operator f modifies G, using those choices, to produce a new G. (CYCLE, on each iteration, selects and subdivides some edge of G, introducing one new vertex and replacing one old edge with two new ones.)

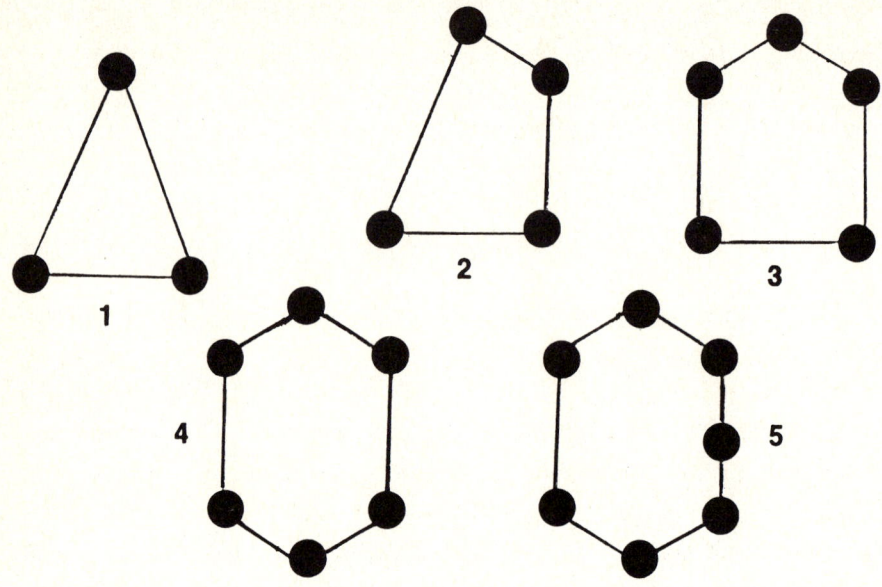

Figure 3

Some Iterations of CYCLE

There is a recursive definition implicit here:
        Every $G \in S$ is in P.
        If $G \in P$ then $f\sigma(G)$ is in P.
        Nothing else is in P.

The algorithm for generating all of P is
        Accept $G \in S$
GROW: Output G
        If σ *fails*
            then *halt*
            else $G \leftarrow f\sigma(G)$
        Go to GROW

The output of this algorithm, under all possible choices of G from S and all possible choices of σ, is precisely P. Note that the operator f is a recursive function, but the selector σ is not even likely to make the same selection on a

subsequent iteration (or even a subsequent run) for a given
input graph. No operator is ever assumed to be applicable to
an arbitrary graph. The selector places restrictions on the
bindings of the variables referred to by the operator.

Figure 3 shows several iterations of CYCLE. Each pictured
graph would be output by the algorithm, and each graph is a
cycle. CYCLE is the cycle-generator and does not halt, since
the modifications can go on indefinitely, i.e., bindings for
the variables in σ can always be found.

There are many kinds of non-determinism in this algorithm,
raising a variety of questions with regard to efficiency and
complexity. First, any G in S is an acceptable input for the
p-generator. In order to guarantee completeness, the
p-generator must begin on each of the graphs in S. Second, any
binding satisfying σ is valid. There are, therefore, many
different sequences of iterations which will construct any
given graph in P. This redundancy is tolerated because it
facilitates manipulation of concepts (particularly inversion,
which appears in the next section). Finally, a given graph
property p may properly have more than one algorithm associated
with it. This sort of non-determinism is to be valued; it
provides additional manipulative facility and is traditionally
found as "equivalent definitions" in mathematics. All of this
"don't care" non-determinism is acknowledged and accepted,
because the goal of this representation is not speed but
manipulative facility. Rarely, in fact, will these
p-generators be required to run.[9]

3.0 CONSTRUCTING DECISION ALGORITHMS FROM DEFINITIONS: INVERSION

IM is still in class. "The graph in Figure 1 is a cycle," says
the teacher. "And in Figure 4 are some others." The
R-language representation for the property of being a cycle,
recall, was

$$\text{CYCLE:} \quad S^{*}_{xvy}(K_3) \text{ where } x,y \in V, v \notin V, xy \in E$$

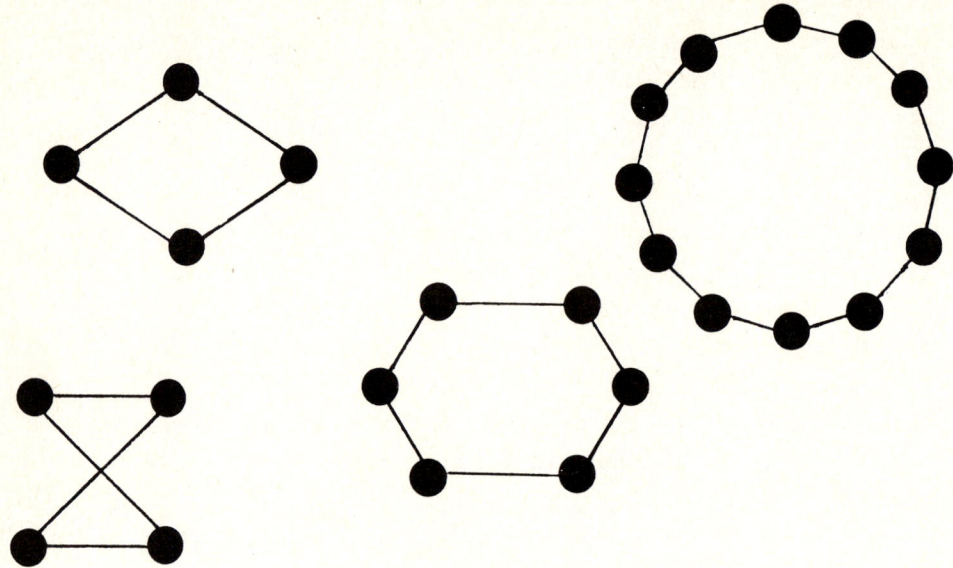

Figure 4

Some Cycles

"In Figure 5," says the teacher, "are some other graphs. Which of them are cycles?" IM rapidly constructs a testing algorithm for cycle identification. R-language representation supports that application of knowledge.

If a graph may be constructed one edge or vertex at a time, it may also be dismembered in the same fashion. Given a p-generator for the expression $<f,S,\sigma>$, under certain circumstances it is possible to calculate an inverse for that expression, call it $<f^{-1},S,\sigma^{-1}>$. This inverse has a semantic interpretation which is also a specialized algorithm, describable by an automaton (a *p-tester*) intended to test graphs for the property p. A p-tester methodically attempts to dismember an input graph until it is again some graph in S. The algorithm for a p-tester reads:

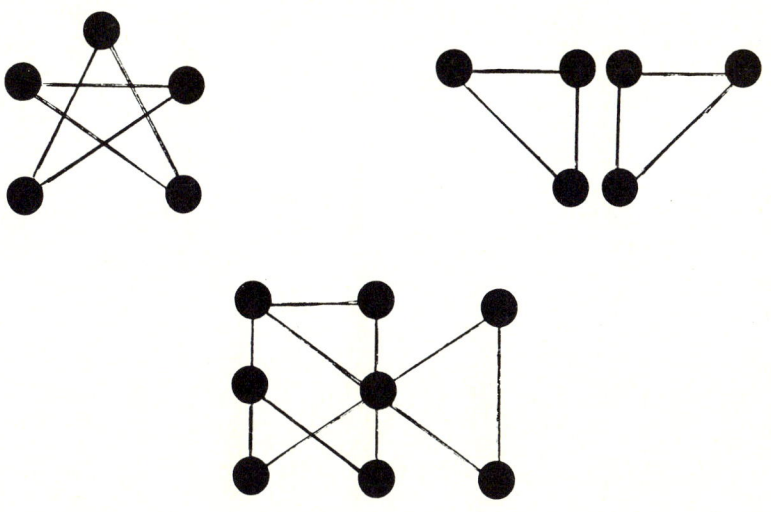

Figure 5

Possible Cycles

```
           Accept G
DECAY:     If G ε S
              then return TRUE and halt
              else if G ∉ S and σ⁻¹ fails
              then return FALSE and halt
              else G <- f⁻¹σ⁻¹(G)
           Go to DECAY
```

A p-generator preserves the "p-ness" of a graph, but promises nothing about its behavior if some G not in P is input.[10] A p-tester, on the other hand, preserves both p-ness and non-p-ness. That is, a p-generator may be stopped after any iteration, yielding a graph with the same truth value for the property being tested as each of the preceding graphs. For example, if p is the property of being a cycle and the graph G is not a cycle, then the graphs $f^{-1}\sigma^{-1}(G)$ and $(f^{-1}\sigma^{-1})^4(G)$, if they exist, will also not be cycles. More formally, a terminal R-expression $<f^{-1}, S, \sigma^{-1}>$ is said to be the *inverse* of another terminal R-expression $<f, S, \sigma>$ if and only if the p-tester associated with $<f^{-1}, S, \sigma^{-1}>$ returns TRUE on all outputs of the p-generator for $<f,S,\sigma>$ and FALSE on all other graphs. The testing algorithm is non-deterministic in its choice of bindings under σ^{-1}. On any given iteration only one set of variables satisfying σ^{-1} is chosen; alternatives need not be explored. Any choice valid under σ^{-1} guarantees a correct result.

As an example, consider the inverse for CYCLE:

$$\text{CYCLE}^{-1}: \quad <S^{-1}_{xvy}, \{K_3\}, \sigma^{-1}>$$

where σ^{-1} = x,y,v ε V, xv,vy ε E, xy ∉ E, d(x) = d(y) = d(v) = 2

On each iteration, CYCLE^{-1} contracts any simple cycle by "unsubdividing", i.e., collapsing a subdivided edge into a single edge. After some iterations, a simple cycle will become isomorphic to K_3 and the cycle-tester will return TRUE. Any non-cycle submitted to the cycle-tester will have its subdivided edges collapsed, and its simple cycles will become isomorphic to K_3. At this point, σ^{-1} will fail (i.e., bindings for x, y and v will not be found) and the cycle-tester will return FALSE.

Note that **any** selection suiting the requirements in σ^{-1} guarantees the correct results, not simply some specific selection. If G was an output of the p-generator, it had a seed graph G_S and a sequence of fσ applications which produced it. When G is submitted to the p-tester, the ultimate seed graph reached need not be G_S, and the dismemberment sequence need not be the reverse of the original fσ construction sequence. There are likely to be many correct testing choices under σ^{-1}. It is the redundancy of the p-generator which supports this "don't care" flexibility in the p-tester. If G has property p, and only if it does, any repeated applications of $f^{-1}\sigma^{-1}$ will return it, in some fashion, to some seed graph of p.

Someone described the meaning of "cycle" to IM, but IM constructed a testing algorithm all alone. In R-language terminology, IM converted a p-generator into a p-tester. If the expression for p permits the automation of such a conversion, the expression is said to be *invertible* and the automated process is called *inversion*. Often, in graph theory, there is no obvious relationship between a testing algorithm for p and the p-generator. There is, at present, one technique for inversion which has been successful on the graph properties expressed in R-language and studied. Its major inversion heuristic is that the vertices and edges involved in the iteration just completed are either immediately identifiable, so that the graph may be returned to G, or belong to a set of possible choices, any of which will move the graph back correctly toward some seed graph of p or FALSE, without necessarily returning to G at all. Thus inversion undoes generation, or what might have been generation.

Primitive	Effect	Representation
N	No change	$N<V,E> = <V,E>$
A_x	Add vertex x	$A_x<V,E> = <V \cup \{x\},E>$
A_{xy}	Add edge xy	$A_{xy}<V,E> = <V,E \cup \{xy\}>$
D_x	Delete vertex x	$D_x<V,E> = <V-\{x\},E>$
D_{xy}	Delete edge xy	$D_{xy}<V,E> = <V,E-\{xy\}>$

Table 1

Some Primitive Operators for R-Grammars

Not every expression will be invertible via this mechanism. In particular, consider a graph property whose expression in an R-language includes I_{xy}, an operator which identifies or merges vertex x with vertex y, leaving only the revised vertex x in the graph and assigning all the adjacencies of y to x. After such a merger occurs there is no indication of which vertex is the revised one, let alone which edges incident with x were attributable to x, to y, or to both of them. Thus an expression whose formulation includes I_{xy} will generally not be susceptible to inversion.

If the operators are kept sufficiently simple, however, there is a technique[11] for the automatic construction of p^{-1} from p. Permit only the primitive operators of Table 1. From these primitive operators, construct composite operators of the form fg (interpreted as "apply g followed by f") and f + g (interpreted as "apply exactly one of f or g"). Both f and g may themselves be composite. (S_{xvy}, in CYCLE, is the composite $D_{xy}A_{xv}A_{vy}A_{v}$.)

The following are five rules for the automatic construction of an inverse $<f^{-1}, S, \sigma^{-1}>$ for a graph property expression $<f, S, \sigma>$. The first four rules are designed to construct f^{-1} from f.

RULE 1
Every primitive operator has an inverse. The inverses are

$$A_x^{-1} = D_x$$

$$A_{xy}^{-1} = D_{xy}$$

$$D_x^{-1} = A_x$$

$$D_{xy}^{-1} = D_{xy}$$

$$N^{-1} = N$$

RULE 2
The inverse of a sequential composite is the inverse of its elements, in the reverse order, i.e.,

$$(fg)^{-1} = g^{-1}f^{-1}$$

For example,

$$(A_{xy}A_y)^{-1} = A_y^{-1}A_{xy}^{-1} = D_y D_{xy}$$

RULE 3

The inverse of an additive composite is the sum of the inverses of its elements, in the same order, i.e.,

$$(f + g)^{-1} = f^{-1} + g^{-1}$$

Selection of either f^{-1} or g^{-1} should guarantee a correct result; both options need not be followed. For example,

$$\left(A_x + A_{yz}\right)^{-1} = A_x^{-1} + A_{yz}^{-1} = D_x + D_{yz}$$

RULE 4

The inverse of an uncertain addition is a tentative deletion, i.e., if the degree $d(x)$ of a vertex x is unknown when f^{-1} arrives at D_x, use

$$A_x^{-1} = D_x^{\#} \quad = D_x \text{ if } d(x) = 0$$
$$= N \text{ else}$$

The fifth rule enables the construction of σ^{-1} from σ, and is a bit more complex. It is here that the inversion technique may fail. Define the **profile** of a vertex or an edge to be a subset of those terminal expressions in some given selection language which describes the vertex or edge correctly, for example "$x \in V, d(x) = 1$."[12] A **pre-profile** is a profile immediately before the application of an operator. Although σ initially constitutes a profile, σ is expanded to σ_{pre}. This new pre-profile excludes ineffectual (equivalent to N) operations. σ_{pre} also includes any properties of the seed preserved under f. A **post-profile** is a profile immediately after the application of an operator. For most cases, the construction of σ^{-1} from σ is embodied in

RULE 5

Let σ be a pre-profile of those variables involved. Expand σ to σ_{pre}. Compute the changes to σ_{pre} caused by f. The new description, σ^{-1}, makes statements about:

- whether or not vertices are in V
- whether or not edges are in V

- whether or not vertices are distinct
- whether or not edges are distinct
- the degree of a vertex
- the maximum degree of any vertex in the graph

In other words, a p-generator uses σ to single out a variable x by its relationship to G and then applies f to x, changing in some fashion the nature of x with respect to G. This new description of x marks it as useful for inversion. What aspects of x (or xy) are significant? Most of the graph properties based on the primitives mentioned here find membership with respect to V and E, distinctness, degree of a vertex and maximum degree of any vertex in the graph to be an adequate perspective. As a simple example, compute the inverse of CYCLE:

$$f^{-1} = S^{-1}_{xvy}$$

$$= \left(D_{xy} A_{xv} A_{vy} A_v\right)^{-1}$$

$$= A_v^{-1} A_{vy}^{-1} A_{xv}^{-1} D_{xy}^{-1}$$

$$= D_v D_{vy} D_{xv} A_{xy}$$

$$\sigma = x,y \in V,\ v \notin V,\ xy \in E$$

$$\sigma_{pre} = x,y \in V,\ v \notin V,\ xy \in E,\ d(x) = d(y) = 2$$

$$\sigma^{-1} = x,y,v \in V,\ xv, yv \in E,\ xy \notin E,\ d(x) = d(y) = d(v) = 2$$

Once a p-generator exists, what guarantee is there that an automatically computable p-tester can be found? The example makes clear that the control mechanism lies in σ^{-1}, the heuristic which identifies the vertices and edges for use in the transformation of the graph. The language Σ may be adequate to write σ for the p-generator but not to write σ^{-1} for the p-tester. A p-tester is really a p-generator run backwards, but the directions for running backwards (f^{-1} and σ^{-1}) are heuristic creations.

Inversion is recognition algorithm construction. It is available because the graph property is expressed in an R-language. Just as there may be several p-generators associated with a given property p, there may also be several p-testers. This multiplicity is once again consistent with the multiplicity of testing algorithms sometimes available for a mathematical property.

4.0 DETECTING NATURAL HIERARCHIES: SUBSUMPTION AND THEOREM PROVING

IM confronts a homework assignment. The first problem reads: "A closed walk which traverses each edge of a graph exactly once and passes through every vertex at least once is called an **Eulerian walk.** An **Eulerian graph** is one for which an Eulerian walk exists. Is every Eulerian graph a cycle? Is every cycle Eulerian?" IM generates some cycles, some Eulerian graphs and some non-Eulerian graphs. All the cycles test Eulerian, but one of the Eulerian graphs fails a test for cycles. Based on the definitions, **and the generated examples**, IM writes, "Every cycle is Eulerian, but not every Eulerian graph is a cycle." On request IM should produce a proof. In the meantime, that is a fine conjecture, reminiscent of the theorem types earlier in this paper.

Given two graph properties p_1 and p_2, property p_1 **subsumes** property p_2 (and the R-expression for p_1 subsumes the R-expression for p_2) if every graph with property p_2 also has property p_1.[13] If p_1 subsumes p_2, p_2 is a special case of p_1. In addition, if property p_1 subsumes property p_2 **and** property p_2 subsumes property p_1, then p_1 and p_2 are **equivalent properties** and their respective R-expressions are equivalent.

One reasonably simple heuristic for testing subsumption under an R-language representation has been identified. Let $<f_1,S_1,\sigma_1>$ be an invertible expression for p_1, and let $<f_2,S_2,\sigma_2>$ be any expression for p_2. Then p_1 subsumes p_2 if:

- f_2 is subsumed by f_1
- a p_1-tester returns TRUE for every $S \in S_2$
- σ_2 is subsumed by σ_1

If S_2 is manageably finite, as is usually the case, it is only necessary to specify how operators and selectors subsume each other. Define selector subsumption first. Let σ_1 and σ_2 be selectors which respectively select, with respect to a graph G, vertex sets V_1 (with cardinality n_1) and V_2 (with cardinality n_2). Denote by $\sigma<v_1,v_2,\ldots,v_n>$ the fact that the vertices $v_1,v_2,\ldots,v_n$, *in the specified order*, satisfy σ. Then selector σ_1 subsumes selector σ_2 if and only if for every set of vertices

$$\{v_1,v_2,\ldots,v_{n_2}\}$$

such that

$$\sigma_2<v_1,v_2,\ldots,v_{n_2}>$$

there is an arrangement with repetition

$$<v'_1,v'_2,\ldots,v'_{n_1}> \text{ from } \{v_1,v_2,\ldots,v_{n_2}\}$$

such that

$$\sigma_1<v'_1,v'_2,\ldots,v'_{n_1}>.$$

That is, selector σ_1 will subsume σ_2 if and only if the description in σ_1 of each vertex v is consistent with and no more restrictive than the description of the corresponding vertex v' in σ_2. Here are several examples of less restrictive descriptions. ("expr" denotes the degree of a vertex or the cardinality of a set.)

- "description 1 on v" is less restrictive than "description 1 and description 2 on v." For example, "v ε V" is less restrictive than "v ε V, vw ε E." The first permits v to be isolated, the second does not.

- "expr < k_1" is less restrictive than "expr < k_2" if $k_1 > k_2$.

- "expr ≥ k" is less restrictive than "expr = k"

Here is an example of selector subsumption:

σ_1: x,y ε V, xy ∉ E, d(x) ≥ 2

σ_2: x,y ε V, xy ∉ E, d(y) > 2, d(x) = 1

From {x,y} such that σ_2<x,y>, arrange <y,x>. Then σ_1<y,x> and σ_1 subsumes σ_2.

Here are six conditions for operator subsumption:

Condition 1
  f subsumes f.

Condition 2
  f + g subsumes f and subsumes g. Clearly f and g are special cases of "f or g."

Condition 3
  f^* subsumes f^k. One may choose to iterate k times, and f^k is a special case of f^*.

Condition 4

f^* subsumes N. One may also choose to iterate f no times, and the null primitive N is a special case of f^*.

Condition 5

$f_1 + g_1$ subsumes $f_2 + g_2$ if f_1 subsumes f_2 and g_1 subsumes g_2. The f's and g's may themselves be composite operators.

Condition 6

$f_1 g_1$ subsumes $f_2 g_2$ if f_1 subsumes f_2 and g_1 subsumes g_2. The f's and g's may themselves be composite operators.

In combination with the identity $f + g = g + f$ for any composite operators f and g, these operator subsumption conditions may be combined in fairly lengthy reasoning procedures. For example, if $f_1 = (f + g^*)(f^2 + g)$ one can rewrite f_1 as:

$$f_1 = f^3 + fg + g*f^2 + g*g$$

Then one can show that f_1 subsumes, among others, each of the following:

f^3

$g^5 f^2$

$(f + g*)f^2$

g

$fg + g$

A great many theorems and conjectures in graph theory are really statements of subsumption or equivalence, presented in Section 2 as Type 1 and Type 2. R-languages are readily applicable to proofs of such theorems. Consider the following simple example: "Every cycle is Eulerian." The proof examines the expressions[14] for the properties p_1:

EULERIAN: $(S_{wvz} + Y_{v_1 v_2 \ldots v_k})^*(K_3)$ where $w, z \in V$, $v \notin V$, $wz \in E$.

$|\{v_1 v_2 \ldots v_k\} \cap V| \geq 1,$

$v_1 v_k \notin E$, $v_i v_{i+1} \notin E$, $i=1,2,\ldots,k-1$, distinct $v_i, i=1,2,\ldots,k$, $k \geq 3$

and p_2

CYCLE: $S^*_{xvy}(K_3)$ where $x,y \in V$, $v \notin V$, $xy \in E$

From $\{x,v,y\}$ such that $\sigma_2 <x,v,y>$, arrange $<x,v,y>$. Since $\sigma_1<x,v,y>$, σ_1 subsumes σ_2. Clearly f_2 is subsumed by f_1, by Condition 2. Because K_3 is the seed graph for p_1, any p_1-tester must return TRUE on K_3. Thus p_1 subsumes p_2 and the theorem is proved.

Subsumption is the relation used to construct mathematical hierarchies. As such, it is crucial to the organization of mathematical knowledge. The $<f,S,\sigma>$ formulation captures both the definitions and the generated graphs IM used for the homework problem on subsumption. The R-language representation even offers some transparency for certain pairs of expressions. Commonality of seed, or of operator, or even of selector, is worthy of notice. Once again, the redundancy of representation becomes an asset. Here, for example, are two expressions for a chain:[15]

CHAIN$_1$: $S^*_{xvy}(K_2)$ where $x,y \in V$, $v \notin V$, $xy \in E$

CHAIN$_2$: $B^*_{xy}(K_2)$ where $x \in V$, $y \notin V$, $d(x) = 1$

CHAIN$_1$ reflects a close kinship with
    CYCLE: $S^*_{xvy}(K_3)$ where $x,y \in V$, $v \notin V$, $xy \in E$

and CHAIN$_2$ reflects a close kinship with
    TREE: $B^*_{xy}(K_1)$ where $x \in V$, $y \notin V$

The two expressions for a chain describe perspectives on the concept; CHAIN$_1$ modifies an initial path internally, CHAIN$_2$ extends it. Both expressions are significant and useful.

5.0 CREATING NEW CONCEPTS: MERGER

IM is still doing homework. Question 2 reads, "A tree is an acyclic, connected graph. What is the smallest tree? How does the number of vertices in a tree compare with the number of its edges?" Once again IM generates graphs, carefully applying the definitions of acyclic and connected. IM constructs a formula: "The number of vertices is exactly one more than the number of edges."

For properties p_1 and p_2 (with respective sets P_1 and P_2) mathematicians frequently explore the property of having both p_1 and p_2. Given a graph property p_1 and a graph property p_2, define their **merger** to be a graph property $p = p_1 \wedge p_2$ (read "p_1 and p_2"), the set of all graphs with both properties. Similarly, the merger of R-expressions $<f_1, S_1, \sigma_1>$ for p_1 and $<f_2, S_2, \sigma_2>$ for p_2 is the new expression $<f, S, \sigma>$ for $p = p_1 \wedge p_2$. Thus a $p_1 \wedge p_2$ - generator must produce precisely the set $P_1 \cap P_2$.

Another strength of the R-language representation is that merger appears to be reasonably amenable to automatic computation. Given expressions for p_1 and p_2, there are principles and techniques for the automatic construction of an expression for $p_1 \wedge p_2$. The claim is not that every merger will have an expression computable from these principles, but that any expression for a merger constructed from these principles results in a p-generator which is both correct and complete. For reasonably complex mergers, the heuristics described here have been very successful in testing.

Many attempts at merger, upon examination, become simple cases of subsumption. This gives rise to:

PRINCIPLE 1
If p_1 subsumes p_2, the merger of p_1 and p_2 is simply p_2.

Recall that p_1 (with expression $<f_1,S_1,\sigma_1>$) subsumes p_2 (with expression $<f_2,S_2,\sigma_2>$) if f_1 subsumes f_2, σ_1 subsumes σ_2, and a p_1-tester returns TRUE for every $S \in S_2$. Consider now variants where subsumption is not possible because one of these conditions fails. If σ_1 does not subsume σ_2, try:

PRINCIPLE 2
If f_1 subsumes f_2 and a p_1-tester returns TRUE for every $S \in S_2$, then the merger is $<f_2,S_2,\sigma>$. A correspondence between the variables of p_1 and the variables of p_2 is asserted by the relation between f_1 and f_2. σ is "σ_1 and σ_2" but eliminates any references to variables not in σ_2. If σ_2 subsumes σ_1, σ will be simply σ_2.

If S_1 is distinct from S_2, it may be possible to apply:

PRINCIPLE 3
If f_1 subsumes f_2, σ_1 subsumes σ_2 and $S_1 \cap S_2 \neq \phi$, then the merger is $<f_2, S_1 \cap S_2, \sigma_2>$. Again assume a proper mapping of the variables.

The most difficult variant is when f_1 does not subsume f_2. A graph generator grows graphs in iterative steps. Denote the change in n (the number of vertices in V) after a single iteration of a p_i-generator as Δn_i, and the change in m (the number of edges in E) as Δm_i. Define Δn and Δm correspondingly for property p.

PRINCIPLE 4
If p is the merger of p_1 and p_2, Δn is the least common multiple of Δn_1 and Δn_2, and Δm of Δm_1 and Δm_2.

Clearly, Principle 4 is only guidance for dealing with uncooperative f's. Here are further suggested techniques for f construction. First, composite operators may obscure the nature of f_1 and f_2; rewrite them in terms of the primitive operators. Second, look for possible subsumption relationships. Third, attempt to create a hybrid f which is a specialization of both f_1 and f_2. This f is formed by specializing f_1 and f_2 until they are equivalent, or one subsumes the other. This series of transforms is guided by the Δn_i's and Δm_i's. A limited list of such specializations follows. The reader should feel free to augment it.

- $f^*_{a,b,\ldots} \Rightarrow (f_{a_1,b_1},\ldots f_{a_2,b_2},\ldots \ldots f_{a_k,b_k},\ldots)^*$

This restricts the number of times f is applied within an iteration to some multiple of k. Subscripts are presumed distinct.

- $f^*_{a,b,\ldots} \Rightarrow f_{a_1,b_1},\ldots f_{a_2,b_2},\ldots \ldots f_{a_k,b_k},\ldots$

This fixes the number of times f is applied within an iteration to exactly k.

- $f^*_{a,b,\ldots} \Rightarrow f^+_{a,b,\ldots}$

This denotes "at least one iteration is required."

- $f^* \Rightarrow N$

This means f is not iterated at all.

- $(f + g)^* \Rightarrow f^* g^*$

  $(f + g)^* \Rightarrow g^* f^*$

These require that the applications of f and g appear in a specific order.

- $(f + g)^* \Rightarrow (f + fg)^*$
  $(f + g)^* \Rightarrow (f + gf)^*$
  $(f + g)^* \Rightarrow (g + fg)^*$
  $(f + g)^* \Rightarrow (g + gf)^*$

These insist that some alternatives may not occur alone.

- $(f + g)^* \Rightarrow f^*$
  $(f + g)^* \Rightarrow g^*$

These eliminate an option.

- $f_{\alpha,\beta,\ldots} \Rightarrow f_{a,b,\ldots}$

This represents a consistent substitution of variable a for α, b for $\beta,\ldots$, within the constraints of σ. For example, if σ does not say $x \neq y$, then A_{xy} may be specialized to A_{xx} or A_{yy}.

The reader may have noticed that these "specializations" are merely subsumption tests applied in reverse, i.e., if f_1 subsumes f_2, then f_2 is a specialization of f_1. As f_1 and f_2 are transformed, σ_1 and σ_2 must be modified accordingly to keep track of the restrictions on newly-introduced variables.

After specialization, it is frequently necessary to verify that f_1 and f_2 are equivalent or that one subsumes the other. Here are some verification rules. Each of the following pairs of expressions may be verified equivalent:

- $f_{a,b,\ldots} f_{a,b,\ldots} \equiv f_{a,b,\ldots}$

    Note that the subscripts are identical, hence the lack of impact on the graph.

- $fN \equiv f$
  $Nf \equiv f$

    The null operator may be ignored.

- $f_{a,b,\ldots} f^{-1}_{a,b,\ldots} \equiv N$

- $f^{-1}_{a,b,\ldots} f_{a,b,\ldots} \equiv N$

An operator and its inverse cancel each other out, as long as they are applied in sequence to the same vertices/edges.

- $f^* f^* \equiv f^*$

  This is a notational equivalent.

- $(f + g)^* \equiv f^*(f + g)^*$
- $(f + g)^* \equiv (f + g)^* g^*$

  These are simplifications.

- $(f + g) \equiv (g + f)$

  This is the inherent commutativity in the iteration choice.

- $f \equiv g$ where g is the defined primary equivalent of the composite f, a verification assumed informally above.

- $A_x f_{a,b,\ldots} \equiv f_{a,b,\ldots} A_x$ if σ prevents x from being a,b,....

  This is a very limited form of commutativity.

- $f^*_{\alpha,\beta,\ldots} f^*_{a,b,\ldots} \equiv f^*_{\alpha,\beta,\ldots}$ if σ permits α = a, β = b,....

  $f^*_{a,b,\ldots} f^*_{\alpha,\beta,\ldots} \equiv f^*_{\alpha,\beta,\ldots}$ if σ permits α = a, β = b,....

  These are principles of absorption.

- $f_{a_1,b_1,\ldots} f_{a_2,b_2,\ldots} \equiv f_{a,b,\ldots}$ if σ can be changed to select variables appropriately.

As an example (more elaborate ones may be found in [Eps]) consider the property "trees with an odd number of vertices."

p_1 = TREE: $B^*_{xy}(K_1)$ where $x \in V$, $y \notin V$

p_2 = ODD-VERTICES: $(A_{xw} + A_y A_z)^*(K_1)$
where $x, w \in V$, distinct $y, z \notin V$

In keeping with the techniques discussed above, first rewrite f_1:

f_1: $(A_{xy} A_y)$

The seeds are identical, but no other subsumption relationships are visible. Calculations show $\Delta n_1 = 1$, $\Delta m_1 = 1$. For p_2, however, there are choices: either $\Delta n_2 = 0$ and $\Delta m_2 = 1$, or $\Delta n_2 = 2$ and $\Delta m_2 = 0$. Now specialize both f_1 and f_2 so that merger is possible. The motivation for the particular specializations given is an attempt to match Δn_1 with Δn_2, and Δm_1 with Δm_2. First push f_1 toward $\Delta n = 2$:

$$f_1^* = (A_{xy} A_y)^* \Rightarrow (f_1^2)^* = (A_{xy} A_y A_{wz} A_z)^*$$

$$\sigma_1 = x \in V, y \notin V \Rightarrow x, w \in V, \text{ distinct } y, z \notin V$$

Note that it is quite legitimate for x and w to be the same, but y and z must be distinct because y is added **after** z and is not in V at the time. Now push f_2 toward $\Delta n = 2$ and $\Delta m = 2$:

$$f_2^* = (g + h)^* = (A_{xw} + A_y A_z)^* \Rightarrow (ggh)^* = (A_{xw} A_{pq} A_y A_z)^*$$

$$\sigma_1 = x, w \in V, \text{ distinct } y, z \notin V \Rightarrow x, w, p, q \in V, \text{ distinct } y, z \notin V$$

Rewrite f_2 (and σ_2) in an attempt to match f_1. In f_2 uniformly replace w with y, p with w, and q with z to get:

$$(A_{xy} A_{wz} A_y A_z)^* \text{ where } x, y, w, z \in V, \text{ distinct } y, z \notin V$$

Because y and z are added during the iteration, $y, z \in V$ is irrelevant and the specialization of f_2 and σ_2 is now

$$(A_{xy}A_{wz}A_yA_z)^* \text{ where } x,w \in V, \text{ distinct } y,z \notin V$$

When contrasted with the specialization of f_1 and σ_1:

$$(A_{xy}A_yA_{wx}A_z)^* \text{ where } x,w \in V, \text{ distinct } y,z \in V$$

it becomes apparent that applying the limited commutativity rule to permute A_y and A_{wx} will demonstrate the equivalence of these two operators.

With their common seed, then, create an expression for the merger p whose associated p-generator produces all trees with an odd number of vertices:

$$p: (A_{xy}A_yA_{wz}A_z)^*(K_1) \text{ where } x,w \in V, \text{ distinct } y,z \notin V$$

Other heuristics arise during the construction of expressions for more elaborate mergers. The discovery of a common seed, when $S_1 \cap S_2 = \phi$, is non-trivial. One reasonably successful heuristic is to let the p-generator with the more elaborate σ (say, p_1) run a bit until it produces a graph (or graphs) on which the p_2-tester returns TRUE. Selective iteration (the transformation under specialization of an expression like f + g + h into hf + hg + h) is useful for constructing an operator when a variable (here one referenced by h) is highly restricted under σ.

How is the R-language representation doing on IM's homework? Under merger, it is possible to construct an expression for "tree" from those for "acyclic" and "connected." The expression for the merger is

$$p_1 = \text{TREE}: \quad B_{xy}^*(K_1) \text{ where } x \in V, y \notin V$$

It is significant that the tree generator does not take the classical generate-and-test approach, which in this case would be to generate an acyclic (or a connected) graph and then test to see if it was connected (acyclic) too. Rather, the new

generator incorporates the test information in some fashion.
(This is, of course, the key to its ability to invert as
well.) Thus multiple mergers (e.g., "cyclic, biconnected
graphs with an even number of vertices and an odd number of
edges") will not necessarily have expressions with less
efficient generators or testers than their component properties
(e.g., cyclic, biconnected, and so forth.)

IM was also asked, "What is the smallest tree?" The smallest[16] example should be in the seed set of the expression for the merger and, indeed, it is K_1. Another question was, "How does the number of vertices in a tree compare with the number of edges?" (This measure of *density* is of great interest in graph theory.) The R-language representation is easily manipulated to solve this problem too. In TREE, $\Delta n = \Delta m = 1$ and initially $n = 1$, $m = 0$. Thus n will always be $m + 1$. Not only does the representation facilitate the creation of a new concept, it can provide detailed information on it.

6.0 EXPLORING

Suppose now that IM is told to construct a graph which has two properties selected at random. If IM chooses acyclic and connected, a tree will result. But if IM attempts to generate a 3-regular[17] graph with an odd number vertices, it will not succeed. All the regular graphs on an odd number of vertices seem to be 2-regular or 4-regular or 6-regular. What's happening here?

The R-language representation is certainly helpful for such a problem. Certain mergers (this one among them) can be *proved* impossible based on the values m and n must assume under the expressions for p_1 and p_2. Thus merger can become a counterexample constructor or a proof technique for the Type 3 statements in Section 2.

In the scenarios above, IM applied graph properties and the merger procedure to examples. On some level, an R-language representation is purely examples. A program designed for discovery in graph theory could use R-language expressions in the following ways:

- generate specific examples of a property
- generate specific examples of a merger
- attempt to force regularities in specific examples
- observe structural similarities in two expressions
- design new expressions and run their generators

AM did much of this in set theory, but with a generate-and-test approach. R-language representation provides error-free examples and the ability to manipulate an entire set of similar objects, i.e., reason about a concept. Discovery in an R-language should be much like IM doodling thoughtfully.

7.0 ADAPTATION

"This morning," the instructor announces, "we will consider a category of objects related to graphs: labelled graphs." IM summons all that newly-acquired knowledge about graph theory, and prepares to modify it.

It is important to be able to extend a successful representation for one area to deal with a closely related area. In [Eps] the R-languages are shown to adapt readily for labelled (or colored) graphs. The R^c-languages and R^e-languages, as they are called, prove IM-like in their epistemological adequacy and manipulative skill. The naturalness of this extension is noteworthy because it suggests that the original representation was a "good fit." In addition, such extendibility is a necessity when modelling the historical development of a body of knowledge. This makes R-languages particularly attractive for work in mathematical theory formation.

8.0   SCOPE, LIMITATIONS AND FUTURE WORK

The adequacy of the R-languages for the goals detailed in Section 1 is an interesting and non-trivial question. The following points are worth raising:

- What kind of graph property has a representation which defines a p-generator?
- What kind of graph property can be decided by a p-tester?
- Are those graph properties adequate for research in graph theory?

These questions are addressed here by examining the Turing machine counterparts of p-generators. A graph will be represented to a Turing machine as an ordered pair of lists, <V,E>, where the vertices are uniquely numbered and then binarily encoded. (There are, of course, other equally acceptable representations. This one, which uses the paper's original definition, is an obvious choice.) Define a graph property p to be *recursively enumerable* if and only if there exists some Turing machine which generates P. Define a graph property p to be *recursive* if and only if there exists some Turing machine which decides[18] P and halts on all inputs.[19]

Consider first the Turing machine counterpart of a p-generator. Within certain constraints, an R-language expression <f,S,σ> is modelled by a three-tape Turing machine. The first tape contains the program to modify the input graph (the information contained in f and σ) and space for computations. As f and σ were defined, they are certainly finite and encodable for a Turing machine. The second tape is for S. As long as the set S is finite or recursively enumerable, the second tape either lists S or encodes the Turing machine which generates S. If S is not finite or recursively enumerable, the R-language expression is implemented by a Turing machine with an oracle which decrees whether or not a given graph is in S. The third tape is for the output, that is, the set P. The Turing machine's program instructs it to select any graph G_1 from S, modify it into some graph G_2, output G_2 and then recurse, to modify G_2 on the next iteration.[20] Thus, if there exists an R-language expression for graph property p with some recursively enumerable S, p is recursively enumerable. If there exists an R-language expression for p and an oracle for S, p is recursively enumerable relative to S.

The p-generator deforms G_1 into G_2, and the p-tester is supposed to undo that transformation, i.e., transform G_2 into G_1 or into some other G_3 from which G_2 might have come. The p-tester $<f^{-1}, S, \sigma^{-1}>$ described here may also be modelled by a three-tape Turing machine, under certain constraints. The first tape contains the program to modify the input graph (the information contained in f^{-1} and σ^{-1}) and space for computations. As f^{-1} and σ^{-1} were defined, they are finite and encodable for a Turing machine. The second tape is for S. If the expression for p is written so that S is finite, the second tape lists S. If the expression for p is recursive, the second tape encodes the Turing machine which accepts S. If S is neither finite nor recursive, an oracle is needed. The third tape is for the output, that is, the decision as to whether or not the input graph has property p. The Turing machine's program instructs it to take as input any graph G_2, test G_2 for membership in S, modify G_2 into some graph G_3 if possible, and then recurse, to input G_3 on the next iteration. The nature of S is clearly significant. If S is finite or recursive, the p-tester has a Turing machine counterpart. If, however, S is only recursively enumerable (or worse), the Turing machine counterpart is in need of an oracle and is recursive relative to S. One way to simplify this problem is to have a metric (e.g., number of vertices) on the graph, which is monotonic decreasing during the execution of the p-tester. Given such a metric, the oracle could be replaced by a Turing machine which grew all the (finitely many) graphs in S the same size as G_2 and compared them with G_2. All the properties expressed in [Eps] do in fact have such a metric, usually number of vertices or number of edges. The labels GROW and DECAY in the algorithms are references to that metric.

The obvious question becomes, are recursive or recursively enumerable graph properties the only ones of interest to mathematicians? In the representation of a graph as a pair of sets <V,E>, E was described as any set of pairs of elements of V. Thus E is any subset of the Cartesian product V X V. If the vertices of V are distinguished by labels, every labelled graph on |V| = n vertices corresponds to some subset of V X V. Isomorphism may be used to place those labelled graphs into equivalence classes. Call the set of those classes Γ. Then the distinct graphs on n vertices are precisely Γ. A graph property defined on graphs *of no more than n vertices* will be a finite set and, therefore, recursive. In addition, a finite number (exactly $2^{|\Gamma|}$) of such graph properties can be defined. Somewhat surprisingly, properties which reference the universe U of all finite graphs are also recursive for bounded n. Thus such properties as "having a k-factor" (a k-regular subgraph) and "extremal Hamiltonian" (one edge short of being Hamiltonian) are also recursive.

Once the size of V is unbounded, however, it is possible to construct a set of graphs (i.e., a graph property) which is not recursively enumerable. For example, let Q be a non-recursively enumerable set of natural numbers. Then

$$G^Q = \{<V,E> \mid E \subseteq V \times V \text{ and } |v| \in Q\}$$

is a non-recursively enumerable graph property. It is interesting that several graph theorists[21] report no knowledge of any non-recursively enumerable graph properties under study. This suggests that such properties, although they exist, are in some sense pathological. From one perspective, this is not surprising. In order for a mathematician to study a graph property, the mathematician must want both to define it and to determine whether or not it occurs. Thus graph properties which arouse interest among mathematicians are expected to be decidable and, therefore, recursive. In this context, a representation schema such as the R-languages, which is limited to recursive and recursively enumerable graph properties seems adequately expressive.

If the existence of a p-generator and a p-tester for every property p remains an open question, Table 2 offers some empirical support for the argument that R-languages are adequate. The table lists 43 properties, of varying difficulty, selected from the benchmark and successfully formulated as R-expressions in [Eps]. An attempt was made to include a broad representative sampling of graph properties from the three texts. Several properties with well-known characterizations (e.g., line graphs as in [Har]) were omitted although they are certainly representable in an R-language. The only graph property attempted for which no R-expression was found is "having diameter k." Three graph properties (self-complementary, uniquely k-colorable and k-edge-colorable) were expressed and proved correct but lack completeness proofs. Current research suggests that a less modest knowledge of graph theory may resolve such difficulties.

What will be the complexity of the algorithms for generating and testing graphs? The implementation of a p-generator or a p-tester will derive its complexity from the representation of G itself. A p-generator (or p-tester) binds and modifies on each iteration. The modification is O(e), where e is bounded by the length of the expression for f (or f^{-1}). It is the matching required by σ (or σ^{-1}) which may be resource-consuming. The speed with which the variables are bound will depend upon the way (or, perhaps, ways) G is stored and, possibly, the size of G.

There are many other interesting open questions. Here is a sampling:

- Does a p-tester exist for each p-generator?

- Inversion, merger and testing for subsumption are more heuristic than algorithmic. What are the necessary and sufficient conditions for these procedures in a given R-language?

- Can R-languages be extended to deal with the following?

    o   Non-redundant generation
    o   Edge weights
    o   Enumeration problems, e.g., finding all the spanning trees of a given graph, or all the distinct k-factors
    o   Properties involving minimal or maximal conditions, e.g., the travelling salesman problem or the Chinese postman problem
    o   Other mathematical domains, e.g., group theory or number theory

- Is it possible to discern from a p-generator that a property is finite?

9.0   CONCLUSION

The primary application currently envisioned for R-languages is as a representation for a knowledge-based system which explores graph theory, the way AM [Len] explored set theory. An implementation is intended which will simulate IM, perhaps an extremely bright IM. Such a system, with the help of experts in graph theory, would construct and explore a semantic network of graph properties.

The syntax of the R-languages successfully exploits its unusual link to the semantics of graph theory. In retrospect, the fact that a single representation can support so many applications in a natural way is not surprising. Poincare wrote, "...to prove even the smallest theorem [we] must use reasoning by recurrence, for that is the only instrument which enables us to

graph	connected graph
edgeless graph	biconnected graph
acyclic graph	k-connected graph
tree	graph on counted vertices
loopfree graph	graph with counted edges
chain	graph with calculated maximum degree
cycle	bipartite graph
star	complete bipartite graph
wheel	k-vertex-covered graph
complete graph	k-independent graph
graph on even number of vertices	k-colored graph
graph on odd number of vertices	k-chromatic graph
graph with even number of edges	graph with vertex covering number k
graph with odd number of edges	graph with circumference k
Eulerian graph	graph with edge covering number k
graph with n vertices	graph with a k-factor
graph with m edges	k-factorable graph
graph of minimum degree k	graph with independence number k
graph of maximum degree k	Hamiltonian graph
pinwheel	planar graph
graph with k components	non-planar graph
even-regular graph	odd-regular graph

Table 2

Graph Properties Studied under Recursive Generation

pass from the finite to the infinite."[Poi] LISP recursion in AM was a beginning. The R-languages, with their flexibility and power, are the next logical step.

FOOTNOTES

[*] This work was done at Rutgers University. I thank N.S. Sridharan for his inspiration and guidance, and Saul Amarel, Tom Mitchell, Marvin Paull, Rick Statman and Ann Yasuhara for their insightful questions and discussion.

[1] Here begins a series of clarifying footnotes, supplementing the text or addressing some relevant but mildly divergent question. The set definition certainly contains a numerical pattern suggestive of a cycle. IM the student drew a reasonable analogy and is at the periphery of the concept of planarity. Although the pictures might be helpful to IM, the isomorphism between them is better indicated by the original ordered pair definition.

[2] Michener [Mic] supports this dependence upon examples. The claim of an alternative, pictorial representation is based on years of teaching and observation, and extends beyond graph theory to examples of any abstract concept.

[3] IM, while learning graph theory, solves many problems typical of mathematical research. Within an environment carefully structured by a good teacher, theorem proving is only part of IM's task.

[4] The distinction between p and P is really syntactic, not semantic. For example, p may represent "acyclic", while P is the set of all acyclic graphs. The context will dictate whether p or P is used.

[5] The work of Boyer and Moore[Boy] on induction proofs is kindred.

[6] The examples throughout this paper are of undirected graphs, but R-languages accommodate directed graphs as well. A walk of a graph G is an alternating sequence of vertices and edges, $v_1, v_1 v_2, v_2, v_2 v_3, v_3, \ldots, v_{k-1}, v_{k-1} v_k, v_k$ beginning and ending with vertices, in which each edge is incident with the two vertices immediately preceding and following it. The abbreviated form is $v_1 v_2 \ldots v_k$. A walk is closed if $v_1 = v_k$, otherwise it is open. A cycle is a closed walk on k vertices, all distinct, with $k \geq 3$. A graph is acyclic if it contains no cycles, i.e., every walk is open.

[7]   A graph $G = \langle V,E \rangle$ is said to be complete if and only if $E = \{(x,y) | x,y \in V, x \neq y\}$, i.e., it contains an edge between every pair of distinct vertices.

[8]   In [Eps] this language is called P.

[9]   The p-generator will not halt if P is infinite. It is, of course, possible that P is a finite set, in which case the p-generator must halt.

[10] All R-expressions should, however, make certain that G is still a graph. That is, when an edge xy is added, σ should force x and y to be in V. Similarly, when vertex x is deleted, σ should force all edges to and from x to be deleted.

[11] This technique is guaranteed at this time only for certain expressions.

[12] There is no requirement that the profile selection language be the same as the selection language of the p-generator. The former is likely to be a superset of the latter. Indeed, the selection of an adequate, but not overly verbose, profile selection language is at the crux of the question of invertibility.

[13] Those reading [Eps] will observe that subsumption was defined oppositely there.

[14] The operator $Y_{v_1 v_2 \ldots v_k}$ denotes the addition to the graph of a cycle on some arbitrary number k of vertices. The selector specifies that these vertices are distinct and at least three in number, that all of the cycle edges are new to the graph, and that at least one of the cycle vertices is not. The ellipsis is not part of the selector notation, but a convenience enabling a clear counting up to k.

[15] A chain is a graph consisting of a single open path on at least two vertices. The length of a chain is one less than the number of its vertices, i.e., $n - 1$.

[16] "Smallest" is ill-defined but typically of great mathematical interest. Both Lenat [Len] and Michener [Mic] provide for it, and justifiably so.

[17] A graph is said to be r-regular if and only if every vertex is of degree r.

[18] A machine which recognizes a property is guaranteed to halt on any graph with the property and report that the graph has the property. A machine which decides a property is guaranteed to halt on any graph and report whether or not the graph has the property.

[19]   One definition views Turing machines as language generators, the other as language deciders. The two views are perfectly compatible (see, for example, [Hop]) and are selected to emphasize the relevant features of R-languages.

[20]   Recall that in order to generate all of P, every element of S must be used to start the p-generator. It may be helpful to imagine a set of machines, one for each element in S, all operating in parallel. S thus must be recursively enumerable. The non-determinism of the algorithm is then not an issue for a Turing machine. See [Hop].

[21]   Personal communication, M. Saks, R. Statman.

REFERENCES

[Bon]   Bondy, J. and Murty, U., *Graph Theory with Applications*, North Holland, New York, 1976.

[Boy]   Boyer, R.S. and Moore, J.S., *A Computational Logic*, Academic Press, New York, 1979.

[Dor]   Dorin, P.M., *Aspects of the Implementation of Sequential Graph Rewriting Systems*, PhD thesis, UCLA, 1982.

[Eps]   Epstein, S. L., *Knowledge Representation in Mathematics: A Case Study in Graph Theory*, PhD thesis, Rutgers University, April, 1983.

[Har]   Harary, F., *Graph Theory*, Addison-Wesley, Reading, Mass., 1972.

[Hop]   Hopcroft, J. E. and Ullman, J. D., *Introduction to Automata Theory, Languages, and Computation*, Addison-Wesley, Reading, Massachusetts, 1979.

[Len]   Lenat, D. B., *AM: An Artificial Intelligence Approach to Discovery in Mathematics as Heuristic Search*, PhD thesis, Stanford, July, 1976.

[Mic]   Michener, E., *Understanding Understanding Mathematics*, Technical Report AI MEMO-488, MIT, August, 1978, LOGO MEMO-50.

[Ore]   Ore, O., *American Mathematical Society Colloquium Publications*, Volume 38: *Theory of Graphs*, American Mathematical Society, Providence, Rhode Island, 1962.

[Pas]   Pascal, B., *Pensees de Pascal*, Editions Garnier Freres, Paris, France, 1964, pages 73-84.

[Poi]   Poincare, H., *Science and Hypothesis*, Dover Publications Inc., New York, 1952.

[Poi2] Poincare, H., L'Intuition et la Logique en Mathematiques, *La Valeur de la Science*, Flammarion, France, 1970, pages 27-40.

[Ros] Rosen, B.K., Deriving Graphs from Graphs by Applying a Production, *Acta Informatica*, 4: 337-357, 1975.

[Wos] Wos,L., Solving Open Questions with an Automated Theorem-proving Program, In *6th Conference on Automated Deduction* edited by D.W. Loveland, pages 1-31, Springer Verlag, New York, 1982. Lecture Notes in Computer Science, vol 138.

SYMBOLIC TRANSLATION AND VERY HIGH LEVEL QUERY LANGUAGES*

W. H. Guier

Johns Hopkins University Applied Physic Laboratory
Johns Hopkins Road
Laurel, Maryland   20707

R. Jernigan

Decision Resource Systems
5595 Vantage Point Road
Columbia, Maryland 21044

* This work has been supported under Navy Contract N00024-85-C-5301

Mathematical statements are usually expressively direct and rigorously unambiguous to those practiced in the notation and area of mathematical application. Mathematical statements of specification are declarative, while, eg., algebraic statements are procedural or even algorithmic. This paper presents an approach to the joining of established mathematical notation with "computer-like" procedural and algorithmic information to provide an integrated means for specifying the desired output of computation processes. This approach differs from previous ones in that the mathematical notation is "unsugared"; ie., the original specification of the process appears only in established mathematical notation. This specification statement is then symbolically translated by computer to equivalent algebraic expressions which are then processed by the computer to yield the desired output. This approach is demonstrated within the application of deductive data base queries and primarily through query examples. Data base queries are formulated de novo into Codd's alpha expression (α-exp) which embodies an expressively direct, non-procedural, and mathematically complete set of retrieval criteria in the first order relational calculus. This α-exp is then translated symbolically into a recent database computer language, Jernigan's ALPS, which is a relational algebra exhibiting many aspects of the first order relational domain calculus. This approach to very high level languages by symbolic translation of a specialized and

unsugared notation such as mathematics is
shown to be a practical one via the choice of
the examples. These examples also show that
the "layering" inherent in this approach
provides the opportunity for introducing
multiple levels of sugaring of the notation
and of procedural "control" of the evaluation
process.

1.0   INTRODUCTION

Any present information processing system is expected to do
more than merely search its database for stored information.
It should have a formal notation system or language in which
the database may be "queried" for information not stored in the
database. The information processing system then retrieves the
answer to the query by logical inference from information which
is contained in the database. Such information processing
systems are termed deductive database systems. The notation or
language in which such queries are formulated for processing is
called an information query language. It is this application
area and processing environment to which we direct your
attention in this paper.

The very powerful query languages available today are
yet another class of application languages which must be
learned by the programmer or investigator who desires to use
such retrieval systems. In this particular case the languages
usually are the result of attempts to 'sugar' the mathematics
of logical inference in the name of being 'user friendly'.
However, user friendliness is an attribute that depends heavily
upon the user's knowledge and background. For investigators
who are familiar with the notation system of formal
mathematical logic, this sugaring of the language for the
mathematically naive user can be very unfriendly. To the
mathematically experienced person, this sugaring of query
languages ignores the wonderfully efficient, expressively
direct, and rigorously exact syntax and semantics of an
existing language which has been refined for over half a
century by investigators focused upon the logic of inferring
new information from old. In this particular application area,
user friendly sugar replaces this mature and nearly universal
notation with a language which is expressively less direct,
narrower in scope, and in the worst cases requires development
of lengthy algorithms to perform primitive mathematical
inferences.

Therefore, the notation of mathematical logic is the
preferred query language for the mathematically experienced
investigator and it seems reasonable to formulate database
queries in this language. At the very minimum, it is
reasonable to not deny the use of logic notation to those who
prefer it. E. F. Codd accomplished this when he introduced in
1970 his alpha expressions into computerized database retrieval
systems, [Codd 1970 1972]. Codd introduced the notion that a
query is a specification of a set (of those database

inferences) to be retrieved. He then formalized this set specification as an alpha expression (α-exp) with a rigorous statement of the semantics of the computer database processing required to satisfy an α-exp query. This semantics was established in terms of an interpretation of first order predicate theory. Codd's pioneering work initiated a growing interest in the logical foundations of database queries and formal logic now plays a significant role in database language studies [Date 1975, Codd 1979, Ullman 1980, Gallaire 1981, Maier 1983]. However, Codd's original work has found its major applications as a meta-language for research in database theory.

Information processing systems must perform tasks other than inferring and retrieving information. They must input new information into the database and allow changes or corrections to be made to the stored information. That is, they must have features which allow maintenance of the database. Database designers also must come to grips with very practical issues such as efficiency and security and integrity of the database. A recent development is the information processing system, ALPS, [Jernigan 1984, 1985, 1986] which can both accept logically constructed data queries and perform all of these pragmatic tasks of information maintenance. ALPS is one of the newer languages where it can be proved that its query component is 'complete', i.e., for every query form in the first order predicate theory of logic there exists an equivalent expression in the query component of ALPS. In fact Codd's formulation of α-exp can be used as a meta-language to prove the logical completeness of ALPS with respect to data queries. In particular, since Codd proved the completeness of α-exp [Codd 1972], the proof that ALPS is logically complete with respect to α-exps establishes two important facts with mathematical rigour and are stated here without proof.

(1) To every query form in first order logic, there exists a query form in α-exps and in ALPS

(2) to every query form in α-exps, there exists an exact equivalent query form in the ALPS which can be considered to be the translation of the α-exp into ALPS.

These existence theorems establish the potential of combining the advantages of formulating data queries in a rigorous and established mathematical notation with the practical advantages of using database processing systems such as ALPS. To realize this potential, one needs only to demonstrate the ability to translate queries (or fragments of queries) into ALPS with sufficient speed and flexibility to be useful.

The major focus of this paper is the demonstration that (a) the mathematical notation of α-exp queries can be translated automatically by the computer at the symbolic level into ALPS and that (b) this translation capability provides a practical tool to the person involved with complicated database inferential queries, eg., in expert systems applications. This demonstration is in the form of examples of data queries that have been carefully selected to be easy to understand yet sufficiently broad in scope to provide convincing demonstrations of the applicability of such dual language approaches to deductive information queries.

Section 2 establishes a simple relational data base that will be used in all the examples to follow. A very brief review of α-exps and the logical calculus used in α-exps is presented as background for the translation of α-expressions shown via examples. The ALPS information processing language is also reviewed to provide the reader with sufficient background to understand the computer processing of the translated query in the examples. Mathematical proofs are beyond the scope of this paper.

2.0   THE EXAMPLE DATA BASE AND QUERY LANGUAGES

2.1   The Example Data Base and its Notation

The suppliers-and-parts data model used in the examples is outlined below, Date [1975].

TABLE I

The Suppliers-and-Parts Data Model

Simple Domains

ID.	Title	Data Type	No.	Example
Sn	SUPPLIER NUMBER	CHARACTER	5	'S1'
Pn	PART NUMBER	CHARACTER	6	'P6'
Q	QUANTITY	NUMERIC	5	4
SN	SUPPLIER NAME	CHARACTER	20	'SMITH'
PN	PART NAME	CHARACTER	20	'BOLT'
L	LOCATION	CHARACTER	15	'LONDON'
St	STATUS	NUMERIC	3	15
Clr	COLOR	CHARACTER	6	'BLUE'
Wt	WEIGHT (lbs)	NUMERIC	4	13

Relations

Name	ID
Suppliers	SR
Parts	PT
Supplies	SP

Example Data Base

Suppliers (SR)
ΔSn ΔSN ΔSt ΔL

S1	SMITH	20	LONDON
S2	JONES	10	PARIS
S3	BLAKE	30	PARIS
S4	CLARK	20	LONDON
S5	ADAMS	30	ATHENS

Parts (PT)
ΔPn ΔPN ΔClr ΔWt

P1	NUT	RED	12
P2	BOLT	GREEN	17
P3	SCREW	BLUE	17
P4	SCREW	RED	14
P5	CAM	BLUE	12
P6	COG	RED	19

Supplies (SP)
ΔSn ΔPn ΔQ

S1	P1	3
S1	P2	2
S1	P3	4
S1	P4	2
S1	P5	1
S1	P6	1
S2	P1	3
S2	P2	4
S3	P3	4
S3	P5	2
S4	P2	2
S4	P4	3
S4	P5	4
S5	P5	5

The following points concerning notation can be seen from the above tables.

Relations are essentially sets of tuple variables whose domains are the cartesian product of the sets of simple component domains. The designation of a relation is the name of the relation followed by the names of the component domains, which are separated from each other by a jot, "∘". This is called "jot" notation. The degree of a relation is the number of the product components. An example is the Supplier relation, SR. The supplier relation has arity 4 and its designation as a relation is SR∘Sn∘SN∘St∘L.

Frequently, domain identifiers, e.g., 'Sn' for supplier number, are used interchangeably with variable identifiers. When variable and domain identifiers are distinguished, variables are prefixed with "Δ" and are separated with the semicolon, ";", e.g., SR∘Sn∘SN∘St∘L(ΔSn;ΔSN;ΔSt;ΔL), where "∘Sn∘SN∘St∘L" are domain identifiers and "ΔSn;ΔSN;ΔSt;ΔL" are the associated variables. The association between domain identifiers is determined by their relative position in the lists, i.e., the first variable is associated with the first domain identifier.

To conform to the typical notation in predicate calculus, the membership predicate of a variable ranging over its domain is written as (<var> ∈ <domain>). This also applies to tuple sets so that a specification of a relation (tuple set) is the membership predicate:

$$(\Delta S; \Delta N; \Delta St; \Delta L \in SR \circ SN \circ SN \circ St \circ L)$$

which is true for every tuple variable in the relation.

2.2 Alpha Expressions

A query syntax based upon Codd's alpha expression (α-exp) has been chosen because it most directly relates to the mathematical definition of the extension of sets and relates to first order predicate theory via the well formed predicate formula, which is the α-exp.

With some simplification, Codd's alpha expression has the syntax:

$$\{(t) (n) : WFF(t)\}.$$

where the braces denote set definition with member tuples, t. A quota, (n), is the number of members of the tuple set to be retrieved. It also is to the left of the colon and may be omitted if all members are desired. The colon denotes "such that", and WFF(t) denotes a well formed formula of the relational calculus. The only free (unquantified) variables, in WFF(t) are the tuple variables, t, representing members of the retrieved tuple set. Membership in the tuple set, i.e., those values of (t) in the data base for which WFF is TRUE. In database applications, of course, these tuple sets represent relations in the database. Therefore, specification for the retrieval of all 4-tuple members of the Supplier relation, SR, in the database is:

$$\{(\Delta Sn;\Delta SN;\Delta St;\Delta L) : (\Delta Sn;\Delta SN;\Delta St;\Delta L \in SR \circ Sn \circ SN \circ St \circ L).\}$$

2.3 ALPS, An APL Logic Programming System

A language for combined deductive data base maintenance, numerical, and logical processing is being explored which retains close kinship with first order mathematical formalisms and accomplishes to a large extent the capabilities listed above for combined applications. This language, ALPS, has its roots in Kowalski [1979].

The implementation is based on APLLOG [JERNIGAN 1984, 1985, 1986] and APLDOT [Kruba 1983].

The reader familiar with PROLOG will find the following points useful in delineating differences between ALPS and PROLOG:

1. The basic clausal form is "A←B", which means that A is true if B is true. "A" is a predicate symbol and is the HEAD of the clause and "B" is the TAIL. The TAIL may contain several predicate symbols separated by logical connectives. Either the HEAD or the TAIL may be empty. If the tail is empty the clause is an assertion of fact and the implication symbol "←" is replaced by a period "."; if the head is empty, the clause is a query and the "←" is replaced by a question mark "?". For example;

"A←B." is a proposition, which may be true
or false;
"A." is an assertion of fact, therefore is
true;
"A?" is a query, which may be true or false.

2. The predicate symbols in the tail clause are
separated by symbols for disjunction "∨" and
conjunction "∧" e.g., "A←B∨C∧D." asserts that A
is true if B is true or if both C and D are
true. Conjunction has precedence over
disjunction.

3. Clausal variables, as in PROLOG, are local to the
clause in which they occur. Variables are
denoted by a leading ,"Δ" in the variable name,
e.g., "ΔA" and "ΔLoc" are variable names. For
example, "A(ΔA;ΔB;ΔLOC;ΔQTY)←B(ΔA;ΔB;ΔLOC;ΔQTY)."
is a proposition with four variables, i.e., arity
4. A query clause that references the clause,
e.g., "A(ΔX;ΔY;ΔZ;Δ1)?", would instantiate the
variables in the query clause to ALL values of
the variables for which the proposition clause
could be determined to be true.

4. A predicate symbol with its associated variables
denote a relation. "A(ΔA;ΔB)" denotes the
relation "A" of the domains denoted by variables
"ΔA" and "ΔB". The domain of "A" is the cross
product of the domains of "ΔA" and "ΔB".

5. In a clause, two predicate symbols connected by
the conjunction symbol, e.g., "B(ΔA;ΔB)∧
C(ΔB;ΔC)", denote the relation that is the
relational JOIN of the two relations denoted by
"B" and "C", i.e., "(ΔA;ΔB;ΔC)".

6. Two predicate symbols connected by the
disjunction symbol, e.g., "B(ΔA;ΔB) ∧ C(ΔB;ΔC)",
denote the relation that is the UNION of the two
relations denoted by "B" and "C", i.e., the
relation if the variables "(ΔA;ΔB;ΔC)".

7. The meaning of a clause is independent of the
order of the conjuncts in the clause, of order of
the conjuncts in the clause, i.e., "A∧B" ≡
"B∧A". However, since conjunction has precedence
over disjunction, "A∧B∨C" ≢ "A∨B∧C", but "A∧B∨C ≡
"C∨B∧A".

8. A predicate in the tail may be negated. For
example, "B(ΔA)∧~C(ΔA)" denotes the set
compliment of C with respect to the set B. In a
proposition, a negated predicate symbol, if used,
must be in the tail, that is, the head cannot be
negated. (This is a temporary restriction that
will be lifted, hopefully, in the future.)

9. A predicate or its associated relation may be modified by functions, which are attached to the predicate by the ",". The functions may be used to effect selections, control projections, or apply user-defined modifications to the relation. Examples of the functions are given in the text of this paper.

10. A query in clausal form can have a head that has no predicate symbol, i.e., HEAD contains only the variable list denoting the relation defined by those variables.

3.0 EXAMPLES

This section presents examples of relational data base queries, their computer translation to a logically related target database language, and their evaluation in the target language processor. Each example contains four parts:

1. brief statement of the database query in natural language,

2. database query as alpha expression,

3. generated ALPS query,

4. tabulated result of the processed database query.

This is the first of two sections. The first presents examples that reduce to a single relational algebra operation, including projection, selection, join, union, intersection, difference and divide. The second section presents examples of typical queries encountered in database usage.

3.1 Projection, Selection, Join

EXAMPLE: 3.1.3. Projection of data set: SR onto L.
"Get locations of the suppliers."

ALPHA EXPRESSION:

$\{(\Delta L) : (\Delta L \in SR \circ L).\}$

ALPS STATEMENT:

$(\Delta L) \leftarrow SR \circ L(\Delta L)?$

QUERY RESULT:

ΔL

LONDON
PARIS
PARIS
LONDON
ATHENS

The projection is defined to delete duplicate tuples from the retrieved list so that, for example, a projection of the Supplies relation, (SP), on two axes, (ΔPn, ΔQ), would eliminate duplicate tuples, e.g., ΔPn;ΔQ=P1,P3. However, the reduction of a domain representing quantity, Q, solely on the basis of eliminating non-duplicates, presents semantic difficulties. Reduction of the Q domain by an operator to compute the TOTAL quantity, would make more sense. ALPS provides the projection function, "p", where, for example, the quantity variable, Q, can be totaled in concert with a projection over Pn.

EXAMPLE: 3.1.4. Projection of a relation of multiple domains
"Find the quantity of each type of part."

ALPHA EXPRESSION:

{(ΔPn;ΔQ):(ΔPn;ΔQ ∈ SP∘Pn∘Q).}

ALPS STATEMENT:

SP∘Pn∘Q(ΔPn;ΔQ), p(ΔPn;tot ΔQ)?

QUERY RESULT:

ΔPn	ΔQ
P1	6
P2	8
P3	8
P4	5
P5	12
P6	1

EXAMPLE: 3.1.5. Selection on part name.
"Select part numbers, colors, and weight of parts named SCREW."

ALPHA EXPRESSION:

{(ΔPn,ΔClr,ΔWt) : ∃ΔPN (ΔPn;ΔPN;ΔClr;ΔWt ∈ PT∘Pn∘PN∘Clr∘Wt)
       ∧ (ΔPN = 'SCREW').}

ALPS STATEMENT:

(ΔPn;ΔClr;ΔWt) ← PT∘Pn∘PN∘Clr∘Wt(ΔPn;ΔPN;ΔClr;ΔWt),
    q(ΔPN eq 'SCREW')?

QUERY RESULT:

ΔPn   ΔClr   ΔWt

P3   BLUE   17
P4   RED   14

EXAMPLE: 3.1.6. Selection with multiple domain specification
"Select part named, SCREW, and weight ≤ 15 pounds."

ALPHA EXPRESSION:

{(ΔPn;ΔClr;ΔWt) : ∃ΔPN (ΔPn;ΔPN;ΔClr;ΔWt ∈ PT∘Pn∘PN∘Clr∘Wt)
        ∧ (ΔPN = 'SCREW') ∧ (ΔWt ≤ 15).}

ALPS STATEMENT:

(ΔPn;ΔClr;ΔWt) ← PT∘Pn∘PN∘Clr∘Wt(ΔPn;ΔPN;ΔClr;ΔWt),
q((ΔPN eq 'SCREW') ∧ ΔWt ≤ 15)?

QUERY RESULT:

ΔPn   ΔClr   ΔWt

P4   RED   14

EXAMPLE: 3.1.7. Retrieve and join two sets
"Retrieve sets SR and SP, join over the common field, Sn."

ALPHA EXPRESSION:

{(ΔSn;ΔSN;ΔSt;ΔL;ΔPn;ΔQ) : (ΔSn;ΔSN;ΔSt;ΔL ∈ SR∘Sn∘SN∘St∘L)
        ∧ (ΔSn;ΔPn;ΔQ ∈ SP∘Sn∘Pn∘Q).}

ALPS STATEMENT:

(ΔSn;ΔSN;ΔSt;ΔL;ΔPn;ΔQ) ← SR∘Sn∘SN∘St∘L(ΔSn;ΔSN;ΔSt;ΔL)
        ∧ SP∘Sn∘Pn∘Q(ΔSn;ΔPn;ΔQ)?

QUERY RESULT:

ΔSn	ΔSN	ΔSt	ΔL	ΔPn	ΔQ
S1	SMITH	20	LONDON	P1	3
S1	SMITH	20	LONDON	P2	2
S1	SMITH	20	LONDON	P3	4
S1	SMITH	20	LONDON	P4	2
S1	SMITH	20	LONDON	P5	1
S1	SMITH	20	LONDON	P6	1
S2	JONES	10	PARIS	P1	3
S2	JONES	10	PARIS	P2	4
S3	BLAKE	30	PARIS	P3	4
S3	BLAKE	30	PARIS	P5	2
S4	CLARK	20	LONDON	P2	2
S4	CLARK	20	LONDON	P4	3
S4	CLARK	20	LONDON	P5	4
S5	ADAMS	30	ATHENS	P5	5

EXAMPLE: 3.1.8. Retrieval of two sets with join and selection
"Retrieve sets SR and SP, select Supplier number=S2."

ALPHA EXPRESSION:

{(ΔSN,ΔSt,ΔL,ΔPn,ΔQ) : ∃ΔSn (ΔSn;ΔSN;ΔSt;ΔL ∈ SR∘Sn∘SN∘St∘L)
            ∧ (ΔSn;ΔPn;ΔQ ∈ SP∘Sn∘Pn∘Q) ∧ (ΔSn = 'S2').}

ALPS STATEMENT:

(ΔSN,ΔSt,ΔL,ΔPn,ΔQ) ← (SR∘Sn∘SN∘St∘L(ΔSn;ΔSN;ΔSt;ΔL)
        ∧ SP∘Sn∘Pn∘Q(ΔSn;ΔPn;ΔQ)),q(,ΔSn eq 'S2').

QUERY RESULT:

ΔSN	ΔSt	ΔL	ΔPn	ΔQ
JONES	10	PARIS	P1	3
JONES	10	PARIS	P2	4

EXAMPLE: 3.1.9. Join of selection, with selection
"Select suppliers and supplies, SR and SP, for those suppliers who supply part P2. "

ALPHA EXPRESSION:

{(ΔSn,ΔSN,ΔL) : (ΔSn;ΔSN;ΔL ∈ SR∘Sn∘SN∘L)
           ∧∃Δv(ΔSn;Δv ∈ SP∘Sn∘Pn) ∧ (Δv='P2').}

ALPS STATEMENT:

(ΔSn;ΔSN;ΔL) ← (SR∘Sn∘SN∘L(ΔSn;ΔSN;ΔL)
        ∧ SP∘Sn∘Pn(ΔSn;Δv)), q(Δv eq 'P2')?

QUERY RESULT:

ΔSn	ΔSN	ΔL
S1	SMITH	LONDON
S2	JONES	PARIS
S4	CLARK	LONDON

EXAMPLE: 3.1.10. Union of two sets, with selection
"Get supplier numbers for those who supply part P1 or P5."

ALPHA EXPRESSION:

{(ΔSn) : ∨/(∃Δv (Δv ∈ {'P1','P5'}) ∧(Δv;ΔSn ∈ SP∘Pn∘Sn)).}

ALPS STATEMENT:

(ΔSn) ← SP∘Pn∘Sn('P1';∘Sn) ∨ SP∘Pn∘Sn('P5';∘Sn)?

QUERY RESULT:

ΔSn

S1
S2
S3
S4
S5

EXAMPLE: 3.1.11. Intersection of two sets
"Get supplier numbers for those who supply both parts, P1 and P5."

ALPHA EXPRESSION:

{(ΔSn) : ∧/(∃ Δv1 (Δv1 ∈ {'P1','P5'}) ∧(Δv1;ΔSn ∈ SP∘Pn∘Sn)).}

ALPS STATEMENT:

(ΔSn) ← SP∘Pn∘Sn('P1';ΔSn) ∧ SP∘Pn∘Sn('P5';ΔSn)?

QUERY RESULT:

ΔSn

S1

EXAMPLE: 3.1.12. Difference
"Get supplier numbers for those who supply part P1 but not P5."

ALPHA EXPRESSION:

{(ΔSn) : ('P1';ΔSn ∈ SP∘Pn∘Sn) ∧ ~('P5';ΔSn ∈ SP∘Pn∘Sn).}

ALPS STATEMENT:

(ΔSn) ← SP∘Pn∘Sn('P1';ΔSn) ∧ ~SP∘Pn∘Sn('P5';ΔSn)?

QUERY RESULT:

ΔSn

S2

3.2 The Relational DIVIDE

EXAMPLE: 3.2.13. Divide of one relation, by a second relation.

"Get supplier numbers of suppliers who supply all parts."

ALPHA EXPRESSION:

{(ΔSn) : ∧/(∃ Δv(Δv ∈ PT∘Pn) ∧ (Δv;ΔSn ∈ SP∘Pn∘Sn)).}

ALPS STATEMENT:

(ΔSn) ← PT∘Pn(ΔPn) ∧ (SP∘Pn∘Sn({ΔPn};ΔSn)).

QUERY RESULT:

ΔSn

S1

EXAMPLE: 3.2.14. Divide with selection
"Get supplier numbers of suppliers who supply parts P1, P4, and P5."

ALPHA EXPRESSION:

{(ΔSn) : ∧/(∃ Δv(Δv ∈ {'P1','P4','P5'})
         ∧ (Δv;ΔSn ∈ SP∘Pn∘Sn)).}

ALPS STATEMENT:

(ΔSn) ← SP∘Pn∘Sn({'P1','P4','P5'};ΔSn).

QUERY RESULT:

ΔSn

S1

EXAMPLE: 3.2.15. Join with divide
"Get supplier names of suppliers who supply all parts."

ALPHA EXPRESSION:

{(ΔSN) : ∃ Δv1 (ΔSN;Δv1 ∈ SR∘SN∘Sn) ∧∧/(∃ Δv2(Δv2 ∈ PT∘Pn)
         ∧ (Δv2;Δv1 ∈ SP∘Pn∘Sn)).}

ALPS STATEMENT:

(ΔSN) ← SR∘SN∘Sn(ΔSN;Δv1) ∧ PT∘Pn(Δv2) ∧ SP∘Pn∘Sn({Δv2};Δv1)?

QUERY RESULT:

ΔSN

SMITH

4.0   TYPICAL DATABASE QUERIES

This section presents a few examples which are routine database queries.

4.1   Queries Without Negation

EXAMPLE: 4.0.16. Retrieval with quota.
"Get the supplier number of any one Paris supplier."

This example uses an user-supplied function, "anyN", to select one tuple.

ALPHA EXPRESSION:

{(ΔS) (1) :(ΔS;'PARIS' ∈ SR∘Sn∘L).}

ALPS STATEMENT:

(ΔS) ← SR∘Sn∘L(ΔS;'PARIS'), q(1 anyN ΔS)?

QUERY RESULT:

ΔS
―――
S3

EXAMPLE: 4.17. Retrieval with Ordering.

"List supplier numbers and status for suppliers in PARIS and in descending order of status."

ALPHA EXPRESSION:

{(ΔSn,ΔSt) : (ΔSn;ΔSt;'PARIS' ∈ SR∘Sn∘St∘L) ∧ (↡ΔSt).}

ALPS STATEMENT:

(ΔSn;ΔSt) ← SR∘Sn∘St∘L(ΔSn;ΔSt;'PARIS'), s(↡ΔSt)?

QUERY RESULT:

ΔSn ΔSt
―――――――
S3   30
S2   10

EXAMPLE: 4.18 Selection by a derived attribute.
"Show supplier with maximum quantity of part P2."

ALPHA EXPRESSION:

{(ΔS) : ∃ Δv (ΔS;'P2';Δv ∈ SP∘Sn∘Pn∘Q) ∧ (max Δv).}

ALPS STATEMENT:

(ΔS) ∈ SP∘Sn∘Pn∘Q(ΔS;'P2';Δv), q(max Δv)?

QUERY RESULT:

ΔS
―――
S2

EXAMPLE: 4.19. Selection across multiple sets.
"Get supplier names for suppliers who supply at least one RED part."

ALPHA EXPRESSION:

{(ΔSN) :∃Δv1(ΔSN;Δv1 ∈ SR∘SN∘Sn∘Q) ∧∃Δv2∃v3(Δv2;Δv3 ∈ SP∘Sn∘Pn)
        ∧∃Δv4∃Δv5(Δv4;Δv5 ∈ PT∘Pn∘Clr)
        ∧ (Δv1=Δv2)∧(Δv3=Δv4)∧(Δv5='RED').}

ALPS STATEMENT:

(ΔSN) ← (SR∘SN∘Sn(ΔSN;Δv2) ∧ SPΔSnΔPn(Δv2;Δv4)
        ∧ PT∘Pn∘Clr(Δv4;Δv5)), q(Δv5 eq 'RED')?

QUERY RESULT:

ΔSN
―――
SMITH
SMITH
SMITH
JONES
CLARK

EXAMPLE: 4.20. Selection using a set against itself
"Get supplier names for suppliers who supply at least one part supplied by supplier S2."

ALPHA EXPRESSION:

{(ΔSN) : ∃ Δv2(ΔSN;Δv2 ∈ SR∘SN∘Sn) ∧ ∃ Δv4(Δv2;Δv4 ∈ SP∘Sn∘Pn)
        ∧∃Δv5(Δv4;Δv5 ∈ SP∘Pn∘Sn) ∧ (Δv5='S2').}

ALPS STATEMENT:

(ΔSN) ← (SR∘SN∘Sn(ΔSN;Δv2) ∧ SP∘Sn∘Pn(Δv2;Δv4)
        ∧ SP∘Pn∘Sn(Δv4;Δv5)), q(Δv5 eq 'S2')?

QUERY RESULT:

ΔSN
―――
SMITH
SMITH
JONES
JONES
CLARK

4.2   Negation

EXAMPLE: 4.3.14. "List supplier numbers for suppliers who do not have bolts."

{(ΔSn) : (ΔSn ∈ SR∘Sn) ∧ ∃ ΔPl (ΔSn;ΔPl ∈ SP∘Sn∘Pn ∧
        ~(ΔPl;'BOLT' ∈ PT∘Pn∘PN)).

(ΔSn) ← SR∘Sn(ΔSn) ∧ (SP∘Sn∘Pn(ΔSn;ΔPl) ∧
        ~PT∘Pn∘PN(ΔPl;'BOLT'))?

ΔSn

S3
S5

EXAMPLE: 4.3.15. "List supplier numbers for suppliers who do not have bolts and screws."

{(ΔPn) : (ΔSn ∈ SR∘Sn) ∧ ~ (∃ ΔP1 (ΔSn;ΔP1 ∈ SP∘Sn∘Pn) ∧
         (ΔP1;'BOLT' ∈ PT∘Pn∘PN) ∧
  ∃ΔP2 (ΔSn;ΔP2 ∈ SP∘Sn∘Pn) ∧ (ΔP2;'SCREW' ∈ PT∘Pn∘PN)).}

(ΔSn) ← SR∘Sn(ΔSn) ∧ ~ ((SP∘Sn∘Pn(ΔSn;ΔP1) ∧ PT∘Pn∘PN(ΔP1;
        'BOLT')) ∧ (SP∘Sn∘Pn(ΔSn;ΔP2) ∧ PT∘Pn∘PN(ΔP2;
        'SCREW')))?

ΔSn

S2
S3
S5

5.0   SUMMARY AND DISCUSSION

5.1   Expressive Directness

Expressive directness is a term used to describe the attributes of a language signifying precision of meaning, succinctness, and scope of allowed discourse. Most people agree that mathematical discourse is expressively direct, and to many investigators, this is a valued attribute of any programming language. It is useful to compare languages for such attributes and this is now briefly considered. The example presented below contains three related query statements.

EXAMPLE: 5.1.21. Comparison of α-expressions, SQL, and ALPS "List part names for all parts obtainable from PARIS."

ALPHA EXPRESSION:

{(ΔPN) : ∃ΔSn∃ΔPn (ΔPN;ΔPn ∈ PT∘PN∘Pn)∧(ΔPn;ΔSn ∈ SP∘Pn∘Sn)
        ∧ (ΔSn;'PARIS' ∈ SR∘Sn∘L).}

ΔPN

NUT
BOLT
SCREW
CAM

SQL EXPRESSION:

```
select   PN
from     PT
where    Pn in
            (select  Pn
             from    SP
             where   Sn in
                        (select  Sn
                         from    SR
                         where   L = 'PARIS')
            )
```

(PN)

NUT
BOLT
SCREW
CAM

ALPS EXPRESSION:

(ΔPN) ← PT∘Pn∘PN(ΔPN;ΔPn) ∧ SP∘Pn∘Sn(ΔPn;Sn) ∧ (SR∘Sn∘L(ΔSn;'PARIS).

ΔPN

NUT
BOLT
SCREW
CAM

The first query listed is an alpha expression. The second query is in the language SQL, which has its roots in the tuple calculus as does alpha expressions [Date 1986]. While the format is different, the semantic structures of the two are strongly related. The third form of the query is in ALPS, which may be considered to either have been written de novo in ALPS or to be the translation of the first form, ie., the α-expression. All three of these queries seem rather efficiently stated, ie., expressively direct, however, the α-expression and ALPS statements are more easily processed by automatic theorem powers.

The major points which these examples are intended to demonstrate are the following.

1. Given an application area for which mathematics is a normal medium of discourse, it is feasible to communicate with computers in this same medium and with only minor changes or additions made to accommodate to the fact that computers are involved in such discourse.

2. Such discourse seems natural to the mathematician; the computer oriented additions to the language are trivial to learn, the typing is not difficult since

the minor inconvenience of using special characters is more than compensated for by the very short text required and, most important, the mathematical investigator is being aided with the drudgery part of his work without the intrusion of unrelated translation activities.

3. By presenting the mathematically oriented investigator with a symbolic translation of his input statements into a more broadly based computer language, ALPS, the investigator at an interactive terminal continually sees at least two ways of specifying his problem (query). This dual mode of specification can provide insight into new ways to more precisely and/or efficiently specify his problem. This seems especially true if one language is primarily a non-procedural one such as the predicate calculus and the other is, for example, based on a strongly procedural algebra. In addition it is very easy for the investigator to intermix discourse in both high level languages if desired.

5.2 CONCLUSIONS

Most fields of mathematics have an accepted syntax (notation) and concomitant semantics that exhibit many of the desirable attributes of a computer language, and

1. the language is widely known to specialists in the applications domain (the mathematical theory), usually including several acceptable alternate notations;

2. it is almost always an efficient and expressively direct language, that being the nature of mathematical discourse;

3. there is usually a strong non-procedural component of the language also because of the nature of mathematical discourse.

Such mathematical applications languages are frequently used successfully for unambiguously defining the semantics of special purpose computer languages. Rarely is mathematical notation used as a computer language per se except, of course, for the universal use of the arithmetic operators in FORTRAN and its successors. The examples of this paper were chosen to demonstrate this capability of mathematical discourse to serve directly as a computer language.

REFERENCES

1. Codd, E. F., A Database Sublanguage Founded in the Relational Calculus, Proc. 1971 ACM SIGFIDET Workshop on Data Description, Access and Control.

2. Codd, E. F., Relational Completeness of Data Base Sublanguages, "Data Base Systems", Courant Computer Science Symposia Series, Vol 6, Prentice Hall, (1972).

3. Codd, E. F., Extending the Relational Database Relational Model to Capture More Meaning, ACM, Vol. 4, No. 4, pp. 397-434 (1979).

4. Date, C. J., "An Introduction to Database Systems", Addison-Wesley, (1975). See especially Ch. 4, Sec. 3.

5. Ullman, J. D. "Principles of Data Base Systems", Computer Science Press, Rockville, Md., (1980).

    a. Data Manipulation Languages for the Relational Model, Ibid, Ch. 4, p. 104 ff.

6. Gallaire, H. J. Minker, J. M. Nicolas, An Overview and Introduction to Logic and Databases, "Logic and Databases", eds. Gallaire and Minker, Plenum Publ. Co., New York, NY, pp. 3-30 (1978).

7. Gallaire, H. J. Minker, J. M. Nicolas, Background for Advances in Data Base Theory, "Advances in Data Base Theory", eds. Gallaire, Minker, and Nicolas, Plenum Publ. Co., New York, NY, pp. 3-21 (1980).

8. Maier, David, "The Theory of Relational Data Bases", Computer Science Press, Rockville, Md. (1983).

9. Reiter, Raymond, Chapter 8: Towards a Logical Reconstruction of Relational Data Base Theory, "On Conceptual Modeling, Perspectives from Artificial Intelligence, Databases, and Programming Languages". Eds. M. L. Brodie, John Mylopoulos, and J. W. Schmidt, Springer-Verlag (1984).

10. Kruba, S. R., "APLDOT - An APL Programmer's Modelling Language", Conf. Proc. APL83, ACM, New York, NY (1983).

11. Jernigan, R., "Logic Programming in APL", Conf. Proc. APL84, ACM, New York, NY (1984).

12. Jernigan, R. and Desai, A., "XIMM - An Expert System for Idle Materials Management: Logic Programming for Corporate Strategies; The Role of Language in Problem Solving - I, eds. Jernigan, Hamill, and Weintraub, Elsevier Science Publishers B. V. (North-Holland) (1985).

13. Jernigan, R. and Eisner, E., "A Generalized Data Base Interface for APL", to be Published in Conference Proceedings, APL86, ACM, New York, NY, 1986.

PROGRAMMING THE PARALLEL PROCESSOR

Gordon Lyon

Center for Computer Systems Engineering
Institute for Computer Sciences and Technology
National Bureau of Standards
Gaithersburg, Maryland 20899

Language pragmatics for efficient parallel programming encompass many things, of which some are familiar from serial machines and others are not. Proceeding discursively, numerous examples illustrate language-level facets selected from parallel performance areas of load balance, granularity, and memory domains. A concluding sketch of a construct for "self-service" shows how an understanding of execution implications might eventually yield a portable language construct.

1.0   PRAGMATICS AND PROGRAMMING LANGUAGES

A programming language has syntax, semantics, and pragmatics:

> The *meaning* associated with syntactically correct instances of language can be viewed from two points of view, the meaning intended by the originator of the sentence, and the meaning retrieved by a receiver. It is not always the case that these two meanings are identical.[LEE83]

The originator's meaning is semantics and its effective meaning through the receiver, *pragmatics*. Pragmatics is what language causes a system to do; the numbers, the time, the resources demanded. To pragmatics falls the burden of accounting for those real-world constraints and economics that render a programming language viable or unacceptable. For example, it is fair to say that the original FORTRAN had excellent pragmatics; essentially its design role was to supplant assembly code, and this it did quite successfully while dramatically simplifying program coding. While emphasis in computational costs has shifted over the decades, the issues of overall outlay and efficiency must always be addressed in one form or another.

1.1   Parallel Computers, Parallel Programming

As computers have pressed the physical limits of component speeds, computational topology has assumed an increasingly important role in machine design. Parallel processing is one manifestation of this. Parallel programming, where in more

than one processor will be available to a single program, is
far less familiar than serial (monoprocessor) computation, and
it can be considerably more constraining. To see this,
consider the paradigm *algorithm::language::machine* which can be
viewed as an expression of instructing a machine via a programming language to perform some task. Most contemporary machines
are serial with one program counter, so that the final target
(with variations) is familiar. Parallel architectures change
this drastically, and in ways not fully understood. Each
parallel architecture has its important special features and
capabilities to be explored. The mapping from language to
topologies is considerably more varied and is often intrusive
throughout the whole development process. As aptly remarked,
"You do not bring [arbitrary] algorithms to these machines."
[MOL86].

The profusion of various parallel architectures (vector, MIMD,
dataflow) presents a challenge to the entire field of computing. Certainly current difficulties hint that no *one* of the
new forms is cheapest, fastest, or most easily programmed, at
least not within a broad a frame of reference.

An ideal programming language would deliver full powers of
hardware parallelism while maintaining expressive capabilities
appropriate to the problem being solved, independent of system
and hardware. This is not generally realizable today. Three
concerns from machine design--balance, domain, and granularity-
-illustrate some current language problems and their programming implications. Load balancing attempts to occupy all
processors of a machine in useful work. Clearly, this is
important whenever an attempt is being made to accelerate an
algorithm that is slow. Secondly, parallel computation accent-
uates architecture topology and the domains it implies. Many
problems in converting old serial programs to parallel versions
lie in memory domains. And third, granularity expresses a
measure of aggregated computation; correctly chosen, it ensures
that system overheads, especially those of synchronization and
communication, do not dominate computations.

2.0   LOAD BALANCE--KEEPING BUSY

Load balancing attempts to keep all processors busy on a
problem. If this is not possible, processors will be starved
in varying degrees for computational work. An assumption in
load balancing is that processors are too expensive to sit
idle. In time this notion will change, much as it has for main
memory.

Two architectures serve as examples for the following discussion of load balancing. Diagrams depicting these are Figures 1-
a and 1-b. The first is a fairly common parallel processing
arrangement, with several processors using a connection network
to reach shared memory. It is often referred to as MIMD for
multiple-instruction, multiple-data; commercial variants are
available. The second, a more radical general purpose dataflow
architecture, has only a few experimental machines working,

mostly within universities [GUR85]. In dataflow, each operation can be considered as an independently schedulable computation that first awaits availability of all of its arguments.

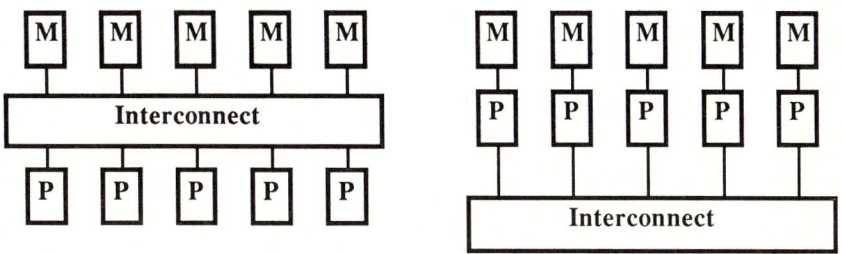

Figure 1-a. Shared-Memory   Figure 1-b. Message-passing

2.1   Static and Dynamic MIMD Balance

Load balancing may be attempted prior to the program's running (static), or on-the-fly (dynamic). Consider first a static allocation problem of pre-scheduling work over n processors. Schwartz [SCH80] observes that to add a list of m numbers requires O(log m) time steps for a grand parallel sum, so that the best way to apportion numbers to be summed on n processors is m = O(n log n), i.e. give each processor O(log n) numbers. In this fashion each of n processors does O(log n) *serial* adds prior to contributing to an overall O(log n) *parallel* summation. The arrangement is reasonably balanced, but the programmer must correctly divide the work for the parallel machine.

In the second, dynamic case, assume that each datum may demand varying degrees of processing time, and that these times are unknown. One highly successful approach uses processes that compute, roughly one to a processor, and a cafeteria-like serving up of data. That is, each process takes a datum, reduces it as needed, and returns to fetch another from the data queue. It should be noted that this self-scheduling can be used as a software implementation of dataflow. (A later section explores the approach as a language construct.) No processor is generally idle until the very end of the data stream. However, as has been pointed out [GOT84, JOR85], if the last datum's need is huge relative to those reduced earlier, the approach may fail to achieve a good average processor balance. Since only one processor can work on the last result, the others simply wait.

2.2   Dataflow: Surfeit and Starvation

The very model of dataflow can lead to a natural load balancing of processing capabilities, but not without an effort outside of that provided by the basic hardware. However, before discussing problems of balance, consider a short explanation of the classical dataflow model (Figure 1-c depicts a typical machine). If the computation A = B + C*E is viewed as a rule of how *values*, and especially tokens representing values, flow, then the following is true. Node "*" is waiting for tokens for C's and E's values. When node "*" has both of these, it can schedule its (short) computation, the result of which is sent to node "+". Node "+" awaits two tokens, one from the multiply, and another for B. It schedules the final computation in the expression. Dependencies during computation are determined by the control graph, a parse of A = B + C*E that is stored in memory M. Values are stored and matched in the token store segment of memory.

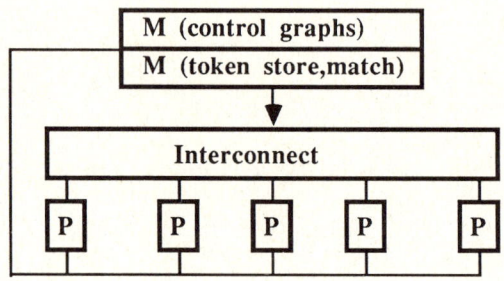

Figure 1-c

Dataflow

The model is not classical serial, for there is no program counter (or even several of them as in MIMD). Execution is conceptually possible whenever all tokens have arrived for a computation node, which means that a large, suitable program could have much work to occupy a machine's computing units. Such a program would have a "bushy" parse tree. The actual computational units are hidden from the programmer, and can be varied in number. Unfortunately, there also arises a dual to the serial bottleneck of having to move all computation through a single processor. In the potentially vast propagation of tokens, some nodes will have prolonged waiting for their full complement of tokens. However, tokens already received must be stored prior to their use in a computation. The danger is deadlock by memory exhaustion; i.e. if incomplete nodes use up all the token storage, then none of them is ever scheduled because this would require even more tokens. The potential for rampant and uncontrolled parallel scheduling reflected in token backup is a serious design consideration for dataflow architectures. Thus, while the serial machine is throttled by its single processor bottleneck, pure dataflow can be choked by too large a bite, a profusion of pending transactions (see [VEG85]).

Despite the foregoing, dataflow can starve as well. Avoiding this embarrassment places demands upon programming system and programmer which equal those of more conventional MIMD

machines. Simply put, a dataflow machine *per se* does not know
how to decompose a problem for good parallel computation. A
programmer or a very smart compiler has to structure the
control graph to get suitable parallelism. Consider the linear
recurrence sum $S(i+1) = a(i)*S(i) + b(i)$. Clever combinings of
terms can accomplish all $S(1)...S(n)$ sums in $2 \log n$ [LAK85].
Nonetheless, any solution, for dataflow or MIMD, must tell what
the orders of the partial summings are. Otherwise, the most
likely code (control graph) is perfectly serial, and takes $O(n)$
time. The programmer's techniques count heavily to accelerate
execution.

3.0   MEMORY DOMAINS--THE INFLUENCE OF TOPOLOGY

Domain signifies classes or partitions that exist among
elements of a computer system. The organization of memory is
an important domain in parallel programming; it is shared by
processors through some common access network, or each
processor is given its own memory, with the network passing
messages from processor to processor. The former case functions similarly to committee members sitting around a working
table as they write draft pages for a joint report; piles of
notes in the center of the table can be read collectively by
members, or sections can be taken by individuals to be
rewritten *in situ*. Message passing is more like a meeting
conducted via telephone or televideo link. Here a natural
structure is imposed by the links themselves (for example,
transmitting large documents may be a nuisance). Both forms
need an adequate rate of information transfer. Their problems
may differ, however. Shared information often suffers from
contention. Message passing may incur routing and transmission
latencies that slow computation.

Because languages reflect underlying realities, it is not
surprising that two very common views of language are strongly
coupled procedures (FORTRAN-like), which share memory, and
weakly coupled objects (as in Smalltalk-80), which send
messages to each other. While claims have been made for a
duality between the two models [LAU78], examination (e.g.,
[HIK85]) suggests that message-passing is the more orderly and
structured of the two. Shared memory has been popular because
it is computationally fast and flexible.

3.1   Implicit and Explicit Shared Memory

Many of the problems in converting older FORTRAN decks to
parallel machines lie not in what the code says but in what it
does not preclude. The unconstrained scope of older FORTRAN
coding styles impedes a parallel decomposition of programs.
Explicit constructs aside (EQUIVALENCE is covered next), the
simple call-by-reference for larger objects (arrays) promotes
memory sharing and therefore, possible contention which must be
accounted for. In the monoprocessing environment, by-reference
parameters save excessive copying. With parallel processing,
such copying may actually be attractive, especially in efficient message-passing domains (next section) where it avoids

contention and side effects. To promote easier automatic translation to parallel code, it has been suggested in the scientific community that a language such as FORTRAN could be extended slightly to express disparate memory domains.

A central problem with shared memory is that certain variables, especially those for synchronization, may generate very heavy traffic. Since only one request to a memory module can be serviced at a time, contention can degrade the whole performance of a system. Notice, however, that the contention is not limited to requests for a single variable. The same problem arises when elements of an array lie in the same memory module; the contention problem is shared among all variables in the module. An attempt to avoid memory bank contention uses random mapping from virtual to real addresses, thereby scattering structure elements among memory modules. In this way, heavy use of a shared structure is dispersed [GOT83]. However, certain language constructs, principally overlays such as EQUIVALENCE in FORTRAN, can cause this scheme some problems. The reason is quite clear. No longer are elements of an array entirely free to be placed anywhere in real memory, since they define locations that obey other constraints. If EQUIVALENCE entities straddle each other as bricks in a wall, any scattering (in real memory) entails double fetching for the split entities. (See Figure 2.) This then burdens the communication network between processors and memory, already an expensive component. Explicit memory overlays are definitely a problem, and should be avoided.

3.2   Weakly-Coupled Domains

A message passing, parallel system can be relatively inexpensive if its communications network is kept simple. This is a central attraction. However, the architecture is then best suited for statically defined objects which communicate among each other occasionally. Clearly, not all problems have independent subcomputations that decompose in such a fashion, nor do all problems hold their topology throughout [KAL85]. Moving large amounts of data or shifting processes to and from private processor memories can be cumbersome and slow. Heavy random global references will also clog the communications network.

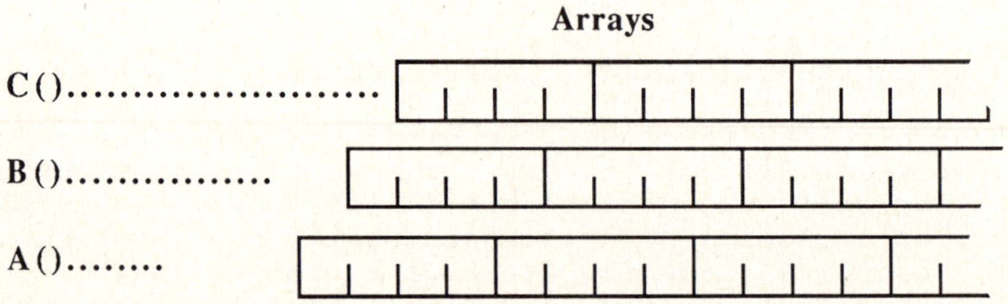

Figure 2

Overlays and Boundaries

Programming for machines with strongly visible topologies will in itself be more special purpose, and by implication, less portable. This is especially true when latencies and transmission rates along channels force one to cater carefully to them in writing programs. However, when message sending is as fast as procedure invocation, local "call-dependencies" can be used to lay out a program loading onto the node space. In this manner a parallel machine that lacks fast (external) i/o can still be very vital to modeling and simulation applications; quick internal "move around" supports necessary communications and external requests are few.

It is quite another circumstance if each process must adroitly avoid interprocessor communication because of excessive overhead. Two tradeoffs appear almost immediately in terms of programming and "move around". General message passing between any pair of nodes involves both routing and forwarding. The inability to connect one node to another directly incurs a need for forwarding, which in turn implies system routing overheads. These may be costly. On the other hand a system whose nodes allow only nearest-neighbor (e.g. N,S,W,E) communication may have very fast local connections, but more distant destinations become a programming responsibility and burden. Some machines, e.g. The Connection Machine(tm), incorporate *both* mechanisms [CON85], letting compilers for higher level languages automatically select which communication avenue is best. Definitely convenient and effective, the approach obviously entails greater original cost.

4.0 GRANULARITY--CONTAINING OVERHEAD

The overheads of a system will dictate that certain operations, e.g. procedure calls, process creations, and synchronizations, not occur at frequencies that let their costs dominate all others. To assure this, chunks of "working code" between the distinguished operations should be large enough to overshadow any overhead burden. Minimal limits on the "chunks" establish a granularity for the system.

"Granularity" connotes several germane elements, the first being a frame-of-reference. When speaking of the "grain" of a system, some aspect of its performance is often implicitly assumed to be the focal point. In software engineering with FORTRAN, one of the most vital FORTRAN mechanisms is the use of procedures and functions to build program modules. For this setting it makes sense to talk of the granularity of procedures and functions since inefficient invocations can not be tolerated and grain is controllable by programming style.

Second is granularity itself. It is defined here in terms of machine major cycles or software level constructs that correlate directly to major cycles. Grain size is the *minimum* amount of computation in the frame of reference that is still considered effective or efficient (a third point, which

follows, refines this). Grain size is not precisely
characterized, but rather is often placed in one of three
categories:

* Fine: Roughly one to seven instructions, e.g.
  {a = a +1; b = c - d / e;}

* Medium: a procedure or function whose code is a
  page or so.

* Coarse: a very large procedure or a whole
  program--several hundred lines of code, with
  calls to other procedures or functions.

Third, granularity implies some limit of acceptance along with
a confidence level for this acceptance. Let t(o) signify in
some appropriate measure the execution overhead of the mechanism highlighted by the frame of reference. Similarly, let t(g)
denote a measure of the time for granules of the system. At 5%
acceptance it is required that "t(o)/t(g)" < 0.05. (The
expression is in quotes, since not much has been explained yet
on the measure.) Then if the granularity, *g*, happens to be
small, one can write *g* = *small* (.05). Furthermore, if all uses
of the mechanism of interest, in each individual use, satisfy
the inequality, one can also attach a 100% confidence to the
criterion *for any run of the program*. Expressed in shorthand,
g = *small* (.05 @ 100%). Both the acceptance limit and level of
confidence are implicit in discussions of granularity. They
are hardly ever mentioned explicitly, although it might be a
good idea if they were, much as one speaks in statistics of
intervals and confidence levels. Acceptance can be defined in
terms of an average of all individual t(o)/t(g), a worst case,
or other measures to suit. Compliance is determined by what is
appropriate given circumstances. Real-time systems clearly
need worst-case with 100% confidence, whereas in other
applications an execution-weighted average that complies at 80%
confidence may suffice.

General purpose hardware is more commonly coarse grain than
fine because this is cheaper. The cost of programming coarse
grain is often more, however, because the granularity forces
program rearrangements [REI85]. As an example of a fine
grained hardware feature, consider context switching on the
HEP-100. It can reschedule a ready process in t(o) = 100
nanoseconds (say the divide functional unit is busy). Since
this rescheduling operation is essentially a context switch
that occurs in 1/8 of the HEP's 800 nanosecond instruction
cycle, it is fair to say that context switching on the machine
is very fine indeed [JOR85]. For comparison, the context switch
of a conventional minicomputer may occupy tens of microseconds,
two orders of magnitude slower.

4.1 MIMD Granules

Because MIMD processes run in parallel, the overhead of
synchronizations and communication is important. On a system
that has procedure calls incurring 6-12 microsecond costs and

task initiations 20-30 microseconds, synchronization overhead can usually be tolerated within a range reaching 75 microseconds. At the range high end, parallel processes should have sizes comparable to those of larger procedures. However, there are contemporary language implementations in which synchronization is over 100 times slower than the range just given. For these implementations, the synchronization mechanism is useful only for communication between machine-sized jobs; the granularity of synchronized modules must be exceedingly coarse, otherwise overhead would swamp the system. Consequently, a language gains little in having a well-structured synchronization construct that is far too slow. It will not be employed in the bulk of the critical code where it is needed. Instead, loops with polling are used, a style of programming that goes back thirty years.

4.2 Abstraction as Controlled Granularity

Many modern languages provide an abstraction mechanism that helps organize the coding effort and enforce consistency. FORTRAN procedures represent the primitive origins of this productive direction. One can view abstractions as each being a specification of some grain size; the granularity can be shrunk to that of an instruction, and some languages encourage this. Unfortunately, the necessary hardware to support a fine-grained programming view is often missing [DAV85]. This is especially pertinent with message passing, which is harder than procedure calling to optimize because it is more dynamic. Such systems thereby acquire reputations of being very slow. In the granularity range of allowed abstract definitions, the smallest sizes must not be matched inappropriately to their underlying machine architecture.

5.0 EVOLUTIONARY STEPS FOR HIGHER LEVEL LANGUAGE

Having presented a number of cases in which parallel processing intrudes rudely into the programmer's world, it is natural to explore accommodations that language might provide. The examples argue that a sound understanding of major execution problems is essential, that a truly practical language design should not arise independent of likely support architecture. An advantage to this conservative approach is that a compiler responsible for a coherent and effective mapping onto machine instructions can actually be written, and a true degree of portability may be possible. This encompasses more than special purpose extensions of a language for one machine, or a language that expresses well a theoretical domain, but it also evolves somewhat slower.

Among topics mentioned, "self-service" has proven workable on both shared memory and message based systems. The paradigm, a software version of dataflow scheduling, seems well suited for general load balancing. For example, see [OLE85] for an evaluation of the dataflow perspective for matrix computations. It is instructive to sketch a language construct for the paradigm, and to examine briefly what responsibilities might

thereby devolve from programmer to compiler. One immediate
point the reader will see is that "self-serve", systematically
generalized, begins to look very similar to a *parallel-FOR*
(e.g., [MIK 84]). Although the two should be combined in a
real language design, this avenue is not pursued.

5.1   Expressing Medium-Grain Dataflow

Operations on tokens in hardware dataflow become ***processes that
consume structures*** for the software construct modeled here.
Granularity is medium. The programmer defines an explicit
structure template and instances of these self-service items
are somehow "served up" to consumer processes. Details of the
serving are hidden. As in a parallel-FOR statement, the served
items can be in a range, a set or generated by a function.
However, the example explores yet another mode, one in which
servicing processes can add to the set of offered data via a
SERVEUP() instruction. There is no explicit "serve me"
request, since this will be handled by formal parameters that
are matched with each automatic serving. The paradigm is:

```
DO (<structure template>)<proc body template>
FOR <structure initialization>.
```

An anonymous procedure body defined after the DO keyword
provides the active mechanism. The system will create as many
processes from this text as makes sense. As each copy
proceeds, it may generate new structures to be consumed. These
it posts through a SERVEUP(<structure>). When an anonymous
procedure (process) is done, it automatically sleeps until
there is something for it to consume. Whenever a process
concludes that all work is complete, it issues an EXIT. This
immediately clears the serving line and renders all further
SERVEUPs as null operations. Eventually all processes fall
asleep. The DO-FOR then terminates.

For slightly more detail of use:

```
DO ({cur:^bucket,par:^bucket})
  { IF cur^.status = full THEN
         ....issue SERVEUPs for further buckets...
    ELSE
         ....suitable wrapup, EXIT issued ...
  }
FOR {root,NIL};
```

starts a bucket search in which a full bucket generates
pointers to several other buckets, one of which may have some
room. The process that finds a bucket with room will stop the
search via an EXIT. The initial {root,NIL} points to the first
bucket and indicates that it has no parent. Each searched
bucket will generate new service entries (if that is appropriate) via SERVEUP. Available unprocessed structures are
automatically served to procedure incarnations. Unnamed, the
structures are available in no other way, and once served
through formal parameters, they disappear. Consequently, only
the abstract properties of the construct will concern the pro-

grammer although he can use the values thus received to build other program structures. For the case in point, a chain from the open bucket to the root could be available after the EXIT.

Given the foregoing, a compiler should understand enough to handle:

1. How many processors are available? Usually a shared memory machine has a system call that returns a count of active processors. Message based systems have similar services, e.g. messages that tell which neighbors are operating on dimensions of the space. Then on shared memory systems with fine grained context switching, a few extra processes will help ensure a good load balance. With more conventional architectures, there should be no more processes than processors. This diminishes context switching losses due to processor contention.

2. How many new processes are really needed? Are there others left over that were not killed off? Some systems have such excessive overhead for process creation that one really does not want to create and kill processes for each minor parallel statement. For this reason, it may help if the processes in the DO statement are in actuality generic, although this would be hidden from the programmer.

3. Does the procedure body ever SERVEUP anything? If not, a warning message is appropriate, although strictly speaking there is no danger. It is just a rather expensive one-shot procedure invocation.

4. What are run time error conditions? The system and the compiled code should catch these errors and report them in terms of the program text where the DO statement lies. The reporting should be uniform whether one or twenty processors are actively working for the program.

While considerable work would have to be invested to smoothly incorporate the DO-FOR, parallel-FOR, and related features into a language, there are obviously many tedious process and processor details in self-service that a compiler could profitably assume, details that are not the same from one machine to another. Programmers might appreciate the help.

6.0 SUMMARY

Although many extravagant claims have been made for contemporary parallel architectures, the examples demonstrate that programmers must remain cognizant of what is being programmed and why. Eventually experiences in catering to parallel machines will yield general insights and paradigms. Care should be exercised to ensure that these paradigms are effectively merged with related programming concepts.

Acknowledgment. R. Carpenter, J. Draper, K. Dymond, and C. Lyon suggested numerous places for improvement in earlier versions.

7.0 REFERENCES

CON85   The Connection Machine(tm). *A More Detailed Look*. Thinking Machines Corporation, Cambridge, Mass., 1985.

DAV85   Davis, A. L. Class lecture remark, Santa Clara College, July, 1985.

GOT83   Gottlieb, A., Grishman, R., Kruskal, C. P., McAuliffe, K. P., Rudolph, L., and Snir, M. "The NYU Ultracomputer--Designing an MIMD shared memory parallel computer." *IEEE Trans. on Computers* C-32, 2 (February, 1983), 175-189.

GOT84   Gottlieb, A. "Avoiding serial bottlenecks in ultraparallel MIMD computers." *Proc., COMPCON '84*, 28th IEEE Computer Society Int. Conf., Feb.27-Mar.1, 1984, 354-359.

GUR85   Gurd, J. R., Kirkham, C. C., and Watson, I. "The Manchester prototype dataflow computer." *Comm. ACM 28*, 1(January, 1985), 34-52.

HIK85   Hikita, T., and Ishihata, K. "A method of program transformation between variable sharing and message passing." *SOFTWARE: Practice and Experience 15*, 7(July, 1985), 677-692.

JOR85   Jordan, H. F. "HEP architecture, programming and performance." Chapter 1.1 in *Parallel MIMD Computation: HEP Supercomputer and Its Applications*. J. S. Kowalik (ed.), The MIT Press, Cambridge, Mass., 1985.

KAL85   Kalos, M. Remarks to the author, February, 1985.

LAK85   Lakshmivarahan, S. and Dhall, S. K. "New parallel algorithms for solving first-order and certain classes of second-order linear recurrences." Report OU-PPI-TR-85-01, School of E.E. and C.S., Univ. of Ok., Norman, Ok., (January, 1985), 29 pp.

LAM85   Lamport, L. "Solved problems, unsolved problems, and non-problems in concurrency." Reprinted in ACM Operating Systems Review 19, (October, 1985), 34-44, from *Third Princ. of Dist. Computing Conf.*

Proceedings, ACM, 1984. {NOTE: The reader must reconcile typographic inconsistencies in and between figures 5 and 6.}

LAU78   Lauer, H. C., and Needham, R. M. "On the duality of operating system structures." *Proc., 2nd Int. Symp. on Op. Sys.*, IRIA (October, 1978).

LEE83   Lee, J. A. N. "Syntax, semantics and pragmatics." in *Encyclopedia of Computer Science and Engineering, 2nd Edition*, (Ralston, A. and Reilly, E. D. Jr., eds.), Van Nostrand Reinhold Co., N.Y., N.Y. 1983, 1473-1474.

MIK84   Miklosko, J., and Kotov, V. E. (eds.). *Algorithms, Software and Hardware of Parallel Computers*, Springer-Verlag, N.Y., N.Y., 1984, p. 80.

MOL86   Moler, C. Discussion comment at NBS on general state of parallel programming, February, 1986.

OLE85   O'Leary, D. P., and Stewart, G. W. "Data-flow algorithms for parallel matrix computations." *Comm. ACM 28*, 8(August, 1985), 840-853.

REI85   Reinhardt, S. "A data-flow approach to multitasking on CRAY X-MP computers." *Proc., 10th ACM Symp. on Op. Sys. Principles*, 1-4 Dec. 1985, in ACM Operating Systems Review 19, (Special issue), 107-114.

SCH80   Schwartz, J. T. "Ultracomputers." *ACM Trans. Prog. Lang. 6*, 4(October, 1980), 484-521.

VEG85   Vegdahl, S. R. "A survey of proposed architectures for the execution of functional languages." *IEEE Trans. on Computers C-33*, 12(December, 1984), 1050-1071.

PANEL:
APPLICATIONS, LANGUAGE, AND ARCHITECTURE:
DIMENSIONS IN PROBLEM SOLVING

PANEL SESSION: APPLICATIONS, LANGUAGE, AND ARCHITECTURE:
DIMENSIONS IN PROBLEM SOLVING

    Panel Chairman: G. Lyon
    Panel Members: J. W. Carr, III
                           R. Jernigan
                           B. Kowalchack
                           A. Lazanoff

LYON

This is an open session where we encourage discussion. I'll start, setting the stage with my own ideas which you are perfectly free to disagree with. So I'll simply continue where I left off, and try to amplify. [Shows title frame which says, "Programming the Parallel Processor - Part II: The Curse of Time" (some laughter)] This is another thread in my paper. It basically has to do with benchmarking and performance analysis work that we're doing at the Bureau of Standards, where we're building special interface cards that monitor certain hardware without in any way perturbing a program when checking its performance; there are no writes-to-memories or anything. So what do I mean by this Grade B thriller title? If we look at architectures, we have a couple of them that are pretty well known. I've alluded to them earlier. There's a shared-memory model that's very common. Increasingly, we're seeing message passing systems, but they've been not quite so popular. In a shared-memory system, what you often have is a bunch of processes on a bus as a typical arrangement. Any processor can get to any of the memory modules. You call things, as you're used to doing; say you call the routine SNARK(). In this case, I've indicated that SNARK() is a parameterless procedure. I've done that deliberately, and I'll get to the point in a minute.

Now, in message passing, you might imagine that your processors are all interconnected but the memory is more private, that is, any given processor has its memory which it's tightly coupled to, but it can't get to the rest of the memory quite so easily. You send messages. Instead of a routine name you have a process name which may in fact designate the processor where it sits. [Send (, A)] Depending on which mappings you choose, there are arguments like those of Lauer and Needham that there is a duality that exists between these two. You can map back and forth from one [procedure calls] to the another [messages], but one is no better or no worse than the other. You may quarrel slightly about the mappings, but what you cannot quarrel about is the "Curse of Time". [Frame shows times for procedure call or message sending, the latter being much slower.] Suppose you can move with impunity from one to the other. The catch is that when you're doing a procedure call with no arguments on most respectable machines, it takes you from 5 to 15 microseconds. With more a loosely coupled message sending scheme, you can see what your frame of reference is for the pragmatics, that is, how much time does it take? How many worlds of computation could go by in the meantime? It's slower by about two decimal orders of magnitude, at <u>least</u>. So, what does that mean in terms of the original applications, language, or hardware...what does the "Curse of Time" mean?

It will back up in certain different ways. In the best of cases, where you have shared memory or messages, all things being equal, it would just be a matter of calling in the other term. You'd change all the "calls" to "sends" or all the "sends" to "calls". It would impact you in terms of language, but not significantly. Editing is not a terribly interesting question for a programmer. On the other hand, if Procurement ordered the wrong kind of machine and you got a message-passing machine with the much slower times I've shown you, then you're going to have to back up considerably, right through the language layer, because algorithms are going to perform terribly. You've been counting on shared-memory performance. You're going to find that the overheads are so terrible, you're going to have to rewrite your algorithms.

That's an example of how I think that you can get by with some variation, say, in the architectural area; or you may not (which is the unfortunate second case). From my own experience, I have in fact been forced to move along this red line. [Line leads back to "algorithm design"] I had an algorithm that was developed on a serial machine; conversion involved doing a parallel hash. Basically the problem was that the hashing algorithm was exceedingly efficient, so that when you went to look up something, the total lookup may have taken only five or six instructions before you actually got it. When you tried to switch to the message passing format, the minimum message passing time was 5 milliseconds - which meant that a whole world could go by before you got your answer back. You may as well not even ask one of the other processors to do it, but rather do it locally. No matter what happened it couldn't have been any worse. The architecture had nothing to do with it, but rather it was the realization.

MCMULLEN

Watching this last set of slides, I had a flashback to early 1960's computing when we were writing big papers on wonderful sorting and hashing and searching and all sorts of algorithms. There was this real feeling of excitement that if we have this better sort or this better search we would get great performance out of our computers. We've shoved all that underneath the table now. If people want to sort they call a sort package and they sort. It's really not interesting anymore. Now you're fumbling with this. How do you handle sorts on a machine with real parallelism or hashing or something like that. With the parallel paradigm you're going to do the same kind of investigations that were happening 20 years ago. How can I get any performance out of this machine that I paid millions of dollars for and make it useful? Do you have a projection that 20 years from now we're going to look back on the parallelism that we are starting to investigate and feel the same way that we feel now about looking at the investigation of sorting and searching that we did 20 years ago?

LYON

I can make it quite specific. What I would like to see is an analogy and a refinement in message passing hardware that represents the great amount of work that's been sunk into the shared memory architecture. My view is that there are a lot of good ideas in message passing, but that it isn't mature right now. People don't know how to do it.

MCMULLEN

My experience with parallelism is that you can certainly crank up things that munch arrays really well. I'm trying to figure out how people are going to deal with all this wonderful parallelism to crank up their compilations. I can't see how to apply running my compiler on your massively parallel computer that has 64,000 separate processors unless each processor is going to compile a separate character out of my program. I don't see how to apply that in any sense, and I'm looking for a projection that we're going to solve that kind of problem or not.

LYON

I can't either. Quite frankly, one of the things that we have programmed in our laboratory is, in fact, a parallel parser. It's performance is just dreadful. The reason is that as you near the top of the parse tree (you can do all the bottom pieces in parallel), there's less and less parallelism but still a lot of things that have to be put together. So the parsing suffers from what is classic: It's the old "architecture is architecture," again. Upward flows in trees choke at the roots. Now it seems that things propagating the other way, that start at the root and go out, are very amenable. For instance, a parallel "make," where if I change this, what depends on this and what depends on that, it keeps branching out and each has to be recompiled. It goes the other direction, away from the root. Pieces basically don't have to be synchronized tightly with each other. A parallel "make" gets practically a linear speed-up. So maybe the problem I said about parsing is bad because, in fact, hardware architectures that use tree communications have this problem and so will any software. It's a graph problem. In which direction you drive the tree means a lot.

It may turn out that what we are going to see, and this is something that we at NBS have been advocating, is that computing is maturing. No longer will you have the universal one-man-band machine. The omnibus, the "I do everything," the "von Neumann savior of the world." In other engineering crafts, for example, in automotive engineering, if someone gives you the specification for a sports car, and then gives you numbers for a dump truck, no one is embarrassed if one can do something the other one can't. You are not worried about the acceleration of the dump truck and the sports car advocate doesn't really care how many cubic meters it can carry. Yet we do in computing.

What we will see is a separation of worlds. For instance, I
could see something like the hypercube architecture with
message passing being very viable if they could get the nearest
neighbor thing efficient -- for certain types of simulation it
doesn't matter. You generate the data at each node. But then
again this is an architectural cluster. It doesn't address all
the problems. One shouldn't be embarrassed by that.

KOWALCHACK

I have an application that we wrote in a language built on one
architecture and then transported to another. I'm going to
tell you our experience of transporting from a VAX 11/780
running Berkeley Unix to an IBM PC running DOS.

Very early in the project we decided that we wanted SUPPORT to
be able to run on a cheap machine. At that point it was a
research tool. It started out as a syntax-directed editor; at
this point there were lots of syntax-directed editors, and we
wanted ours to be able to do something different. We wanted it
to be an effective tool to develop programs, but we wanted it
to operate on inexpensive hardware. Of course, we wanted it to
be easy to use. I shouldn't use the word easy, but we know it
is. We also wanted it to provide rapid response to the user.

We found that transporting it to the IBM PC really wasn't that
bad. We wrote it in Berkeley Pascal. We have something like
22 Pascal modules, and we were very cautious about writing in
standard Pascal, not using any extensions that Berkeley might
have enhanced Pascal with. The original transport took about a
week. We did have three problems. I'll talk about one hard
problem.

When we were running on Berkeley Unix we had to have two C
modules to interact with the file system and check legality of
file names that we added into SUPPORT; that is, save programs
that we had saved as files and wanted to add back into
SUPPORT. Also, keyboard interrupts had to be handled through a
C routine. When we transported onto the PC, Microsoft handled
those things for us, so we really didn't have to worry about
it.

The way we built SUPPORT, we made it very much language-
independent. In order to do that, we modularized the
program. The Pascal interpreter is separate from the program-
building routines which build the program tree. It is totally
separate from our window system, which traipses through the
tree and builds a linked list of what should be on the screen
at that time and actually saves a view of the screen. On the
VAX this is a perfectly acceptable way of doing it. It seems a
little inefficient that every time we change the cursor, we are
traipsing back through the tree and rebuilding this display
list. Actually when we go to write it out we only write out
what we need to write. When we transported onto the PC, this
refresh routine actually was very slow. It took about three
seconds every time it had to refresh the screen. This was
because we were going from our SUPPORT window and IO manager,

through the Microsoft IO manager, through the PC DOS version, which then wrote to the screen buffers. So we just eliminated several steps there and we made our window manager write directly to the screen. It was an easy process.

One of the other things we had to deal with when we transported it was the segment of architecture that the PC has. The way the PC handles things is that it has a 64K segmented data space, and Microsoft Pascal uses the 64K data space addressed through a 16-bit pointer. We call it a short pointer. Of course, the 64K was not enough space in which to keep all of SUPPORT and to build programs trees. So we had to go through a bit of manipulation to also access the long pointer heap. Basically, what we did was to write a new routine to access the long pointer heap and to dispose of it. So it really turned out not to be much trouble to transport onto the PC.

Memory space is one of our biggest problems going from this wonderful VAX 11/780 with all the space that we could possible want onto the PC's 256K memory. We really had to start thinking about what space we were wasting. As it turned out, PC DOS takes up 24K, SUPPORT code takes up 101K, the runtime Library 24K, etc. So before even starting to build a program, we were already using 187K of memory. On a 256K machine, that only left us with 69K, which doesn't seem to be much space for a significant program.

But please remember that this is a development environment. With 69K of memory, our program tree enables us to have about a 550-line program. That 256K restriction really is on our freshman class, because that is all the memory we have on the PC's that are available for their use. But in the freshman class, it's turning out that 550 lines is plenty of space for their introduction programs. We have been promised more memory, and we are waiting anxiously so that we don't have to be to concerned with that limitation.

We have gone in and changed a few things, like condensing our program nodes: Where we might have had 4 billion flags to mark different things in our program tree, we have condensed it to a set now. We saved 3 bytes for every program node. On a 640K machine we can write about a 3000-line program. We feel that is a fair amount to use for a development environment; if you modularize your program, a module should not get much larger than that, if even that large. SUPPORT is a 20,000-line program, and I think our largest module is 1,800 lines. We could actually fit and debug our modules on this.
Efficiency. When we ran a test program, which is a loop counter and IO routine that counts from 1 to 10,000 and outputs the number at the end -- there is no IO, it's just internal computation -- we found on a compiled version that we didn't fare that well. Using the binary tree structure for the program trees, the interpreter touches every program node three times. It tends to slow down our interpreter. But being a development environment and not a real-time system, we figure that it's fair, and as you go onto a more sophisticated system like the PC/AT, the interpretation time narrows down to 39

seconds, which is pretty competitive for interpreted versions of Pascal.

CARR

How does your system compare with Turbo Pascal as far as productivity?

KOWALCHACK

We haven't run any comparisons yet, but it is something that we are hoping to do. I'm sure Turbo Pascal is a little bit faster.

CARR

That is a good economic question.

I've been interested in trying to understand the relationship between hardware and software. Among the important things: It has been hard in the past to understand how VLSI is designed, even though its design must be analogous to the design of programs but does not appear that way on the surface. It appears either easier or more difficult, depending on how and from where one looks at it.

I use the standard "axiom" (which is not true but approximately true) of the "logical equivalence of hardware and software" to work from. One would expect, of course, that VLSI design would probably be a great deal like programming design. Many of the people who come into VLSI design from the computer science part of the undertaking have programming as their background. So when one reads about program and hardware design, or sees it in action, one tends to say: "they copied this," or "they copied that," or "they haven't copied that, why not?"

The first thing that is interesting is that there are programming-like languages in VLSI design which are being used and experimented with. There are both low level languages at the level of the rectangle which is written on the surface of the wafer chip, and there are high level functional languages. For example, the use of LISP and of ADA are among the attempts which are being tried.

In particular, one can note that there are several simultaneous interpretations as far as the semantics of such a high level language is concerned. One language may yield many simulations and many fabrications. This means (to me at least) that one language has many different semantics, depending upon the pragmatic parts of what is going on.

Of course, the reason that these different semantics are evident is that hardware design has more constraints, and less fixed structure, than software design. For example, if one uses a personal computer, one doesn't worry about too much power: "blowing out the chips" by running the counters too fast, or anything like that. That problem has been designed out by the designers; there is no power difficulty. The timing has been set at a stage where there is ordinarily (changing crystals aside) no way to run the system hardware faster. Therefore the problems of optimization are left at the programming level, a little higher, and easier to do.

These problems of optimization do play a very important part in VLSI design, including the problem of minimization of chip area. We've heard today that program designers at Maryland are worried about an "equivalent" of area on a chip, which is the number of stored instructions in an IBM PC program. Thus, this sort of optimization continues to appear in software design; but as the cost of memory comes down, it doesn't now play as important a role.

There are at least three or more different semantic structures, for each higher level language, which are being interpreted: timing, simulation, power, area, among others. Of course, interpretation goes on sequentially, because up until recently only sequential machines were being used in design. (Now designers are beginning to use concurrent machines to do this.)

My former student, Danilo Gajeski at Illinois, who is very deeply interested in silicon compilers, points out that the design process in VLSI is a "daisy chain, priority-interrupt" process, in which the designs are propagated by the design process from top down, upper level to lower levels, in more and more detail. When a constraint at a lower level is violated at some level, an interrupt is sent back up the chain, and the design must be "refurbished" in order to satisfy the lower level's constraint.

This sort of vertical movement, of course, does occur in software design, but it is not as obvious. One does not often see diagrams which indicate there is an (inverted) tree-like structure in which designers of software are going down and coming back up as their designs meet and violate constraints which are unacceptable. In general, these sorts of constraints (certainly not power and area) do not play as important a role in the software process.

The "hardware design programs" which are developed, of course, turn out to be able to allow parameterization. These parameterizations are generally physical, and also in some sense functional, dealing mainly with geometry (length and width of certain portions of the chip) and certain aspects of power, which can be changed by changing lengths and widths of rectangles, etc. Thus in the up and down design process, it is possible to change those parameters which change the physical and geometric structure that one has. From such programs have begun to appear "design generators," which are built by variable-for-constant substitution in a set of designs that have been made by hand. This is sometimes discussed in texts on programming design.

In general, some of these procedures are used with "software programs," but the emphasis on optimization, including

minimization of area, which is there always in VLSI, makes for
a much stronger need for these processes. There is also a
second design constraint which is that "one must have the
desired chip out by such and such date or it will be passe'"
(sometimes said of software programs as well). So these two
constraints, one of elapsed design time, and the second one of
the actual speed and power and area of the chip (where area
determines yield and cost), are basically always all-important.

Another thing that is apparent from watching what has been
developed in these silicon compilers is that, as in operating
systems, the structure of the "environment" produces the
structure of the design. Whatever is meant here by
"environment," intuitively to me it is the hardware and
software system in which the process of design is being carried
out, and the fabrication system in which it's to be
manufactured. To a certain extent, then, only certain types of
design will be accomplished successfully at the present time
because only certain types of (most often) sequential computers
and languages are used. If one ignores CRAY I's which are
available to only a few, only certain types of simpler
computers and operating systems are available to designers.
For example, the UNIX system at Berkeley (as an "environment")
has created as the result of its structure a system called
MAGIC, which has only a certain interactive sequential
behavior. Some minor co-routine behavior is used in the design
process.

The system called "Flavors," which works with LISP, is an
object-oriented programming scheme possibly able to be added to
the LISP machines of the future. It has created the beginnings
of two alternative design systems: one at Symbolics with Neil
Weste and his group, another one at Bell Labs with Kowalski and
others. The Flavors-Smalltalk type of structure is, in a
sense, both an operating system and a language. It has its own
strong effect on the nature of the design process. It may be
that this object-oriented procedure will turn out to be the one
that gets the most interesting future design results. It may
not be completely successful but it will make some progress.

The last thing to mention is the beginning of a joint hardware-
software design process. I mention two papers jointly by a
group of graduate students at Dartmouth and Toronto given at
COMPCON in San Francisco, 1986. The most interesting one was
an interactive compiler which designed digital signal
processing systems. This consisted of a combination of digital
signal processing chips and memory and software. All of these
are put together by the interactive compiler user, based on the
constraints which are necessary for this particular structure.
The original IBM PC Junior had a ROM program storage device
which could be plugged in at the side of the computer. There
was hope (now disappeared) that many programs and operating
systems were going to be plugged into this machine. One can
recognize that the standard bus of the IBM PC is at present the
hardware-software highway for much of American computing. One
can also thus recognize that the future of intermixing hardware
and software is very much dependent on groups like IBM and

INTEL and Motorola which have the potential of developing "VLSI buses" where information -- procedures and data -- can be connected in a simple fashion.

Carver Mead has talked in his most glowing way of the not always apparent future where people will go to photography-like shops, turn in floppy disks, and out will pop chips which they will put into their own machines. This will take part of the programming load caused by the problems of message passing and storage passing and put it into hardware.

Now, sooner or later, some analogous organizational structure like that will occur (but it may not be physically like that at all). There will be the ability to move program and data from software down into hardware. This ability will be based fundamentally on the fact: if you write a program, somehow it should be transferable, translatable over into hardware, built under the control of a computer-aided-design and manufacturing process which may now be being developed around VLSI.

JERNIGAN

About 4 years ago, John Dobbs, who was then a vice-president of Analogic Corporation, noted to Sandy Friedman that array processors were hard to program. It took from six months to a year from the time an array processor was delivered to a client before the client was able to do any useful work on it. Sandy Friedman responded, "Well, I've got an array language that doesn't run very well on any machine." He was speaking of APL. They decided to get together.

Their approach was to write an interpreter that runs in a Motorola 68000 that has the task of interpreting APL code and performing certain of the lexical tasks. It would stage the array processor, which would carry out all computation.

Now the question is, "Can other languages be substitued for APL?" The answer to that is a somewhat cautious yes. What is proposed as a future direction is that there are essentially two kinds of processors. One is the language processor, a machine that will understand the language. It does the parsing and the lexing, and it stages everything for a processor that is designed to carry out the computation. By swapping the parser, you can swap in a different language.

There are well understood algorithms that are used repeatedly. John Carr talked about pushing some of them down into VLSI. I think that is what we are coming to. Things like relational join operations in APL are fairly simple because there are some arithmetic computations and character computations that have been understood for several years. These have been pushed down inside microcode on some computers.

The design philosophy that we are using here in the JHU/APL Space Department with the MIS system is that we will push details of well understood algorithms away from the user. These are covered with language that can be processed by

specialized processors. I think we are moving toward
specialized processors for language parsing and specialized
processors for algorithms. The language processors can be
swapped to meet individual tastes. The algorithmic processors
can serve a variety of language processors.

LAZANOFF

The Supercomputing Research Center in Lanham, Maryland, is only
about a year old. Consequently, all of us have come from
somewhere else in recent memory. My background gets me into
this forum because I've provided Gordon Lyon with some computer
time on a hypercube architecture. We have one of those and a
couple other funny computers that we play with.

I thought I'd take a perspective of looking at language from
perhaps a more pure user vantage point. Over the years any
number languages have grown up and been developed by people
with solutions for providing new programming facilities as
concepts and software have advanced. And yet we still have
this curious thing called FORTRAN still hanging around us.
There have been any number of people over the years that I have
run into who think that FORTRAN ought to be allowed to die and
to go on to the next-generation languages. Well, FORTRAN still
hasn't died. However the standards process is trying to evolve
yet another version of the language, and I think its an
interesting process to consider for anyone who wants to see a
language grow and develop. What we see is that even without a
standard, people want to interchange codes; and it's not just
people in the research environment, people at different
universities wanting to exchange codes. Also, it is not just
to the same mainframe, but to any kind of vendor mainframe that
people have access to. There is also an entire software
industry of people developing applications for other people to
use.

I have in the back of my mind, because of some very personal
experience with this, an application like NASTRAN, which was
originally funded by NASA Goddard Lab back in the early
'70's. That cost us something like two or three million
dollars. It has about 500,000 lines of code. It probably runs
on about two dozen different vendors' mainframes or mini-
computers today. I guess it runs on everything from Apollo to
Cray and Cyber 205. What that says is you have to have strong
language support. There's got to be a basis by which a
language can support a very large system. Chiefly, the users
do not modify NASTRAN, because they want the expertise that
this structure analysis package delivers. So most of the users
see NASTRAN only as a form of solving a problem with which they
specify input. But if you have to run NASTRAN and put it on a
system somewhere, you've got to have a language that allows you
to get that thing running in a reasonable period of time. A
NASTRAN conversion from one system to another today might take
a year to two years. I don't even know, for example, that they
have solved the problem of how to run it on a Unix system. So
despite what might be called the rampaging growth of Unix into
a lot of environments, some people probably have yet to deal

with the fact that they may not be able to do structural analysis problems under it.

But the part I wanted to get to is the standard process today that's trying to produce the 8X (and some people contend that X is now a hexadecimal number). It has now approached FORTRAN from the point of view of trying to provide a number of new facilities in a language. Those facilities try to accomplish vector notation and array notation. There was an attempt a while ago to get concepts of multiprocessing and multitasking into the language (which, the last time I looked at a standards document for 8X, were not in the language). They got thrown out of the standard process early on. The current language, if you read it, looks like it's got a little bit of Pascal, and a little bit of Algol has been drawn into the language. Several major vendors, IBM and DEC included, have said they're just not going to support the standard. Other users are upset because the standard has introduced the concept of deprecating features. What that means is that there are some things they'd like to get rid of in the language that they don't have the nerve to take out right now. But they want to leave it in there and say, if you use it we're not going to guarantee that it's going to be in the next standard (whatever that means).

How do you evolve a language, and what are your goals in evolving a language? This is the question that is involved in language development. For a language like Fortran, which has built up millions of lines of code over about 27 or 28 years, there are literally hundreds of thousands of people who program with it. There are major programming systems around the world, and I'd say that one has to really understand why people use certain features in the language: because they can achieve a certain degree of portability; or because they're able to do certain functions that perhaps the standards people haven't blessed yet or haven't agreed to bless yet. But the real, practical world of developing a programming system says that you've got to be able to work with this thing even if it doesn't port that readily. People have developed good programming styles.

What I'd like to conclude with is to say that one needs to be able to have languages that run on a number of different architectures; the benefits are obvious to everybody. You need to really understand what users are trying to get done, not say to yourself that because you don't like a feature, it shouldn't go in there. I hope I've stirred up a hornet's nest!

WEINTRAUB

I think it's Dijkstra who said, "I don't know what language you will be programming in the 1990's, but I know what we'll call it: Fortran." I remember picking up in our library here the NBS document from about four or five years ago on matrix manipulation in Fortran, in which they were basically trying to do what they did for the Cyber, which is to put APL into Fortran and make it part of the standard. It was all I could do not to return my lunch in the cafeteria.

The other thing is the question of portability -- what is in the standard and what's not. Again on Fortran, I remember someone here got very upset because he did what I think everyone has done at one time or another, which was a call routine of argument 4, and in the routine, it reset the parameter variable. From then on, whenever he added 4 to anything it was 7, and he was absolutely furious because he had been programming in Fortran, he said, for 15 years and he'd never run into that. It turned out that in the version of Fortran that he'd been working on, for that specific case where you had a literal, it had not done a pass-by-address. And in fact he was right; he had not been caught by it before. My point concerns a standard language which isn't completely standard. A comment was made before about the little things in Pascal, the strings that don't get extended. We're now seeing it in APL, which is also 20 years old and now has several very different dialects. Even going with one vendor from one version to another, you have major different things happening. I don't see how we're ever going to have real transportability except through program transformation by editing, but that doesn't seem to be a major industrial focus. It ought to be possible to write an interactive editor which, given the differences between the two languages, would look for the cases and grab them.

BLUM

A lot of what we're talking about is what you'd probably call high technology -- taking software, imbedding it in hardware, using multiple processors, using parallelism, and so on. There is this terrible investment that we have in obsolescence; Fortran is one example, COBOL is another example. The obsolescence is in the existing code, the existing libraries, the existing training. If you suddenly came up with something that was entirely different -- for example, some people say that fourth generation languages are an order of magnitude better than COBOL -- what do you do with all the people who only know how to program COBOL; what do you do with all the libraries that exist; what do you do with all the knowledge that's already encoded only in COBOL that only a COBOL compiler can understand? Are we doing the right thing in terms of looking for bridge technologies, that is, things that get us from where we are now socially, politically, in terms of the user environment, to where we want to get, where we can use these new high technology things that we're trying to develop? Clearly, languages would seem to be an effective way of gracefully getting up from the old way of doing things to the new way of doing things in a somewhat transparent way.

JERNIGAN

I think there are two aspects of your question. One is what do we do with all of that code that has to be maintained, somewhat volatile application code. What I'm addressing with that particular category is the volume of code that I've seen in my many years when I was doing Algol and FORTRAN and COBOL, and now see in APL, that is very application-specific, but contains things that some of the higher level languages now subsume.

Another category of code is the one you will see represented if you look into math libraries. Some of the math functions are not going to change now or forever. And they may be written in Fortran or assembly language; it doesn't matter what they're written in, from a user's standpoint. Those things we can carry around with us for a long time. But when I look at some applications that are coded in COBOL, and I think of some of the higher level languages we have coming down the pike, like some of the versions of PROLOG that are available, I think it is cheaper to rewrite in the new higher level languages and throw away the old applications than it is to try to maintain some of those older programs.

WEINTRAUB

The assumption there is that someone understands what that program is supposed to do. If you look at Weinberg's book on software psychology where he talks about that, one of the things that happened was there were features in the programs that no one understood, because they'd been written in assembler originally and transformed from assembler to COBOL to whatever, PL/1, etc. And it wasn't until the people took out the features during rewriting that disasters occurred.

JERNIGAN

Well, if I can quote a controller of a corporation, "I know damn well what that program is supposed to do; it's you programmers who don't understand what it's supposed to do."

BLUM

Just a counterexample. Larry Druffle's brother-in-law works for an insurance company, and each policy has its own COBOL program. The fine print is in the program, and after a while it makes errors in two directions -- those that hurt the company, which no one ever corrects, and those that hurt the customer, and here somebody raises a flag and those get corrected. After a while there are so many patches in the system that the knowledge of what that policy is, for the life of that policy, is the program; no one else knows how to do it. So, it's really hard to redo things.

It's also hard when you have a backlog to say let's rewrite everything in a brand new way. I wanted to raise the issue of the need for bridging technologies, in which you really have to retrain people. You can't say, well, we're going to stop doing everything while we learn a new way, because the risk is too high. Management would really much prefer to live with its two-year backlog than to stop everything and start to do something in a brand new way, which, if it fails, leads to a six-year backlog rather than the two-year backlog.

MCMULLEN

But we have to handle that problem in some sense. There are parts stores that don't have carburetors for Model T's any more. You just stop stocking COBOL programs or stop running them at some point, because you can't get somebody to fix it, and you bridge, by brute force, to the new technology. You write the program over again, because you can't get it to work, and you can't get the parts, and you can't get the programmer. It may take fifteen years before we stop stocking those carburetors for the Model T, but there is a lifetime after which it's going to die.

JERNIGAN

In response to that particular question, there is a bank that has 40 million lines of COBOL code operational. A bank cannot afford not to be operational for any minute during the day. It may be bad code, but it's going to live for a long time, because it is there, and it works. Software tends not to wear out. A friend of mine, Nick Zvegintzov, made the analogy with aluminum: The can may not be useful anymore, but the aluminum itself stays useful. COBOL is very much the same way. The can that it sits in may need to be replaced, but the aluminum itself stays good.

LAZANOFF

I think that for some applications that have to do with safety problems, such as reactor analysis problems and aircraft problems, as long as a particular aircraft is flying or a particular reactor is running, the code that was used to do the safety analysis on that object probably has to live for the duration of the object.

SLATER

Returning to the analogy of the Model T, people went out and bought the new cars because they liked them better. Now I presume all of us here like other languages better than COBOL; I like any other language better than COBOL. There's a whole world out there that loves COBOL. I've a friend who has written six programs that run at high IPL on the VAX in COBOL, etc. One of the questions that I think really needs to be addressed is how do you change the psychology of the world out there? We can say COBOL is no good as long as we want, but if everybody else likes it, even if we enacted it into law, we'd have this prohibition, and people would smuggle COBOL code. How do we get people to abandon COBOL code? Even if we can show them how to do it, we can prove to them it's better to do it, it doesn't mean they're going to do it.

JERNIGAN

Why would you want to?

SLATER

Because, new ways of doing things <u>are</u> better and faster, and more productive.

JERNIGAN

If you could demonstrate that to people controlling the purse strings of the corporations around the world, they would abandon COBOL. They would achieve your objective.

LYON

My remark would be that you could probably get rid of COBOL as you want if, like the Model T, it wore out, so that you had a choice whether you had to replace it with another Model T or with something a little bit "spiffier". But, I guess I do agree. From my experience, a rather large insurance company threatened to sue anyone they could get hold of who was trying to improve COBOL and was going to gum up all the lines of code they had (which led to much sputtering and running around). The fact is, the code is there, and it works, and it works as well as it ever did. The parts don't wear out. Maybe we should have languages for the FOR statement, so that it gets looser, and sloppier over the years. You either have to buy a new FOR statement or move on to something else. That's sort of the problem.

HENDLER

One of the things that did not get said early in the panel, that I was expecting to hear, was that there is a high relationship between language, application, and architecture. In fact I've seen architectures built to run to specific languages. I've seen languages designed for new architectures. I've seen applications that put demands on languages and cause the languages to change. I've seen languages that opened up new application areas. So I see those as highly linked, and the way I think I can bring this back to our concept is that the languages aren't going anywhere else, but the computers are. So, one of my questions is, should we be concentrating on the new architectures and making sure that our new languages are more compatible with them? Let us show off these architectures, and therefore, the COBOL will sort of go away, because when it's time to replace your $50,000 computer, you can either spend $50,000 for a large time-sharing thing with one big processor, or you can buy the spiffy new 64,000 processor machine, which will run those operations 10^{12} times faster.

LYON

There's been sort of a history of doomed machines that have had to run emulators of RPG, which undermines your line of thought, even though I'm highly sympathetic to it. But the expense.... PL/1, to some extent, was brought in and touted to help sell a line of machines.

HENDLER

It wasn't the language that was designed for a machine. It was designed as a new language and it would run on that machine, but it wasn't a language specifically designed for that exact architecture, to the nth degree.

LYON

Let's take one that was targeted tighter, then. The people who did the original Star 100, which I guess became the Cyber 203, and eventually the 205, really had APL in mind when they did it. They nailed that architecture as well as they thought they could. Unfortunately, the customer didn't want the language, so then they backed up to FORTRAN. It would have been an interesting experiment.

LAZANOFF

Let me make a few more comments about COBOL and the conversion question. I have been on the vendor's side of the issue of trying to represent a new COBOL compiler, just taking existing COBOL programs and moving them over to another machine. We thought we had this hot, good COBOL. We discovered that we didn't have any of the other applications the application shop needed to support their own programs. That is, the customer's computational environment wasn't just COBOL programs, it was a whole host of other software that was available to them in that system. You can't just walk up to somebody and say, here's a machine that has something that's got a nicer language than what you're used to, and then the customer doesn't have any of the support environment that goes with it.

The other part is that any major business will tell you it probably cost them several hundred thousand or a million dollars to even think about converting the existing programs, and they might just decide to weight their procurement evaluation of your computer with that amount of money and see whether your system still holds up. And they might also worry about whether there are people adequately trained to use the new language. They might worry about where they're going to get employees who can support that. The employees themselves might worry about whether or not they can get jobs elsewhere in their industry if they're not current in the language and the systems of their industry. It's a very difficult problem.

JERNIGAN

Let me respond to something Dave Weintraub said. I think you illustrate something very important to recognize, that very often an application gets wedded to a particular installation in a way that seems somewhat independent of the machine and the software that you have purchased from the vendor. I can point to several examples of that, that I'm currently dealing with -- one right here at the Laboratory, where we have a system we want to move from an MVS to a VM system that's sitting right next to it, and we're running as fast as we can to do that, but at the same time, the application is progressing faster than that. We see we want to do that, but it just seems to keep inching away from us, and the systems do look somewhat alike to us and we're running APL which is very transportable, but we can't transport it tomorrow, and we might not be able to transport it this calendar year. They don't know how to deal with that.

WEINTRAUB

I was at one of the original meetings where we were discussing this. I had the same kind of concept, that we were going to talk about architectures and languages for architectures; actually, there are also problem architectures, and I'll use that to bridge back. Morgan Stanley gave up its COBOL and is now using APL and some very advanced database language, and it is running circles around all the other investment banks in New York, to the point where First Boston, which has luckily had an APL expert on board, is now beginning to tout the same kind of things. What's happening is that that portion of the banking industry which had millions of dollars invested in COBOL is being forced to move because one company said, "We're using more up-to-date languages, and we just let go half of our programming staff, and we're still working and doing fifty times the work we were before." If someone else shows the technology will work for them and starts getting your customers, you'll change rather than lose all your customers, or you'll go out of business. Unfortunately, I think those of us who are mainly academics lose sight of that.

As for the question of the machine-specific architectures, I think what's gotten me is that we saw this massively parallel processor. The problems are there, the machine architecture is there; but our ability to set the problems in our minds so that they can be solved efficiently on those architectures requires languages the rules for which haven't even been defined yet. One advantage APL had in becoming a computer language was that it wasn't written as a computer language. Ken Iverson was trying to describe some mathematical formulations and he came up with a notation system which happened to be very handy to help him think. Then they said, "Gee, let's put this on a computer", and from what I understand, he originally objected, because it was taking away his pure language. The same thing is going to happen with these massively parallel machines and these massively parallel problems. We have to come up with a way of thinking about them, and from that will evolve a computer language, I hope. Because, if the language evolves first, it's going to constrain the way we're allowed to think about this problem in our minds, not on the machine, but in our minds. When I'm programming and I have to stop and think, if I want to add 50 numbers it requires this Do loop, that's going to slow me down; if I go +On, it's done. The same kind of thing happens when you're starting to think of parallel processing: Once we develop the notation, the language will follow; if the language comes first, we're going to be stuck.

JERNIGAN

Let me comment on Morgan Stanley. I don't know the details internally in that particular bank, but I know a couple of other banks, and I would dare suggest that you get a very different view of what language is being used in a corporation when you visit the corporate headquarters than you get when you visit the operations center.

RICH

Since the topic is architecture, it seems more natural to choose houses than Model T Fords for analogies. It is the case that the house I live in is subject to tremendous improvements in engineering, one way or another. If it were built as a sphere, for example, then I would get a lot more volume for the same amount of area to heat and cool. If it were built of different materials, I wouldn't have to worry about putting asbestos down between the sheathing and the inside partitions. It was built in 1955, and it's really very out-of-date architecture. I am not going to be persuaded by any arguments like that, however, to burn the house down and get a new one built at what it would cost at today's prices. And I think I am very much interested in people who tell me how to live more comfortably in that house, and if I'm going to buy another house, God forbid, some other time, then I would look at architectural innovations, but I doubt very much that I'd be willing to move into a sphere.

I think one of the things that the kinds of people gathered in this room tend to forget is that they are not only not representative of the population of the country as a whole, they are not even representative of the bulk of the programmers who work seven and a half hours every day, not counting coffee breaks and lunch. What seems to us more elegant and more user-friendly, easier, does not necessarily seem that way to a person who has been rewriting the same payroll program for the last 15 years. Coming to the question of how to persuade people to do things, if you really want to persuade the people, and not persuade their bosses who will then force the people, I think you have to find things that are in fact easier and user-friendly for the people who are going to use them, not for us.

LYON

One of the things that was brought up earlier was about libraries. Sometimes even the simplest things cause you a nuisance. For instance, FORTRAN and PL/1 put arrays in memory in different ways. One is stored by row, the other by columns. This leaves you with a certain problem in maintaining a library, because you have your choice of a couple of copies or having some sort of interface between them. It's a case, in any event, where supporting two different languages is a little more difficult than it need be, just for what seem to be historical reasons. Another thing is that one might be sort of tempted -- by the modern programming environment -- to take some of the ideas that Bonnie Kowalchack is talking about and pushing on students. For instance, a Cornell one has been used for teaching. I've seen one or two others from Wisconsin. After you use them a little bit, you discover that they have a lot of of strength.

You could imagine, since they are often template-driven, that you could throw off "brave new languages" rather quickly; and you say, "I'll make surface structure some exotic new thing and you can twiddle with it." The programming environment will support it all and make sure it is all written right. The target language, the intermediate language, will be FORTRAN or COBOL. That is, I'll now use that FORTRAN or COBOL no longer as my writing language, but as an intermediate, and then do a compilation. That's OK, but the trouble is, then you've got a problem of runtime support. You have done it on some exotic environment, but it really still is the same old COBOL that's running, and the error messages come. Anyone who has ever used a preprocessor knows what squirrelly error messages you get. Then you need some fancy runtime system to catch those error messages and filter them. But taking the language that you are currently using and pushing it down one level and calling it an intermediate target does have its attractions, as well as some fairly strong drawbacks.

TAYLOR

Over 20 years of watching people argue about computing languages of various kinds, primarily the better known ones, and talk about architectures of various kinds, and seeing machines come along, two things keep coming back to me. The first one is, I wonder if there isn't a boundary on the kind and number of things we can do with the kinds of computers we've managed to invent so far. And in some ways these early languages don't do a terribly bad job of reflecting that subset of activities. Therefore it's not quite the issue we make of it. Why don't we get rid of all these languages and bring in the newer ones? That is, there may be more of a fit between what is possible and what these languages enable us to do than we like to admit. That's one side of this thing about architecture and languages and ideas that interests me.

The other one is, I would like to see the parallel processor idea brought down to a much lower level like a coprocessor or a triprocessor problem where it would be more useful to me. I've got 16 machines that have 8087 and 8086's or some other combination. I think that problem has another dimension to it that we don't address very well, either. That is, I sometimes think we all feel it is better to save a million hours of meteorological computation for one meteorological institution than it is to save a million hours of computation time for two million people divided up into half an hour apiece.

LYON

There may be an experiment on your question about to run. The hypercube has a number of realizations, and one of them approaches it considerably differently from some of the other implementations of that architecture. They treat it as a co-processor. At least they tell you that you're supposed to be able to. You write FORTRAN. You're not to worry architecturally about how it handles anything. They say you're going to lose 20% of the architecture capability, but don't worry about it. Now, we at NBS have one of these machines in a building adjacent to us, and so we are going to be pattering our little feet down the hall to give it a try. Currently the compiler has some bugs. That machine will have 64 nodes per board, and you can stick a good number of boards into it. That is fairly impressive, but the idea is you are not supposed to worry about it, it's just a coprocessor. Just FORTRAN code, they say. Sounds interesting.

PROGRAMMING LANGUAGE ENVIRONMENTS

**AMPLE: A PROGRAMMING LANGUAGE ENVIRONMENT
FOR AUTOMATED MANUFACTURING**

J. C. Boudreaux

Center for Manufacturing Engineering
National Bureau of Standards
Gaithersburg, Maryland 20899

This paper describes the Automated Manufacturing Programming Language Environment (AMPLE) system, being developed within the Center for Manufacturing Engineering of the National Bureau of Standards. The development of the AMPLE system is being undertaken for two primary reasons: to provide a precise, conceptually transparent language for the construction of control interfaces to industrial manufacturing processes; and to address the technical and economic requirements of small-batch flexible manufacturing systems. The specific goals of the language design effort are to provide workstation programmers with a high-level programming environment to aid in the process of part manufacturing, and to provide an integrated system of software tools for translating process planning information into equipment-level programs.

1.0 INTRODUCTION

This paper is the first in a series of reports being developed within the Center for Manufacturing Engineering of the National Bureau of Standards to define the Automated Manufacturing Programming Language Environment (AMPLE). The purpose of this report is to provide concise overview of AMPLE Version 0.1 in order to encourage technical discussion and review of the basic design principles while the system is still flexible enough to be able to accommodate changes.

Work on the AMPLE project has been surrounded by a larger and more comprehensive project which investigates the design of advanced automated manufacturing systems. This project, embodied in the Automated Manufacturing Research Facility (AMRF) of the National Bureau of Standards, has provided an invaluable source of empirical data and practical experience.

From the inception of the AMPLE project in October 1984, the design of the system has been deliberately coupled with the development of prototypes. There have been two prototypes.

The first was built during the initial design phase, and the second, now being finished, is a more elaborately worked companion to Version 0.1. Both prototypes have been built in FranzLISP, a currently popular dialect of LISP.

We also recognized the importance of software tools which allow users to verify AMPLE products. Though an important long-term objective is to develop a fully automated, proof-based verification system, such a system is presently beyond our capabilities. The Version 0.1 prototype allows users to validate programs by computer-generated visualizations produced by a Workstation Animation Package and an NC Part Program Verification System.

The development of AMPLE is being undertaken for two primary reasons: to provide a precise, conceptually transparent mechanism for the construction of control interfaces to industrial manufacturing processes; and to define a uniform environment which supports the efficient bundling of software packages into user-extensible computer-integrated manufacturing systems.

Like every other computer language, AMPLE requires a model of computation which provides an operational characterization of its linguistic constructions. One completely general model of computation is the abstract machine first described in the 1930's by Alan Turing. Turing machines are very powerful, yet very austere, models of computation. A Turing machine is a set of states, a set of "tape" letters, a tape infinite to the right such that each cell contains a "tape" letter, and a transition table. This model is completely general, or universal, just because anything that can be computed can be computed on a Turing machine -- given sufficient amounts of time and a sufficiently clever mode of representation.

However, there are fundamental differences between traditional models of computation and those which are needed to represent the operation of flexible manufacturing workstations. The salient feature of this new and as yet only imperfectly grasped class of models, which for want of a better name I will call the non-Turing class, is that success or failure may be determined by the occurrence or non-occurrence of preferred states in the physical universe, and not by such computer-oriented measures as side effects on store! That is, success in this context is a matter of setting in motion those causal chains, and only those causal chains, which have the highest initial probability of bringing about the preferred states.

In order to understand the AMPLE model, we need to have a clear idea of an automated manufacturing workstation. Though there are many variants, we may suppose that every workstation is centered on a numerically controlled (NC) machine, such as a horizontal or vertical mill, a lathe, or a coordinate-measuring machine, cf. Jablonowski /9/ and Mason and Freeman /10/. The phrase "NC" is intended to imply that all machining operations, especially those relative motions of the tool which modify the part's geometry or material condition, are performed under the direction of a user-defined program. Such programs are executed by an embedded computer, called the NC machine's controller. NC part programs may be written in a FORTRAN-level language, called APT, cf. ANSI X3.37-1977 /3/. APT programs are not only used to specify the path which the cutting tool is to traverse, but also the rate of the traversal and a variety of auxiliary operations, such as adjusting the flow of coolants during machining. Since parts are usually designed to specific engineering tolerances, it is obviously essential that the exact position and orientation of the part be precisely determined. This is accomplished by fastening the part in a suitable designed fixture, such as a vise. Work holding fixtures may be mounted on one or more pallets, which are shuttled into proper position for either fixturing the part or presenting the part for machining. Finally, all of the implied transfers of material within an automated workstation are carried out bye a programmable industrial robot, cf. Edkins /7/.

Though the details may differ from case to case, it is a straightforward job to describe the overt action which an automated workstation would have to perform to manufacture a specific part. Assuming that that part is made available to the workstation, say by direct delivery by a material handling system, and that the part satisfies all of the relevant preconditions, i.e., it is the right size, shape, and so on, then the part must be *LOAD*'ed, which means that it must be moved from its initial location to the work holding device, fixtured, and then shuttled into proper position. Once the fixtured part has been properly positioned, it may then be *MACHINE*'d as specified by the stored NC program. Since several machining operations may be performed by the same workstation, and since these operations may involve different part surfaces, it may be necessary to *REFIXTURE* the part. One way to do this is to shuttle the part out, tell the robot to acquire the part, tell the robot to present the correct face, and then to repeat the fixturing operation with the re-oriented part. After all of these operations have been completed, the final step is to *UNLOAD* the part and to return it to the material handling system for delivery to the next workstation for additional processing, if any is required.

This idea is at best a rough approximation to what is going on. The actual situation is much more complicated. Since automated workstations are intended to operate with infrequent human supervisory intervention, they must be equipped with the capacity to interpret commands and sensory feedback with respect to an internal world model, cf. Albus /1/, and Albus, Barbera, and Nagel /2/. However, the need for self-monitoring, especially in the context of error-recovery, presupposes that the workstation's world model includes some internal representation of the workstation itself. This world model constitutes the central kernel of the AMPLE system, hereafter called AMPLE/core. Put succinctly, the function of AMPLE/core is to maintain formally precise representations of all physical objects and processes in the manufacturing domain:

- ***parts***, including representations for geometric attributes, topological attributes, tolerance and dimensioning data, and administrative data;

- ***devices***, including NC-machines, fixtures and specialized work holding devices, NC-machine tools and tool-changing devices, robots, grippers and other end-effectors;

- ***sensors***, which may either be atomic sensors, such as contact switches, or more complicated sensory systems consisting of a network of simpler sensors; and

- ***processes***, which are associated with manufacturing devices and provide the methods for bringing about physical changes in the workstation or the manufactured part.

Because of its central importance, the syntax and semantics of AMPLE/core, Version 0.1, will be described in a Language Reference Manual now being prepared for publication by the National Bureau of Standards. In the remaining sections of this paper, each of these classes of entities will be discussed. Since this discussion presupposes some familiarity with FranzLISP data structures, I will conclude this introductory section with a brief survey of this topic. Should more information be required, the reader may consult Wilensky /12/.

A common feature of almost all dialects of LISP is an interactive interpreter which presents the user with a comparatively simple interface. From the user's perspective, the FranzLISP system consists of an interface which signals its availability by printing a prompt symbol. When the user responds by keying in an legal LISP expression, the interpreter immediately returns the value of that expression on the next line. Should the user wish to introduce a symbol, then this new symbol and its current value is stored in a symbol table, usually called the **"oblist"**.

Though FranzLISP provides few useful data types, including **fixnum** (integer), **flonum** (float), **string**, and **list**, the direct availability of the **oblist** allows LISP programmers to invent and support very powerful typing mechanisms, as has already been explained in Boudreaux /5/. Recalling that a list is a data object whose "head" is an arbitrary LISP object and whose "tail" is itself a list, a type symbol may be defined by associating a symbolic name with a LISP object, usually a list, and then embedding some keyword, like **"record"** or **"array"**, in a specific place within the object to characterize the manner in which the "tail" components are to be processed. This raises an important consideration. Though LISP objects are very easy to compute with, even experienced LISP programmers notice that the piles of parentheses arising in even modestly complicated lists are difficult to read. To circumvent this problem, AMPLE allows the user to specify a so-called display-form which is judged to be visually clearer and easier to read. In this paper, I have used a display-form which is vaguely Ada-like,

though this is entirely a matter of personal style. To avoid
confusion on this point, it is very important to emphasize that
the only difference between the display-form of an AMPLE/core
object and its internal LISP form is in the shape and relative
placement of its enclosing parentheses. From the syntactic
point of view, both forms have been expressly designed to be
structurally isomorphic.

Suppose, for example, we wanted to define a type **POINT**, then we
would probably want to construct a list whose display-form in
AMPLE would be:

>   **typedef POINT is**
>
>   **record**
>   **X-ord : float;**
>   **Y-ord : float;**
>   **Name : string;**
>   **end record;**

In this case, we are using the **"record"** typing mechanism.
Since every record type is a finite sequence of fields, each of
which has a field name and a corresponding type, one obvious
FranzLISP object which seems to express the same information as
definition of **POINT** is

>   **((X-ord float)(Y-ord float)(Name string))**

A very nice feature of this representation is that we can move
from one field specification to the next by processing each
component in turn, or to use LISP jargon, we move from one
field specification to the next by **cdr**-ing down the list, and
then **car**-ing the resulting value, i.e., the **car** of the above
list is:

>   **(X-ord float)**

Once we have the field specification, then another application
of **car** yields the field name, and an application **cdr** followed
by an application of **car**, which is usually condensed to **cadr**,
yields the field type.

The representation of this information is still not enough. We
also need to associate the field sequence with the type name
POINT, and we also have to keep in mind that **POINT** was defined
by using the **"record"** mechanism. One way to do this, though by
no means the only way, is to construct the following Lisp
object:

>   **(POINT record**
>   **((X-ord float)**
>   **(Y-ord float)**
>   **(Name string))).**

which shows the close analogy between the AMPLE/core representation and the structure of the AMPLE display-form. Internal
representations for other AMPLE/core types such as enumeration

types, sequences, and arrays, may be handled in an analogous fashion. Thus, the job of finding a representation for enumeration types is very simple indeed. Suppose we consider the type **BOOLEAN**:

     typedef BOOLEAN is (true false);

then a reasonable approach is to associate the list of values with the type name as follows:

     (BOOLEAN enumeration (true false))

Sequences differ from arrays only in the sense that arrays have both an upper and lower bound for each of their index sets, whereas sequences have only a lower bound, that is, a smallest but no largest index value. For example,

    typedef 4X3-MATRIX is array ((1 4) (1 3)) of float;

defines a type of 4X3 matrices which may be used for transformations and rotations in three dimensional space. The list **((1 4)(1 3))** expresses the index set of the array. Note that the length of the list is the rank of the array, i.e., the number of dimensions, and each component of the index list expresses first the lower bound and then the upper bound.

This is the barest outline of the representational issues and I will have more to say about it in the sequel, particularly in Section 5 where I will introduce nets as appropriate representations of processes in AMPLE/core. But for now let's begin our discussion of the classes of entities in AMPLE/core with the class of manufactured parts.

2.0 MANUFACTURED PARTS

Parts are entities that are directly modified in the manufacturing process. Thus, each part is created in several manufacturing steps or stages, beginning with raw stock, which is the part's initial state, and ending with the finished part. From the initial state to the finished part there is a complicated network of intermediates states, each one of which is obtained from its predecessor by the selective application of a specific manufacturing process.

The techniques for representing parts in AMPLE/core is a complicated study which can only be briefly outlined here. The general policy in this case is to adopt, where possible, existing national and international standards. Some important examples are cited below.

Part geometry data provide the information necessary to characterize the geometry of the part. Data of this type may be represented by using wireframe data structures, cf. the Initial Graphics Exchange Standard (IGES) /11/. The defining characteristic of wireframe systems is that the geometry of parts is represented by points, lines, curves, circles, and so on. More complicated geometric features are described by splicing together simpler features or by introducing spline functions, i.e., piecewise continuous polynomial interpolation functions. It is at times preferable to describe the geometric attributes of parts by using more elaborate data structures, including boundary representations (B-reps) and the tree-like structures of constructive solid geometry (CGS). The following typedefs give the general flavor of the representation of geometric types in AMPLE/core:

```
typedef COORDINATE is record
     identifier : string;
         X-ord : float;
         Y-ord : float;
         Z-ord : float;
end record;

typedef VECTOR is record
     identifier : string;
        i, j, k : float st i**2 + j**2 + k**2 = 1.0;
         length : float st length ≥ 0.0;
end record;
```

This example shows the specific application of the "types-as-predicates" paradigm in AMPLE/core. This paradigm has been discussed in Boudreaux /5/, 116-118.

```
typedef SPHERE is record
     identifier : string;
         center : coordinate;
  radius-vector : vector;
end record;
```

These cases are merely examples of how geometric types are defined. More complicated examples could be presented, but this would serve no useful purpose. It is also a straightforward exercise to define the topological attributes of parts, that is, those attributes which indicate the connectivity of the part's components. Thus, the part, as a topological object, is resolved into faces; each face is resolved into an ordered collection of bounding edges; and each edge is resolved into bounding vertices.

AMPLE/core representations of geometric and topological attributes are well-known and generally accepted. However, there are classes of attributes which are much less clearly understood, specifically, dimensioning and tolerancing, annotations and administrative data, and part functionality. Let's briefly consider each of these hard cases.

To be useful in the manufacturing process, geometric attributes must be properly dimensioned. Dimensioning data give information about the magnitude or size of selected features of the part so that all other sizes and shapes can be determined without calculating or assuming the magnitude of any unrepresented dimensions. Since it is not possible to produce exact dimensions, tolerancing data must also be included. Conventional tolerances may be expressed as allowable errors on the dimension, e.g., 1.00 ± 0.05 mm specifies a dimensional variation which is constrained to lie in the interval 0.95 to 1.05 mm. Methods for minimizing cumulative error in dimensional tolerances are described in ANSI Y14.5M-1982 /4/. In addition to conventional tolerancing, other methods maybe used in part design specifications. One frequently cited example is geometric tolerancing, which specifies tolerances of a part's basic geometric characteristics. Basic geometric characteristics include: straightness, flatness, roundness, cylindricity, parallelism, perpendicularity, angularity, concentricity, and symmetry.

Non-geometric data serve to enrich the representation of the manufactured part by providing other essential design information. Annotations of this kind will include such information as the material type of the part, detailed descriptions of the surface finish on specified surfaces, and critical inspection points.

Finally, information will be needed about part functionality, that is, about those attributes which the part must possess in order to perform its specified function within the integrated system. Data elements characterizing a part's functional attributes will allow the production of parts which, though not optimal, are at least functionally adequate. Though an exhaustive list of functional attributes is not readily available, any such list would be likely to include such candidates as material strength and hardness, wear and corrosion resistance, and also the anticipated useful lifetime.

The fundamental principle which guides the design of the AMPLE/core representation of manufactured parts is that every part must have some determinate properties and attributes which permit it to perform the specific function for which it was designed. This is true of manufactured parts which have been designed to fit within larger units, like gears and other single-block pieces, and also for such large-scale assemblies as airplanes and nuclear reactors, which may be among the most complicated entities ever consciously designed by mankind.

In this context, it is essential to determine by objective standards well before final integration and assembly that each part is able to play its assigned role. If one considers the actual probability of failure, it is self-evident that the utility of the final product is strongly dependent upon the precision and reliability of its components.

In order to be guaranteed that the product will indeed do its job, what we must have is a clear and useful statement from the designer of part specifications, including not only a statement of the dimensioning scheme of the part, but also a description of permitted variations of features, which are given as tolerances. There is no question that the internal structure of such product specifications is a very difficult matter to describe in a few words, but the general picture is clear enough.

The specifications of a part may be thought of as a complicated property, expressed in a language such as the first-order logic, which the part either satisfies or does not satisfy. In this model, the specifications are designed to be simple boolean tests which the part either passes or fails. Of course, this assumes that the specifications are well-enough defined that those parts that pass will perform up to -- and maybe slightly beyond -- the demands placed upon them through their active work life in the final assembled product.

Once a set of specifications has been defined and verified, then the ultimate goal for all of the manufacturing processes that will yield that part is unambiguously determined. At this point it is possible to use an inferential method called backtracking to generate subordinate goals for each of the component processes. The method of reasoning is quite similar throughout. At each level new subgoals are spawned such that if the processes at that level satisfy the individual subgoals, then the goal set for the next higher level will automatically be satisfied.

3.0 MANUFACTURING DEVICES

Devices are entities that are used to modify parts. Every device is either an atomic device or a compound device. The fundamental distinction between these entities is that atomic devices are not composed of entities that are themselves devices. Compound devices have components which are themselves devices; they can be commanded to perform any one of a number of operations; and they may be in any one of a number of distinct states. Let's consider a specific example, written in AMPLE/core display-form. To avoid unnecessary complexity, the first case that we'll look at is the definition of a vise-fixture:

```
typedef VISE_FIXTURE is device
    components are
        left_jaw is atomic;
        right_jaw is atomic;
    end components;

operations are
    OPEN [yawn-distance : float];
    CLOSE [yawn-distance : float];
end operations;

states are
    IS_OPEN : boolean;
    IS_CLOSED : boolean;
end states;
end device;
```

This type definition says that vise-fixtures are a family of devices whose components consist of left and right jaws, both of which are in turn atomic devices, that vise-fixtures must at least be able to respond to two kinds of commands, **OPEN** and

CLOSE, and that vise-fixtures have only two internal states, **IS_OPEN** and **IS_CLOSED**, both of which are Boolean-valued.

It's important to understand the structure of the operation section a bit more accurately. First, every item consists of a main verb, say **OPEN**, which may be followed by a sequence of zero or more qualifying phrases. In this example, each main verb is followed by one phrase, which is flanked by square brackets:

>   **OPEN [yawn-distance : float];**

The square brackets say that the enclosed expression is an optional ingredient which maybe legally omitted. The intended interpretation of the bracket expression is easy enough to read: "yawn-distance" is an expression, or better a *parameter*, which may be assigned any floating point data value. Of course, this is really not a very useful parameterization of **OPEN**, since it allows for very stupid typing errors to be the occasion of bothersome run-time errors. The first thing that we'd like to do is to restrict the admissible floating values to lie within a certain range:

>   **OPEN [yawn-distance : float range 0.0 .. 10.0];**

which restricts the value of the parameter to the specified range. Secondly, we'd like to be able to determine a default value of the parameter in the case in which no actual value is passed in. This can be accomplished as follows:

>   **OPEN [yawn-distance : float range 0.0 .. 10.0 default 1.0]**

which says that an unaccompanied **OPEN** operation is to trigger the same series of actions as would have been triggered by associating the value 1.0 to the parameter **yawn-distance**.

But what does **OPEN** mean? An obvious question, but one that will take a bit of work to answer! Let's begin with what various audiences have told me is the most difficult notion to understand. **OPEN** and **CLOSE** are not reserved words of the AMPLE language, that is, their sense cannot be determined in advance by the designer of the language. After all, there is a limitless supply of devices, each of which possesses its own highly characteristic motions, and it is in terms of the control of these characteristic motions that the device is able to be put to useful work. But unless something very odd is afoot, the meaning of the following verb phrase is clear:

>   **OPEN yawn-distance => 5.0;**

means that the vise-fixture is to open its jaws until the distance between the facing jaw surfaces, as computed along the common surface normal is 5.0 units. This statement expresses what is usually called a post-condition, that is, a condition that is expected to be satisfied at the conclusion of the operation. Statements of this sort do partially -- but only partially -- define the meaning of operations like this. In addition, one should also consider pre-conditions, i.e., statements which may be used to characterize the condition of the world -- or at least some small part of it -- just before the operation is performed. In this case, there is a very large family of possible pre-conditions, but all seem to have to do with the inter-surface gap, i.e., the **"yawn"**. From the formal point of view, understanding the meaning of an operation is being able to construct a functional association between pre-conditions and post-conditions.

With this discussion in mind, it should be a straightforward exercise to interpret the following more complicated device typedef:

```
typedef ROBOT is device

    components are
       end_effector is device;
       wrist is atomic device;
    end components;

operations are

    ACQUIRE part-or-tool : phobj [AT location];
    MOVE part-or-tool : phobj [FROM location]
       TO location;

    RELEASE [END_AT location];

    TRANSFER [part-or-tool : phobj]
            [FROM location]
            [TO location];
            [END_AT location];

    ATTACH grip : end_effector [FROM location]
            [END_AT location];

    DETACH grip : end_effector [TO location]
            [END_AT location];

    EXCHANGE [grip-1 : end_effector] [TO location]
            FOR grip-2 : end_effector
            [FROM location]
            [END_AT location];

    CLEAR [DROP_AT location]
            [END_AT location];

    PAUSE;

    HOME;

end operations;

states are
    IDLE : boolean;
    COMMAND_EXECUTING : boolean;
```

```
            COMMAND_FINISHED : boolean;
            CANT_DO : boolean;
        end states;

    end device;
```

The AMPLE/core display-form neatly illustrates the underlying abstraction of type definitions. Notice that the only conceptually important components of the class of robots is a wrist and some end-effector. There will undoubtedly be other articulated joints, but they are only significant as intermediate movers. From the perspective of this type definition, the final goal states may be characterized by the location, i.e., position and orientation, of the wrist or end-effector.

4.0   SENSORS

An actual manufacturing environment consists of physical objects and processes, and the causal chains that they set in motion. Sensors are input-like mechanisms which allow the real-time adaptive control of manufacturing processes. More specifically, information about the current condition of the parts and devices is collected by the sensors and then passed in a properly encoded form to the control software. Control and guidance decisions are then based in part upon this sensory information. Though the importance of sensors in automated manufacturing is obvious, the current version of the AMPLE Version 0.1 prototype has not yet been extended to include devices of this class. Hence, the ideas presented in this section should be taken as a provisional sketch of this area of AMPLE/core.

Sensors may be grouped in many ways, but for our present purposes the most useful way is to group them into primitive sensors and compound sensors.

Primitive sensors consist of three layers: actuators, transducers, and A-to-D converters. The actuator is an interface with the physical environment that is selectively reactive to certain ranges of physical stimuli. The transducer converts the time series of stimuli on the actuator interfaces into an electrical signal. The A-to-D (analog-to-digital) converter periodically samples the signal and then represents its value by mapping it into a pre-selected range of values. In many cases, the range of values will form a discrete set of scalar values which is similar to an enumeration type. In other cases, the yield of the A-to-D converter will be some well-defined compound data type.

The information needed to represent atomic sensors includes a precise definition of the data type of the values yielded by the sensor's A-to-D converter; the identity of the physical quantity being measured; and the effective thresholds, time delays, hysteresis effects, and other important computational properties of the sensor for the purpose of real-time correction of sensory information.

Compound sensors are composed of spatio-temporally distributed atomic sensors. In the simplest cases, the atomic sensors are ordered on some regular design, for example, a planar lattice, and each of the component sensors is of the same type. That is, the values of each are drawn from the same base enumeration type. In more complicated cases, compound sensors are built on different types of atomic sensors and have a rather more complicated temporal regime.

The information needed to adequately describe a compound sensor includes an enumeration of the atomic sensors which constitute it, and a description of the intended spatio-temporal network which binds the atomic sensors together.

Because of its importance, the AMPLE/core representation of sensors is now being intensively investigated. The results of our current efforts will be presented at a later time. For a very thorough examination of the theory of the integration of sensory data within a real-time control system, the reader may consult Albus /1/; for another perspective, see Henderson and Shilcrat /8/.

5.0   PROCESSES

In order to represent actual workstations in AMPLE/core, it is not sufficient to have a typedef for all of their component devices and sensors. It is also necessary to recognize the fact that actual workstations are complicated aggregates of physical objects, and as such that they have the same kinds of physical properties and attributes as do manufacturing parts. That is, they have shape, size, some definite location in the world coordinate system, and so on. More specifically, each the range of operations that may be actually performed by an actual device is constrained and limited by its physical construction. For example, consider the effect on robot trajectory of the limitations on admissible joint angles. The means to represent this mass of data in AMPLE/core is by building a semantic network and then linking it to a symbolic name. The LISP object consisting of a symbolic name and a semantic network of this kind, will be called a configuration.

If a device is an ingredient of a configuration, then all of the components of that device are also ingredients of that configuration. When ordered by the component relation, the devices of a configuration form a tree whose root is the configuration itself and whose leaves are atomic devices. Hence, once a symbolic name has been associated with the configuration, then each of its ingredient devices can be uniquely identified by a pathname. For example, if **"HWS"** is the symbolic name of a configuration which includes an horizontal milling machine and a robot, then

HWS/robot

is a pathname designating the robot, and

HWS/robot/end-effector

is a pathname designating the robot's end-effector. Instead of the pathname notation, which makes use of the component section of the corresponding typedefs, the AMPLE programmer could choose to introduce another symbolic name. Given the utility of the *oblist* of FranzLISP, the user can introduce new symbolic names almost without limit.

The AMPLE/core object which represents process objects is constructed from basic linguistic units which are functionally analogous to program statements:

<configuration-pathname> ":" <command-sequence>

where the initial component is the component of the configuration which is being directed to perform the action which is introduced in the second component of the pair. The internal syntactic structure of each member of the command-sequence is either one of the operations associated with the device in the typedef or a previously written AMPLE program:

HWS/robot: ACQUIRE part-or-tool => PARTNO-A34;
HWS/robot: ACQUIRE part-or-tool => TOOLNO-788;

In this example, the parameters are mandatory, or to use more traditional grammatical terminology, the main verb of the command is transitive in that a direct object must be supplied. There are also intransitive verbs which are syntactically forbidden to have direct objects:

HWS/robot: HOME;

which directs the robot to return to that position and orientation which it has been taught to recognize as **"home"**.

The supposition that we must make is that the configuration component addressed in the pathname, can be commanded to perform the action or series of actions specified in the verb phrase. In the AMPLE system, this supposition will be decided by table lookup. Therefore, it is essential that a complete list of admissible main verbs be associated with each configuration ingredient.

The mechanism for associating performable actions with AMPLE verb phrases is called *parametrization*. Parametrization is achieved by forming a suitable template in the native language of the device controller. In the simplest case, executable control code may be generated from the template by performing global substitution on embedded variables. Another plausible model of parametrization is a variant of the familiar mechanism by which argument values are passed into subroutines. There are subtle differences between different argument-passing mechanisms, i.e., pass by reference, pass by value, and so on, but these distinctions need not detain us here.

The structural organization of AMPLE programs is obviously a crucial topic which can only be touched upon here. All AMPLE programs are specific instances of the abstract net type which is equivalent in expressive power to Petri nets. The key to their structure is an underlying combinatorial object, say a (di)graph whose nodes are connected by (directed) edges, and then a list of functions associated by a putprop-like mechanism with each node. Suppose that we choose to represent digraphs by means of the adjacency relation between its nodes, which may be illustrated by the following LISP object:

(A (B C) B (D) C (D) D)

such that the list following each symbolic node is an exhaustive enumeration of that node's immediate successors, then an application of putprop could be used to associate some computation with the node. The nodes of the digraph will be called **"boxes"** and the contents of boxes are sequences of AMPLE processes.

The underlying model of execution requires that each box in a program net have some definite state. As with Petri nets, the significant aspects of the program net can be represented by the motions of control tokens. That is, when a program net is initiated, a single token is passed to the token-holder of all those boxes that have no immediate predecessors. These boxes are then said to be enabled. All subsequent markings of the program net are determined by the following "enabling" rule: once all operations in an activated box are successfully terminated, then one token is removed from that box's token holder, and one token is placed in the token-holders of all of the box's immediate successors.

The rules governing the activation of enabled boxes are a bit more complicated. For our present purposes, let it suffice to say that any number, including all, of the enabled boxes may be assumed to be activated concurrently. One important implication of this assumption is that the only effective control that the AMPLE programmer has over the order of execution is that which is forced by the "enabling" rule, given the intrinsic combinatorial connectivity of the digraph.

In subsequent investigations, more sophisticated rules will be considered for the enabling of boxes and then their subsequent activation. These rules will be functionally dependent not only on the termination or non-termination of a box's predecessors in the program net, but also on the current state of the workstation environment. This implies that there will be complicated interactions between rules for moving tokens and the sensor system. But even in these more difficult cases, the same model of execution will be preserved.

To this point, we have been discussing the properties of program nets without considering the actual content of the constituent boxes. As might be expected, the contents of boxes is subject to very strict (semantic) rules. First, the contents of every box must be addressed to one and only one

device in the workstation configuration. This then is the
physical object which is the implied subject of all of the
box's imperative verb phrases. Second, the processes within a
box are performed sequentially, that is, in the order in which
they have been written. The following piece of code may be
taken as an example of the possible contents of a single box:

```
    HWS/robot : ACQUIRE part-or-tool => PT-A37;
                MOVE part-or-tool => PT-A37 TO
location'buff(1);
                RELEASE END_AT buff-safe;
                HOME;
```

This simple AMPLE program will **ACQUIRE** PT-A37, whose location,
orientation, and grip points are defined in the AMRF database,
and then **MOVE** that part to slot 1 of the buffer, whose location
is defined under the configuration attribute "location". After
RELEASE'ing the part, **HWS/robot** goes **HOME**.

There is no reason to group all of these process in a single
box. All things being equal, the code just given would achieve
essentially the same effect as the following multi-box program:

```
    HWS/robot : ACQUIRE part-or-tool => PT-A37;

    HWS/robot : MOVE part-or-tool => PT-A37 TO
location'buff(1);
                RELEASE END_AT buff-safe;

    HWS/robot : HOME;
```

This example is one in which the actions are inherently
sequential, but obviously sequentiality is merely an especially
simple digraph. There are many other structural possibilities.

The detection of errors, which is the primary mechanism for
shifting from one processing regime to another, is accomplished
by interaction with the sensory system. But this is a complicated area which is currently under active -- and intense --
investigation. One apparently reasonable alternative is to
adopt a variant of the exception handling mechanism of Ada, but
this approach yields dangerously complicated control structures, that is, control structures whose semantic interpretation is very hard.

6.0   CONCLUSIONS

Much work has already been done to implement the notions
described in this paper, but much more needs to be done before
we have any right to be confident that AMPLE provides an
acceptable solution to the problems in the field of automated
manufacturing. In my opinion, a sure sign of the quantity of
work remaining is the fact that the objects in AMPLE/core are
still enormously complicated. This may be explained in part by
the complexity of the target domain, but it also suggests that
new clarifying insights are needed.

BIBLIOGRAPHY

1. Albus, J. S. *Brains, Behavior, and Robotics*. McGraw-Hill; 1981.

2. Albus, J. S., Barbera, A. J., Nagel, R. N. "Theory and Practice of Hierarchical Control," *23rd IEEE Computer Society International Conference*, September 1981, 18-39.

3. ANSI X3.37-1977, "Programming Language APT," American National Standards Institute, Inc.; 1977.

4. ANSI Y14.5M-1982, "Dimensioning and Tolerancing," The American Society of Mechanical Engineers; 1983.

5. Boudreaux, J. C. "Problem Solving and the Evolution of Programming Languages," in R. Jernigan, B. W. Hamill, D. M. Weintraub, *The Role of Language in Problem Solving-I*, North-Holland, 1985; 103-126.

6. "CAM-I's Illustrated Glossary of Workpiece Form Features," Computer Aided Manufacturing-International, Inc., Arlington, TX; R-80-PPP-02.1, revised May 1981.

7. Edkins, M. "Linking industrial robots and machine tools," in A. Pugh, *Robotic Technology*, Peregrinus; 1983.

8. Henderson, T. and Shilcrat, E. "Logical Sensor Systems," *Journal of Robotic Systems*, vol 1(1984), 169-193.

9. Jablonowski, J. "What's new in machining centers," *American Machinist*, Special Report 763, February 1984;95-114.

10. Mason, F. and Freeman, N. B. "Turing centers come of age," *American Machinist*, Special Report 773, February 1985; 97-116.

11. Smith, B. M., et al. Initial Graphics Exchange Specification (IGES), Version 2.0, U.S. Department of Commerce, National Bureau of Standards, NBSIR 82-2631(AF).

12. Wilensky, R. *LISPcraft*, W. W. Norton; 1984.

QUESTION AND ANSWER PERIOD

DOYLE

I've seen demonstrations of CAD/CAM systems where an engineer will design a part, do finite element analysis, check it, and flip back and forth until he's got it. In the end, he'll generate an NC program, which then goes out and does the machining operation. How do you fit in with that?

BOUDREAUX

AMPLE is a programming language environment, that is, an umbrella under which all of the CAD/CAM and CAE functions that you've mentioned are arranged. Specifically, the CAD design of parts and the generation of NC part programs is presently being provided by a commercially available system called Auto-Trol. One important new component that my colleagues and I are working on is an automated verification system.

DOYLE

No, you've got to try it. You go out and machine the part and see what happens.

BOUDREAUX

Well, that's one way to do it, if you don't mind machining through the back of your machine tool on occasion.

DOYLE

What about the geometry of the robot's positions, and things like that?

BOUDREAUX

Internally, robot positioning is accomplished by means of a kinematic model of a 6-degree-of-freedom robot arm. Once the final position and orientation of the end-effector are specified in the world (workstation) coordinate system, then the necessary angles for each joint are calculated directly. The model ensures that no joint limits are exceeded. Not only does AMPLE generate control code to cause these motions to take place, but it also generates parameters for the AMPLE Animation Package (AWAP) which allows the programmer to preview all of the motions, both the motions of the robot as well as other devices in the workstation. The kinematic model and AWAP were developed at the National Bureau of Standards.

DRS.
A LANGUAGE-ORIENTED DIAGNOSTIC RUN-TIME SYSTEM

Bonnie Kowalchack and Marvin V. Zelkowitz

Department of Computer Science
University of Maryland
College Park, Maryland 20742

Programming languages were primarily designed to help a programmer write source code. The role of programming languages has been broadened, with uses extending from the specification phase to the debugging phase of the software life cycle. This paper describes Drs., a diagnostic system that is part of a Pascal development environment called SUPPORT, which runs on Berkeley Unix systems and IBM PC's. Drs. is language-oriented, it uses the source code and Pascal syntax to invoke various diagnostic facilities. Drs. uses multiple windows and visual cursor control to coordinate user interaction with the system.

1.0   INTRODUCTION

The role of language is important in all facets of program development. In the earliest days of programming, the significance of programming languages was primarily confined to writing the source code. Current research is extending the role of language from the specification and development phases to the later testing and debugging phase of the software life cycle. This paper discusses the role of a programming language as an aid to the testing and debugging of programs. Traditionally, computer systems include separate command and operational languages, such as an operating system command language used to invoke programs and an application programming language used to solve problems. A few systems have been built in the last few years which merge the two concepts. For example, the C-shell command language in UNIX has many C language features, and allows the user to "think C" for both C program development and execution. The distinction between the command and operational languages is blurring, and an integrated system with unified command syntax is the goal of many researchers.

A Pascal development system, called SUPPORT [ZELK84], has been implemented at the University of Maryland. Drs., a diagnostic system that aids the user during debugging and testing of a program has been built as a part of SUPPORT. Drs. accepts commands in a Pascal syntax, and responds to the user via formatted data. Unlike many other debuggers, the user only needs to know the Pascal language, not the underlying machine representation of Pascal data.

In the next section of this paper, an overview of Drs., a brief introduction to the SUPPORT environment and a short description of the SUPPORT Pascal interpreter states are presented. In section 3, a more detailed explanation of the capabilities of Drs. is given.

2.0   OVERVIEW

2.1   Features of Drs.

Drs. is a language-oriented debugging environment engineered to display program execution in a manner that is intuitive to the user. The need for a separate debugging command language is minimized, since any Pascal statement can be executed within the environment of a halted program. The actual Pascal source code is used to invoke debugging features in Drs.

SUPPORT is oriented around windows (see Figure 1). It separates Pascal data declarations from the program text by displaying data and text in two different windows. Drs. also has data debugging windows which are separate from the text debugging views. Data structures can be viewed as formatted Pascal data through the Run-time Display window and the Variable Display window. Scalar data only can be viewed interactively through the Variable Display window. Both user-defined types and scalars can be investigated in the Run-time Display window. The Program Trace and Coverage Trace use the source code to display execution views of the program.

2.2.   The Support System

SUPPORT is an integrated environment used to build Pascal programs [ZELK84] [LYON84]. It contains a syntax directed editor, similar to other such projects (e.g., [FISC84], [GARL84], [REIS84], [TEIT80]). The window system of SUPPORT is designed to provide multiple views of a program's development cycle (see Figure 1). These include views of the program text, data declarations, a message window, an input view, execution output and various debugging windows. In addition to the syntax directed editor, SUPPORT contains the following major pieces: a LALR parser for adding source text, a character-oriented editor for editing programs, a Pascal interpreter for program execution, and Drs., the diagnostic run-time system described in this paper. During program creation, SUPPORT builds a program as a binary tree. That is, as a program tree is created, a non-terminal is replaced by the right hand side of its production. Consider the production rule for the while statement which has the right-hand side definition,

"WHILE <expression> DO <statement>".

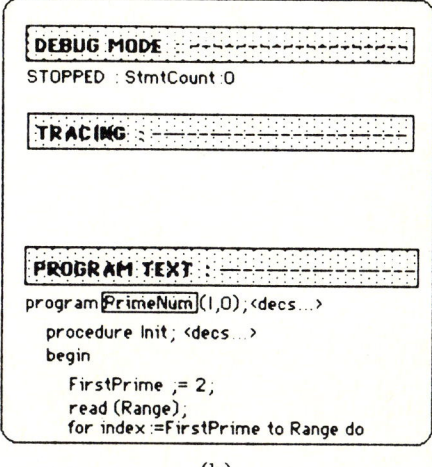

```
 PROGRAM TEXT :  ------------
program PrimeNum (I,0); <decs...>
   procedure Init; <decs...>
   begin
      FirstPrime := 2;
      read (Range);
      for index :=FirstPrime to Range do
         sieve[index] := true;
   end;
   procedure FindPrime; <decs...>
      procedure NotPrime; <decs...>
      begin
         while factor *multiple <Range do
         begin
            if sieve[factor *multiple] then
            begin
```

(a)

(b)

Figure 1

(a) SUPPORT starts with a window displaying program text.
(b) Windows open as horizontal bands on the screen. The window consists of a window header and appropriate text.

The non-terminal <while statement> is replaced by this right-hand side definition, its left son becomes the non-terminal <expression>, and its right son becomes the non-terminal <statement> (see Figure 2).

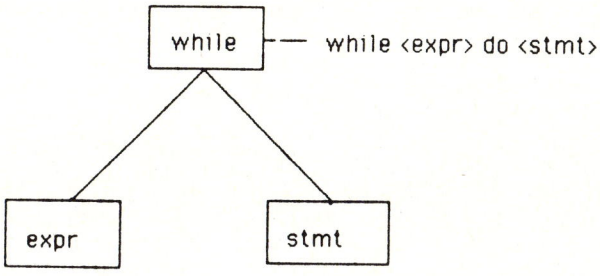

Figure 2

Binary parse tree for the WHILE statement.

A user can move the cursor onto a non-terminal and expand it into program text either by selecting an appropriate response from a menu or by typing in text which is verified by SUPPORT's LALR parser. Cursor motion operates via the cursor arrow keys on the keyboard or by typing a command preceded by a prompt character. After each command, the screen is refreshed by a

tree-walking algorithm which builds a text display list and
prints those lines which have been altered since the last
refresh operation. Information in the tree includes the
formatting code to "pretty print" the source text. The program
can be saved in its internal tree representation or in its
source listing format. The SUPPORT environment is fully
integrated, allowing the user to switch between program
building, editing, execution, and debugging without the need to
load other packages, change environments or even remember a new
set of commands. This promotes a natural human-engineered
interface for a programmer.

Implemented as 20,000 source lines which include 28 modules in
Pascal and 2 in C, SUPPORT runs on Unix 4.2bsd systems and on
IBM PC's. A PC with 256K of memory can process about a 600
line program, while a 640K machine can process about a 3200
line program. Thus, it can handle moderately complex single
user programs.

2.3. Interpreter Modes

Because the various functions that Drs. provides are closely
linked with the SUPPORT interpreter, a brief description of the
interpreter modes is given for reference. If a program has not
yet been executed, or has normally completed execution, the
interpreter is in "OFF" mode. When a program is running, it is
in "ON" mode. If execution is suspended for any reason, the
interpreter is in a "SUSPENDED" mode. There are suspended
modes for each of the following conditions: a program error;
output filling the output window; a Breakpoint set by the user;
Incremental Execution to halt the program after each statement.

Unless suspended because of a program error, a program can be
restarted from the suspended point. While a program is
suspended, debugging features can be turned off or on, program
code can be inspected, and in many situations, code can be
altered.

3.0   DETAILS OF DRS.

3.1   Using Pascal Syntax to Debug Code

Often during debugging, a user wishes to change the value of a
variable, insert another statement or observe new execution
results. Modifying the source code to accomplish these tasks
has the disadvantage of having to later edit the code to remove
these statements. Debuggers often allow a user to perform some
of these tasks when specified by a separate command language.
The cost of using such a package is learning yet another series
of commands with limited functionality.

Drs. does not require a separate debugging command language,
since any Pascal statement can be executed within the environment of the halted program. This is achieved via Immediate
Execution. While execution is suspended, any syntactically
correct Pascal statement may be typed and will be automatically

interpreted. Immediate Execution allows the programmer to change or display variable values, and execute procedure calls within the currently executing scope of the program. When Immediate Execution is initiated, Drs. responds with the prompt "TYPE TEXT:". At this point, the user enters any Pascal statement to be executed (see Figure 3). This action can be repeated as many times as desired.

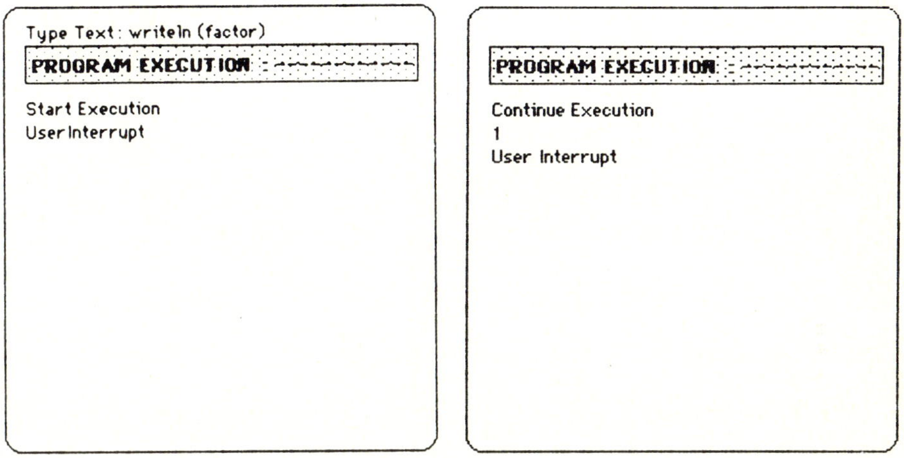

```
┌─────────────────────────────────┐   ┌─────────────────────────────────┐
│ Type Text: writeln (factor)     │   │                                 │
│ ╔═══════════════════════════╗   │   │ ╔═══════════════════════════╗   │
│ ║ PROGRAM EXECUTION         ║   │   │ ║ PROGRAM EXECUTION         ║   │
│ ╚═══════════════════════════╝   │   │ ╚═══════════════════════════╝   │
│ Start Execution                 │   │ Continue Execution              │
│ User Interrupt                  │   │ 1                               │
│                                 │   │ User Interrupt                  │
│                                 │   │                                 │
└─────────────────────────────────┘   └─────────────────────────────────┘
            (a)                                    (b)
```

Figure 3

(a) After invoking Immediate Execution which yields the prompt "Type Text:", the user types a statement to be executed.
(b) The statement is executed and output is displayed in the execution window.

Program Tracing and Incremental execution are temporarily turned off when Immediate Execution is invoked. The current state of the program tree (the part of the code where interpretation was suspended) is saved, and the tree is cut. The newly added program text is then parsed, and if it is a legal statement, the interpreter pointers are reset to make this the next statement. The Pascal interpreter is then invoked. After executing this statement, the interpreter pointers are restored, the program tree is rebuilt to its original state, and the debugging options that were switched off are turned on again. At this point, execution may be continued as before, another statement may be immediately executed, or anything allowed during suspended execution may occur.

3.2   Using Program Text to Debug Code

Because the programmer is developing a source program in the SUPPORT environment, the program text is almost always displayed on the screen. With this in mind, Drs. allows several debugging features, that are described in this section, to be invoked by moving the cursor onto actual program constructs in the user's source code, rather than using a debugging command language.

3.2.1   Program Execution Tracing

Debugging a program requires that the programmer understand the flow of executing statements. The typical method of monitoring this is by either adding WRITELNs or debugging commands to the source code. This method is usually slow, tedious and often ineffective unless a myriad of debugging code is added. Also, the programmer must return to the code and delete all the added debugging commands once the problem has been found. Typical trace debuggers just print a sequence of statement numbers as execution progresses. In Drs., when the Program Execution Trace window is opened, the program text is displayed and the currently interpreting statement is highlighted and updated as execution proceeds. This allows the user to watch the flow of execution by observing the actual program code, not just messages describing the condition of the code.

While executing, the header line of the window is continuously updated to indicate the procedures that are running. As a procedure or function call is made, this new name is added to the list displayed in the header line. When the procedure or function is exited, the routine name disappears from the list (see Figure 4). This displays a dynamic record of procedural changes, and hence an overall outline of the program flow.

The window which displays traced execution contains the program text. As the program is interpreted, each statement is displayed in normal infix notation, but traced as it is executed in postfix notation. For example, when executing an assignment statement such as

> factor := factor + 1;

the entire statement is first highlighted.

> **factor := factor + 1**;

As the statement is interpreted, the Trace window explicitly displays the order in which the statement sections are executing. First, the expressions on the right side of the statement are evaluated

> factor := **factor + 1**;
> factor := **factor** + 1;
> factor := factor + **1**;

then the destination is checked for type constraints

> **factor** := factor + 1;

and then the assignment is made. The next statement to be executed is then highlighted.

Displaying the statement execution in postfix notation presents more information about execution than just highlighting or pointing to the entire statement (e.g.,[MAC84]). It also serves as an instructional device to the novice programmer.

```
┌─────────────────────────────────────┐   ┌─────────────────────────────────────┐
│ TRACING : [PrimeNum] [Init] ------  │   │ TRACING : [PrimeNum]------------    │
│ program PrimeNum (I,O); <decs...>   │   │  Init (Range, FirstPrime);          │
│   procedure Init; <decs...>         │   │  FindPrime (Range, FirstPrime);     │
│   begin                             │   │  writeln ('These are the prime numbers │
│     FirstPrime := 2;                │   │             between', FirstPrime, 'and', │
│     read (Range);                   │   │             Range)                  │
│     for index := FirstPrime to Range do │ │ end.                              │
│ PROGRAM EXECUTION : ------------    │   │ PROGRAM EXECUTION : ------------    │
│ Start Execution                     │   │ Start Execution                     │
│                                     │   │                                     │
└─────────────────────────────────────┘   └─────────────────────────────────────┘
              (a)                                        (b)
```

Figure 4

(a) Program Trace window showing two levels of procedure calls in the header line (PrimeNum and Init).
(b) After execution of Init is completed and control returns to PrimeNum Init is removed from the header line.

The beginner can view the executing program code and obtain a clearer idea of how the program is actually interpreted. Each piece of code that is highlighted during execution is a valid cursor position in the SUPPORT environment. Consequently, the source code itself is used to dynamically display the trace.

3.2.2   Coverage Tracing

A universal problem when programming, is insuring that all the code written is pertinent; that is, that it actually is executed. It is common to write a block of code that is never used. The Coverage Trace window allows the user to view the program text at any time in the SUPPORT environment, to determine which statements have been executed. When the Coverage Trace window is opened, the program text is displayed, and any section of the program that has been interpreted in the last execution of the current editing session, will be highlighted (see Figure 5). Thus, if program execution terminates successfully, the user can easily view any section of code that is not used. Also, if the program terminates unsuccessfully, the user has a simple means of tracking down the code which caused the crash. If the program currently in the editor has never been executed, none of the code will be highlighted.

3.2.3 Breakpoints

Breakpoints can be set at or removed from any statement in the program text. Drs. allows the user to move the cursor onto the Pascal statement in the program code and set the breakpoint. The user does not need to search through the code for a line

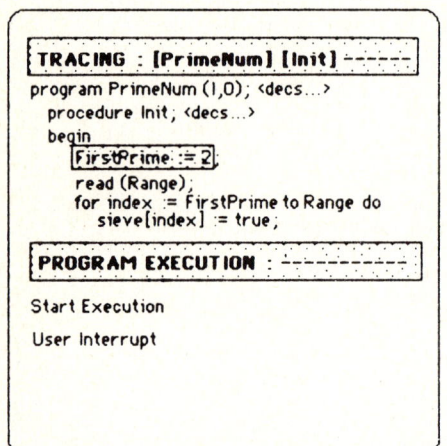 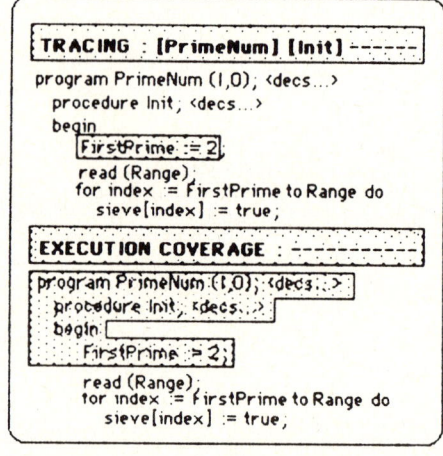

(a) (b)

Figure 5

(a) The Trace window displays the currently executing code while the Execution window displays the output.
(b) The Coverage window is opened, replacing the output window. The Coverage window highlights all parts of the code that have been executed up to the point of the interrupt.

number; the text itself is used to mark the stopping point. When a breakpoint is set, the interpreter will stop immediately before the execution of the marked statement.

3.2.4 Incremental Execution

Incremental Execution causes the interpreter to stop before every program statement. After each statement is executed, the interpreter mode is checked. If in Incremental mode, the interpreter will stop and wait for a carriage return. While suspended between statements, any of the other debugging features can be invoked.

3.3 Displaying Pascal Data Structures

As explained above, the execution control flow monitoring features can be invoked through the Pascal source code window. In a similar manner, Data can be inspected via data declaration windows which are described in the following sections.

3.3.1 Variable Display

Often program errors are caused by incorrect values in variables that are used for control flow. Locating the incorrect assignments is typically done by inserting WRITELN statements into the code to print the values assigned to a variable. Not only is this tedious, but it also requires the programmer to go back into the code to remove the added statements. With the Variable Display window, viewing scalar variable assignments can be done interactively and does not require that temporary statements be added to the code. The variable names and values are displayed as formatted Pascal data, not in the internal machine representation. Variables are marked for tracing by moving the cursor onto the variable in the program text, and marking the variable. The user does not have to re-type a variable name or procedure name; he just needs to point to the desired variable in the program code.

When the variable is initially marked for tracing, the variable name and it's scope name are displayed. Variables can be marked when the interpreter is in off or suspended mode. As a program executes, the variable's value is updated immediately after each assignment to it (see Figure 6).

3.3.2 Run-Time Display

Pascal, like many other high level languages, provides a user with the capability to define complex types not originally specified in the language, yet only a few debuggers have facilities to inspect the values of these types (e.g.,[MYER80], [SCHA80]). In order to view user-defined types, a programmer must insert specific lines of code into the program, and even then cannot always directly display their values.

The variables associated with any current environment can be viewed when the Run-time Display window is opened. This is accomplished by searching information from the interpreter's run-time stack. When the interpreter is suspended, the header line contains a list of the current procedures in execution (see Figure 7). This gives the user a visually intuitive feel for the sequence of calls causing scope changes in the program, up to the point of the interrupt. The currently displayed scope name is always highlighted. This serves as a quick reminder of which scope's variables are being inspected.

When execution is suspended, a list of the variables in the currently interrupted scope is displayed as formatted Pascal data. This list is analogous to the top of the run-time stack. The user can scroll through the list of variables by using the arrow keys on the keyboard. Scope changing is done by moving the cursor into the header line and moving right or left by the arrow keys [SHNE85]. The display window is automatically updated with the variable list of the newly highlighted scope name (see Figure 7).

The cursor arrow keys are used in essentially the same manner in the Data windows as in the Program Text windows. This

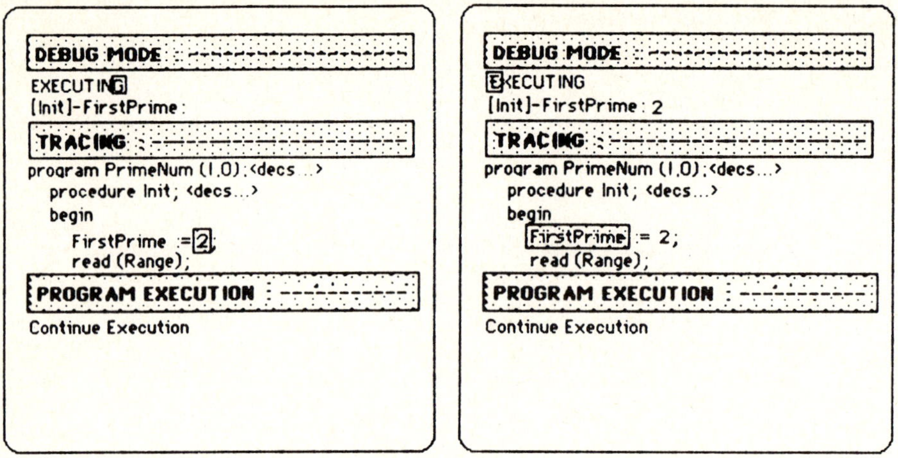

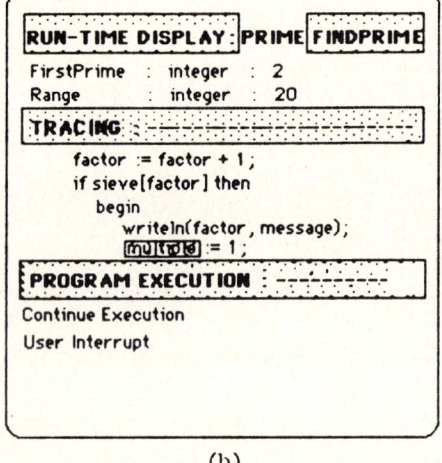

Figure 6

(a) The program is executing directly before an assignment to a variable that is marked for tracing.
(b) The assignment statement is executed and the value is updated in the variable trace window.

Figure 7

(a) The run-time window is displaying the top scope values.
(b) The cursor is moved onto the previous scope and the variables of the new scope are immediately displayed.

avoids the confusion of learning new commands for different environment modes, and figuring out which mode is current before an action can take place. The up-arrow and down-arrow keys move the cursor to the previous and next line in the Data

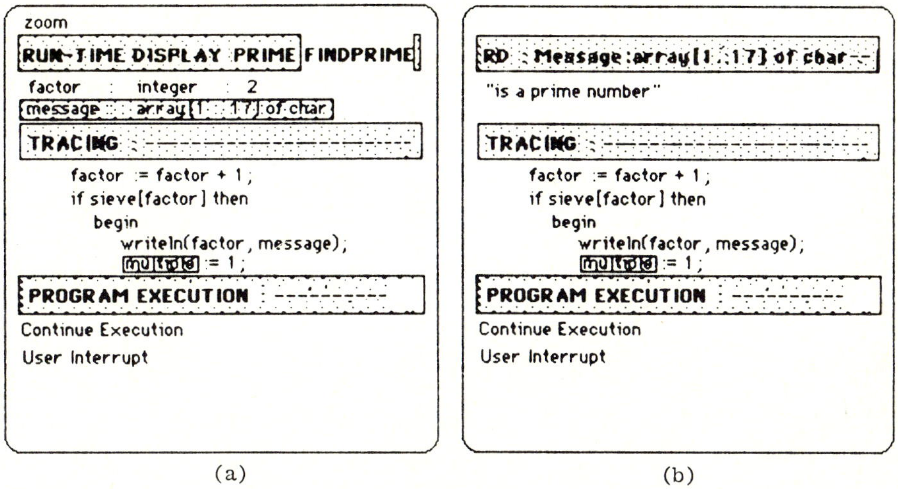

Figure 8

(a) The cursor is sitting on a string variable and declaration.
(b) The zoom command displays the variable name and declaration in the header line and the value of the string in the window.

windows and to the previous and next program construct in the Program Text windows. Similarly, the right-arrow and left-arrow keys move to the previous and next scope in the header line, and in the Program Text windows move to the previous and next program non-terminal.

The type definition of a variable is displayed along with the name in the run-time window. If the variable is a simple type, its value is also displayed at this time. If it is a more complex type, the user can display the value of the variable by moving the cursor onto the variable of interest and performing the "zoom" operation (see Figure 8). The header line will contain the scope name, the variable name and the type declaration. The window will contain the value of the variable of interest. To return to the original list of variables, the user simply invokes the "pan" command. The "pan" and "zoom" commands in the Run-time window are analogous to those commands in the Program Text window. For program text, the "pan" command elides a program section and the "zoom" command displays the entire section of code that was previously hidden by the "pan" command.

4.0 CONCLUSIONS

Drs. is a language-oriented diagnostic run-time system for the Pascal language. It is built into SUPPORT, a Pascal development environment, implemented at the University of Maryland. Drs., as is SUPPORT in general, is viewed through a set of windows, controlled via the cursor arrows on the keyboard. Drs. displays multiple views of program code during execution, both dynamic and snapshot. This includes Program Tracing of the flow of control, Program Coverage during suspended execution, interactive Variable Tracing, and interaction with the Run-time Variables on the stack. Statements can be interpreted within a suspended execution environment without being added to the code, via Immediate Execution. This facility allows the user to directly utilize the source language rather than learn a new set of commands, and prevents the need to insert extra statements into the code which must later be removed.

With the maximum output of interactive information displayed on the screen (both the Variable Trace window and the Program Trace window on together), Drs. runs at a speed which allows a user to successfully observe program flow. If the user desires a closer monitoring of interpretation, Incremental Execution and Breakpoints are useful.

Drs. is a diagnostic system which utilizes the program text as the input language. The commands are coordinated with those of the SUPPORT system, hence the user need only learn one set of commands to operate the entire integrated programming environment.

SUPPORT is now in use at the University of Maryland on IBM PC's. It is used for the Freshman Pascal for Computer Science majors. Early reactions to the idea are favorable but it is too early for any qualitative results.

5.0 ACKNOWLEDGEMENTS

Partial support for this research was provided by Air Force Office of Scientific Research grant F49620-85-K-00018 to the University of Maryland. Work on the original DEC System 10 version of SUPPORT and on the original DEC VAX 11/780 version began at the Institute for Computer Sciences and Technology of the National Bureau of Standards. Marty Branstad and Gordon Lyon, of NBS, participated in the early design of SUPPORT. Jennifer Drapkin, Larry Herman, David Itkin and Michael Maggio worked on the current version of SUPPORT.

REFERENCES

[FISC84] Fischer, C., Pal, A., Stock, D. L., Johnson, G. F, and Mauney, J. The POE language-based editor project, ACM SIGSOFT Symposium on Practical Software Development Systems, Pittsburgh, PA, April, 1984, (ACM SIGSOFT Notes 9,3 (May, 1984) 21- 29).

[GARL84] Garlan, D. B., and Miller, P. L. GNOME: An introductory programming environment based on a family of structured editors, ACM SIGSOFT Symposium on Practical Software Development Systems, Pittsburgh, PA, April, 1984, (ACM SIGSOFT Notes 9,3 (May, 1984) 42-48).

[LYON84]   Lyon, G., Zelkowitz, M., Elgot, J., Itkin, D., Kowalchack, B., and Maggio, M. Dialogue mechanisms in a table top programming environment, IEEE Fall CompCon 1984, Arlington, VA, Sept, 1984 (Proceedings 33-39) Sept, 1984.

[MAC84]   Macintosh Pascal Users' Guide, Apple Computer Inc. and Think Technologies Inc. 1984.

[MYER80]   Myers, B. A. Displaying data structures for interactive debugging, XEROX Palo Alto Research Center, CSL-80-7, June 1980.

[REIS84]   Reiss, S. Graphical development with PECAN program development systems, ACM SIGSOFT Symposium on Practical Software Development Systems, Pittsburgh, PA, April, 1984, (ACM SIGSOFT Notes 9,3 (May, 1984) 30-41).

[SCHA80]   Schach, S. R. A portable trace for the Pascal heap, Software Practice and Experience, Vol 10, 421-426, 1980.

[SHNE85]   Shneiderman, B., private communications.

[TEIT80]   Teitlebaum, T. The Cornell Program Synthesizer: A tutorial introduction, Dept. of Computer Science, Cornell Univ., Ithaca, N.Y. 1980.

[ZELK84]   Zelkowitz, M. V. A small contribution to editing with a syntax directed editor, ACM SIGSOFT Symposium on Practical Software Development Systems, Pittsburgh, PA, April, 1984, (ACM SIGSOFT Notes 9,3 (May, 1984) 1-6).

QUESTION AND ANSWER PERIOD

LOCKER

How many different windows can be on the screen simultaneously?

KOWALCHACK

We don't allow any window to have less than five lines of window text in it. So that allows three windows at one time on the PC.

LOCKER

So how many covered windows are still around floating in the system?

KOWALCHACK

There are about seven windows, maybe eight. The user has to open them. I think during any debugging session, having three of the debugging windows open at one time gives the user a good view of the program.

THE EFFECT OF GRAPHICAL REPRESENTATION OF PROGRAMMING ON THE CONCEPTUAL BUGS IN NOVICES' PROGRAMS: A COMPARISON OF FPL AND PASCAL

Nancy Cunniff, Robert P. Taylor, and Steven Taylor

Center for Intelligent Tools in Education
Department of Communication, Computing and
Instructional Technology in Education
Teachers College Columbia University
New York, New York 10027

The effect of programming language on the conceptual bugs in novices' programs was studied. Using the graphically represented programming language FPL, students wrote programs to solve a specific problem. The solutions were analyzed and compared to Pascal programs written by students at Yale University in an earlier study. The findings suggest that although some conceptual bugs appear to be language-independent, there seems to be a relationship between language and the occurrence of several types of conceptual bugs. The results indicate that FPL may help novice programmers avoid certain conceptual bugs often observed in Pascal programs. We believe that the graphical representation of FPL may be responsible for some of the differences we observed. Further research is underway to investigate this more fully.

INTRODUCTION

Introductory programming instruction should foster an understanding of the conceptual basis of programming and the development of an ability to solve common programming problems. Studying student performance in programming is one way to appropriately inform the process of designing instruction to achieve these goals. Student performance includes the commission of errors of various kinds and recent work at Yale University has shown study of this area of performance to be rewarding (Soloway, Erlich & Black, 1983; Spohrer, Soloway & Pope, 1985; Spohrer et al., 1984, 1985). That work analyzed programs written in Pascal by students in introductory programming courses and developed a method for classifying and explaining commonly occurring bugs.

At Teachers College we have long been concerned with the improvement of instruction in introductory programming and have developed a unique software vehicle, FPL (First Programming Language) for teaching programming to beginners (Russman and

Taylor, 1975; Taylor, 1977, 1982, 1985). Since proper
understanding of students' errors can also guide us in the
ongoing improvement of FPL, we are always interested in knowing
more about such errors. The Yale research so attracted us that
we decided to begin trying to replicate some of it,
substituting work in FPL for work in Pascal.

We recently reported the results of the first piece of that
replication attempt (Cunniff, Taylor & Black, 1985). It
suggests that novice programmers using FPL may be able to avoid
some of the common bugs observed in similar programs written by
beginners in Pascal. Specifically, beginners working in FPL
avoided certain bugs related to BEGIN END usage in Pascal and
they made fewer bugs in initializing and updating of variables.

Since that first study proved so interesting, we decided to
continue the analysis of FPL by applying a second, more recent
approach developed at Yale. This paper reports these results
and compares the bug patterns observed in FPL programs with
those described in corresponding Yale work on Pascal
programming (Spohrer et al., 1985).

This paper proceeds as follows. First it describes the
language FPL. Next, the bug analysis method developed at Yale
is described. Following that, it catalogues and analyzes the
bugs we found in FPL programs written by novices and compare
them with those reported in a parallel study conducted at
Yale. Finally, it presents our conclusions and the
implications we see for further research.

FIRST PROGRAMMING LANGUAGE

FPL was developed at Teachers College, Columbia University to
teach structured programming to beginners who possessed little
formal problem solving experience. FPL was developed in
response to the needs of such beginners for a programming
language that would help them understand the processes involved
in computing, while giving them a language which allowed them
to write complex programs (Russman and Taylor, 1975).

A Graphical Approach to Programming

One of the unique aspects of FPL is that it is a graphic
language; that is, FPL is built around a set of 11 icons which
are graphical representations of programming concepts. Each
icon represents a specific programming action/concept. Eight
of the icons include text, the variables and constants of the
program. The FPL icons without text imply the flow of control
of a program; the text provides specific values for
manipulation. Figure 1 illustrates the FPL icons and their
corresponding Pascal translations.

A program in FPL consists of icons connected to indicate flow
of control. This unique spatial layout results in a program
"listing" that is actually a drawing. This drawing can be read
in map-like fashion, providing the programmer with a clear
indication of the flow of the program. Conversely, classical

programming languages result in sequential, prose-like program listings which can sometimes hide the flow of control.

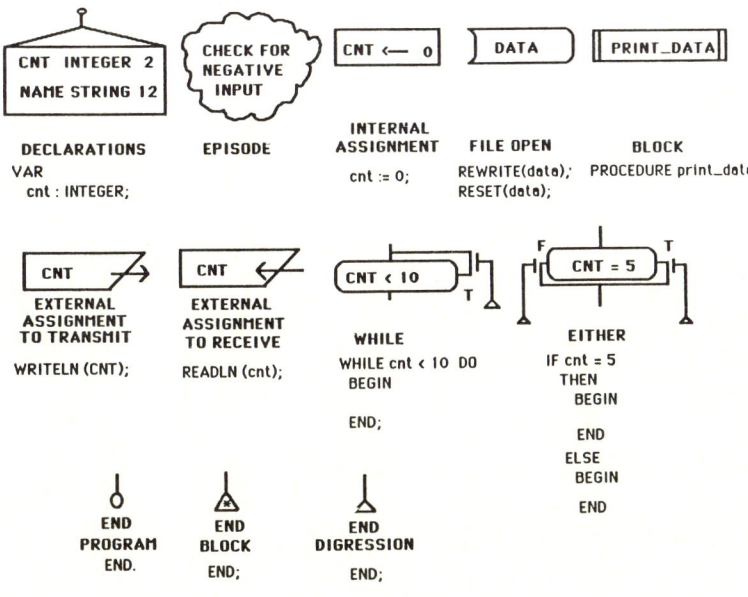

Figure 1

FPL Icons with Pascal Translations

Representation of Programming Structures

FPL is a "thorough introduction to the basic logic structures involved in all programming" (Taylor, 1982, p. vi). Its design focuses on the premise that there is essentially only a small set of concepts involved in all of computer programming. While most languages have multiple structures that can be used to implement similar computing actions, FPL provides just one structure for each major concept. Consequently the student needs to learn only eleven structures in order to write complex programs. This design decision was based on the hypothesis that limiting the number of programming structures that students had to learn would result in better understanding. If students did not have to make decisions about which of several apparently similar structures to use, those structures available would be used more accurately. See Taylor (1982, 1985) for a further discussion of this design.

The FPL Software

Versions of FPL currently run on the DEC20, the VAX and he IBM-PC. These implementations present the user with an interactive graphical interface which presents each programming icon as the user indicates what will occur next in the program flow. The

student enters a program using the FPL software and, upon
completion, the FPL system generates a drawing and an
executable version of the student's program. For comparison
purposes, figure 2 depicts an FPL and a Pascal solution to the
same programming problem.

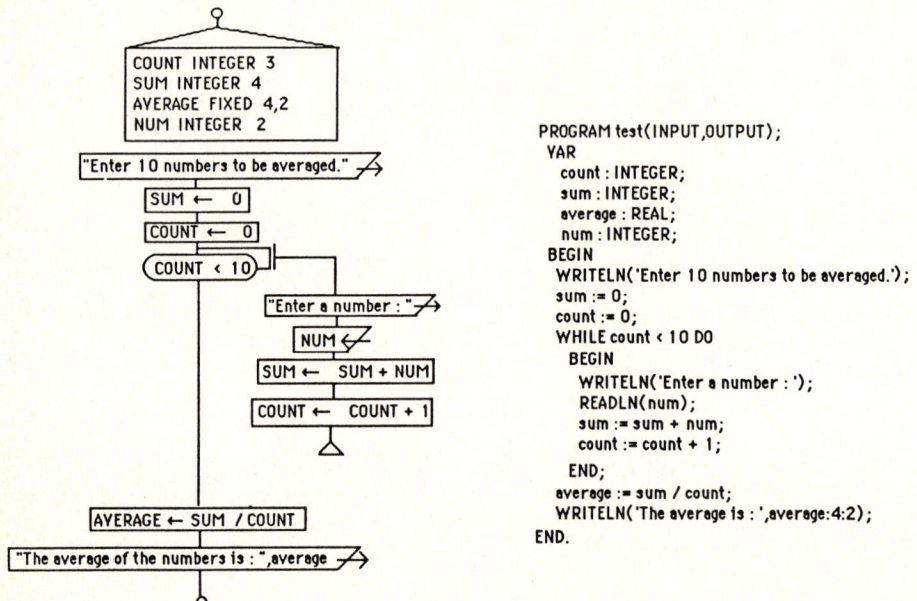

Figure 2

FPL Program and Pascal Translation

CONCEPTUAL BUGS IN NOVICES PROGRAMS

Development of programming skill involves learning syntactic
and conceptual rules. The correct use of a combination of
these two sets of rules can result in errorless programs;
misuse of the rules results in "buggy" programs. Though they
differ for each language and each implementation, syntax rules
are definitive and finite. Although they can cause difficulty
for beginners, bugs related to syntax can be detected and
explained (to some degree) by the compiler or interpreter.

Conversely, conceptual rules (encompassing logic structures and
rules of programming discourse) are more difficult to define;
consequently they are more difficult to teach and learn. Bugs
caused by failure to follow conceptual rules are often hard to
locate and eliminate. They may surface only under certain
input conditions, and, when they do, it may not be clear how
to correct them. Because of this, it is pedagogically
important to understand why and where conceptual bugs commonly
occur so that rules about conceptual bugs can be defined for
novices.

Elliot Soloway and his colleagues at Yale have been studying
bugs in programs written by novice programmers and have
developed a method for analyzing these bugs. Their early work
in bug classification focused on counting and categorizing
conceptual bugs (Johnson, Soloway, Cutler and Draper, 1983).
Recently, they have developed an integrated bug analysis
approach that studies more than just the occurrence of bugs.
This scheme analyzes bugs in relationship to a student's
programming goals and the plans that the student apparently
intended to use. This work is based on the belief that
understanding *why* bugs occur is more important than merely
knowing that they *do* occur, and that an understanding of the
programmer's intentions can aid in accurate analysis of bugs
(Soloway et al., 1983).

They argue that bugs are "properties of the relationship
between programs and intentions ... A programming plan is a
procedure or strategy for realizing intentions in code"
(Soloway and Erlich, 1984). Taking the student's goals and
plans into consideration can help in the understanding and
explaining of the bugs in specific programs. This can lead to
development of broader-based knowledge of students'
misconceptions about the conceptual basis of programming.

To analyze the conceptual bugs, Soloway and his colleagues have
developed an approach which uses "Goal-and-Plan" (GAP) trees to
depict problem solutions. Goal-Plan analysis of conceptual
bugs is subdivided into five categories which are used for bug
classification.

Goal and Plan Trees

A GAP Tree is a schematic diagram of all of the programming
plans which have been used to solve a particular problem
(GOAL). Once a GAP tree has been constructed, a specific
programming solution can be identified by tracing the branches
of the tree which were used in the solution. Bug analysis
using the GAP approach relates specific bugs to specific
programming goals and plans. Consequently, although two bugs
may appear to be similar, an attempt is made to identify more
clearly the cause of the bug rather than just count the
occurrences. This approach is described in detail in *Bug
Catalogue: II, III, IV* (Spohrer et al., 1985). There, novice
programmers' Pascal solutions to several programming problems
are analyzed in detail via GAP tree representations.

Types of Conceptual Bugs

"Exactly what constitutes a bug is not always clear. Some
variations actually cause a program to function incorrectly,
while others are simply inefficient or stylistically
undesirable" (Spohrer et al., 1985, p. 3). Novice programmers
often think of "bugs" as only those problems which prevent
their program from compiling (syntactic bugs) or those which
cause run-time failure. They are unaware of the fact that
there is more to a bug than meets the eye. Many bugs do not
cause program failure or incorrect output, but reflect

misconceptions about program requirements or rules of programming discourse.

To provide a framework for identifying, understanding and explaining conceptual bugs, Spohrer et al. have delineated five categories of conceptual bugs:

> TYPE I: The program does not work or it violates explicit problem specifications
>
> TYPE II: The program violates implicit problem specifications.
>
> TYPE III: The program has redundant, inefficient or totally superfluous fragments of code.
>
> TYPE IV: The program uses an unpreferred plan.
>
> TYPE V: The program uses additional plans to achieve goals which were not asked for, or uses an incorrect plan which cannot achieve the desired goal (1985, p. 4-5).

AN ANALYSIS OF BUGS IN FPL PROGRAMS

Our earlier work suggested that FPL helps students avoid several types of conceptual bugs. That study was based on an early approach to bug classification used at Yale (Johnson et al., 1984). The work at Yale suggested to us that because FPL's design limits students' decisions regarding programming structures, it may help students implement certain programming plans with fewer bugs. We hypothesized that students programming in FPL would have fewer bugs in the actual implementation of some standard programming plans. To test this hypothesis, we chose the "Electric Bill Problem" (see Table 1), one of the problems used in the studies at Yale, and collected FPL solutions to it. Our analysis is based on a comparison of the results of their students' Pascal programs with the FPL programs written by students at Teachers College.

METHOD

Subjects

For this preliminary study, programs were collected from thirteen students enrolled in introductory programming courses at Teachers College. These courses were for non-computer science majors; the majority of the students had little, if any, programming background. Though FPL is the major instructional language, used for most of the students' early programming, all these students also had some experience with Pascal and/or BASIC.

Materials

We analyzed the first computer-compiled FPL solution to the "Electric Bill Problem" written by each student. Figure 3 shows one student's program. We used the terminology and bug explanations outlined by Spohrer et al. (1985) for our analysis. In the discussion of the programs, goals will be identified by "G:" followed by a description of the goal (e.g., G:INPUT). Plans will be preceded by "P:" (e.g., P:PROMPT-EACH).

> An electric company charges its customers by the kilowatt hour (KWH) for electricity used. The cost per KWH decreases as a customer uses more electricity according to the following rate schedule:
>
> 9 cents per KWH for the first 350 KWH
> 6 cents per KWH for the next 250 KWH
> 5 cents per KWH for the next 200 KWH
> 3 cents per KWH for all KWH over 800 KWH
>
> Write a program that reads a customer number and the number of kilowatt hours used by the customer.
>
> Remember to prompt the user to input the ID and KWH used, for example:
> PLEASE INPUT YOUR ID AND KWH USD:
> 23456
> 774.5
>
> Remember to label your output, for example:
> CUSTOMER: 23456
> KWH used : 774.5
> COST: $55.23
>
> Suggestions:
> (1) If you want to say .09 in your program, you should say **0.09**
> (2) In FPL you can only have 2 claims in an EITHER.

Table 1

The "Electric Bill Problem"

Procedure

We analyzed the programs based on the programming goals suggested in the Yale study: VALID-DATA-ENTRY (G:VDE), CALCULATION (G:CALC), and OUTPUT (G:OUTPUT). During the initial analysis of the FPL programs we constructed a GAP tree (see Figure 4) based on a compilation of all of the actual programming plans used by the students to solve the problem in FPL.

RESULTS AND INTERPRETATION

A total of 13 programs were collected and analyzed. Based on the bug descriptions in *Bug Catalogue: II, III, IV,* we observed a total of 42 bugs (see Table 2) in the FPL programs (an average of 3.2 bugs per program). In comparison, in the 61 Pascal programs analyzed by Spohrer et al., 1985 there were 266 total bugs with an average of 4.4 bugs per program. See Table 3 for a summary of FPL and Pascal bugs.

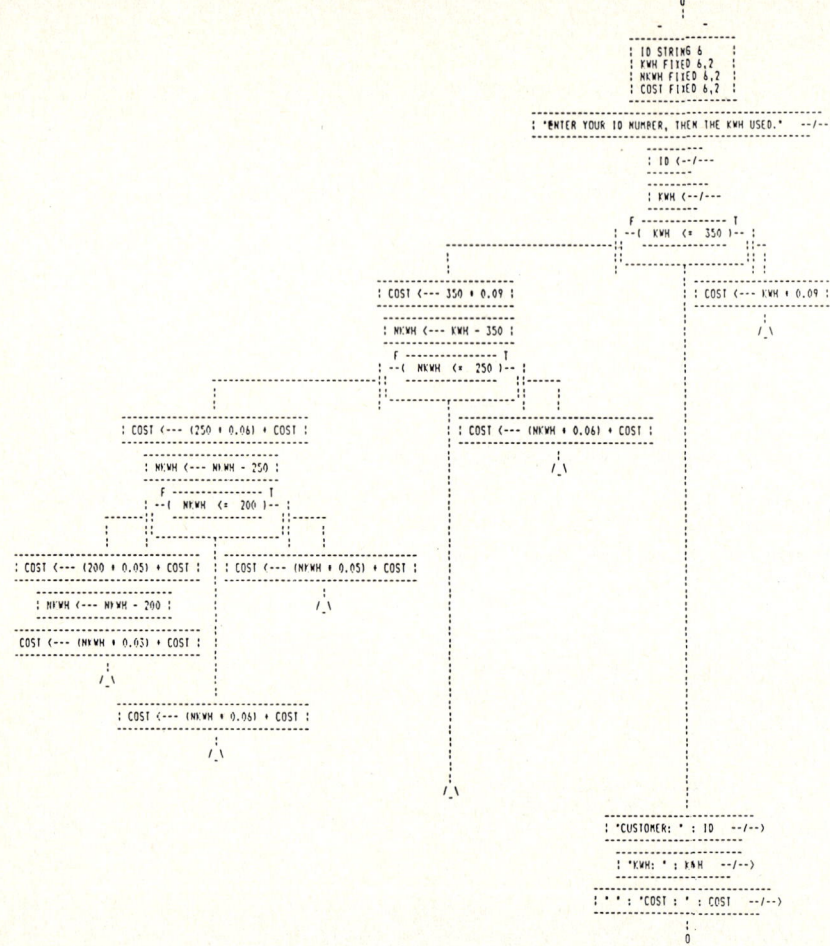

Figure 3

A Student's Solution to the Electric Bill Problem

Our most striking observation is that the 79% of the FPL bugs were related to G:VDE compared to only 44% of the Pascal bugs. Because of the disproportionate distribution of bugs, we reexamined the bugs related to the G:VDE, in an attempt to define the causes and identify possible preventive instructional action.

G:VDE Bugs

In this section we will discuss the 33 FPL and the 116 Pascal bugs related to G:VDE. This goal encompassed such diverse actions as declaration of variables, reading input, and checking for valid data. There were bugs related to each of

these subgoals, but the majority of the FPL bugs were of two
types, choice of programming plans for getting input and
guarding against invalid data.

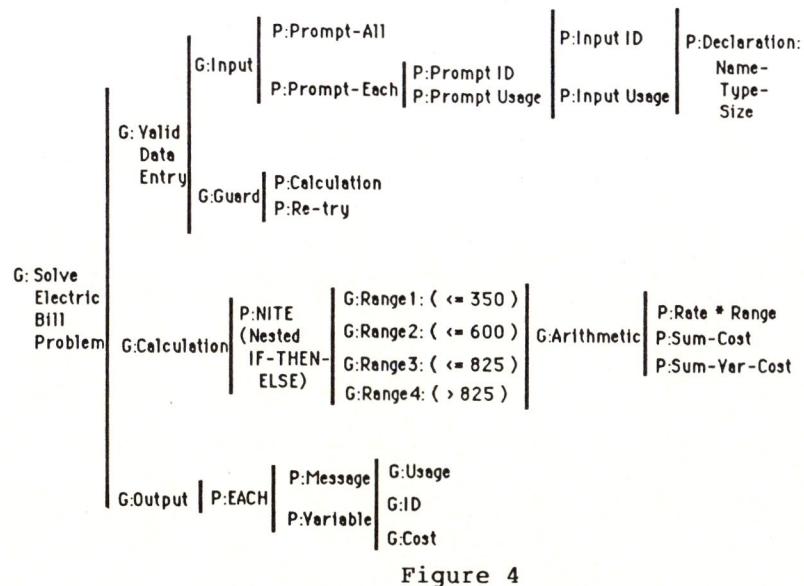

Figure 4

Goals and Plans Used in FPL Solutions
to the Electric Bill Problem

"Unpreferred" Plans

Of the 33 FPL bugs under investigation, 24% (8) fell into the
category of "unpreferred plans" for achieving G:INPUT.
Specifically, this "bug" was the use of individual prompts for
each input (P:PROMPT-EACH) required rather than using one
prompt (P:PROMPT-ALL) and reading in both inputs. (See Figure
5 for examples of both programming plans for this goal.)

Although the problem description used one prompt, most of our
students (62%) used the programming plan that is emphasized in
our courses. This plan requires the use of appropriate prompts
for each input in order to avoid any possible confusion by the
user. Our students' consistent use of this plan indicated that
they had successfully learned a programming plan for achieving
G:INPUT.

Further analysis indicated that all of the FPL students and 98%
of the Pascal students implemented their chosen plan for
G:INPUT without error. We decided that the choice of
programming plan was not really a bug for our students.
Instead, the choice of an alternate plan indicated that the
students really had internalized the programming plan for
G:INPUT that they had been taught. We consequently decided not

to consider this as a bug, and discounted it from the totals in further interpretation.

FPL#	/FREQ		TYPE	PASCAL #/FREQ
2	4	G:VDE:G:INPUT:G:KWH::MALFORMED DCL (INTEGER FOR FIXED)	II	15/5
3	2	G:VDE:G:INPUT::SPURIOUS INIT (ID,COST,KWH)	III	------
4	1	G:VDE:G:INPUT::SPURIOUS INIT (KHW,COST)	III	------
5	1	G:VDE:G:INPUT::SPURIOUS INIT (COST)	III	--------
6	1	G:VDE:G:INPUT:G:LOOP (UNCALLED FOR PLAN)	V	------
7	1	G:OUTPUT:G:KWH,ID,COST::MISSING VARIABLE	I	49/1
8	1	G:OUTPUT::MISSING G:COST	I	------
9	1	G:CALC:G:ARITH::SPURIOUS UPDATE	I	------
10	1	G:CALC::MALFORMED G:RANGE2 (INCORRECT CONST)	I	26/2
11	1	G:CALC:G:RANGE1:G:GUARD::MALFORMED CONDITIONAL (< FOR <=)	I	21/3
12	1	G:VDE:G:GUARD::MISPLACED INPUT (INPUT INSIDED GUARD)	I	48/1
13	1	G:VDE:G:GUARD::MALFORMED GUARD (WHILE FOR EITHER)	I	--------
14	1	G:CALC::MALFORMED PLAN (RUNNING-TOT)	I	17/4
15	1	G:VDE:G:INPUT:G:ID::MALFORMED DCL (SIZE)	II	--------
16	1	G:VDE:G:INPUT:G:COST::MALFORMED DCL (SIZE)	II	--------
17	1	G:CALC:G:RANGE2,3:G:GUARD::MALFORMED CONDITIONAL	III	10/11
18	1	G:CALC:G:RANGE4::SPURIOUS G:GUARD	III	2/26
19	1	G:OUTPUT::G:AVERAGE(UNCALLED FOR PLAN)	V	--------

Table 2

Types and Frequency of Bugs

CHECKING FOR VALID DATA

In our earlier study, we found that the most frequent bug in both FPL and Pascal was a failure to guard against invalid input. We concluded that this was a language-independent bug, and that further investigation was necessary in order to understand the reasons for its frequency and ways of avoiding it (Cunniff et al., 1985). The present study has shed light on this bug situation.

	FPL	PASCAL
# PROGRAMS	13	61
# BUGS	42	266
AVERAGE	3.2	4.4

BUGS BY CONCEPTUAL TYPE

	FPL		PASCAL	
TYPE I	20	(48%)	117	(44%)
TYPE II	6	(14%)	55	(21%)
TYPE III	6	(14%)	46	(17%)
TYPE IV	8	(19%)	36	(13.5%)
TYPE V	2	(5%)	12	(4.5%)

BUGS BY PROGRAMMING GOAL AFFECTED

	FPL		PASCAL	
GOAL: VDE	33	(79%)	116	(44%)
GOAL: CALC	6	(14%)	73	(27%)
GOAL: OUTPUT	3	(7%)	77	(29%)

Table 3

FPL and PASCAL Bugs: Total Occurrences

After discounting the bugs for "unpreferred plans," we were left with 25 FPL bugs and 85 Pascal bugs still related to G:VDE. Investigation of these bugs revealed that in the FPL programs almost half (48%) were caused by failure to check for invalid input and guard against calculation of a bill for a negative input for KWH. All but one of the FPL programs exhibited this bug. Interestingly, of the 85 Pascal bugs related to VALID-DATA-ENTRY, only 9% (10 bugs) were MISSING GUARD BUGS. We surmised that this considerable discrepancy might be also explained by the instruction given our students.

As we suspected, checking for valid data has not been emphasized in the introductory courses taken by these subjects, therefore it would be unexpected for them to employ such a guard in their programs. By contrast, we have some indication from reading other problems used in the programming courses at Yale, that an awareness of invalid data is emphasized in these courses (e.g., Spohrer et al., 1985, p. 84). We think that this instructional emphasis may account for the fact that so many of the Pascal students employed a check for valid data.

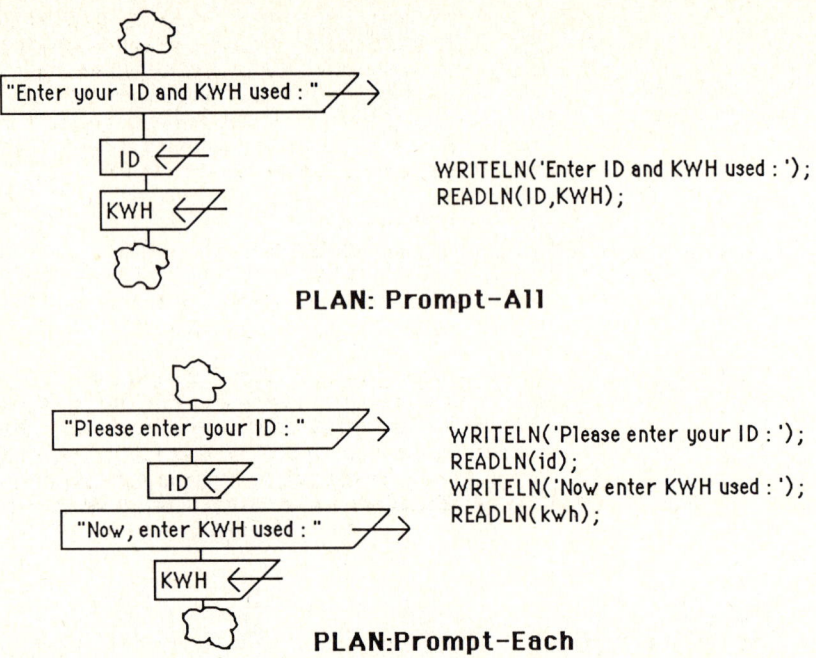

Figure 5

Plans for GOAL:Input

It seems that the novice programmer is initially unaware of the need to guard against invalid input. Such checking requires the programmer to be acutely aware of the possible actions of the potential user, maintaining multiple points of view while programming. Pea (1984) has labelled bugs relating to such situations "egocentrism bugs," suggesting that the novice programmer thinks the computer can fill in missing information in much the same way as a human listener does.

Our results seem to indicate that unless students are taught to check for valid data, they will not implement guards in their programs. Consequently, we feel that MISSING GUARD bugs are directly related to instruction rather than either student misconceptions or language design. We therefore further adjusted the bug totals, eliminating these "bugs" from consideration, too.

BONA FIDE BUGS

With the elimination of the bugs discussed above, we were left with 22 bugs in the FPL programs (an average of 1.69 per program) and 225 Pascal bugs (an average of 3.69 per program). Although we have analyzed only a small number of programs, this large difference in average number of bugs may

suggest that the use of FPL results in fewer bugs in a
student's initial programming session. Table 4 summarizes the
distribution of these remaining bugs by GOAL and by TYPE.

	FPL	PASCAL
# PROGRAMS	13	61
# BUGS	22	225
AVERAGE	1.69	3.69

BUGS BY CONCEPTUAL TYPE

	FPL		PASCAL	
TYPE I	8	(37%)	107	(48%)
TYPE II	6	(27%)	55	(24.5%)
TYPE III	6	(27%)	46	(20.5%)
TYPE IV	0	(---)	5	(2%)
TYPE V	2	(9%)	12	(5%)

BUGS BY PROGRAMMING GOAL AFFECTED

	FPL		PASCAL	
GOAL: VDE	13	(69%)	85	(38%)
GOAL: CALC	6	(27%)	73	(34%)
GOAL: OUTPUT	3	(14%)	77	(32%)

Table 4

FPL and Pascal "Bona-Fide" Bugs

The remaining bugs will be examined and discussed in terms of
the three major programming goals of the Electric Bill problem,
G:VDE, G:CALC, and G:OUTPUT. We will propose explanations of
the most frequently observed bugs, and make some suggestions
about the effect that language may have had upon the occurrence
of these bugs.

Goal:Input

The Pascal bugs were equally distributed over the three major
program goals; the majority of the FPL bugs still fell into the
GOAL:INPUT category.

Most of the G:VDE bugs in FPL (46%) were related to the
declaration of variables (G:VDE:G:INPUT::MALFORMED
DECLARATION). This was also a fairly common Pascal bug (31% of
the G:VDE bugs). This may reflect novices' uncertainty about
the specificity of data types. It also may be partially
explained by FPL's requirement that when declaring a variable,

the user must not only specify the dataname and type, but must also indicate the maximum size of the variable (e.g., ID INTEGER 5 indicates that the dataname ID can be assigned an INTEGER value up to and including five digits). This approach may reduce the number of bugs related to output (specifically of data typed REAL in Pascal) but seems to increase the bugs related to input.

The results suggest that dealing with input, specifically in an interactive program, may be problematic for novices. The variety of bugs in this area and the small number of programs analyzed prevents us from isolating a specific cause of confusion, but suggests that programming plans for dealing with the general goal of data entry may require more instructional emphasis.

Goal:Output

Only 14% of the FPL bugs were related to the goal of output, in comparison to 32% of the Pascal bugs. We think this is a result of FPL's inclusion of a decimal data type (called FIXED), requiring the programmer to define the fields of a real number at the time of declaration. In Pascal, this field definition must be included in the output statements. Although this feature of FPL accounted for a small number of G:VDE bugs (that is, incorrect size declaration), 51% of the Pascal G:OUTPUT bugs were caused by missing or inaccurate field specification. This is a language-specific bug indicating a limitation of Pascal for the types of problems beginners are assigned. The problem is apparently eliminated by FPL's incorporation of the data type FIXED.

Goal:Calculation

The third goal involved in the Electric Bill problem was that of the calculation (G:CALC) of the BILL. To accomplish this goal, the student was expected to use a series of nested EITHERs in FPL and a NESTED-IF-THEN-ELSE (P:NITE) in Pascal. All of the FPL solutions used the appropriate plan while only 82% of the 61 Pascal programs implemented the preferred plan. We think that this may be a direct result of the design of FPL, which provides only one structure for decision making.

Although the percentage of bugs related to G:CALC were approximately the same in FPL and PASCAL (27% in FPL, 34% in Pascal) the distribution of the bugs was quite different. Of the FPL bugs, 33% were directly related to the formation of the EITHER, while 67% were arithmetic (e.g., incorrect constants or relational symbols).The pattern of bugs in the Pascal programs was almost exactly the opposite. Of the 73 bugs in the Pascal) solutions, 69% were related to the formation of the IF-THEN-ELSE structure while only 31% were arithmetic in nature.

The arithmetic bugs in both languages seem to be caused by misreading or misunderstanding the problem (using incorrect constants for range delimiters) and failing to use appropriate arithmetic symbols (parentheses for determining order of operations, < for <=). It seems plausible that these bugs are not related to programming at all, but reflect students' computational and problem solving misconceptions. Conversely, bugs in structuring of the EITHER and the IF-THEN-ELSE are directly related to an understanding of the programming language.

CONCLUSION

Based on the small number of programs analyzed, it is not possible to make definitive judgments about the relationship of programming language and non-syntactic bugs. However the results of this preliminary study suggest that novices using FPL make fewer conceptual bugs than students using Pascal and also suggest several interesting implications for the teaching of programming:

1. Some G:VDE bugs may generally be language-independent (related to instruction and experience) and not reducible by choice of programming language. This possibility suggests that such bugs are caused by misconception and not misuse of language features.

    One approach for remediating this problem may be to provide novices with experiences using and testing others' programs rather than merely creating their own.

2. Some G:OUTPUT bugs are language-specific (related to the idiosyncracies of languages). The structure of FPL apparently eliminates an output bug frequently observed in Pascal (failure to specify field size in output of data typed REAL). Eliminating the cause of any frequently occurring bug is certainly desirable. Although this may seem to be a trivial bug, it is obviously an indication of student misunderstanding which can be eliminated.

    Identification of common language-specific bugs should, in the long run, lead to the modification of language features. A short-term solution for programming instruction is selection of an alternative introductory language.

3. The implementation of programming plans for decision making involves the integration of many programming concepts. FPL's single decision-making structure (the EITHER) apparently makes implementation of such complex actions easier for novices. When novices must choose from among a set of functionally related and overlapping constructs as they must with Pascal (i.e., IF...THEN and IF...THEN...ELSE) they are likely to err. Our results suggest that FPL's simple, non-overlapping concept embodiment is less confusing for beginners.

This study suggests that FPL may make learning programming easier for novices. We think that our preliminary results suggest that another study, with a much larger group of students, would prove very rewarding. We plan to pursue this. We have also begun to investigate whether FPL's iconic structure makes programming concepts easier to understand and remember.

One point that should not be overlooked is that our results, together with those reported from Yale, indicate that certain frequently occurring bugs seem to be language-independent. This implies that the content of introductory programming courses should not have coding issues as a sole focus. Rather, there should be multiple foci, including problem solving and human-computer interaction.

Finally, our results have emphasized to us the importance of multi-language studies for research on the learning and teaching of programming. It seems clear that such studies will point out advantages and disadvantages of specific languages, and will lead us to a better understanding of students' conceptual development.

REFERENCES

Cunniff, N., Taylor, R. P., and Black, J. B. (1985). *Does programming language affect the types of conceptual bugs in novices' programs? A comparison of FPL and Pascal.* Proceedings of SIGCHI '86, pp 175-182.

Johnson, W. L., Soloway, E., Cutler, B., & Draper, S. (1983). *Bug Catalogue I.* (Tech. Rep. No. 286). New Haven CT: Yale University, Department of Computer Science.

Pea, R. D. (1984). *Language independent conceptual "bugs" in novice programming.* (Tech. Rep. No. 31). NY: Bank Street College, Center for Children and Technology.

Russman, G. M. & Taylor, R. P. (1975). A compiler-free approach to developing fundamental programming skills. In O. Lecarme & R. Lewis (Eds.), *Computers in education* (pp. 63-67).

Soloway, E. & Erlich, K. (1984). Empirical studies of programming knowledge. *IEEE Transactions on Software Engineering.* SE-11:3. pp. 267-275.

Soloway, E., Erlich, K. & Black J. B. (1983). Beyond numbers: Don't ask "How many"... ask "Why." *Proceedings of SIGCHI'83.* 240-246.

Spohrer, J., Soloway, E. & Pope, E. (1985). A goal-plan analysis of buggy Pascal programs. *Human Computer Interaction 1*, pp. 163 - 207.

Spohrer, J., Pope, E., Lipman, M., Sack, W., Freiman, S., Littman, D., Johnson, L., & Soloway, E. (1984). *Bugs in novice programs and misconceptions in novice programmers*. New Haven, CT: Yale University, Department of Computer Science.

Spohrer, J., Pope, E., Lipman, M., Sack, W., Freiman, S., Littman, D., Johnson, L. & Soloway, E. (1985). *Bug Catalogue: II, III, IV.* (Tech. Rep. No. 386). New Haven, CT: Yale University, Department of Computer Science.

Spohrer, J., Soloway, E. & Pope, E. (1985). Where the bugs are. *Proceedings of CHI'85*, pp. 47-53.

Taylor, R. P. (1977). Teaching programming to beginners. *SIGCSE Bulletin.* 9 :1, pp. 88-92.

Taylor, R. P. (1982). *Programming primer*. Reading, MA: Addison-Wesley.

Taylor, R. P. (1985). *FPL: Graphical representation of classical programming*. (Manuscript in submission.)

QUESTION AND ANSWER PERIOD

RICH

This question has to do with a number of comments that were made both yesterday and today about the difficulties of displaying complicated pictures on small screens. I think I saw in your list of boxes one with two lines on each end which was labeled BLOCK. Does that mean that I can summarize one of these detail pictures as a block and get a top down view of my whole program?

CUNNIFF

Yes.

RICH

Could you say a word about how useful your students find that?

CUNNIFF

At the moment that is only a part of the pencil and paper version of FPL; we're just getting it running up on the system. They use it quite frequently in their planning and it helps to narrow down the scope of the whole program. You can have a whole series of procedure calls, and the procedures on your paper can be on another page and you can go and look at them. It turns out to be a really useful way of organizing things for them.

BOUDREAUX

It strikes me that the system that you've described here is one which makes use of icons, pictures which are intended to give the people who use the system a conceptual idea. Have you tested the effect of different representations, different icons if you have a concept like iteration? Have you tested the effect of using different pictures and how that affects the students' errors?

TAYLOR

We haven't done any Shneiderman research on that. What we've done is less formal. This system has been around for a long time in paper and pencil form, and the development of it was based on student errors with original conceptions, the way we represented things like WHILE and EITHER. We've done some quick research lately and we expect to follow it up in the fall with more extended work on long-time users to see what they remember. We have found that they seem to remember what the symbols stood for, but they can't tell you what the names were anymore.

The other aspect of that which is interesting -- there was an IEEE issue on computer graphics about a year ago, I think, in which somebody from DEC summarized some information on iconic representation and talked about abstract, representational, and sort of in-between as being the three options. Again, there's no research on it; that's why we're interested in this whole area and try to get as much out of it as we can to help ourselves and others understand. It appears, from crude research at least, that if the people can accept the idea, if it's clear enough to be acceptable, it doesn't really have to look like, say, a loop to represent repetition as long as it's a clear idea. So what we've modified over a long period of time were those return passes and everything, so that you can see the difference between the WHILE and the EITHER, for example. Apart from that, we're going to do more research on that but don't have any hard data; that was done by examining student papers and seeing what they did wrong.

LANGUAGES AND SOFTWARE PARTS
FOR ELLIPTIC BOUNDARY-VALUE PROBLEMS

Ronald F. Boisvert

Center for Applied Mathematics
National Bureau of Standards
Gaithersburg, Maryland 20899

Advances in numerical analysis have lead to the development of software for solving increasingly complex mathematical problems. Unfortunately, this has meant an increase in the complexity of the user interface, especially in the case of subprograms in general-purpose, procedural languages like Fortran where such software is almost exclusively available. As a result, high-level applications-oriented interfaces to such software are beginning to emerge. In this paper we describe such a system, called ELLPACK, for elliptic boundary-value problems. The ELLPACK system is characterized by a carefully-designed software parts technology for the problem domain combined with a high-level language which allows users to declare problem components using natural mathematical notation and to easily invoke modules for various stages of the solution process. We also describe how ELLPACK is being used as the kernel for sophisticated problem-solving environments involving graphics workstations, expert systems, and supercomputer networks.

1.0   LANGUAGES AND MATHEMATICAL SOFTWARE PARTS

1.1   Mathematical Software

The packaging of algorithms for the solution of mathematical problems as portable Fortran subprograms has been vigourously exploited by the mathematical software community over the past 15 years. The success of commercial libraries such as IMSL [1] and NAG [9] attests to the widespread acceptance of this technique in the scientific community. Advances in numerical analysis over these years have lead to the ability to solve more and more complex problems; unfortunately these problems have become more and more difficult to specify within the confines of general-purpose procedural languages such as Fortran. The following examples illustrate this problem.

Evaluation of special functions
Computation of scalar-valued functions fits naturally into the subprogram model. A Fortran function call like Y = BESJ0(X) might be used to evaluate the 0-th order Bessel function of the first kind at the point X.

Evaluation of definite integrals
We wish to compute the value of the definite integral of a continuous function of one variable over a bounded interval to within a given tolerance. This is a much more difficult problem; one of the inputs is a function whose form is not known a priori. The user interface is still readily handled within the confines of Fortran, however. A subroutine call like CALL INTGRL (FCN,A,B,TOL,RESULT,INFO) might be used to integrate FCN(X) on the interval [A,B] to tolerance TOL; the answer is returned in RESULT and an error code is returned in INFO.

Solution of partial differential equations
Here the problem might be to determine a function u(x,y) which satisfies a certain differential equation on an irregular bounded region in the plane on whose boundaries certain side conditions must be satisfied. In spite of the difficulty of this problem, Fortran subprograms for solving it are now becoming available [5]. Unfortunately, there is little support within Fortran for naturally describing such problems. The domain may be described implicitly by storing information in a two-dimensional array which corresponds to points on a covering grid. Multiple functions need to be written for coefficients of the differential equations and for each of the boundary conditions. The solution might be returned as a set of values at grid points. Such an interface is quite detailed, easily requiring a subprogram call of 30 to 40 arguments, and is certainly unnatural from a mathematical viewpoint.

1.2   Very-High-Level Languages

One solution to this problem is to increase the power of the programming language. Most languages currently used for scientific computing allow one to naturally express constructs at the level of algebra and trigonometry, whereas complex mathematical problems require the ability to express objects used in the calculus such as derivatives and integrals, and correspondingly high-level operators to manipulate them; algorithms for their solution require matrices and vectors, along with associated operators of linear algebra. Rice [14] has detailed the types of facilities that would be required by such a language. (Such facilities could be built into a language with support for abstract data types, like ADA or Pascal-SC [10].)

A new language however would require the large and carefully crafted body of mathematical software now available be redesigned and rewritten. A more modest approach is to extend Fortran (through the use of a preprocessor) so that this software is more easily accessible. IMSL Inc. has produced such an interface to their subroutine library [15]. IMSL's PROTRAN has declarations for vectors and matrices along with

simple linear algebraic operators for manipulating them, as
well as complex problem-solving statements like APPROXIMATE
(for data fitting), INTEGRATE (for numerical integration), and
DIFEQU (for solving ordinary differential equations). The
PROTRAN preprocessor translates these statements into calls on
appropriate routines from the IMSL library.

1.3   Software Parts Technology

In order for such a system to be built, the underlying software
must conform to certain standards. Such standards for the
reusability of software are the basis for a software parts
technology [2,18]. Simply stated, a software part is a program
for performing a well-defined computational task. The form of
its input and output are rigidly set in such a way that various
parts can be joined together to perform more complex tasks. Of
course, a necessary condition is that the target problem area
be naturally decomposible into subtasks which are each useful
in a variety of contexts. The software tools of the UNIX
system, for example, are components of a reusable software
parts technology for a software development system.

A software part has three identifiable components (see Fig.
1). The prologue first determines whether its input is
admissible; it then transforms its input into a form more
suitable to the algorithm which it employs. The nucleus
performs the computational task associated with the part.
Finally, the epilogue transforms the output of the algorithm
into the standard format required by parts of its type.

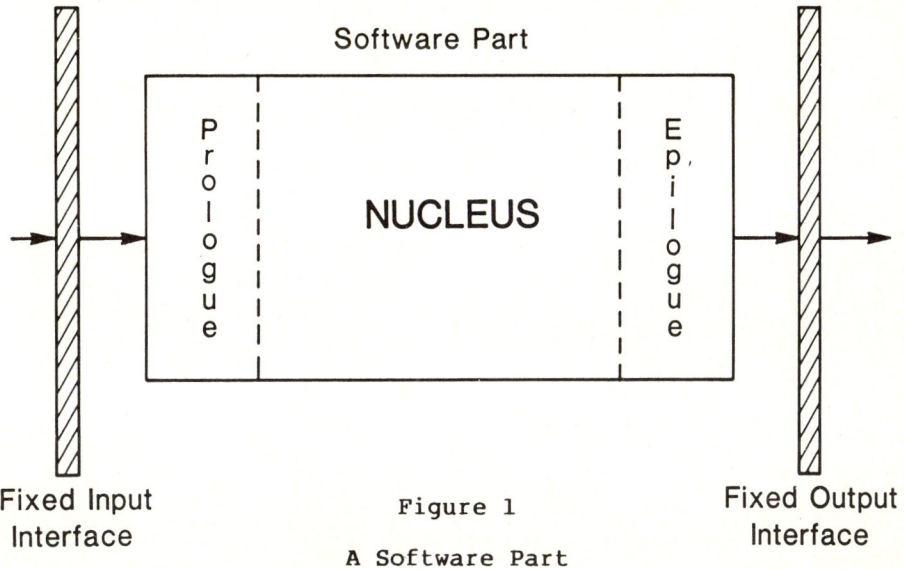

Figure 1

A Software Part

There are several other requirements for reusability. The
algorithm must be robust; it must perform well near the
boundaries of its problem domain; it should be able to detect

failure and fail gracefully. Documentation for the part must be provided which explains clearly what the part does and how it does it. Performance of the part must have been systematically measured and reported.

1.4 Problem-Solving Environments

A problem-solving environment (PSE) is the result of combining a rich collection of software parts for a particular applications area with a very-high-level user interface. Several such systems have existed within the statistical community for a number of years, e.g. DATAPLOT [8] and MINITAB [17]. Few such systems currently exist within the mathematical software community; a notable exception is MATLAB [11], an interactive PSE built on software from the widely-used LINPACK subroutine package [7].

In the remainder of this paper we describe the ELLPACK system in some detail. ELLPACK is a PSE which solves elliptic boundary-value problems. We begin with a short introduction to the problem area and then briefly outline the nature of the ELLPACK language and its problem-solving modules. We conclude with a discussion of how the ELLPACK system affects the nature of elliptic problem solving and the possible role of such a system in more sophisticated PSEs with access to distributed computing networks and expert systems.

2.0 ELLIPTIC BOUNDARY-VALUE PROBLEMS

Elliptic boundary-value problems describe the equilibrium states of physical systems. These problems require the determination of a function which satisfies a given differential equation inside a bounded region along with additional conditions on the boundary of the region. Such problems occur regularly in the physical sciences and engineering. For example, the solution to such a problem might represent the temperature distribution in a room in which some walls are held at certain fixed temperatures and other walls insulated, or the lateral deflection of a (nearly horizontal) membrane stretched over a rigid frame and supporting a given load. In this section we briefly describe the basic components of such problems and the numerical methods which solve them. For simplicity we restrict ourselves to linear second-order equations defined on two-dimensional regions.

2.1 Problem Components

The most general linear second-order elliptic equation takes the form

$$au_{xx} + 2bu_{xy} + cu_{yy} + du_x + eu_y + fu = g$$

where a, b, c, d, e, f, g, and u are each functions of x and y, and subscripts denote partial differentiation. (The condition $b^2 < ac$ must be satisfied for "ellipticity".) Much terminology is associated with such equations. For example, if a=c=1,

b=d=e=0 and f is constant we have the Helmholtz equation; if in
addition f=0 we have Poisson's equation, and if g=0 also we
have Laplace's equation.

In an elliptic boundary-value problem one is given all functions except u, whose value must be determined in the interior
of a given bounded two-dimensional region called the domain.
In order for the problem to have a unique solution certain
additional conditions must be specified along the boundary of
the region. The most general form of such a condition is

$$pu_n + qu = r$$

where p, q, and r are functions of x and y, and subscript n
denotes the derivative of u in the direction of the outward-
pointing normal vector to the boundary. When p=0 we have a so-
called Dirichlet problem, and when q=0 we have a Neumann
problem.

The actual "answer" sought from such a problem depends heavily
upon the application. Typical examples are a plot of the function u over the domain, the value of u at a few isolated
points, the derivatives of u along the boundary, or the
integral of u along a certain path. The choice of numerical
method is often affected by the desired output, and general-
purpose software for such problems must have some way of
accommodating such user needs.

2.2   Numerical Methods

There a now a great variety of techniques for the numerical
solution to elliptic boundary-value problems, and we cannot
hope to adequately describe them here; see [3] for a recent
survey. Instead we shall briefly outline the basic components
of most methods in order to aid the understanding of the
functionality of the ELLPACK system.

Most numerical methods are composed of two distinct phases:
discretization and solution. In the discretization phase the
continuous problem is replaced by a discrete one which is more
amenable to computer solution, i.e., the solution of a system
of linear algebraic equations. The algebraic system is solved
in the solution phase. There are a large variety of numerical
methods for each of these phases.

Discretization methods are based upon the imposition of a grid
over the domain. Finite difference discretizations replace the
differential equation at each grid point by a difference equation approximating it; the unknowns in the system are the
values of the solution at the grid points. There are many
different ways to approximate a differential equation by finite
differences, and each leads to a discretization with different
properties. Finite element discretizations write the solution
as a linear combination of piecewise polynomial functions with
unknown coefficients. The requirement that the coefficients be
chosen so that the resulting function is a best approximation
to the solution again leads to a system of linear algebraic

equations whose unknowns are the desired coefficients. Of course, there are various ways to measure the "goodness" of an approximating function, and these lead to quite distinct discretizations.

The system of linear algebraic equations obtained in the discretization phase is nearly always very large and sparse (i.e., most of the elements of the corresponding matrix are zero). Solution methods can be divided into two classes: direct and iterative. Direct methods are generally based upon Gauss elimination, but are always modified to account for sparsity, such modifications being complicated by the fact that new non-zeros are generated during the course of the computation. Iterative methods have the advantage that no extra non-zeros are generated during the course of the computation and hence storage management is less of a problem, but the exact solution is not obtained in a finite time, and hence considerable effort has been expended to design iterative methods which converge quickly and to develop criteria with which to decide whether a solution with a desired accuracy has been attained.

Several other operations are routinely found as components of numerical methods for elliptic problems. For example, solution phase algorithms can often be improved greatly by a reordering of equations and unknowns; many such reorderings are possible. Initial approximations for the solution are necessary when iterative methods are used; these may be specified, or generated automatically by some rough approximation method.

3.0   ELLPACK

The ELLPACK project began in 1975 with the aim of developing an environment to facilitate the exchange of software parts for elliptic problems among numerical analysts. The project has had some 13 principle participants from both universities and scientific laboratories since that time, with substantial contributions from about 20 others; the project was coordinated by John R. Rice of Purdue University. The great complexity of the resulting Fortran software parts environment lead to the development of a preprocessor which allowed users to describe elliptic problems in a more natural way and to invoke software parts by simply giving their name. The preprocessor generates a Fortran program which sets up the initial interface and calls the necessary software parts (problem-solving modules). The entire system, including the preprocessor and some 50 problem-solving modules, is written in portable Fortran.

ELLPACK solves general linear elliptic problems with general linear boundary conditions on general two-dimensional domains and in three-dimensional boxes. The nature of the language design, however, has led to the ability to solve many more complicated problems than were envisioned in the original design. ELLPACK has now been distributed to well over 200 sites worldwide, and has been found quite useful in solving routine to moderately difficult problems encountered in applications, for teaching courses in the numerical analysis of

partial differential equations, and for experimental studies of
the performance of numerical methods and software for elliptic
problems.

In this section we will briefly describe the ELLPACK language,
the nature of the software parts technology underlying it, and
the construction of the language preprocessor. Complete
details on the use and the implementation of ELLPACK may be
found in [12].

3.1   Language Elements

An ELLPACK program is divided into segments; the basic segments
are summarized below.

EQUATION
Declaration. Defines the partial differential equation using
mathematical notation. The keywords UXX, UX, etc. refer to the
derivative of the solution function U; coefficients may be any
Fortran arithmetic expressions. Example: UXX + 5*UYY -
F(X,Y)*U = EXP(X+Y).

BOUNDARY
Declaration. Defines the problem domain and the boundary
conditions which must be satisfied there. The boundary is
divided into a sequence of smooth pieces which join up
continuously; these are described parametrically. There are
shorthands for rectangular domains and for straight line pieces
in nonrectangular ones. Example: U=0 ON X=COS(PI*T),
Y=SIN(PI*T), FOR T=0 TO 1.

GRID
Executable. Places a user-defined grid on the domain.
Example: 13 X POINTS 0 TO 1 $ 25 Y POINTS -1 TO 1. Both
uniformly-spaced and non-uniformly spaced grid may be
specified.

DISCRETIZE
Executable. Calls a discretization module specified by the
user. This module generates a system of linear algebraic
equations which is a discrete representation of the problem.
Many such modules are available.

SOLVE
Executable. Calls a solution module specified by the user.
This module solves the linear algebraic system. Many such
modules are available.

OUTPUT
Executable. Generates printed and plotted output selected by
the user. After a SOLVE segment is executed the functions U,
UX, UXX, etc. become defined, and may be used as arguments to
the TABLE and PLOT verbs of the output segment. Any
user-defined function of two real variables defined on the
domain can be printed or plotted in this way. Example:
TABLE(UY) $ PLOT(U)

SUBPROGRAMS
Declaration. User-defined Fortran subprograms. Functions referred to in the EQUATION, BOUNDARY, and OUTPUT segments are defined here.

ELLPACK syntax is best illustrated with an example. The following ELLPACK program generates a contour plot of the function satisfying Laplace's equation with Dirichlet boundary conditions on the quarter of the unit circle in the first quadrant. The problem is discretized using standard finite differences (5-POINT STAR) and the linear system is solved using Jacobi iteration with conjugate gradient acceleration (JACOBI CG).

```
*        ---------------------------------------------
*            SAMPLE ELLPACK SOLUTION OF LAPLACE'S EQUATION
*        ---------------------------------------------

EQUATION.    UXX + UYY = 0

BOUNDARY.    U=G(X)         ON X=COS(T), Y=SIN(T) FOR T=0 TO PI/2
             U=1-Y          ON LINE 0,1 TO 0,0
             U=1-X          ON LINE 0,0 TO 1,0

GRID.        33 X POINTS    0 TO 1
             33 Y POINTS    0 TO 1

DIS.         5-POINT STAR
SOLVE.       JACOBI CG (ITMAX=200)

OUTPUT.      PLOT(U)

SUB.
             REAL FUNCTION G(X)
             REAL X, S, PIOV2
             S = ACOS(X)
             PIOV2 = 2.0*ATAN(1.0)
             G = S*(PIOV2-S)
             RETURN
             END
END.
```

Note that segments may be made up of several statements, each separated by a newline (or $). Segment names must start in column one; the rest of the segment is in free format. Comments are denoted by a *. Segment names may be abbreviated to three characters. The last line of an ELLPACK program is END. Modules may have keyword parameters, and all parameters have defaults; the parameter ITMAX specifies the maximum number of iterations to perform. Arithmetic expressions use Fortran syntax; the unknown function is denoted by U and its derivatives by UX, UXY, etc. The SUBPROGRAMS segment defines user functions referred to elsewhere in the program. There are several additional types of problem-solving modules and language segments to invoke them. With the INDEX segment users specify a module which renumbers the equations and unknowns of the linear system; such renumberings often greatly speed up

solution algorithms. Some algorithms for special problems
(e.g., the Helmholtz equation on a rectangle) do not have a
clear delineation between discretization and solution; multi-
grid and Fourier methods are of this type. Such combination
modules are invoked with the TRIPLE segment. It is often
desirable to perform various ancillary tasks when solving
elliptic equations. Examples of these are computing the
eigenvalues of the discretization matrix, displaying the
nonzero pattern of the discretization matrix, and providing an
initial estimate of the solution for an iterative methods. The
PROCEDURE segment is used to invoke modules of this type.

3.2 Preprocessor Design

The ELLPACK preprocessor reads an ELLPACK program and translates it into a Fortran program which performs all the
requested tasks; the generated Fortran program is called the
ELLPACK control program. The preprocessor does its job in
three phases (see Fig. 2):

System Definition
Read a file which describes the characteristics of the problem-
solving modules.

Analysis
Read the user's ELLPACK program and parse it to determine the
characteristics of the problem to be solved and the sequence of
modules to be executed.

Code Generation
Generate the ELLPACK control program.

The first and third phases are accomplished by executing a
Fortran-aware macro processor [16]. In phase one a macro is
read which initializes the preprocessor's symbol table and
provides macro definitions for Fortran code to be generated for
all the modules in the current ELLPACK system. During the
second phase the symbol table is updated with information
describing the elliptic problem to be solved and the problem-
solving modules to be invoked. In the final phase a macro
giving the form of the control program is read and expanded
based upon the final contents of the symbol table. The files
read during the first and third phase are called templates. A
major portion of the lexical/syntactic analyser which makes up
the second preprocessing phase is generated automatically by a
compiler-compiler system called PG [6], which is specifically
designed for the generation of Fortran preprocessors.

The major advantage of this design is the ease with which the
ELLPACK system can be changed. Substantial changes to the form
of the control program, including addition and deletion of
problem-solving modules, can be made by simply changing the
template files; no change to the grammar which defines the
language is usually necessary.

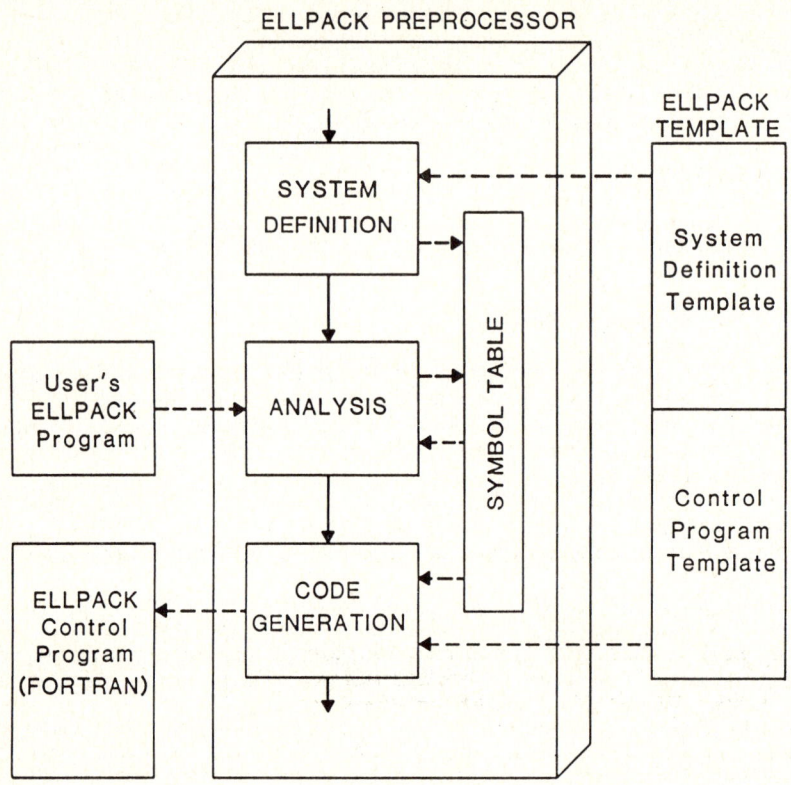

Figure 2

Organization of the ELLPACK preprocessor

3.3 ELLPACK Software Parts Environment

The ELLPACK system is a successful realization of a software parts technology for elliptic boundary-value problems. Within the ELLPACK environment there are seven module types and five inter-module interfaces. The ELLPACK module interfaces are:

Problem Definition
The inital interface. Describes the partial differential equation, the domain, boundary conditions, the user-specified grid, and a number of global control variables. (Generated by the ELLPACK control program).

Discrete Domain
A discrete representation of the domain. Relates all grid points to the domain and describes all boundary-grid intersections. (Generated by the domain processor.)

Discrete Operator
A discrete representation of the differential equation and
boundary conditions. This is a system of linear algebraic
equations in a particular sparse storage format. (Generated by
discretization modules.)

Equation/Unknown Reordering
Permutation vectors giving an alternate ordering for equations
and unknowns of the linear algebraic system. (Generated by
renumbering modules.)

Linear Algebraic Solution
The solution vector to the linear algebraic system. (Generated
by solution modules and triple modules.)

Modules of a given type read variables from a specific initial
interface and write all variables at a specific final interface. The five basic module types are illustrated in Figure 3
along with their starting interfaces, stopping interfaces, and
the ELLPACK language segment which invokes them. Two additional module types are defined: triple modules, which begin at the
discrete domain interface and end at linear algebraic solution,
are used to implement fast elliptic solvers for specialized
problems, and procedure modules, which may read any interface
and write none, are used to perform various utility tasks. In
all, the system has 9 discretization modules, 7 reordering
modules, 18 solution modules, 16 triple modules, and 11
procedure modules.

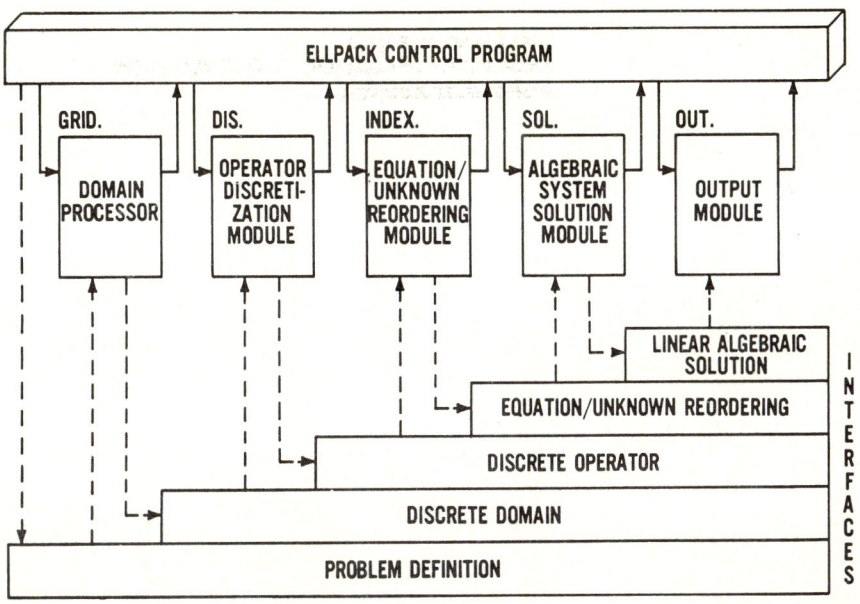

Figure 3

Modules and Interfaces in ELLPACK

The ELLPACK Contributor's Guide (Part 4 of [12]) provides a
detailed specification of the data structures which make up
these interfaces. Part 2 of [12] presents a detailed description of each of the modules which make up the ELLPACK system,
and Part 3 of this same book presents a detailed performance
evaluation of ELLPACK modules.

3.4   Advanced Language Elements

The ELLPACK language as described in section 3.1 provides the
ability to easily declare elliptic problems and to invoke
software parts for their solution, but the range of problems
which can be solved within the confines of the language is
still quite modest. The principle reason for this is that the
language has no control structures other than sequential module
execution. The simplest way to make control structures available in a Fortran-based preprocessor is to allow "crutch-
coding" in Fortran. This is implemented using the following
additional ELLPACK segments.

FORTRAN
Executable. Contains executable Fortran statements which are
copied into the ELLPACK control program.

DECLARE
Declaration. Contains Fortran declarations which are copied
into the ELLPACK control program.

This simple change to the language (the Fortran statements are
not parsed by ELLPACK) has allowed the ELLPACK software parts
to be used in much more complex ways to solve many problems far
beyond the scope of ELLPACK's original design. For example,
problems with interior interfaces, nonlinear problems, time-
dependent problems, and coupled systems of elliptic equations
have all been solved in this way.

One way to solve such problems in ELLPACK is to employ a
solution strategy based upon the iterative solution of a single
linear equation. As a very simple example we will consider the
problem of finding the function $u(x,y)$ which satisfies the
equation

$$u_{xx} + u_{yy} - (x^2+y^2)e^{-xy}u^2 = 0$$

for $0<x<1$, $0<y<1$, with boundary conditions $u=1$ for $x=0$, $y=0$,
$u=\exp(y)$ for $x=1$, and $u=\exp(x)$ for $y=1$. This is a nonlinear
problem. The simplest algorithm for solving such a problem,
known as Picard or fixed-point iteration, is summarized as
follows.

1. Guess u_0

2. For $i = 0,1,2,\ldots$ until converged do:

2a. Solve $u_{xx} + u_{yy} = (x^2+y^2)e^{-xy}u_i^2$ for u

2b. Set $u_{i+1} = u$

The solution has converged when two successive solutions of 2a are the same. In ELLPACK step 1 is accomplished by the triple module SET which defines the solution function u(x,y) to be a user-selected function. As long as u(x,y) is defined before the equation is referenced we may use it in the right-hand side of the EQUATION segment as in step 2a. This is now a linear elliptic equation which ELLPACK problem-solving modules can solve directly. Since the function u(x,y) is automatically updated each time a solution or triple module is executed, step 2 is accomplished by simply solving the elliptic problem declared in ELLPACK repeatedly. Loop control is accomplished with the FORTRAN segment. An auxiliary array UOLD is declared to save the solution from the last iteration to monitor convergence. The following ELLPACK program implements this algorithm.

```
*         ------------------------------------
*              PICARD ITERATION FOR NONLINEAR PROBLEM
*         ------------------------------------

DECLARE.
              REAL UOLD(11,11)

EQUATION.
              UXX + UYY  =   (X**2 + Y**2)*EXP(-X*Y)*U(X,Y)**2

BOUNDARY.
              U = 1.0        ON   X = 0.0
                             ON   Y = 0.0
              U = EXP(Y)     ON   X = 1.0
              U = EXP(X)     ON   Y = 1.0

GRID.    11 X POINTS    $   11 Y POINTS

*        INITIALIZE PICARD ITERATION
TRI.     SET (U=ZERO)
FOR.
              DO 100 ITER = 1,6
*             SOLVE LINEAR PROBLEM WITH A FAST-DIRECT METHOD
TRI.          FISHPAK HELMHOLTZ
FOR.
*             PRINT MAX CHANGE IN SOLUTION FROM LAST ITERATION
              PRINT *, ITER,DIFMAX(UOLD,11)

  100         CONTINUE

OUTPUT.  TABLE(U)

SUB.
         REAL FUNCTION DIFMAX (UOLD,NPTS)
C
C   RETURN MAX CHANGE IN CURRENT SOLUTION FROM UOLD,
C   THEN SAVE CURRENT SOLUTION IN UOLD.
C   UOLD SET TO ZERO ON FIRST CALL.
C
              (... Fortran code omitted ...)
END.
```

The following results for this problem were obtained on a Cyber 180/855.

Iteration	Max Change in U
1	2.7E+0
2	7.3E-2
3	5.2E-3
4	3.5E-4
5	2.3E-5
6	1.5E-6

4.0   DISCUSSION

4.1   Effect on Problem-Solving

ELLPACK provides several clear advantages for solving elliptic problems. Foremost is the ready access to a substantial collection of state-of-the-art software parts for this problem area. This is quite important for (a) learning about the properties of numerical methods, (b) experimenting with various methods on model problems before embarking on the solution of a difficult problem, and (c) verifying the solution obtained to an application problem by a second, completely different numerical method. Having a large number of different numerical algorithms at one's disposal is particularly important in an application field in which no single numerical method is sufficiently robust to handle all problems posed for solution.

High-level user interfaces to software parts collections of this type are necessary since the detailed programming necessary to simply describe the target problem is sufficiently complex to discourage use of the parts. One programming effort analysis of the ELLPACK language showed increases in programmer productivity of from 10 to 50 when compared to direct access to the ELLPACK software parts through Fortran [13]. Special-purpose applications-oriented extension to an existing language is an expedient way to implement such a user interface in way likely to be accepted in the short term. A careful language design will allow sufficient flexibility to permit users to combine the parts in novel ways to solve problems well beyond the scope of the original problem class.

4.2   Future Problem-Solving Environments

The ELLPACK system has provided an invaluable tool with which to study the nature of problem-solving environments. I briefly describe several ways in which ELLPACK has been used (or has figured prominently in plans) to construct advanced problem-solving environments of various types.

<u>Performance Evaluation of Software Parts</u>

One of the original motivations for the development of ELLPACK was the prospect of using it for experimental performance evaluation of software for elliptic problems. This involves solving many different elliptic problems with many different numerical methods on many different grids. ELLPACK provided the necessary software parts and an easy way to describe test problems. However, producing the hundreds of ELLPACK programs required to solve all problems by all methods on all grids was still prohibitive.

To solve this problem an integrated performance evaluation system was built around ELLPACK; see Fig. 4. First, a database of test problems was built. An ELLPACK program generator was developed to translate a concise description of a numerical experiment ("solve problems A, B, C, D, E by methods F, G, H using grids I, J, K, L, M, N") to a sequence of ELLPACK programs. Each such problem is then solved and performance indicators (such as measures of accuracy, efficiency, memory usage, etc.) are stored in another database. Other programs access performance data from the database, generating various statistical analyses. The design of the performance evaluation system is detailed in [4]. Data from many thousands of elliptic problem solutions have now been logged in the performance database. Such data could not have been easily generated without access to a software parts technology such as ELLPACK.

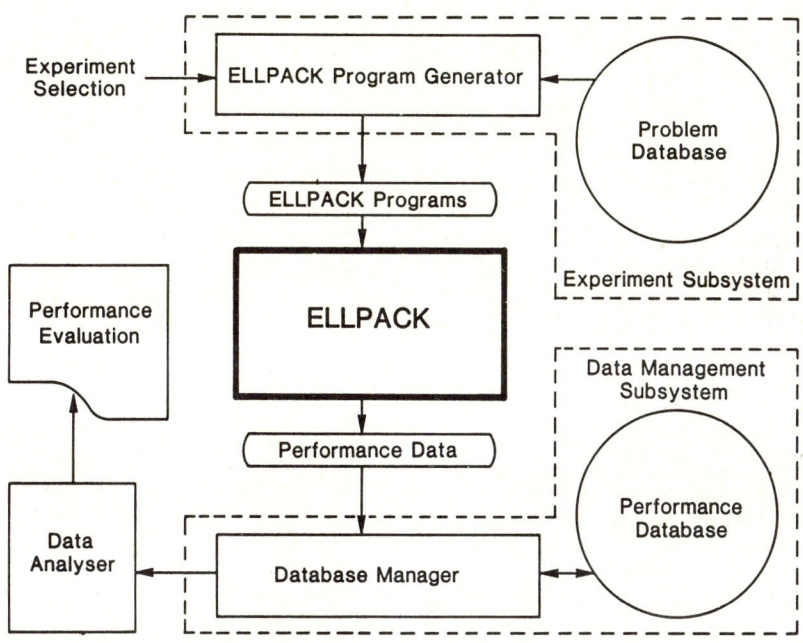

Figure 4

A Performance Evaluation System Based On ELLPACK

Interactive Elliptic Solvers for Specialized Applications

The ELLPACK system described above is primarily batch oriented. However, the ELLPACK control program generated by the preprocessor may contain user-supplied Fortran statements which obtain input from the user at run-time. Thus, ELLPACK programmers can build specialized application programs which obtain various parameters from users, solve a particular related differential equation and produce output in a form suitable to the application. A new, experimental feature of the ELLPACK language, the MENU segment, allows ELLPACK programmers to define menus to be displayed at run-time with selected ELLPACK segments executed based upon the user's menu selections. This greatly eases the production of interactive ELLPACK programs.

Wayne Dyksen of Purdue University has combined the use of menus with a sophisticated graphics workstation to develop some novel elliptic problem-solving environments. These systems allow the problem to be solved and a plot of the answer to be saved in a window; the problem can be re-solved by another method with the results compared visually. Computational grids can also be visualized in this way, and the domain re-gridded using various graphics input devices.

Expert Elliptic Solver

When scientists and engineers use ELLPACK to solve "real world" problems they are often overwhelmed by the abundance of problem-solving modules. Since performance of algorithms for a given elliptic problem is not easily ascertained a priori, even by a well-trained numerical analyst, choosing the best algorithm is not easy to do. In addition, most problem-solving modules have restrictions on their use and, although these restrictions are carefully documented in [12], it remains a tedious task to even determine all the possible legal module combinations which may be used for a given problem. Moreover, most users are unfamiliar with many modern numerical methods for these problems, and thus often choose a less desirable method for their problem only because it is more familiar.

An obvious approach is to develop an expert ELLPACK assistant to aid in problem analysis and method selection. The knowledge base for such a system would contain (a) properties of well-posed elliptic boundary value problems, (b) properties of numerical methods, (c) properties of ELLPACK problem-solving modules, (d) complete documentation for ELLPACK modules, and (e) the performance evaluation data described above. The expertise system would make a symbolic analysis of a given elliptic problem and then, with the aid of an inference system, would determine the best solution strategy based upon various selection rules. When there is only limited information about the elliptic problem a statistical analysis of data from related problems in the performance evaluation database would be undertaken.

Distributed Elliptic Expert

Another factor to consider in solving an elliptic problem is the hardware on which the solution algorithm is to execute. Some problems which have very large resource requirements are more suited to a large mainframe than to a small local workstation. Some numerical methods admit specialized variants for vector or parallel processors with very different performance characteristics; specialized versions of ELLPACK for such machines are currently under development.

Information about the availablity and performance of ELLPACK problem-solving modules on a number of different computing devices could also be part of the knowledge base of an elliptic expert. If, in addition, a network connecting all these machines were available, then an expert elliptic assistant could select the best method and computer on which to solve the problem and then submit a job to ELLPACK on the appropriate system. In this case additional information about network bandwidths and current workloads of each machine would be needed in order to more accurately estimate turnaround. The organization of such a system is depicted in Fig. 5.

ACKNOWLEDGEMENTS

The development of the ELLPACK system was a cooperative project involving many researchers supported by a variety of institutions; see [12] for a complete listing. The design and development of interactive ELLPACK and the expert elliptic solvers described in section 4 are being undertaken by W. R. Dyksen, E. N. Houstis, C. Ribbens, J. R. Rice and colleagues at Purdue University.

DISCLAIMER

Certain proprietary products have been referenced in this paper in order to fully describe the ELLPACK system and its relation to other developments in mathematical software. Identification of such products does not imply recommendation or endorsement by the National Bureau of Standards.

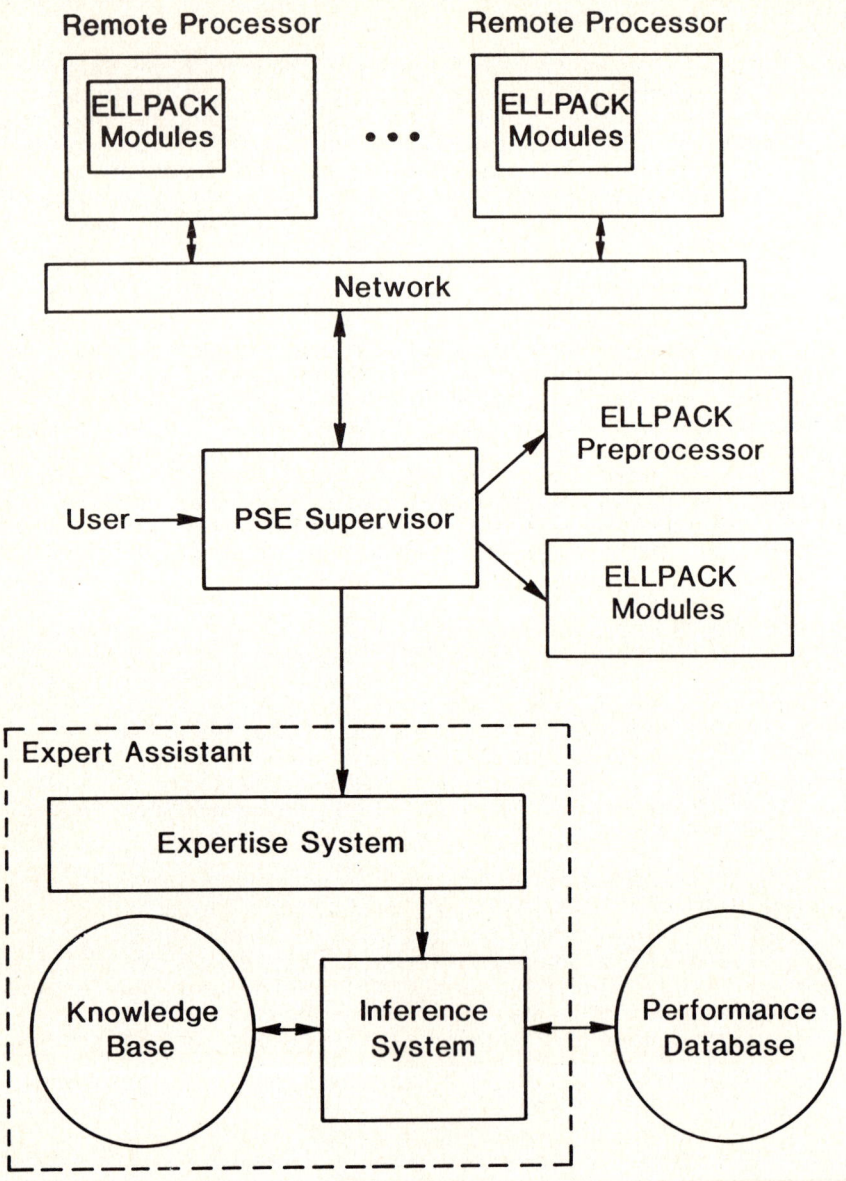

Figure 5

An Advanced Elliptic Problem-Solving Environment

REFERENCES

[1] T.J. Aird, The IMSL library, in *Sources and Development of Mathematical Software* (W. Cowell, ed.), Prentice-Hall, Englewood Cliffs, NJ, 1984, 264-301.

[2] J.C. Batz, P.M. Cohen, S.T. Redwine, and J.R. Rice, The application-specific task area, *IEEE Computer* 16 (1983), no. 11, 78-85.

[3] G. Birkhoff and R.E. Lynch, *Numerical Solution of Elliptic Problems*, SIAM, Philadelphia, 1984.

[4] R.F. Boisvert, E.N. Houstis, and J.R. Rice, A system for the performance evaluation of partial differential equations software, *IEEE Trans. Softw. Engng.* 5 (1979), 418-425.

[5] R.F. Boisvert and R.A. Sweet, Mathematical software for elliptic boundary-value problems, in *Sources and Development of Mathematical Software* (W. Cowell, ed.), Prentice-Hall, Englewood Cliffs, NJ, 1984, 200-263.

[6] J.F. Brophy, The PG system, in *Solving Elliptic Problems Using ELLPACK* (J.R. Rice and R.F. Boisvert), Springer-Verlag, New York, 1985, 455-467.

[7] J.J. Dongarra, C.B. Moler, J.R. Bunch, and G.W. Stewart, *LINPACK Users' Guide*, SIAM, Philadelphia, 1979.

[8] J.J. Filliben, DATAPLOT --- Introduction and Overview, National Bureau of Standards, SP 667, 1984.

[9] B. Ford and J.C.T. Poole, The evolving NAG library service, in *Sources and Development of Mathematical Software* (W. Cowell, ed.), Prentice-Hall, Englewood Cliffs, NJ, 1984, 375-398.

[10] J.W. von Gudenberg, PASCAL-SC: A Pascal extension for scientific computation, in *Proceedings of the 10th IMACS World Congress on System Simulation and Scientific Computation*, vol. 1, Aug. 1982, 404-406.

[11] C.B. Moler, MATLAB User's Guide, Univ. New Mexico Tech. Report CS81-1 (revised), 1982.

[12] J.R. Rice and R.F. Boisvert, *Solving Elliptic Problems with ELLPACK*, Springer-Verlag, New York, 1985.

[13] J.R. Rice, A programming effort analysis of the ELLPACK language, *SIGNUM Newsletter* 14 (1979), no. 1, 109-111.

[14] J.R. Rice, Programming language facilities for numerical computation, MRC Technical Summary Report

#2033, Mathematics Research Center, University of Wisconsin, January 1980, 29 pages.

[15] J.R. Rice, <u>Numerical Methods, Software, and Analysis</u>, McGraw-Hill, New York, 1983.

[16] J.R. Rice, C. Ribbens, and W.A. Ward, Algorithm 622. A Simple Macro Processor, <u>ACM Trans. Math. Softw.</u> 10 (1984), 410-416.

[17] T.A. Ryan, Jr., B. L. Joiner, and B.F. Ryan, Minitab Reference Manual, Minitab Project, 1982.

[18] A.I. Wasserman and S. Gutz, The future of programming, <u>Comm. ACM</u> 25 (1982), 196-206.

QUESTION AND ANSWER PERIOD

LYON

Since you mentioned parallel processors, what machines have you considered? I understand that the implementation of some numerical methods for these machines, matrix computations in particular, are still up in the air.

BOISVERT

One way of handling parallel processors in a distributed ELLPACK environment would be to replace the ELLPACK problem-solving modules on each parallel computer by ones rewritten specifically for that machine. The ELLPACK group at Purdue is also investigating other strategies; the parallel machine which they are concentrating on is the FLEX. The topic of matrix algorithms for parallel computers is now attracting a lot of interest in the numerical analysis community. Although much progress has been made, there are still many open problems.

BOUDREAUX

It seems to me that this work has two important aspects. First, you're showing us ways of using a rational environment, a reasonable environment, proven and tested software programs, in this case written in Fortran. I think it's interesting, because it allows us to preserve wealth that's already expressed in these languages, and I think that in that sense, work that you've done shows us the direction that things ought to take in the future in other kinds of environments, not only for elliptic problems. The second thing is, having built an environment at one level of capacity, it seems to me that the thrust of your work is to develop a more intelligent environment to make use of those resources that we have expressed in Fortran. Are you keeping careful notes as to how you're building this environment? I'm interested in hearing more about the actual techniques that you're using to get at the kind of things that mathematicians know when they sit there to use the system. I think that's a very exciting piece of work.

BOISVERT

A paper describing the overall design of the elliptic expert is now being written at Purdue and should appear shortly. A prototype of the expert ELLPACK advisor is now running at Purdue. It will be very interesting to see how that develops.

PANEL:
OPEN QUESTIONS:
AN AGENDA FOR
LANGUAGE IN PROBLEM SOLVING

PANEL SESSION: OPEN QUESTIONS: AN AGENDA FOR LANGUAGE IN PROBLEM SOLVING

           Panel Chairman: B. I. Blum
           Panel Members: G. Arango
                            R. Jernigan
                            B. Shneiderman

BLUM

This is the last session of this symposium. It should try to tie things together and say what is really important. There are some open questions. We are concerned with an agenda for language and problem solving. That's the title of this panel, and it has two key words.

Language--what do we mean by language? Is it a sequence of sentences as in natural language or mathematical notation? Or when we was about programs and computers, are we talking also about pictographic representations? We had a paper earlier today that was about the use of graphics. In my paper, there's a section called "Diagrams Considered Harmful." My personal feeling is that when it comes to something large and complex, diagrams obscure more than they help. However, for things such as training or teaching the semantics of programming, representations are appropriate for explaining how systems work, for understanding concepts. And finally, we should recognize that, with most computer language usage, we are also concerned with interacting and communicating. The dynamics are as important as the static expression of the language. Clearly, bit map displays, color, and pointing devices are changing our perceptions of how to interact.

What do we mean by problem solving? I have a feeling that many participants talk about problem solving, but mean they want to implement a computer solution; write a computer program for.... I personally feel that programming is an artifact of our times. That is, we don't know a better way of doing it; but sooner or later we will find better implementation methods, and we won't be writing programs anymore. Users will use computers. Engineers will develop the software instructions; only they will use programming languages. Personally, I'm more interested in the design of system solutions, that is, how one captures the knowledge of particular applications. That is how I define problem solving.

Going back to last night's excellent presentation and Alice B. Toklas and Gertrude Stein, we have to ask what are the questions. Only after we know the questions can we find the answers. This is a very varied group. There are many different interests. It is difficult for us to say how we're going to find those answers unless we can start to articulate the questions. I'll start with this, "What's the process?" If the process is creation, we're building something. After we build it we have to evaluate it in some way. Generally the way we evaluate is subjective: it's nice; it's better than x. The process also might be one of discovery. There are some fundamental rules, fundamental concepts and we're trying to identify what those rules and concepts are. These are very different processes.

We also have many different cultures. Historically, computer science evolved from mathematics, formalisms, logic. AI represents a different school; it looks at some less well-defined objects: knowledge representation, planning, inference. People see problems in different ways. There is a continuum that goes from well defined mathematical computation problems to abstract symbolic problems. Obviously, no single problem solving paradigm can address (or be meaningful for) all users.

We started looking for the question and so far only have found more questions. That is not unusual. For example, we once had a conference to decide what medical informatics is. Is it a collection of rules or tools? In other words, is the focus for medical informatics the fact that we're all using the same tool (a computer), or are there some fundamental rules that we all should be using? One of the people put it in the sense of, "Is this a methods science or a systems science?" The systems science tries to find the answers, the method science tries to define the methods that can be used. It's not clear to me where we are with respect to the problem solving question. Are we focusing on language, on computers, on people, on interactions, whatever? In medical informatics we clearly found there was a dual evaluation standard. For a hundred years medicine had been learning how to conduct clinical trials and perform empirical research. When it came to computers, however, it was "I love it" or "I hate it." Because nobody ever published a paper on "I hate it," there was the clear implication that there was tremendous personal involvement and bias in the evaluations. I think that this same phenomenon is present in our analysis of problem solving using computers. Our emotions get in the way.

Let me conclude with a personal reference. I am in the process of developing something I call an environment for building systems. When I look at what I am trying to do, I see that all the questions are very large; I don't know how to decompose them. (Dealing with big issues is fun; a partial solution may be more satisfying than failing to solve a very small one.) Everything I do is subjective. It is an art; you might call it a hobby. When I try to measure things, there are no golden rules; when I measure I always use local metrics. Everything is very domain sensitive. If you can do the same thing that I can do, then there is a basis for comparison; if you do something slightly different from what I do, then the results are difficult to compare. This allows me to stake out my turf and reign supreme. Maybe that is our approach to problem solving.

But, to return to Alice B. Toklas. Is there a question? I'm sure that there must be. Frankly, I have trouble formalizing and evaluating what I am doing with respect to problem solving. Perhaps it is my background in medical informatics, but to me much of my work can be characterized by a Koren cartoon in The New Yorker. It shows a grotesque mask, 20 feet tall, with its proud owners explaining, "Its mere possession is immensely satisfying." I try to hide this in my papers, but that's the way I feel about my work. If you want anything more qualitative or quantitative, I will pass your request on to our next speaker.

ARANGO

Picking up where Bruce left, I want to emphasize in this brief presentation the need to make explicit that type of knowledge he has, the type of art he has and that he permanently applies in the problem solving task of developing tools, in systems, or environments. One of the things that we see in software engineering or in the computing industry today is that software systems are the most formal objects that we have around. Because we've been working on the formalization for so many years, we've gotten to the point where we can actually have them put into libraries and reuse them. One of the lessons learned is that reusing software is not easy. Reusing code is not easy. For example, if you have a set of needs and you have a solution for that set of needs, when your needs change a little bit, just to adjust the solution to fulfill the new needs is a very expensive process; we call it maintenance in software engineering. It's supposed to account for 80% of the investment in large projects. The point is that you cannot reuse some resource even if it has been captured formally unless you have some idea of a rationale of how that product was generated.

In my previous talk, I was referring to domain theories as a way of capturing the type of domain-specific knowledge that Bruce was referring to. Now, my vision of the future is that, just as we have collected algorithms of the ACM as a source of problem solving methods, we should have the collected domain theories of the ACM. There's a tremendous wealth of knowledge in systems, in the minds of problem solvers, in texts, and from the point of view of constructing software. We are not really using that knowledge. We need to capture it in a formal way and to study the problem of how to evolve this product so that it can feed our needs by providing a rationale, a scaffolding of how those theories came about.

I saw a poster on the stairs outside with a phrase by Isaac Newton that says something like, "I could see farther than others because I stood on the shoulders of giants." In software engineering, we are standing on the toes of each other. It's time to apply the example of the applied sciences where, as Professor Rich was saying yesterday, we don't consider something to be scientific until it has been published; that is, until it has been captured in a way where other people can look at it, validate it, reuse it. That has to happen in software engineering, too. We have to capture the problem solving knowledge that's already there. I'm not talking about finding out new ways of doing things; just capturing and formalizing what we think, what we already know, and making it public in a way that other people can reuse it.

SHNEIDERMAN

My goal this morning is to offer a vision of a possible direction for the development of new systems, new languages if you will, and my hearing of the talks in this conference has encouraged me to concentrate on this particular topic rather than go on to some of the additional ones I had on my list. The notion I want to talk about I've given the term "direct manipulation." My understanding emerged from observing what users of interactive systems liked and what they didn't like over a period of many years. Sometimes I perceive myself as a movie critic of interactive systems, getting to see many systems. Often people say I've got to show you this system and describe how terrible it is. But from time to time someone is eager to show me how wonderful a particular system is. This occurred six or more years ago when people began to show me display editors and were excited about how display editors were superior to the traditional line oriented editors. There was a great feeling of enthusiasm and the comment that, "once you've tried this you'll never want to use anything else again."

I tried to sort out what it was that gave such a great sense of satisfaction, and I think it was, for one, the visual display of the object of interest and the large enough format to see a full page of text, say, 66 lines. Secondly, what they were referring to was the WYSIWYG principle -- what-you-see-is-what-you-get -- so that on the display screen they could see the boldface, centering, indentation, and the layout of paragraphs. Compare this to the old-fashioned kind of editors or formatters like nroff, troff, script, scribe, which have a very strange set of notations that you must put in to effect bold facing, at-sign b left paren and then at-sign b, right paren, or something like that. Inevitably, you forget the at-sign b, right paren, and two-thirds of your document is then in boldface or the wrong font size, etc.; a terrible waste, an embarrassment, and a distraction.

Also, consider the use of the delete key, for example. Put the cursor on a character, press delete, it's gone, and the rest of the characters move in to fill the space. If you continue to do it, the letters jiggle over, in fact, grabbing words from the next line where necessary to present a continuous representation of that world of objects. That's in contrast with bizarre change commands: change space, slash, old string, slash, new string, slash--just a frustrating annoyance.

When you look at professional users of those systems, a third to a half of their commands are in error in one form or another; a terrible waste of time. Much better to operate the delete key or simply type the insert with all the characters moving over to provide space for the new characters. This provides a great sense of confirmation: I'm trying to put a character in. I put it in, and in fact it goes there; not some strange change or insert command where you have to issue yet a further command to see what happens once you're done. So, those are some of the principles about display editors, and in fact there's confirmation of their efficacy; Terry Roberts' fine dissertation and several other studies showed a cut of one-half in the learning time for display editors over command, line-oriented editors, and a doubling of productivity. That's a strong phenomenon. It was nice to see it confirmed by the empirical evaluation.

Other places where one finds direct manipulation are video games, my favorite examples. Pacman has a great clarity of the illusion of the world of action. You simply move the joystick to the right and the Pacman goes right. If the Pacman is against the right hand wall and you push right, you don't get error message number 407, or hex addresses or crash the system; it just sits there. There's no need for an error message, because the visual representation of the world of action is apparent to the user. This is done the way that Nancy described this morning. You avoid the errors; you prevent users from making errors. The video game designers really have the clue. Early on, they were designing systems where the actions were in the task domain; they were not syntactic; they were not computer domain related; they were in the task domain. You forget that you're using a computer, and you're in the world of Pacman or any of these other video games.

Another favorite example is driving a car where you turn left and in fact the car goes left. If you've gone too far you turn back. Imagine driving by typing "left 30 degrees" then typing "undo" if you need to back out. It's laughable but that's really the state of many contemporary office automation tools.

These principles seem to be the underlying ones for direct manipulation. The visual display of the objects and the actions in the task domain, rapid incremental and reversible actions. Immediate presentation of the results without having to issue other commands. Some by-products are that there are fewer errors, that there's low syntactic learning, and low computer domain knowledge that's necessary.

I think these visual worlds are a little bit hard for us to create. We're stuck in the old languages like Ada or Prolog or Lisp or Fortran or Basic. The linear syntactic forms imprison us in a way. I think there's a great power in these languages, but we're only beginning to discover the ways of giving greater power with direct manipulation. I think it offers a very appealing alternative for many task domains. I do counsel you if you're going to try this to try it out on two or three or four design projects because it takes a while to break free from the older thought processes.

Let me just report one example. A few months ago someone was showing me his design of a project management system of which he was very proud. It had a graphical interface, it used Gantt charts, with horizontal bars that showed for each of the tasks how many weeks it required. The designer was very pleased to show me how nicely it appeared on the screen. I said fine, tell me more. If one task is going to take a week-longer, how do I change it? He was really proud to show me that there were in fact two levels; there was the command level and the menu level; that in the command level he had designed an elaborate syntax to lengthen or shorten a particular project. And he showed me also his error messages which captured the errors in the months or the dates, or if the month identified 7/30 was in fact not the correct one, it gave very effective feedback. There was a whole subsystem for dealing with the commands. Then there was also a version with the menus which he said for the novice user would be very effective; they'd just have to choose from the menus which task, lengthening and shortening and dates. It was well designed. But I pointed out, here you've got this graphical display, in fact there was a mouse there, why can't you, for example, put the mouse cursor on the end of that bar chart, click once and drag that bar one week to the right and let it sit there when you let go. Essentially, the only syntax is the notion that you have a handle at the end of these bars and that you can drag them, and that it could only go along the line (there were week-long schedules) so you could drop it only on week-long changes, and it prevented errors. There were no error messages then, there was no syntax to learn, nothing to type, and furthermore, I think more importantly, you preserve the operator's attention in the task domain. The visual representation was appropriate, but I suggested the addition of the motion of dragging the bar or lengthening it.

Well, the first response, of course, was resistance: "We couldn't do that." There was a lot of huffing and puffing about why that couldn't be done. It took a while to settle down until we talked it through, till he could accept the idea, because it meant changes to the code and redesign and a lot of effort that had been invested. In fact, the more effort that's required, the harder it is to change. That's why the commitment is strongest to these traditional languages by the most sincere devotees of those languages. It's most hard to make them see these new possibilities.

Those are the positive sides; I should say there are cautions. These direct manipulation notions are still novel. It is a little hard to get into them the first few times, but now I can hardly think of any other way of doing it. There are difficulties in implementation, because the traditional languages don't always make it easy, and there are real questions about how one does programming within direct manipulation. The Macintosh interface does direct manipulation for file commands, but it is hard to do programming with it. One of our efforts has been something called direct manipulation DOS, where we provided some of those operations on an IBM PC. I would like to encourage participants in this conference to think visually, to keep an open mind to these possibilities, and I hope that by next year's conference we'll have a whole series of presentations that excite us all about the possibilities of more visual language.

JERNIGAN

I'll start off with a story, and forgive me if I've bored you with this story before. About 10 years ago I went for a job interview with the US Railway Association. In the process of interviewing, I was ushered into the office of the Vice President of Finance of that organization: kind of a big, palatial office, 2000 square feet. He was sitting there like he had been there all night, had his shoes off, shirt sleeves rolled up, sat down on the couch, put his feet up. The first words he said to me were, "I hate computers." He didn't say, "Hello, how are you." He just said, "I hate computers." I asked why. He said, "We take models, financial models we understand very well, we give them to the programmers, they run down the hall, and the first thing they do is lose them in the computer and we never see them again."

During this conference, or symposium, we've seen several examples of how you can see the effects of what you've done. This runs a range of graphical representations from the systems that deal with the novice, like the system we saw this morning, the one that Bonnie Kowalchack demonstrated to us yesterday, that are designed for the beginning programmer to learn something about how the computer works. Probably, extensions of these would be able to expand them all to the level where a very experienced programmer would be able to use something like that for his level of problem solving. For example, the kind of graphics that Jack Boudreaux showed us in the AMPLE system to demonstrate to the parts programmer what the effect of his programs were. We assume we've got something of an expert there, who still needs the same kind of desire to see what the results of his actions are. Ben's suggestion is that there are probably ways that we can extend this direct manipulation concept so maybe we could put a wand on the robot and move the arm around. Maybe we can capture that information; it is indeed a possibility. We are not nearly as far from it today as we were five years ago, I think we've got some better ideas about how to that.

Another thing we've seen in this conference is the kind of textual representation, the algorithmic representation or scheme for it, for problems that are maybe a little bit elusive. Susan Epstein is addressing an area where we may not have a language sitting on any of our desks right now. So there are efforts to reach out and capture with a notation system some kind of representation system concepts that might be a little bit elusive to us if we had to program them using some of the existing languages that we have today. A comment was made during the break that the system Guier was demonstrating seems rather cumbersome. In the way it was presented, it was a rather cumbersome way of writing programs. There are conceptual coverings that you can add, a notable one being something like QBE; Peter Gray says in his book on "Logic, Algebra and Data Bases" that QBE is very much like Prolog. The control structures that execute it are very much the same, but the representation that we have is very different. There are, essentially, two kinds of representations that we are looking at; somehow I think they will either all come together as one or one will be a covering of the other. One is the textual, the linguistic representation of a problem, and the other is covering. The emphasis today is on graphics as a representation of the effect, not of the cause; i.e., we use graphics to demonstrate the effect of our actions, of our writing code.

In my opening comments for this symposium, I made the observation that I sometimes am not sure whether language is the appropriate model for dealing with computers or whether the tool box is the appropriate model. Well, we've had two and one-half days of papers on how to somehow deal with this subject. I assume that we've all reached the point now so that when I count 1, 2, 3, and ask you what is the role of language in problem solving, we will be able to recite in unison what that role is. "1, 2, 3...." You'll notice I didn't respond either. I think I have an idea of what that role is. I think that language is a mechanism, i.e., notation system, we use for reasoning. I find when I have a problem I sit down with my pencil and I start making hen scratches on a piece of paper. They might only be intelligible to me, but they tend to help me somehow to organize my thoughts. When I sit down at the terminal, I have to express them more explicitly because it's not going to accept my hen scratches and the pieces that I've left out. I've organized my thoughts, and I have a fairly good understanding about how I'm going to proceed with solving the problem. I also use warm bodies I find laying around in offices. I walk in and say, "I've got a problem I want to explain." I start trying to explain to this unfortunate person what my solution is going to be, and very often I find that this process of explanation helps me to work out in my own mind what the solution ought to be.

BLUM

We now are open for questions or answers.

GIESZL

I'd like to ask Ben if he has any comments on how to use direct manipulation on a fairly serious medical diagnostic program other than by having pointers to parts of the body or something?

SHNEIDERMAN

I don't want to trivialize the problem by saying here is the answer. The first level, pointing to the body, seems like a good demonstration, but I think the reality is probably deeper. I think, and I had some discussion with Jim Reggia on our faculty about it, what you need to do is tell me what your theory of disease is. Give your model. I'm not sure whether you are looking at chemical imbalances, viral infections, or endocrinology. Show me a representation on the screen of endocrinology -- the flows and levels of various hormones in the body -- and then allow the operator to play with those levels.

This idea is extremely well suited for expert systems. Direct manipulation is relevant because most of the expert system user interfaces are the old teletype designs. They're really primitive.

That's a fundamental mistake of many of the expert system designs. The CAI people make the same mistake. I think what you want to create is a visual representation, a model. I sometimes call this "visi-rules" because you can play with the levels of inputs and watch what happens to the output. As I maybe change the level of some hormone in the body, I can see how it is going to lead to a change. One other example is a little more playful, but I think has the same message. This is "visi-cooking." In the world of cooking there are lots of inputs like flour, eggs, butter, and so on. Then there are intermediate things like the size and shape of the pan and the temperature, and then there are the outcomes. I'd like to be able to play with the levels of the inputs and watch how blueberry pancakes turn into blueberry cookies as I add more flour or change the temperature. I think that physicians and other people will come to these systems when they have an environment for exploration. But, if you don't have a model, you don't know what you are talking about.

BLUM

The question was really on the use of graphics with expert systems. ONCOCIN is a system for oncology (cancer patients) that's being developed by Ted Shortliffe and his group at Stanford. In the last few years they began to emphasize graphics. The model they use is the one in which a cancer researcher has a form that he has to fill out. What they have done is to draw a picture of the form and put it on the screen of a work station. The picture contains a diagram of the body where you can indicate the sites of the tumors. There are also lines that explode into what are called flow sheets, that is, tabular displays. The user enters today's data as collected for use in treating the patient, and the system uses that as an input to the protocols, which are written in the form of rules. ONCOCIN recommends therapy and is able to provide explanations and advice.

We at Hopkins also did something similar, but we did it in a different way. We used a data processing paradigm. In the Hopkins case, the tool is used every day; there is no way to take care of the patients without using this. Therefore, we designed our system to look like any other piece of paper that the care providers normally use. It is surprising to see the kinds of things emphasized in an operational situation when everybody has to use a system every day. In our case, we restricted features of the system in order to avoid potentially high risk situations and also to reinforce education. For example, at Hopkins, because most users are in training, it would be inappropriate to get people too reliant upon a tool that won't be available to them when they leave. In a (tool development) research setting, of course, one would have entirely different objectives and resultant products.

Thus, I think that each case illustrates an extension of what you're calling direct manipulation. Each system uses tools that seem natural in its respective work environment. Manipulation of these objects has a direct analogue to the use of the objects that preceded them. The model that Ben talks of includes both the knowledge and the environment of application.

SHNEIDERMAN

Let me underscore Bruce's comment. I think that Shortliffe got to this early because he was working on these systems for years and years and also because he conducted empirical studies about the use of the previous versions. He got quickly to understand that they weren't going to use the old designs, and he came up with these new concepts.

I make a subtle distinction between visual and graphic. They may sometimes be graphics, as in diagrams of the body, but that's the small part. The forms are a visual presentation, and I think that's what is important. You don't always have to go to jazzy graphics. Display editors are not graphics; they are visual presentations in my world.

EPSTEIN

I see commonalities here with my own work. I was doing prototype and deformation; I began with a graph that had a property, and deformed it in some fashion retaining that property. When you talk about the graph of the organizational structure or the graph of project development, you are beginning with a prototype and making a visual deformation. The same thing occurs in a medical system, or even in Jack's system for the machine tooling problem. When I identify the prototype and the legal deformations in my graphs, all I have are vertices and edges. Jack has more toys in his arsenal. If he can specify the object and then specify how this object may be used to deform the prototype, he should have a very solid handle on visual manipulation. The same transformation applies with text line editors and object editors.

SHNEIDERMAN

I think that what is happening is that people in various domains, such as graph theory or text editing, are discovering ways of making visual presentations of not only the objects but the actions. I suspect it is harder to make visual presentations of the potential actions.

EPSTEIN

You only saw some of the parameters. One of the most interesting parameters is the idea of merging two nodes in a graph. There are also operations defined on subportions of a graph. You can identify something in chunks. When I said prototype and deformation I meant both. The deformation is equally important; it's what you call an "operation."

SHNEIDERMAN

A certain amount of play and explanation is a part of these systems.

EPSTEIN

We call that doodling.

WEINTRAUB

A couple of thoughts occurred to me. One is that as one of the organizers (although I was only on the program committee this time), I'd say we flunked. I think it would have been better if we had pushed companies like Microsoft and Macintosh, etc., to have a couple of representatives here to discuss the industry side, the mass market side of human engineering.

Another comment. Direct manipulation is the language for a lot of people these days. What's meant by direct manipulation? Now, last year we had a paper on the use of the subjunctive in computer programming. The idea was to use the computer to model the computer. If I move forward five feet, will I still be standing here, or will I be at the bottom of a cliff? "Keep on walking until, if I took another step, I would be over the edge of the cliff." Before coming here this morning, we got into a thing working with WORD. WORD is one of these systems that I presume everyone has seen even if they haven't used it. (There are a lot of systems like it.) You get your text at the top and you can use the mouse to select a whole bunch of different options. Now here is the problem. We remembered that there was a submenu which allowed us to do what we wanted to do. What we had to do was go through one-by-one each of the menus, because we didn't have the reference card; it was buried under the desk. We went through each menu and submenu until we finally found the submenu we were looking for. How much nicer would it have been to be able to say "OK, what would happen here? Show me a table of my submenus," and to be able to do that at different points.

The point is that direct manipulation does not only mean text editing; it also means graphics editing. It also means design of tabular information in such a way that operations which the user would want to do can be easily brought back.

Putting in a plug for the Washington Software Psychology Society (which I'm surprised you haven't done, Ben), there was a talk at the Software Psychology Society where the following question came up. DEC had built a Word Processor, and one of its features was a key to transpose two letters. Now, professional touch typists are taught to never look at the keyboard; you have to teach them every single command and where it is on the keyboard, because they will not look. (I've seen the secretaries here, they will not look at the keyboard; when they are using the symbol tables they will look at the symbol template. Even if we have the thing right on the key, they won't look at the keys. It's an ingrained thing apparently taught by whip in secretarial school.) On the other hand, those of us who look at the keyboard can see those commands. Thus, simple things, like labelling what keys to use, may be really handy for us, but not good for the "professionals."

The point is, you have to think of the operations that are going to be done by the user, and what will be more efficient for the user. To have a whole extra set of commands which you then have to sort out in your mind to do something simple, as opposed to just doing it directly is inefficient. By having the reverse-letter scheme, DEC wasted a command which not only filled up a slot on the keyboard, but more importantly, filled up a slot in the typist's mind saying, "Now, let's see I've got 14 different things I can do, and one of them I'm never going to use, but I have to remember it anyway, because otherwise I'll hit that key by accident." The point is, if we think of direct manipulation as a language, it's a language with many dynamic dialects. Except for the question that just came up a minute ago, it's not clear to me that it's really being addressed within the direct manipulation community.

JERNIGAN

In the discussion about correcting two characters, when you retype two characters, that is a form of direct manipulation. Whereas, to touch a key that says SWAP, I don't know if that would be very direct, or not. It seems that its manipulation is somewhat indirect. It probably depends on where your fingers are at the time. I'm intrigued by commercials we see on television now about new high-tech airplanes where they've given the pilot the ability to talk to the airplane. They can say "fire it," or "forget it."

WEINTRAUB

That comment reminds me of a classic, and I'll just quote it here. The proof of your confidence in software engineering: You get on an airplane and an announcement comes on the speaker that says, "Ladies and Gentlemen, this is your pilot. I am not here. Your plane is being flown by an excellent software system developed by your company." The question is, do you stay on the plane, or do you run off at top speed?

SHNEIDERMAN

I appreciate your comments and examples. The notion of direct manipulation is a very general one. There are lots of ways in which we have to get deeper to understand it. We have been spending a lot of time just trying to understand where we need to have a mouse, or a touchscreen, or a joy stick, or numbered keys, or lettered keys. In the ergonomic literature there's a term called "stimulus-response compatibility" which describes some aspects of direct manipulation. We're under way in trying to understand the application of these ideas to user interfaces.

JERNIGAN

In terms of the immediate world, where do we see some practical limitations on direct manipulation? Some of the systems Ben has described are systems that have been programmed by programmers using a technique other than direct manipulation, where the end users may not have the requirement to do anything that could not be described with direct manipulation.

SHNEIDERMAN

It is very hard to say what are the limits of any possible idea. It's true that the Macintosh interface is not created using the Macintosh interface; it's created in a Pascal-like language. There are in the Macintosh some systems which allow you minimal kinds of programming in that environment, and we're beginning to discover how to accomplish it.

I think, for example, of robot programming. There is one community which is developing traditional languages for doing robots, but there is another community developing direct manipulation of robots. You take the robot, you pull it over here, and you make it lift something, and you record the sequence of actions. Or you spray paint the car door and you record that. Now, can we then manipulate the output and save the sequence? Can we have it go faster or slower, or edit portions of that sequence in some way? In computer-aided design in manufacturing, where in the past programs were written to do things, now they're done visually. There are instances where progress is happening, and we're still waiting to find out what emerges. I don't think we're going to get rid of Pascal quickly, but I think we're going to make tasks available, power available, to larger numbers of people fairly rapidly. There will always be some things which will be using direct manipulation.

BLUM

I tried to make the distinction between applications and implementation. I think that when we talk about direct manipulation, we're really talking about applications, even though it may be the specialized application of implementation. I think that we will always have very formal, probably mathematical, structures for implementation. We're always going to have to live with this. I also think that the technology is moving so that we are now looking for more innovative ways to do our applications and make them easier for our people to use. Here there is less a perception of using a computer as a computer, and less a perception of having to write programs to use a computer, than before. Therefore, application domains really will define what kinds of functions and associated direct manipulations are appropriate.

SHNEIDERMAN

I tend to agree that direct manipulation feels most comfortable when there's a task domain or application domain that's relevant. It seems to have the greatest benefits there. Yet I must say I'm constantly surprised by how clever people have been able to do direct manipulation things for applications that you might consider systems programming or other domains that you might think you need assembly or some other low-level language, or Pascal, to deal with. I think we're still breaking free from it, and I don't know how far we can go. That's really the question.

SLATER

I'm reminded of way back in the middle ages when I was in high school, taking English and studying the sonnet form, which is, in writing, the most user-unfriendly thing possible. And yet, it certainly gives great creations. As we talk about user-friendly, should we not consider the issue that by being too friendly to the user, letting the user manipulate things too easily and too quickly, we encourage the user not to think? How do we balance that trade-off? I think one of the reasons I got along so well with Lisp is that there's no way you're going to write Lisp without thinking.

SHNEIDERMAN

I've heard that before. There are parts of me that are sympathetic to it, but I think overall, I would rather make things easier. I think it was Whitehead's quote which says the progress of civilization is measured by the things we can do without thinking. We can do great and powerful things with just small actions that enable us not to get lazy but, in fact, to apply ambition and to do even more bold things. So I think that by making life easier for the users, we will overall benefit them by giving them greater power. Yes, I know there are lots of terrible dangers of making life too easy, and the arguments about hand calculators are also applied there.

In the old days, printed books were seen as harmful because people would lose their skill at memorization. I guess Arthur Fuehrmann, years ago at NCC, made this lengthy condemnation of writing-assisted instruction in showing why writing and printed documents were going to destroy education. The parallels to computer-assisted instruction were carefully demonstrated. I understand the concerns, I'm aware of them.

There are other dangers. If we make computers too much fun, people will spend all their time with their computers, rather than their wives or husbands or kids. So, let's keep the dangers in mind, but let's not have them impede us in producing gifts that empower people to carry out their dreams and give them the opportunity to create, and allow them to help other people, and to learn, as well.

BLUM

Gordon talked about pragmatics as basically the difference between what was said and what was understood. If we think in terms of an implementation desire and an implementation result, we then can think about the difference between those two things, that gap, as pragmatics. To the extent that we have cumbersome tools, we stand more of a chance to lose things in the transformation. The smaller we can get those gaps, the more we can allow people to think about the problem they want to solve rather than how they have to solve it. In that sense, the more and the better tools that we have, the better off we are.

SLATER

That's why I used the example of a sonnet, because you have to do a lot of thinking about the tool; and yet, a lot of very great literature got written in that form, even though the tool itself demands a lot of thinking about it.

SHNEIDERMAN

True, and great sculptures were made by hand-carving tools and whittling knives; but I certainly would like to see power saws and tools for building houses. I don't think we have to restrict ourselves.

LOCKER

I would like to go back to the theme of the symposium: language and problem solving. If we were to formalize it, what would it mean that we want something that's called "A" to do something that's called "B"? I think we should ask ourselves what problem solving is before we start looking to what kind of tools or which language we are going to design or develop to aid in problem solving.

I would like to use a distinction between a knowledge base and a domain theory. When we have a knowledge base, we have a known set of facts and known sets of rules that organize them. There may be a difference in organizing them, but still, a set of rules helps us organize all the facts that are available. On the other hand, we can have a theory. A theory means that we have a set of facts, but a lot of other facts that are not explained later by that set of rules. So we use a theory to extrapolate, interpolate, in order to find new facts that we hadn't known. It enables us to set up a new set of rules and to go somewhere to an unknown place.

What it really comes down to, in my point of view, is that solving is going to an unknown spot that we haven't dealt with before--for example, the thing Ben Shneiderman brought up, about what would happen if I manipulate a line, have it become longer or shorter. But how is this going to affect my organization to create new facts? I have to go back and look at what kind of truths I think will help us in this kind of thing. How would you relate to that thing, is that the correct approach, and then, how would you go about setting up the tool kits of things or whatever is going to be?

ARANGO

Ben Shneiderman used a metaphor about driving. I'd say that problem solving is like the situation of moving around in a car. In this conference, we have been talking a lot about language in the sense of the body of the car: say, the wheel, and the gauges; the fact that it has windows and we can see the environment; those kinds of parts of the car. If you don't have seats and steering wheel, you won't go very far.

But if you don't have an engine in the car, you won't go very far either; no matter which model of a car you have. In many of the talks, I have seen the tendency to address issues of, say, the shape of the body, how seats can be made more comfortable, how we need windows so we can see the environment, and that we need mirrors. There also is this engine, this power, that makes a problem solving process move, and it has to do with conceptual structures. The essence of problem solving is maybe that engine. We have concentrated too much on the body part, or the interfaces, or the notations, without paying enough attention to what's in that engine, what is the actual power of problem solving techniques, tools, conceptualizations, and how they are captured in language. What can we do for learning more about them?

JERNIGAN

I think the value of some of the explorations in some of the newer languages is that they offer a conceptual covering of concepts that are linguistic devices that permit us to use concepts that we can make part of our tool kit or part of our language without having to revisit the detail of how to code those concepts. I remember back in the late 60's how great it was when we had a computer delivered that had a SORT callable from Cobol programs. We didn't have to write sort programs anymore. It's kind of an archaic art now, but back 15 years ago, that was a skill you had to have if you were going to be a programmer. Now we don't have to worry about that. Now we're starting to look at things like relational join operations, logical inferences, quick access to databases, use of mathematical libraries, use of graphics, all in a very easy way. I think we've ratcheted ourselves up several levels in our tools or in our linguistic ability.

WHITFORD

I have a question related to direct manipulation. It has more to do with the choice between pictorial or textual representation. To preface this, I was thinking of the concept of 2300 bolts. It could be expressed textually or symbolically, very quickly, just by writing down the numbers. It also can be expressed with a picture. It seems to me that choices in representing a concept such as that depends upon the user's questions and the actions they are about to take depending on what they see. If the action is to change the number of bolts, then a textual representation might be more appropriate to manipulate. But what if their action is something at a higher level, maybe thinking about bolts in a bin, or something like that, and the number isn't important, just that there's a quantity there? I'm wondering if we need a better sense of when is a textual or symbolic convention more appropriate or more efficient, and when is iconic, something that derives from something we already know or sense about the natural world, better?

SHNEIDERMAN

Bravo, you're right on target. There's danger that some graphic representation, iconic representation, makes the task more difficult. One of our studies was tabular data compared with bar charts. We did not find that pie charts are especially bad, by the way, but bar charts, and histograms, and plots do have some role, and it does depend on the task. If you're looking to see if a sequence in data shows an increasing trend, visual presentation is really nice, but if you're asked to find the percentage difference from the start to the finish, it may take a little more time, and may be less accurate with the visual presentation. So, our paper by Powers, Sashley, Sanchez, and Shneiderman, was published in Machine Studies two years ago, but there's a recent very good review by Gary Dixon and friends from the University of Minneapolis that appeared in the Communications of the ACM about three or four months ago that covered their recent studies as well as a review of the previous ones. The evidence is that tabular data are very effective in many cases, and you have to work hard to find the right cases where business charts or graphics are winners. Business graphics are appreciated, they look nice, they are fun, they are impressive, but for doing particular tasks, they may be slower and more error-prone. The task orientation is very important.

Let me generalize to the question of icons versus text. I am not a great fan of icons, really, but I think you have to take a balanced view. I think highway signs are a good sort of comparison. Sometimes words are better. "Yield" is hard to show a picture for, but if you have a curve in the road with an entering driveway, it's very hard to have words to describe it. So you need to find a balance. Now, the dangers with icons are that if you have many of them that people are not familiar with, they become very difficult to use. One of the terrible problems with iconic languages is that there's no lexicographic order. You can't go look them up in an index that has alphabetical order. If you've ever used the IBM 3270 series terminals, they have these funny error messages on the bottom: various lightning bolts or little men flapping their hands. You try to find out what they mean and flip through the little booklet, but it takes a long time to make sense of those.

The argument that says icons are international in language and therefore save us in production costs is a weak one. I think we have to find the best representation. It may be words in some cases.

I like icons and pictures when you can do things to them, not
just that they represent a word. You can bring two icons
together forming a new object, or by their position or placement, indicate something. A favorite example is dragging a
document into a printer icon and as the document prints it goes
into the printer and comes out the bottom. You can see how
much of the document has been printed already. You have to
look for the ways of using the icons, not just pictures as
opposed to text.

WHITFORD

Do you think that it's ever useful to have both representations
available at different levels?

SHNEIDERMAN

Yes, often. Another important disadvantage of icons is that
they can take more space on the screen than text. And that can
be a serious impediment. I think you have to weigh those
trade-offs. We've gone to an extreme in the Macintosh environment where you have these icons. You can only fit some 20 on a
screen, but you can get a list of 50 in a tabular display. For
many tasks, that's an advantage. The Xerox Star icons have
both words and pictures. Again, reflection on what the level
of knowledge of the users is, and how much time you have to
train them, are important components.

BLUM

It's partly a matter of scaling. There are some problems where
a limited number of icon symbols, or whatever, can be used
effectively. However, graph theory was defined without necessarily relying on pictures. One learns Euclidian geometry
using pictures only to help you understand the concepts. When
we are doing things like developing large complex systems, the
diagrams are effective ways of explaining and illustrating, but
not for defining or controlling. Think of all the diagrams we
saw in everybody's viewgraphs today. None of them could in any
sense be used formally. However, when you are limited to a
small number of operations, then icons, symbols, etc., can be
very effective.

CARR

I want to comment on creativity and constraint, which has been
mentioned, maybe not in those two terms, but is very important.
I base whatever comments I make on trying to understand hardware design from the point of view of VLSI CAD/CAM sort of
behaviour.

If you watch hardware designers, you will find over a period of
the last half dozen years that, as the systems are developed
and pose more constraints on the capability of the designer,
they begin to have a higher productivity. This seems to
indicate that as with most problems, or sets of problems, there
is a sort of fundamental minimal representation of the problem

and of the solution. If you can concentrate the effort of the
human being within this minimal set, whether it's very simple
graphical representation or whether it's topological or whether
it's a numerical structure in metric space, and so forth -- if
you can concentrate the user on that set of representations and
keep them from wandering away into places where it is of no
value to them, then you will get a higher productivity.

Another example. When I use Pascal, I have no desire to worry
about the syntax of Pascal. In fact, I hesitate to believe
that I have it. I would like a language syntax directed
sensitive attitude that will allow me not to make any mistakes
in Pascal. If I want to go try something else, I'll go to
another environment. It is that sort of restraint which I
think keeps us from writing sonnets on work time. It's okay to
write sonnets, but not when we're trying to solve other
particular problems.

SHNEIDERMAN

I'm in agreement. That's the puzzle. In structured
programming we threw out the "go to" statement and gave greater
power by having less there. I find it nicely summarized in the
Bauhaus motto which was "Form is freedom." When you have a
form in a structure to work in, you have the freedom to be
creative.

EPSTEIN

Let me just suggest that not only can a visual display give you
a picture of the object, it can also curtail search. I'll take
plane geometry as an example. Gelernter's program proved that
looking at the diagram offered tremendous guidance in
controlling search. It's exactly the kind of constraint that
Dr. Carr was just speaking about. I'm saying that somehow
control-constraint is embedded in pictorial diagrams. We would
be very reluctant to code these diagrams into a program. Yet,
in the plane geometry example, the dictates of Euclidian
geometry severely curtail the ways that we can draw
relationships.

CUNNIFF

Just as different tasks require different representations,
different learners and different users require different
representations. It's not saying that one is necessarily
better than the other; it's saying that one may be better for
me than it is for someone else in the room, and that it should
be our responsibility to keep that in mind when designing
systems, languages, problem solving domains of ways to
interact, because different people will be using them. The
bottom line is really how productive can we humans be with
these machines? We can only be that productive if it fits in
some way with the way we behave.

AUTHOR INDEX

Adrion, W.   167 168 **177**
Ahuja, S.   54 **66**
Aird, T. J.   **429**
Albus, J. S.   361 371 **375**
Allen, J.   49 **66** 205
Alterman, R.   227 229 **241**
Amarel, S.   168 169 **177**
Anderson, J. R.   202 **205 241**
Angluin, D.   **113**
Arango, G.   161ff 435 437 450
Arens, Y.   **258**
Ashcroft, E. A.   124 127 129 **131 132**
Bach, E.   **44**
Balzer, R.   **113** 163 175 **177**
Barbera, A. J.   361 **375**
Barr, A.   **177**
Barstow, D.   6 **22** 114 163 166 **177**
Barwise, J.   153 **158**
Batz, J. C.   **429**
Bauer, F.   **114**
Baxter, I.   **177**
Begg, I.   185 **195**
Binford, T.   **90**
Birkhoff, G.   **429**
Black, J. B.   201 391 392 **406**
Blum, B. I.   3 **22 23** 348 349 435 442 443 447 448 452
Bobrow, D.   **46** 67
Boisvert, R. F.   411 **429**
Bonar, J.   **258**
Bondy, J.   **299**
Borges Neto, J.   **196**
Borgida, A.   163 **178**
Boudreaux, J. C.   133 138 145 147 151 **158** 359 362 365 **375** 376 441
Boyer, R. S.   297 **299**
Brachman, R. J.   30 **44 45**
Branstad, M.   **177**
Bresnan, J.   38 **44**
Brison, S. J.   190 **196**
Brooks, R.   218 **259**
Brophy, J. F.   **429**
Brown, J. S.   59 60 159 240 **241** 259
Bruce, B.   3 24 31 **44** 210 211 218 437 444
Buchanan, B.   173 **178**
Bunch, J. R.   227 337 **429** 445
Burton, R. R.   64 **66**
Carbonell, J.   89 104 105 **114**
Carnap, R.   133 137 138 **159** 173 174 **178**
Carr, J. W.   337 342 345 452 453
Chapman, J. P.   186 **195**

Chapman, L. J.	186 195
Charniak, E.	49 50 52 **66** 227 228 229 232 239 240 241
Cherniavsky, J.	177
Chin, D.	**46** 258
Chu, B.	53 **66**
Clancey, W.	173 178
Clark, E. V.	195
Clark, H. H.	186 187 195
Clocks, W. F.	131
Coccia, C.	**90**
Codd, E. F.	301 302 303 306 319
Cohen, P. M.	**429**
Colby, K. M.	49 **67**
Collins, A. M.	**46** **67** 202 **205**
Conrad, M.	89
Cote, R.	89
Creswell, M. J.	131
Cunniff, N.	391 392 400 **406** 453
Curtis, B.	6 **22** 259
Cutler, B.	**395 406**
Dahl, V.	23 29 **44**
Darden, L.	71 72 88 89 **219**
Dascal, M.	183 186 187 188 189 191 **195** 196
Dasigi, V. R.	49 **68** 201 210 218
Date, C. J.	233 303 304 317 **319** 344
Davis, A. L.	**332**
Davis, R.	173 178
DeMarco,	7
DeMillo, R.	174 178
Denny, P. J.	185 **195**
Dershowitz, N.	114
Desai, A.	319
Deutsch, M.	167 **178**
De Kleer, J.	**159**
Dhall, S. K.	**332**
Dijkstra, E. W.	14 18 23 347
Dongarra, J. J.	**429**
Dorin, P. M.	**299**
Doyle, J.	177 178
Draper, S.	332 395 **406**
Dreyfus, H.	164 **178**
Dunham, G.	**90**
Duran, J.	178
Edkins, M.	361 375
Ehrlich, K.	258 259
Eiselt, K. P.	229 **241**
Eisner, E.	319
Elgot, J.	**389**
Elstein, A. S.	9 18 **22**
Eng, J.	**22** 71 90 177 178 **179**
Epstein, S. L.	201 261 299 301 441 444 445 453
Erlich, K.	391 **395 406**
Evans, J.	185 186 192 193 194 **196** 197
Evans, L.	**91**
Fahlman, S. E.	228 230 231 **241**
Fairley, R. E.	23

Faustini, A. A.	119 131
Feigenbaum, E.	177
Fickas, S.	163 178
Fidel, R.	90
Fillenbaum, S.	184 196
Filliben, J. J.	429
Fillmore, C.	31 44
Fink, P.	173 178
Fischer, C.	388
Ford, B.	45 429
Forman, I.	259
Francozo, E.	196
Freeman, D.	161 167ff 177ff 360 375
Frege, G.	134
Freiman, S.	407
Gallaire,	303 319
Garlan, D. B.	388
Gehani, N.	167 179
Geiss, M. C.	184 196
Goedel, K.	147
Goodman, N.	23 136 137 146 159
Good, M. I.	258
Gottlieb, A.	332
Granger, R. H.	227 229 241
Grice, H. P.	184 196
Grishman, R.	332
Grossman, F.	245
Grosz, B.	49 66
Gurd, J. R.	332
Guttag, S.	114
Gutz, S.	430
Hamill, B. W.	158 201 210 218 319 375
Harary, F.	299
Harman, G.	188 196
Harris, M. D.	49 66
Hausen, HL.	167 179
Hayes, P.	133 148 150 157 159
Hedetniemi	23
Hempel, C.	170 171 179
Henderson, T.	371 375
Hendler, J. A.	227 229 241 351 352
Henle, M.	184 196
Hersh, H.	258
Hesse, H.	153
Hikita, T.	332
Hinton, G. E.	241
Hirst, G. J.	228 240 241
Hobbs, J. R.	133 134 159 259
Holbrook, J. K.	229 241
Hopcroft, J. E.	299
Horning, J. J.	114
Horn, B.	90
Horowitz, E.	23
Houstis, E. N.	427 429
Howden, W.	167 179
Huet, G.	103 114
Hughes, G. F.	131

Author Index

Humphrey, S.   90
Hunter, I. M. L.   186 **196** 261
Ihara, H.   202 205
Ishihata, K.   332
Issacson, E.   131
Itkin, D.   **388** 389
Jablonowski, J.   360 375
Jackson, M. A.   7 14 **23** 217
Jernigan, R.   158 301ff 337ff 375 435 441 446 447 450
Johnson, G. F.   388
Johnson, L.   407
Johnson, W. L.   395ff 406
Johnson-Laird, P. N.   186 **195** 196 197
Joiner, B. L.   430
Jones, S. J.   258 305 310 311 315
Jordan, H. F.   332
Jorring, U.   114
Kahneman, D.   184 197
Kahn, G.   175 179
Kalos, M.   332
Kaplan, R. M.   29 38 **44**
Katz, B.   90
Kay, M.   29 31 **44** **45** 46
Keller, H.   131
Kemper, A.   23
Kirkham, C. C.   332
Klerer, M.   245 **258** 259
Knuth, D. E.   255 258
Kolers, P. A.   190 196
Kotov, V. E.   333
Kowalchack, B.   337 340 342 354 377 **389** 390 441
Kruba, S. R.   306 319
Kruskal, C. P.   332
Kubovy, M.   191 196
Laird, J. E.   115
Lakshmivarahan, S.   332
Lamport, L.   332
Landin, P. J.   120 121 124 **132**
Lang, B.   103 **114** 137 184 191 **195** 333 449
Lauer, H. C.   333 337
Lazanoff, A.   337 346 350 352
Lee, J. A. N.   333
Lehman, M. M.   4 5 11 **22**
Leite, J. C.   179
Lenat, D. B.   178 264 298 **299**
Lipman, M.   407
Lipton, R.   178
Litman, D.   49 66
Littman, D.   407
Lowry, M.   90
Lusth, J.   178
Lynch, R. E.   429
Lyon, G.   321 332 337 339 346 351 352 354 355 **388** 389
MacKay, D. M.   203 205
Maggio, M.   388 389
Maida, A. S.   30 45

Maier, D.	303 319
Martins, J.	416
Martin, C. E.	229 231 242
Mason, F.	360 375
Massively, T. J.	231 232 241 339 353
Maull, N.	88 89
Mauney, J.	388
May, J.	258
McAuliffe, K. P.	332
McCarthy, J.	120 121 132 133 142 159
McCluhan, M.	260
McCord, M. C.	29 44 45
McDermott, D.	50 66
McDermott, J.	179
McGettrick, A.	179
McGill, M.	90
McKay, D.	29 45 46
Mellish, C. S.	131
Meltzer, B.	115 159 177
Meyer, B.	259
Michener, E.	297 298 299
Michie, D.	115 159 177
Miklosko, J.	333
Miller, P. L.	388
Minker, H. J.	319
Minsky, M.	90 159
Mitchell, T. M.	89 114 115 206 207 297
Moler, C. B.	333 429
Moore, J. S.	179 297 299
Moore, R. C.	159
Morgan, J. L.	196 353 354
Mostowski, A.	180
Murty, U.	299
Myers, B. A.	389
Nagel, R. N.	361 375
Narasimhan, B.	23
Naur, P.	258
Nau, D. S.	67
Neal, J. G.	27 29 35 37 38 39 40 41 45 46
Neches, R.	176 179
Needham, R. M.	333 337
Neighbors, J.	161 162 179
Newell, A.	9 17 22 99 115 187 196 205
Nicolas, J. M.	319
Nilsson, N. J.	209 210
Niwa, K.	202 205
Norvig, P.	227 229 239 240 241
Nowlan, S.	179
Ore, O.	265 299
Orr, K.	7 18 23
Osgood, C. E.	186 187 196
O'Leary, D. P.	333
Pacak, M.	90
Pal, A.	388
Papert, S.	90
Paris, S. G.	197
Parnas, D.	23

Partsch, H.   162 179
Pascal, B.   265 299
Pea, R. D.   402 406
Peng, Y.   50 52 53 61 66 67
Pereira, F. C. N.   29 31 45 46
Perlis, A.   178
Perlman, G.   256 259
Perry, J.   153 158
Piaget, J.   203 205
Pidgeon, C.   177
Plotkin, G.   115
Poincare, H.   266 295 299 300
Polya, G.   169 179
Poole, J. C. T.   429
Pope, E.   391 406 407
Pople, H.   50 67
Potts, G. R.   187 194 195 197
Pratt, A.   90
Quillian, M. R.   202 205 227 228 229 230 232 235 242
Quine, W. V.   29 45 47 146
Rada, R.   71 72 76 90 219
Ramsey, F. P.   144
Redwine, S. T.   429n
Reggia, J. A.   49 50 52 55 57 66 67 218 219 442
Reif, J.   115
Reinhardt, S.   333
Reisner, P.   258 259
Reiss, S.   389
Reiter, R.   319
Rescher, N.   171 179
Resnick, B.   222
Ribbens, C.   427 430
Rice, J. R.   412 416 427 429 430
Rich, C.   100 115
Rich, R. P.   201ff 354 437
Rieger, C.   49 67
Riesbeck, C. K.   229 231 242
Robinson, R. M.   180
Rosenbloom, P. S.   115
Rosen, B. K.   300
Rubinstein, R.   258
Rudolph, L.   332
Rumelhart, D. E.   49 67
Russell, B.   144
Russman, G. M.   391 392 406
Rustin, R.   44
Ryan, B. F.   430
Ryan, T. A., Jr.   430
Sacerdoti, E.   115
Sack, W.   407
Salmon, N. U.   159
Salton, G.   90
Sasaki, K.   202 205
Schach, S. R.   389
Schank, R. C.   49 53 67
Scherlis, W. L.   95 114 115 201 211 218 222
Scholz, K. W.   187 194 195 197

Schwartz, J. T.	**259** 323 333
Scott, D. S.	95 **115** 219
Sejnowski, T.	**241**
Sells, S. B.	185 **197**
Shapiro, S. C.	27 29 30 32 34 41 **45** **46**
Shilcrat, E.	371 **375**
Shneiderman, B.	201ff 442ff
Shortliffe, E.	178 443 444
Shulman, L. S.	**22**
Sidner, C.	49 **67**
Sigillito, V. G.	**23**
Simon, H. A.	9 17 **22** 187 **196**
Sneed, J.	165 166 **180**
Snir, M.	**332**
Soloway, E.	258 **259** 391 395 **406 407**
Sowa, J. F.	**22** 150 **159** 163 166 **180**
Sparafka, S. A.	**22**
Spohrer, J.	391 392 395 396 397 401 **406 407**
Steinbruggen, R.	**179**
Stenning, V.	5 **22**
Stewart, G. W.	**333 429**
Stock, D. L.	364 **388**
Suppes, P.	164 165 173 **180**
Swartout, W.	**179**
Sweet, R. A.	**429**
Tarski, A.	134 139 140 165 **180**
Taylor, R. P.	355 391 392 393 **406 407**
Teitlebaum, T.	**389**
Tennant, H.	49 **67**
Thomason, R.	**132**
Turner, D. A.	126 **132**
Turski, W. M.	5 8 **22** 26
Tversky, A.	184 **197**
Ullman, J. D.	299 303 **319**
Vegdahl, S. R.	**333**
von Gudenberg, J. W.	**429**
Wadge, W. W.	119 124 131 **132**
Wang, P. Y.	**67**
Ward, W. A.	24 39 **430**
Warren, D. H. D.	29 31 **45 46**
Wason, P. C.	184 185 186 192 194 **195** **196** **197**
Wasserman, A. I.	179 **430**
Waters, R. C.	**115**
Watson, I,	**332**
Webber, B. L.	**47**
Weintraub, D.	**158** 319 347 349 352 353 375 445 446
Weizman, E.	186 **196**
Whitehead, A. N.	**144**
Whiteside, J. A.	**258**
Whorf, B. L.	204 **205**
Wilensky, R.	28 **46** 138 **159** 258 362 **375**
Wile, D. S.	**258**
Wilks,	49 **66**
Wing, J. M.	**114**
Winograd, T.	49 **67**
Winston, P.	**44** 84 **90**
Wittgenstein, L.	141 **159** 189 190

Wixon, D. R.	258		
Woods, W. A.	30	46	205
Woodworth, R. S.	185	197	
Wos, L.	264	300	
Yigal, A.	46	258	
Zave, P.	23		
Zelkowitz, M. V.	377	389	
Zwicky, A. M.	184	196	

SUBJECT INDEX

abduction	49ff 219
abstract data types	15 110 412
abstraction	4ff 96ff 146 163 167 329 370
abstraction mechanism	329
abstraction transformation	5 11
acceptance limit	328
Ada	249 254 342 374 412 439
ALGOL	255 347 348
algorithmic domain	7
alternative logics	183
ambiguity resolution	245 249
AMPLE	359ff
analogical reasoning	72 103 105 107 108
analogy	52 72 84 89 90 95ff 142 157 158 209 213 217 218 219 222 297 301 339 350 363
anthropomorphic	120 256
anthropomorphism	257
APL	24 99 218 306 319 345 347 348 349 352 353
APLDOT	306 319
APLLOG	306
application domain	3 6 7 21 25 161 169 170 176 249 256 447
application generators	11 13 23
application space	3 4 6 9 11
appositive	34 40 41 42 43
architecture topology	322
arrays	126 325 339 354 364
artificial intelligence	4 6 27 44 45 49 66 80 89 90 114 115 159 163 164 177 178 202 210 211 227 241 299 319
artificial language	256
assertion	30 35 40 41 59 60 62 203 306 307
associative long-term memory	9
attention	49ff 191ff
attributes	39 55 57 59 60 64 68 167 316 318 362 365 366 371
automated manufacturing research	359
automated programmer	245 246
automatic programming	6 22 114 212
automatic translation	326
backtracking	16 29 98 112 367
BASIC	7 18 31 50 96 97 109 119 121 126 144 183 187 215 217 249 260 306 323 359 366 372 393 396 414 415 417 421 439
behavioral models	11 12 14

behavioral specification 15
bibliographic retrieval 73
bit-mapped displays 18
bottom-up 14 214
bucket search 330
CAD/CAM 376 452
CALSPAN 27
categories 29ff 64 69 73 138 222 250 328 395 396
change order 6
chunking 17 99 115
chunking principle 17
chunks of information 9
chunks of knowledge 17
COBOL 7 217 2ff 348ff 450
coding styles 325
cognition 9 17 21 66 96 100 150 196 197 203 210 211 256 263 277
cognitive complexity 253
cognitive model 228 249 253 254 255
cognitive operations 190
cognitive process 4 16 25
cognitive psychology 189 202
cognitive science 6 22 45 46 66 196 202 241
color graphics 18
communications 46 89 90 131 178 242 326 327 339 389 451
competence and performance 184
complexity measure 15
computation node 324
computational topology 321
conditional reasoning 186 192
connection machine 327 332
connectives 32 45 138 139 141 197 306
constraints 12 16 26 40 97 105 106 116 157 173 175 176 231 232 285 291 292 321 326 342 343 344 382 452
contention problem 326
centextual analysis 245 249
contextual factors 184 191
contextual influence 241
context-free 43 164
context-sensitive 35 43 50 158
control structures 21 245 249 251 374 422 441
coreferentiality 34 42 43
correctness 24 52 101 105 120 167 168 229 230 250
co-text 186
creativity 452
cue acquisition 9 10
cue interpretation 10
data flow diagram 16
data structures 110 127 240 362 364 365 378 384 389 422

dataflow	124 132 322ff
dataflow architecture	322
DBMS	12
DDL	95
debugging	377ff
decomposition	86 138 325
design process	4 97 98 212 343 344
determinateness	38 39
determiner	38 39 40 41 42
diagramming techniques	17
direct manipulation	215 438ff
disturbing factors	183 184
documentation	169 218 414 426
duality	86 325 333 337
dual-process theory	194
editor	96 115 132 340 348 378 383 388 389
effectiveness	164 168 169 202 204
efficiency	120 167 231 269 303 321 341 425
elliptic boundary-value problems	411 414 415 420 429
entity diagrams	18
entity-relationship model	16
environment	4 6 7 20 21 23 45 66 123 152 184 190 191 195 210 236 246 255 256 262 263 297 302 325 341ff 359 360 370 373 376 377ff 414 416 420 428 431 436 443 444 447 450 453
equivalence	143 254 261 280 288 293 325 326 342
executable representation	250
executable specification	250
expert systems	28 50 55 56 65 66 67 95 164 173ff 211 218 303 411 414 443
extensibility	28 205 206 207
feedback	25 245 249 254 255 257 361 440
formal logic	158 264 303
formal notation	169 302
FORTH	49 52 73 101 205 223 261 289 337 376 453
FORTRAN	7 119 120 126 127 222 249 255 256 258 260 318 321 325 326 327 329 346ff 411ff 439
fourth generation languages	348
frame	31 32 35 40 80 88 113 133 203 234 260 322 327 328 337 346 364 414 427
frame of reference	327
FranzLISP	133ff 360 362 363 372
functional structure	39
gradualness	73 90
grammar	38 40 44 45 56 57 66 259 265ff 273 419

granularity	172 176 321 322 327 328 329 330
graph theory	207 208 221 261ff 444 452
graphical representations	18 392 441 451
heuristic domain	7
heuristic search	209 299
heuristics	7 12 14 16 20 21 197 206 207 209 239 240 264 282 288
hierarchical	14 15 16 20 71 73 111 202 375
high-level language	411
HOS	3
human problem solving	6 22 188 196 209 210
hypothesis evaluation	10
hypothesis generation	10 87
ICON	184 343 344 392 393 452
identifiers	31 33 41 305
idioms	99 204
images	51
implementation space	4 7
implicit knowledge	241
individuals	134ff 164 165 211 325
inference	27ff 49ff 99 113 143 149 193 209 210 218 219 230 241 302 426 436
information processing system	9 302 303
intensional logic	119 121 123 124 125 131
interactive information systems	18
interpretations	32 35 53 141 195 254 342
kernel	27ff 361 411
knowledge acquisition	89 175 179 181
knowledge bases	55 56 65 71 72 73 75 78 87 96 101 107 207 212
knowledge representation	27 30 43 45 65 86 89 205 212 228 262 263 299 436
lambda expression	143 152
language constructs	250 253 326
language design	245ff 329 330 359 402 416 424
language expression	122 267 291 292
language properties	3
language tokens	251
learning process	9
level of abstraction	13 14 17 20 111
level of confidence	328
levels of representation	18 19
lexeme	31 33
lexical marking	186
lexical category	35
lexical functional	38 44
linguistic characteristics	249
linguistic competence	185
linguistic entities	35 165
linguistic factors in reasoning	192
linguistic input	187 188 190
linguistic model	256
linguistic output	187 188 190

linguistic representations	3
linguistic structure	245 249 254
linguistics	195 202
LISP	7 45 57 80 90 120 132 133ff 297 342 344 360 362 363 371 372 373 439 448
load balancing	322 323 329
logic	29 30 44 45 67 119ff 133ff 164ff 183 187 196 229 264 299 302 303 306 319 345 366 393 394 436 441
logic programming	306 319
logical competence	183 184
logical notations	21
logical structure	187 193
long-term memory	9 10
low level languages	342
machine learning	79 89 114 115
Macintosh	389 440 445 447 452
manipulation	124 166 168 215 269 319 341 347 392 438ff
mappings	47 202 337
marker passing	52 53 60
markers	66 227ff
matching bias	192 193 194
mathematical notation	246 251 301 303 318 411 417 435
medical problem solving	22
medical subject headings mesh	73 86
medical systems	215
mental processes	9 188 190
mental representation	44 189 190 196
message passing	325 326 327 329 332 337 338 339 340 345
meta language	27 28 29 42 43 44 303
MIMD	322 323 324 325 328 332
MIRROR	260
model	3 5 28 29 49ff 90 114 131 134 140 141 147 164ff 186 187 196 210 217 219 228 229 231 239 240 241 245ff 262 304 319 323 324 337 350 351 354 360 361 367 372 373 376 412 424 442 443 444 445 450
modifiers	45
morphemes	31 59 60
morphology	73
MYCIN	173
natural artificial language	256
natural language	27ff 49ff 76 78 119 122 125 135 174 187 204 206 209 210 211 219 227 228 229 250 256 257 259 260 263 301 308 435
natural logic	183
natural notation	260
natural representations	16

naturalness principle 187
negation 138 139 141 183 184 185 313 315
network 12 13 15 16 27ff 44ff 52 53 60 63 67 73 124 170 202 227ff 264 295 322 325 326 362 364 371 411 414 427
nodes 12 13 20 30 31 32 33 41 63 74 108 110 203 209 227ff 324 327 341 356 373 444
non-linguistic signs 188
non-procedural languages 11
notation 15 17 20 110 111 136 139 142 151 162 166 169 245ff 298 301 302 303 304 305 318 347 353 372 382 383 411 417 435 441 442
notational forms 246
ontology 133 136 137 147 158
organization of memory 325
output format 249 255 256
parallel architectures 241 322 331
parallel computers 321 333 431
parallel decomposition 325
parallel processing 321 322 325 329 353
parallel programming 321 325 333
parallelism 131 227 231 241 322 325 338 339 348 366
parallel-FOR statement 330
parse tree 33 40 324 339 379
parsing 29 43 45 79 96 229 241 242 339 345
PARSNIP 27ff
Pascal 119 120 123 124 255 265 299 340 341 342 347 348 377ff 391ff 429 447 448 453
pattern matching 103
pattern recognition 9
philosophy 71 89 132 158 195 260 345
physics 3 137 159 165 210ff
portability 246 329 347 348
pragmatic factors 183 184 185 190 194
pragmatics 15 187 188 189 190 195 196 321 333 337 448 449
precision 21 316 366
predicate calculus 32 120 122 211 220 261 264 305 318
predicate logic 30 164
predicates 135ff 365
prime numbers 130
Principia Mathematica 144
problem 3ff 27 28 44 47 50ff 76 80 90 97ff 119ff 133 158 162ff 183ff 201ff 232ff 245ff 261ff 318 319 322 323 325 326 337ff 362 375 382 383 391ff 411ff 435ff

problem solving space	4 9 10 215
problem spaces	3 4 16 17
problem specification	162 217 245 246 247 250 251 253
procedural language	124
producer-consumer	29
program coding	321
program synthesis	114
programming environment	210 246 255 256 354 355 359 388 389
programming language	25 66 101 120 124 132 212 246 249 254 255 256 259 316 321 322 359 375 376 377 391 392 405 406 412 429
programming language design	255
programming languages	15 119 120 121 131 132 158 163 246 249 250 256 258 259 319 321 375 377 393 435
programming style	327
PROLOG	29 121 131 306 307 349 439 441
propositions	31 137 159 166
psychology	22 189 195 196 197 202 203 221 349 350 445
psychopragmatics	189 190 195
quantification	30 44ff 49 135 138 141ff
real-world constraints	321
reasoning	27 28 29 49 50 71ff 103 105 107 108 126 158 169 183ff 280 295 301 367 442
referencing	42 43
regularity	206 207 208 301
reification	5 14 25 257
relational calculus	301 306 319
relational data base	304 308 319
relations	29ff 72 84 86 87 136 137 140 163 164 165 175 176 219 305 306 307
representation	3ff 27ff 57ff 64 71ff 88 96ff 101 111 113 115 133 153 154 161ff 177 186 189 190 196 202ff 218 228ff 234 245ff 258 261ff 264ff 291 360ff 371 378 380 385 391ff 395 407ff 417 420ff 435ff 441 452 453
requirements specification	5
reusability	109 168 178 413
rewrite rules	34ff
robots	133 362 370 375 447
rule-based systems	51 177
schema	9 10 67 104 106 144 145 147 162 163 203 294
self-service	321 329 330 331
semantic knowledge	42
semantic net	63

semantics	15 29 34 35 36 44 53 66 120 123 139 141 146 159 162 163 166 171 174 175 196 230 253 264 295 302 303 318 321 333 342 362 435
semiotic systems	188
serial bottleneck	324
serial machine	231 324 338
shared memory	322 325 326 329 331 332 338 339
shared memory machine	331
short-term memory	9 191
side effects	123 326 360
silicon	343 344
slots	35 45 234
Smalltalk	344
SNePS	29ff
sociopragmatics	190
software engineering	22 23 113 114 115 162ff 220 258 259 327 406 437 446
software maintenance	177
software process	3ff 343
software process models	3
software systems	161 162 169 255 437
solver	10 81 85 171 246
specification	4 5 6 7 15 20 97 98 101 111 114 120 162 163 175 176 177 179 217 245ff 301ff 329 339 363 375 377 404 422
state change	13
strategy	29 53 59 71 72 84 85 110 116 179 191 249 395 422 426
strings	29ff 151 170 187 188 256 348 351
string-category	35
string-reference	40
structural models	11 12 15 20
structural representation	13
structural specification	15
structure	3ff 30ff 52ff 72 73 74 86 95ff 131 133ff 161ff 185 187 188 193 203 204 208 212 219 234 245 249 250 254 255 259 325 326 330 341ff 363 366 368 372 373 393 404 405 406 444 453
structured programming	23 392 453
structuring	101 111 405
subjunctive	445
substrings	31 41
support architecture	329
symbols	33 60 140 151 164 251 253 254 255 256 306 307 404 408 452
synchronization	322 326 329

syntactic flexibility	251 253
syntactic knowledge	33
syntax	15 29ff 49 53 64 67 69 100 120 196 245 246 249 264 295 302 306 318 321 333 362 377 378 380 389 394 418 440 453
systems analysis	9 177
teacher-user	34ff
the automated programmer system	245 246
theorem proving	204 261 262 277 297
theory formation	169 290
theory of deductive reasoning	189
theory of types	144
three-valued logic	44
tokens	31 35 251 253 324 330 373
tool box	442
transformations	3ff 99 107 114 116 120 163
transition network	12
tree structure	16 73 74 131 341
turing machine	291 292 299 360
types	110 111 144 146 233 359ff 378 385 412
typing	362 363
unification-based	45
universals	44 134 135 136 138 142
unix	28 46 131 258 340 344 346 377 380 413
unix consultant	28
user-oriented	246 249 256 258
utterances	28 32 35 37 40 43
validation	5 24 25 161ff
validation obligation	5
verification	5 6 24 25 101 106 107 113 167 168 177 178 185 246 249 256 285 286 360 376
verification tasks	185
video games	439
VLSI	121 342 343 344 345 452
waterfall flow	4

RAYMOND H. FOGLER LIBRARY
DATE DUE

BOOKS ARE SUBJECT TO
RECALL AFTER TWO WEEKS